The
Origin and Evolution
of
New Businesses

The
Origin and Evolution
of
New Businesses

AMAR V. BHIDÉ

OXFORD
UNIVERSITY PRESS
2000

OXFORD
UNIVERSITY PRESS

Oxford   New York
Athens   Auckland   Bangkok   Bogotá   Buenos Aires
Calcutta   Cape Town   Chennai   Dar es Salaam   Delhi   Florence
Hong Kong   Istanbul   Karachi   Kuala Lumpur   Madrid   Melbourne
Mexico City   Mumbai   Nairobi   Paris   São Paulo   Singapore
Taipei   Tokyo   Toronto   Warsaw

and associated companies
Berlin   Ibadan

Published by Oxford University Press, Inc.
198 Madison Avenue, New York, New York 10016

Oxford is a registered trademark of Oxford University Press

Library of Congress Cataloging-in-Publication Data

Bhidé, Amar, 1955–
The origin and evolution of new businesses / Amar Bhidé.
p.   cm.   Includes bibliographical references and index.
ISBN 0–19–513144–4
1. New business enterprises.   2. Entrepreneurship.   I. Title.
HD62.5.B49   2000   658.1'1—dc21   99–38239

3 5 7 9 8 6 4 2

Printed in the United States of America
on acid-free paper

To the memory of my parents,
for their example of courage and enterprise
and unquestioning love

Contents

Preface

This effort to demystify and organize our thinking about entrepreneurs through systematic research has practical roots. I undertook the research that has led to this book to address a problem in business education. Courses in entrepreneurship have gained great popularity as increasing numbers of students want to start and build their own businesses. In 1979, the year I graduated from the M.B.A. program at Harvard Business School (HBS), a solitary course in starting new ventures attracted fewer than one hundred students from a graduating class of about eight hundred. In 1996, nine courses filled more than fourteen hundred student seats from a class of nine hundred. Similarly, Stanford's business school reports that more than 90 percent of its M.B.A. students now elect at least one course in entrepreneurship. We still lack, however, a solid base of ideas for such courses. Over the past half century, business schools have devoted considerable resources to studying the entrepreneurial activities of large companies—how Merck develops new drugs and Intel new microprocessors, how Disney produces and markets *The Little Mermaid* and McDonald's introduces Big Macs in China. Little effort has been devoted to systematic research about starting and growing new businesses.

Researchers have focused on the initiatives of large corporations for several reasons. As business schools and research in the United States came of age in the 1950s and 1960s, large corporations dominated the economic landscape. According to the historian Alfred Chandler, a "new form of capitalism," the "large managerial business enterprise," appeared in the last half of the nineteenth century.[1] This new form, which was controlled by a hierarchy of salaried executives rather than the owners, "dominated the core industries in the United States"[2] by the end of World War I, and by the 1960s it became ubiquitous. In 1967 John Kenneth Galbraith observed that the five hundred largest corporations produced nearly half the goods and services annually available in the United States. He wrote: "Seventy years ago the corporation was still confined to those industries—railroading, steamboating, steel-making, petroleum recovery and refining, some mining—where, it seemed, production had to be on a large scale. Now it also sells groceries, mills grain, publishes newspapers, and provides public entertainment, all activities that were once the province of the individual proprietor or the insignificant firm."[3]

Large corporations represented as dynamic an economic force as the individual entrepreneurs who had initially founded them. The economist Joseph Schumpeter had regarded the rise of the large corporations as inevitable and forecast that such a development would doom capitalism by stifling the "innovative energy" of the individual entrepreneur. "The perfectly bureaucratized giant industrial unit," Schumpeter wrote, "not only ousts the small- or medium-sized firm and expropriates its owners, but in the end it also ousts the entrepreneur and expropriates the bourgeoisie as a class which in the process stands to lose not only its income but also what is infinitely more important, its function."[4] Economist Frank Knight, a Schumpeter contemporary, also believed that managers who did not own a significant share of the enterprise would be much more conservative and risk-averse than the founding entrepreneurs. In fact, large corporations undertook entrepreneurial functions remarkably well. They introduced jet engines, television sets, plastics, pharmaceuticals, mainframe computers, and a host of new products. Domestic companies ventured overseas and became multinational. They also experimented with and adopted new forms of decentralized organizations to accommodate their increasing size and scope. Schumpeter's "perfectly bureaucratized giant industrial units," to use Chandler's words, "provided a fundamental dynamic or force for change in the capitalist economies"—a transformation "which brought the most rapid economic growth in the history of mankind."[5]

The growth and dynamism of large corporations seemed to reduce the relevance of the individual entrepreneur. At the turn of the twentieth century, Galbraith wrote in 1967, "the corporation was the instrument of its owners and a projection of their personalities. The names of these principals—Carnegie, Rockefeller, Harriman, Mellon, Guggenheim, Ford—were known across the land."[6] By the time of Galbraith's writing, the heads of the great corporations were unknown ("Not for a generation have people outside Detroit and the automobile industry known the name of the current head of General Motors"[7]) and owned no appreciable share of the enterprise. The importance of these "organization men" and the corporations they controlled made the individual entrepreneur a less compelling subject of inquiry.

The increasingly *routinized* nature of corporate initiatives suited the norms and aspirations of business scholars. Starting a new venture, Frank Knight wrote in 1921, involved "an intuitive judgment." How entrepreneurs reach a decision, he wrote, was a "scientifically unfathomable mystery. We must simply fall back upon a 'capacity' in the intelligent animal to form a more or less correct judgment about things, an intuitive sense of values."[8] The modern corporation sought to make the process less mysterious. Innovation, Schumpeter wrote in 1942, "is being reduced to routine. Technological progress is increasingly becoming the work of trained specialists who turn out what is required to make it work in predictable ways."9 Compared to what William J. Baumol calls the "untidy decision processes"10 of the individual entrepreneur, routinized corporate initiatives provided greater opportunities for systematic inquiry.

Some researchers built a symbiotic relationship with their subjects. The large corporation's approach to new initiatives could be documented and evaluated by scholars in finance, marketing, strategy, and other such business disciplines. Conversely, scholars developed and refined tools for corporate decision-makers. For example, finance professors helped propagate the use of Net Present Value analysis. As scholars developed even more sophisticated tools such as option analysis, companies such as Merck would use them to manage their portfolio of R&D investments.

Scholars found reliable data on large companies more readily available. Start-ups number in the hundreds of thousands annually and are prone to disappear soon after they are launched. Their financial records are private and often poorly maintained. Large companies are much less numerous and more stable. Audited, standardized, and public accounting data allow researchers to test hypotheses through intercompany and historical comparisons. Stock market prices provide another objective yardstick for testing theories. A researcher such as R. P. Rumelt, for instance, could make a case against unrelated diversification by examining extensive data on the diversification strategies of one hundred of the largest five hundred industrial corporations in the United States.11

The economics of studying large corporations were more attractive. The rise of the large corporation created a significant demand for trained professional managers. This was met by a manyfold increase in the capacity and number of M.B.A. and other business programs. For example, in 1956, a total of 138 institutions in the United States granted 4,266 master's degrees in business. In 1990, a total of 668 institutions granted 77,203 master's degrees.12 During the same period, the number of bachelor's degrees in business rose from approximately 50,000 per year to about 250,000. The curricula for such programs, and the underlying research, were naturally orientated to the problems and practices of large companies.

Management consulting firms, whose research budgets now rival those of the leading business schools, also found it more rewarding to serve large companies, where the same effort yielded higher fees and more prestige. When Marvin Bower and his two partners launched the management consulting firm McKinsey & Co, in 1939, they initially served small companies but then quickly cultivated larger clients who could pay higher fees. The higher fees allowed McKinsey to recruit high-quality consultants and invest in intellectual capital, which in turn helped secure more large clients. McKinsey is now a high-profile recruiter at the top business schools, spends more than $50 million per year on building knowledge, has a worldwide roster of prestigious clients—and continues to avoid the start-ups and small companies who cannot pay its fees.

Entrepreneurs have now recaptured the popular imagination. Increasingly, ambitious young men and women dream of starting their own businesses rather than rising through the corporate ranks. Politicians look to start-ups for jobs and economic growth. The renewed interest has generated a significant demand for systematic knowledge about the distinctive features of individual entrepreneurship. The supply of systematic knowledge about new business has not, however, matched the increased demand.

The resurgence of entrepreneurs derives in part from the tempering of the unrealistic beliefs about large corporations. Managerial capitalism, to use Alfred Chandler's term, did not eliminate entrepreneurial capitalism. Owner-managed companies, which receded to the background after World War II, still accounted for nearly half of the economic activity. The new products and markets developed by Ken Olsen's Digital and Edwin Land's Polaroid were on a par with those developed by the professionally managed IBM and Kodak. Start-ups created new industries, such as xerography and cable television. Harvard Business School, known as the West Point of capitalism, produced at least as many entrepreneurs as captains of big business enterprises. Howard H. Stevenson's 1983 survey of M.B.A.'s shows that more than a third of HBS alumni, from classes as far back as 1942, were self-employed. About half worked in businesses with fewer than five hundred employees, while only 6 percent worked in companies with more than a hundred thousand employees.[13]

Although the school celebrated graduates such as Robert McNamara, president of Ford Motor Company, students were more ambivalent about careers in large corporations. Charles D. Orth's 1963 book *Social Structure and Learning Climate: The First Year at the Harvard Business School* noted a conflict between the goals of HBS and the aspirations of matriculating students. The students' image of success, according to Orth, reflected "the promoter/entrepreneur archetype" rather than the "administrator/manager image implied by the professional standards the School has generated. The financial genius, the tax law manipulator, the 'wheeler-dealer,' and the supersalesman images are as much or more the admired stereotypes to some students as . . . [the] managers on whose training the School has concentrated." Through a questionnaire Orth administered to incoming students, he found only 55 percent indicated a commitment to "an administrative career"; the others were "interested in entrepreneurial opportunities" or unsure of what they wanted to do after graduation.[14]

Events in the 1970s shook common beliefs about the omnipotence of large corporations. "The big corporations," Galbraith once wrote, "do not lose money." In the recession of 1957, he noted, "not one of the largest U.S. corporations failed to turn a profit. Only one of the largest 200 finished the year in the red." Subsequently, however, large firms were no longer immune to losses. Penn Central filed for bankruptcy; Lockheed and Chrysler were spared this fate by federal bailouts. In the recession of 1982, eight of the top one hundred industrial companies and twenty-one of the largest two hundred ended the year with a deficit. Employment in large companies topped out as well. In 1979 David L. Birch published a study that claimed that small firms generated 66 percent of all new jobs created in the United States, whereas "middle sized and large firms, on balance, provided relatively few new jobs."[15]

With the 1980s, start-ups and entrepreneurs became fashionable again. Bernard Goldhirsh launched *Inc.*, "the magazine for growing companies," in 1979; by 1996 *Inc.* had reached a circulation of 659,263 in North America compared to 893,945 for *Business Week*; 804,754 for *Fortune*; and 783,456 for *Forbes*.[16] *Inc.*'s growth attracted competitors such as *Entrepreneur* and *Success*. Interest in entrepreneurship soared on business school campuses. According to data compiled by Jerome Katz in 1991, a couple dozen accredited business schools in the United States offered some coursework in entrepreneurship. In 1998, a total of 120 offered it as a major. "Driven by student and alumni demand," Ethan Bronner wrote in the *New York Times* in 1998, "no field is hotter today in business studies than that of entrepreneurship."[17]

The obstacles to serious research on entrepreneurs, however, remain. On the practical side it is still difficult to get reliable data. The financial rewards for developing expertise on new and growing businesses remain low—large companies continue to have a greater capacity to pay for expert advice than small companies do. The conceptual problem is just as serious. Long neglect has left the field with few well-framed hypotheses that researchers can confirm or modify.

Indeed, many believe that the critical aspects of entrepreneurship lie beyond the scope of scholarly inquiry. Baumol suggests that "there is a sort of Heisenberg principle that holds for entrepreneurial acts." If reported in detail, "such an act is no longer entrepreneurial."[18] Others argue that the performance of new businesses depends on factors that cannot be studied and taught systematically. Philip Thurston remarked in a colloquium on teaching entrepreneurship that, after a decade of teaching in the field, he had found that "education in business administration [was], at best, a minor factor in successful business start-ups."[19] At the same colloquium, another veteran teacher, Arch Dooley, expressed the conviction that the academic profession did not know "whether any educational activities can in any direct sense aid significantly in the development of the crucial ingredients of entrepreneurial success." Dooley had interviewed successful entrepreneurs to identify the factors they believed had contributed most decisively to their success. Their answers, which pertained to timing, guts, determination, luck, and so on, did not parallel the subject matter typically encountered in academic programs.[20]

Business schools now have alumni, according to Bronner, "donating truckloads of dollars to set up centers and chairs in entrepreneurship, yet there are no scholars to fill them." The number of entrepreneurship chairs has grown from eighteen in 1980 to more than two hundred, but dozens remain empty, because business schools cannot easily find candidates with the academic credentials they consider necessary to fill them. As of September 1998, New York University's business school had four endowed chairs in entrepreneurship, of which two were unfilled. The school's dean, George Daly, told Bronner that he saw "entrepreneurship as a word in search of a meaning in the academic sense."[21]

The growing demand for entrepreneurship courses is often met by hiring adjunct or part-time faculty. Compared to other disciplines, the number of new researchers being trained is small. Jerry Katz, of St. Louis University, has compiled a list of universities in North America and Europe that have a doctoral program or doctoral students in fields such as entrepreneurship, small business, family business, and small and medium-sized enterprise studies. In 1998, according to Katz, only five schools—Wharton, Georgia, Calgary, the European Doctoral Program in Entrepreneurship, and the Joenkoeping International Business School in Sweden—offered formal doctoral programs in entrepreneurship. Another two dozen schools offered doctorates in a conventional area but provided "support through research, classes, faculty or infrastructure for students to specialize their research and teaching in entrepreneurship."[22] The combined total of 29 schools compares to 132 accredited schools with doctoral programs. Also noteworthy is the number of top-ranking schools that do not have doctoral programs or students in entrepreneurship. Of the top twenty business schools in *U.S. News & World Report* 1998 rankings, only five—Harvard, NYU, North Carolina, UCLA, and Wharton—were on Katz's list.

The study of venture capital (VC) and VC-backed companies represents one exception to the general neglect of new business by academics. The topic is well suited to the norms of scholarly inquiry. VC-backed start-ups represent an intriguing combination of individual enterprise and professional management. The VC-backed model involves market research, business plans, experienced founders, and professional venture capitalists who provide advice, oversight, and significant financing. Compaq Computer provides an example of a start-up that successfully followed this model. Compaq's founders, Rod Canion, Jim Harris, and Bill Murto, had all been senior managers at Texas Instruments, and they had a well-formulated plan to take on IBM with a technologically superior product. Seasoned investor Ben Rosen helped Canion raise $20 million in start-up capital—funds that allowed the new business to behave like a large, sophisticated company from the start. Canion could attract experienced managers by offering them generous salaries and participation in a stock option plan. Compaq also had a national dealer network established within a year of exhibiting its first prototype. Sales totaled more than $100 million in the first year.

Start-ups such as Compaq bear a close relationship to the large modern corporation. In many ways the VC phenomenon represents a variant of managerial capitalism, and its study a logical extension of business research. Like the decision-makers in large companies, venture capitalists try to use systematic procedures and criteria for making investments and provide capital under well-specified terms. They back experienced entrepreneurs like Canion who bring to their ventures the professional management practices of large corporations. Modern theories of finance, organization behavior, strategy, and so on provide convenient frameworks for analyzing the capital structures, contracts, and investments in VC-backed firms. Researchers can secure and analyze data about the VC industry. Like large companies, venture capitalists comprise a finite, identifiable universe. They try to develop systematic routines and objective criteria for making investments and use well-documented contracts. Venture Economics and other organizations publish data on their investments and rates of return.

But whereas studying venture capital fits the existing norms and styles of academic research, it provides limited insights about the typical entrepreneur and start-up. As we will see, venture capitalists invest in exceptional entrepreneurs and ventures. Very few start-ups qualify for VC funding. Of the nearly million new businesses formed each year in the United States, VCs fund only a few hundred. Compaq represents the exception rather than the rule for start-ups. Most businesses, as exemplified by HP, Dell Computers, and Gateway (who now compete head to head against Compaq in the PC market), start out with limited funds, limited professional management, and, limited planning. And in this crucial area of the undercapitalized and improvised new business we have little systematic knowledge.

I began studying new businesses in 1988, when I joined the HBS faculty to teach a course in entrepreneurship. I had little background in the field. Apart from two unsuccessful attempts to start a venture, I was mainly steeped in the corporate approach to business. I had received my M.B.A. at Harvard in 1979, before start-ups became fashionable. The logic and rationality of the corporate paradigm entranced me. I then worked for five years at McKinsey & Co., where I tried to apply and refine the theories I had learned at business school. A doctorate in business administration followed, wherein I researched hostile takeovers of large, diversified corporations. Now I confronted the task of teaching students about starting and growing their own, usually small, businesses.

I had some clues that suggested that the business school approach required significant modification for the world of start-ups. At McKinsey I had discovered that business school theories that were based on studies of large industrial companies did not easily transfer to the free-wheeling world of finance and investment banking. The traditional model of competitive strategy called for companies to seek sustainable advantages over competitors by preemptively investing in assets such as proprietary technologies, brand names, or high-volume plants. As described in my 1986 article "Hustle as Strategy,"[23] the ease of imitation and fungibility of resources in many financial businesses prevent firms from establishing sustainable advantages. Profitability is more a function of tactical and operational ability ("hustle") than of superior long-term strategy in the traditional sense. Casual observation suggested that execution might be of greater importance than strategy in start-ups as well.

My doctoral dissertation, too, had shown clear differences between takeovers undertaken by individuals—the "raiders" of the 1980s—and corporate mergers. CEOs of large corporations rarely made hostile tender offers and claimed their mergers would provide strategic or synergistic benefits. Hostile transactions were typically undertaken by entrepreneurs who sought quick returns, usually through the sale of unrelated assets, to raise financing for their deals; synergies or long-term business strategy did not interest them.

In the following decade I tried to make a contribution to entrepreneurship education by systematically identifying the differences between how individuals and large companies undertake new initiatives. I published course notes, case studies, and *Harvard Business Review* articles, all with a pedagogical or prescriptive bent. My purpose here is to integrate ideas initially developed to help individuals start and grow their own businesses, to provide a coherent explanation, based on systematic observation, of an important phenomenon. This synthesis, which pulls together the concrete experiences of the several hundred entrepreneurs, deliberately excludes explicit "how to's" to focus attention on what entrepreneurs do and to put their role into a broader economic context. Those who read between the lines to infer practical advice should do so in conjunction with my earlier writings.

This inquiry, which looks at entrepreneurs mainly from an economic point of view, represents an effort to complement rather than challenge existing economic theories. I address questions of economic import that lie outside the traditional boundaries of the discipline. To do so, I rely on theories and constructs drawn from a variety of fields, ranging from agency theory to experimental psychology. Few of us, however, have a deep understanding of all these theories and can relate easily to their specialized terminology. I have, therefore, sought to work with just the landmark, well-accepted ideas from these fields and to use their specialized terms sparingly. I have also grappled with colloquial explanations of entrepreneurial success based on terms such as "determination" and "persistence." Rather than ignore such seemingly ambiguous ideas, I have tried to give them precise meanings in the context of the specific tasks and functions that entrepreneurs perform. Hopefully, the effort will be regarded not as a mélange of the naive and the arcane but as an effort to use the best ideas available today* to explain an important and complex phenomenon.

Finally, this book provides provisional maps rather than a definitive work on new businesses. After many years of exploring the territory, I cannot claim to have identified all the principal features, let alone all the details. I offer plausible conjectures drawn from my research rather than firm conclusions. Others should challenge and modify the conjectures or formulate their own. Research in this important arena has been held back by a chicken-and-egg problem: Scholars avoid the field because it doesn't have a well-defined theory, but such a theory cannot spontaneously emerge without their efforts. I hope the frameworks and hypotheses suggested here will help break the deadlock and stimulate the careful scholarship the topic deserves.

---

* I hope to give back a little to the fields I have borrowed ideas from. For instance, "behavioral" economists who study deviations from rational behavior and decision-making often associate these deviations with undesirable consequences, such as excessively volatile financial markets, overinvestment, and even the formation of cults. This research suggests novel ways in which the "coginitive mistakes" identified by the behavioral economists play an important role in a socially valuable activity. Similarly, my analysis of improvised start-ups adds a different perspective to the problem of financial contracting. Existing theory emphasizes the problems that information asymmetries cause in contracts between the users and the suppliers of capital. Here we will see that irreducible uncertainty due to the absence of critical information represents the main constraint in financing many start-ups.

Acknowledgments

I cannot exaggerate, or even accurately describe, Howard Stevenson's contribution. Howard has had such a profound influence on my worldview that a great many of the ideas expressed in this book very likely derive from my subconscious restatement of his wisdom. He has also been an extraordinary mentor who has unstintingly given me his time, loyalty, and support.

David Chaffetz made copious notes in the course of many airplane journeys. Besides providing insightful suggestions about the ideas and arguments, David served as de facto editor and writing coach. Discussions with Srikant Datar helped me formulate the "investment-uncertainty-profit" framework I used in Part I. Iain Cockburn, Pankaj Ghemawat, Myra Hart, Josh Lerner, Mike Roberts, Steve Kaplan, and Hank Reiling read several drafts, identified my sins of omission and commission, helped clean up the language and logic, and provided data and references. Bill Sahlman's comments helped me think about the overall message and positioning of this book. Bruce Scott's suggestions and encouraging words about my rough early drafts kept me going forward.

Several colleagues at Harvard Business School also gave generously of their time and expertise, notably Chris Argyris, Joe Badaracco, Carliss Baldwin, Jon Biotti, James Heskett, Linda Hill, Herminia Ibarra, Robert Kaplan, David Kotchen, Walter Kuemmerle, Warren McFarlan, Richard Tedlow, and Karen Wruck. Lunches, e-mail, and snail mail correspondence with Olivier Blanchard, Glenn Hubbard, Andrei Shleifer, Jeremy Stein, and Robert Shiller served as valuable quality control mechanisms. Sid Balachandra, John Deighton, Ashish Nanda, V. G. Narayanan, Gus Stuart, and George Wu spent many hours answering various technical questions.

Deaver Brown, John Case, Paul De Rosa, Paul Eckbo, Richard Floor, George Gendron, Alan Kennedy, Roger Kline, Marcia Radosevich, David Roux, and Susan Webber provided a reality check by comparing my observations against their practical business experience and knowledge.

Research associate Kevin Hinton helped organize and conduct most of the interviews with entrepreneurs that this book draws on. Laura Pochop helped complete the interviews and analysis of the data. Charlene Niles of *Inc.* magazine and Joanne Guiniven of McKinsey & Co. provided information from their databases. Julie Yao took charge in the final months of this project and made its completion into a breeze. Students from my M.B.A. classes wrote more than two hundred papers that I have drawn on and helped test and refine my ideas about entrepreneurs. Ken MacLeod of Oxford University Press has been very responsive and a pleasure to work with. Rebecca Kohn edited the manuscript with a light and thoughtful hand. Roberta Brown typed large portions of the manuscript and kept my professional life in order.

Former HBS dean John McArthur has been an enthusiastic supporter; his successor, Kim Clark, and my research director, Teresa Amabile, arranged for the resources needed to see this work through to completion.

As ever, my sister Gauri provided rocklike support and many excellent meals. Ashley Wodtke's company and understanding helped me get started and saw me through much of the first iteration. Her mother, Carol Cross Wodtke, volunteered her artistic talents for the illustrations. My daughter Lila provided a delightful Saturday distraction as she grew from a toddler to a self-possessed pre-K lady. My mother's affection and example kept me going through a difficult period. She passed away, alas, just ten days after I had turned in the final draft.

To all of you, my heartfelt thanks. Your help has gone far beyond the call of professional obligation and friendship. I hope I can make it up to you someday.

The
Origin and Evolution
of
New Businesses

Introduction

Entrepreneurs who start and build new businesses are more celebrated than studied. They embody, in the popular imagination and in the eyes of some scholars, the virtues of "boldness, ingenuity, leadership, persistence and determination."[1] Policymakers see them as a crucial source of employment and productivity growth. Yet our systematic knowledge of how entrepreneurs start and grow their businesses is limited. The activity does not occupy a prominent place in the study of business and economics. Cliché and anecdote—or laments about the ineffable nature of entrepreneurship—dominate the discourse about new and fledgling businesses.

This book examines the nature of the opportunities that entrepreneurs pursue, the problems and tasks they face, the traits and skills they require, and the social and economic contributions they make. It identifies the special features of the poorly mapped terrain of new and growing businesses by comparing it to the more systematically researched world of large companies. The great variety we find among new businesses makes it difficult to go beyond trite generalizations. Their common features stand out when placed against initiatives undertaken by established companies, such as the development of new products, processes, and markets.

The investment-uncertainty-profit diagram (see Fig. IN.1) illustrates the main propositions explored in this book. We will see that new businesses (such as Microsoft in 1975), evolving or transitional businesses (Microsoft in the mid-1980s), and large well-established corporations (Microsoft in the 1990s) pursue opportunities with different levels of irreducible uncertainty, investment requirements, and likely profit. At the

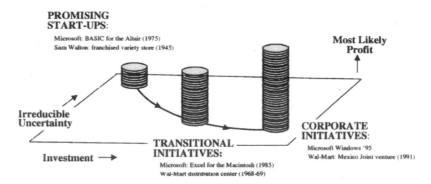

PROMISING START-UPS:
Microsoft: BASIC for the Altair (1975)
Sam Walton: franchised variety store (1945)

Most Likely Profit

Irreducible Uncertainty

Investment →

TRANSITIONAL INITIATIVES:
Microsoft: Excel for the Macintosh (1985)
Wal-Mart distribution center (1968-69)

CORPORATE INITIATIVES:
Microsoft Windows '95
Wal-Mart: Mexico Joint venture (1991)

Figure IN.1. Investment, Uncertainty, and Profit

start-up stage, entrepreneurs such as Bill Gates and Paul Allen, the cofounders of Microsoft, pursue highly uncertain projects that do not require much up-front investment and that are unlikely to generate large profits. In order to grow, entrepreneurs invest in larger and somewhat less uncertain projects. When companies such as Microsoft eventually reach maturity, they focus on initiatives that require significant up-front investment—with commensurately large expected profits—and relatively low uncertainty.

Changes in the nature of opportunities lead to changes in the problems entrepreneurs face and the tasks they must perform. The founders of new businesses, who face significant capital constraints and great uncertainty, rely on opportunistic adaptation to unexpected events. As businesses grow and commit more resources to less uncertain initiatives (i.e., with more defined risks and returns), the opportunism gives way to systematic attempts to anticipate and plan for the long term. New tasks entail changes in the necessary traits and skills. In the beginning, a high tolerance for ambiguity and capacity for adaptation are crucial; the subsequent evolution of a business turns on the entrepreneurs' ability to formulate and implement a long-term strategy; and, in the large, mature corporation, the success of new initiatives depends on a diffused organizational capability rather than the talents of the top decision-makers.

The tendency of businesses of different sizes and maturity to specialize in different—and often complementary—initiatives has important implications for the social good. It affects the development of new technologies and markets and how they interact with the existing economic structures.

This thumbnail sketch raises questions about the lineage and supporting evidence for my propositions: What relationship do these ideas bear to the existing literature? What research are they based on? The remainder of this Introduction addresses these questions and provides an overview of the chapters that follow.

1. Economic Theory

This book examines the birth and evolution of firms primarily from an economic point of view and relies extensively on terms and findings drawn from the economic literature. Economic theory does not, however, provide its basic frame of reference. As we will see, there is a considerable disjoint between the concrete efforts of entrepreneurs to start and build businesses and the central concerns of contemporary economic research. Many of the variables studied in this book lie outside the domain of modern economics.

Entrepreneurs do not play a prominent role in modern economic theory. Economist William J. Baumol observes that entrepreneurs made "frequent but shadowy" appearances in the writings of classical economists but have now "virtually disappeared from the theoretical literature."[2] References to entrepreneurs in formal economic theory are "scanty or more often totally absent." The theory assumes "entrepreneurless" firms with a management group that "reacts mechanically to changes imposed on it by fortuitous external developments."[3] It "offers no promise of being able to deal effectively with the description and analysis of the entrepreneurial function."[4]

Baumol and some other economists have provided roughly similar explanations for why the theory found in standard college economic texts excludes the entrepreneur. The sidebar "The 'Disappearance' of the Entrepreneur" summarizes Humberto Barreto's argument that the roles classical economists used to attribute to entrepreneurs "simply cannot exist within the framework of orthodox economic theory." According to Barreto, the critical assumptions required to make the theory work, such as perfectly informed and rational decision-making, leave no room for the classical entrepreneurial functions of coordination, arbitrage, innovation, and uncertainty bearing.

Basic microeconomic theory involves a trade-off. It specifies precisely the equilibrium that leads to an optimal allocation of society's resources. The familiar price and quantity model tells us that the point at which the demand curve intersects with the supply curve represents the most socially desirable equilibrium. And it predicts that with many rational and informed buyers and sellers, the market will reach this equilibrium. The theory does not attempt to explain, however, how an equilibrium changes. The innovative activity of entrepreneurs analyzed by Schumpeter that moves supply and demand curves lies outside the model.

Advanced theories—of the sort that students encounter in graduate economic programs rather than core college courses—do modify the assumptions that, according to Barreto, preclude entrepreneurial functions. Agency theory, "behavioral" economics, Industrial Organization (IO), and other such subfields analyze the consequences of incomplete or asymmetric information, decision-makers who are only "boundedly" rational, and oligopolistic

The "Disappearance" of the Entrepreneur

Barreto classifies the roles played by the entrepreneur in the history of economic thought into the four categories of coordination, arbitrage, innovation, and uncertainty bearing. The entrepreneur as *coordinator* dates back to Jean-Baptiste Say, a French political economist of the early nineteenth century. According to Say, the entrepreneur hires and combines factors of production (such as land, capital, and labor) and serves as "the link of communication" between the "various classes of producers" and between the "producer and the consumer." The entrepreneur therefore is "the center of many bearings and relations."[5]

Some economists from the "Austrian" school attribute the role of *arbitrage* to entrepreneurs. According to Israel Kirzner, "the 'pure' entrepreneur observes the opportunity to sell something at a higher price than that at which he can buy it."[6] By recognizing and acting on opportunities for arbitrage profit, the entrepreneur moves markets toward equilibrium.

Other "Austrians" treat the entrepreneur as an *innovator* who disrupts the existing order and market equilibrium. According to Joseph Schumpeter, who popularized this view, entrepreneurs undertake "new combinations of productive means," creating new products, methods of production, markets, supply sources, or forms of organization. The new combinations lead to the "creative destruction" of the old order and bring about economic change and growth. Schumpeter's entrepreneurs do not, however, bear the risks of their innovations: "Risk obviously always falls on the owner of the means of production or of the money-capital which was paid for them, hence never on the entrepreneur as such."[7]

The entrepreneur's *uncertainty-bearing* role may be traced back to Richard Cantillon, an eighteenth-century French economist. Cantillon suggested that entrepreneurs performed the vital economic function of committing to buy inputs without knowing how much customers would pay for their end products. For example, farmers paid fixed sums for their inputs, with the hope of realizing prices in excess of their costs; "carriers" bought the farmers' produce, which they would "carry" to the city for sale at an uncertain price to wholesalers; wholesalers then faced uncertain prices in their transactions with retailers and retailers with their customers. This chain of speculation and risk-bearing (rather than arbitrage) was the key to the market system. Frank Knight refined the risk-bearing idea to argue that profit represents the entrepreneur's reward for assuming responsibility for unmeasurable and unquantifiable risk, which he called "uncertainty."[8]

These varied theories, according to Barreto, shared one "fundamental characteristic," namely, "the central position granted to the entrepreneurial function." In all the theories, "the disappearance of the entrepreneur would bring the market system to a halt."[9] Moreover, Barreto's analysis suggests that all four entrepreneurial functions were incorporated, at least to some degree, in the development of microeconomic theory in the early neoclassical era (between 1870 and 1914). For instance, Léon Walras (whom Barreto calls "the father of neoclassical economics"[10]) incorporated functions of coordination and arbitrage in his theories. Alfred Marshall's theories were "eclectic": His entrepreneurs were coordinators, arbitrageurs, innovators, and uncertainty bearers, "depending on the matter at hand."[11] Irving Fisher analyzed the entrepreneur's uncertainty-bearing role, and for John Bates Clark, "the entrepreneur as arbitrageur was an indispensable element in a progressive dynamic economy."[12]

In the mature neoclassical era (from 1914 to the early 1930s), according to Barreto, "two of the greatest authors on entrepreneurship—Joseph Schumpeter and Frank Knight—gained broad recognition and acceptance."[13] Neoclassical theory, which became "orthodox economic theory" during this period, retained the entrepreneur as "a key agent"[14] in explaining the market system. But in the modern microeconomic era, which began in the early 1930s, the entrepreneur suddenly and rapidly "disappeared." "Entrepreneurial considerations," Barreto writes, "no longer played a fundamental role in the orthodox theoretical explanation of the market system ... the word 'entrepreneur' was sometimes used, but it lost any special meaning ... the fruitful theories of innovation, uncertainty bearing, coordination and arbitrage were downplayed or totally neglected."[15]

The rapid evolution of modern microeconomics led to "the ultimate fulfillment, in economics of a perfectly interlocking, self-contained model";[16] prior neoclassical theories had inconsistent elements. But the core assumptions of the refined model—of a "production" function that precisely defined the output that would result from a set of inputs, of perfect information, and of rational choice—preclude incorporation of any of the traditional entrepreneurial roles. Coordination, arbitrage, innovation, and uncertainty-bearing have no place in a world populated with perfectly informed, perfectly rational agents.[17] Any relaxation of the core assumptions destroys the integrated consistent nature of the models; as Barreto puts it, the choice between a model whose pieces "fit perfectly together to form a grand, unified whole" and entrepreneurial functions is "an 'either-or' proposition; there is no marginal adjustment, no happy medium." It is due to this stark choice that "the entrepreneur has been removed from the orthodox explanatory scheme."[18]

industry structures. But assumptions that allow for entrepreneurial activity do not necessarily lead to its inclusion. Many of the theories share the equilibrium orientation of standard microeconomics, albeit with a twist: They predict the misallocation rather than the optimal use of resources. The models suggest that markets with asymmetric information (as in secondhand cars, when sellers are better informed than buyers) do not clear at optimal prices. Irrational investors who "overreact" or "underreact" to information engender excessive volatility in stock prices. Oligopolies with market power restrict supply and charge prices that are higher than the socially optimal ones we would find under perfect competition.

As with the basic microeconomics they seek to extend, many of the advanced theories do not focus on changes in the fundamental determinants of market outcomes.* Standard IO models assume that the number and size of competitors in an industry (like the demand and supply curves of basic microeconomics) are largely determined by the available technology and consumer tastes.[19] The models can predict what happens when technologies and tastes change but not why such changes take place. Only a subset of the advanced theories focuses on the purposive development of new technologies and wants. And compared to Schumpeter and Knight, who analyzed the psyche and motivations of entrepreneurs, the modern theories of economic change take a more stylized approach to the individuals and businesses that undertake new initiatives. Differences in entrepreneurial drive and ability do not lead to differences in the outcomes predicted by these theories.

In pointing out the variables that economists usually leave out of their theories (or treat as exogenous factors) I do not mean to attack modern economic research. All theory involves simplification and starts with some exogenous factors or givens. Any predictive model relies on the unexplained state of its independent variables to forecast the value of its dependent variable. Economists choose their independent and dependent variables to address problems they consider important and that they can study with techniques that conform to the norms of their discipline. This book seeks to use and complement their theories, not to challenge their predictions. It combines the ideas from classical works about entrepreneurial functions and the modern literature with the type of case studies

---

* Apparently the advanced models trade off more realistic assumptions for less certain predictions. For instance, the basic model tells us exactly what to expect under conditions of perfect competition. According to the economist Fisher, models of imperfect or oligopolistic competition lead us to conclude only this: "A great many outcomes are known to be possible—with outcomes depending on what variables the oligopolists use and how they form conjectures about each other" (Fisher [1989], p. 117). The theory generates, Fisher continues, "a large number of stories, each one an anecdote describing what might happen in some particular situation" rather than "a full, coherent formal theory of what must happen or a theory that tells us how what happens depends on well defined measurable variables" (Fisher [1989], p. 118).

that economists do not typically use. The concrete activities of entrepreneurs that it examines have considerable economic significance but lie outside the domain of normal economic analysis.

2. Business Research

Whereas economic theory provides many of the specific tools we will use to study the subject, the organizing framework of this book derives from business or management research. As we will see, the "entrepreneurial" functions of innovation, risk-bearing, and so on represent a central concern of business or management research. And although we cannot directly apply its findings—which deal mainly with initiatives undertaken by large companies—to businesses started by individual entrepreneurs, the research provides a crucial backdrop.

The research of business has become a noteworthy form of economic inquiry in the past few decades. Business schools (and some consulting firms) now devote at least as much effort to the study of economic phenomena as do departments of economics. The research staff and budgets of the economics faculties at Berkeley, Chicago, Harvard, MIT, Northwestern, Pennsylvania, Stanford, and Yale are matched or exceeded by those of their business schools. Among the twenty universities that house the most prestigious economics departments in the United States, as ranked by the 1997 Gourman Report, only Princeton does not have a business school.[20] The leading management-consulting firms also now have research budgets comparable to those of the leading business schools.

Although it is not so labeled, the distinctive feature of virtually all the research and instruction in business schools is its emphasis on entrepreneurial functions. Outsiders do not always appreciate the pervasive interest in entrepreneurial functions. According to the economist Baumol, business schools that would like to provide training in entrepreneurship "usually succeed in imparting only the skills of the manager."[21] Baumol defines the manager as "the individual who oversees the ongoing efficiency of continuing processes,"[22] in contrast to the entrepreneur, who undertakes novel or nonroutine activities. In fact, although they grant degrees in the humdrum-sounding activity of administration, business schools have little interest in maintaining existing equilibriums. Business schools do not secure their clientele by offering instruction on how to keep things they way they are. Rather, like Schumpeterian entrepreneurs, they focus on the innovative activities businesses undertake to increase their profits.

The curricula and research of business schools focus on the development of new products, processes, and forms of organizations, on the management of the attendant risks, and on the coordination of several functions and inputs—activities that line up with classical definitions of entrepreneurial functions. The entrepreneurial orientation goes beyond obvious research of technology and R&D; it permeates all business disciplines. Research in the field of marketing, for instance, investigates the development of new products or forms of distribution. Finance studies how companies evaluate and fund risky new activities. Even cost accounting and transfer pricing, seemingly remote from matters entrepreneurial, typically derive their importance from changes in a company's product mix and the coordination of multiple organizational units.

The focus on entrepreneurial functions often makes business research less precise and internally consistent than mainstream economic research. We encounter many theories with diverse origins and that use different terms and may offer conflicting prescriptions. They can lack the "well defined, measurable variables"[23] that the economist Fisher demands of good theory.* (Michael Porter, for instance, suggests that "differentiated" and "cost-leadership" strategies dominate a "stuck in the middle" approach.) Although it is sometimes tempting, we should not attribute the imprecision of the constructs found in business theories to the gullibility of their consumers or to the intellectual sloppiness of their producers. As the consumers seem to instinctively appreciate, some ambiguity is unavoidable in theories concerned with new sources of profit rather than with the analysis of equilibrium conditions. A reliable, precisely defined formula for making a profit is a logical impossibility. Nor can we expect what Fisher calls a "generalizing theory" that "proceeds from wide assumptions to inevitable consequences."[24] Business school theories are necessarily, in Fisher's terms, "exemplifying theories" that "suggestively reveal the possibility of certain phenomena"[25]—that is, they describe what *can* happen rather than what *must* happen.

The perception that business schools focus on maintaining the existing order probably derives from their interest in the *routinized* initiatives undertaken by large corporations rather than on new businesses started by entrepreneurs. Large companies, Baumol wrote in 1993, have transformed innovation into a "routine and predictable process" that "lends itself to the humdrum talents of capable managers."[26] In a number of industries, Baumol observes, managers do not rely on "the fortuitous appearance of new ideas." Rather, they "treat the generation of new techniques and, even more, of new products as a *routine,* albeit critical, element of their operations, one that is built into the company's organization and budgeted like any of its other activities."[27]

Companies often prepare "a menu of possible inventions from which the proposed developments are selected by another process that has also been made routine." Baumol cites the example of Eastman Kodak, which uses computers to generate "pseudo photographs" with variation in contrast, brightness, balance of colors, and so on. Kodak then polls panels of

---

* We should, note, however that some basic constructs in economic theory, such as the demand curve, also cannot be directly observed or measured.

consumers and professional photographers to decide "which of the computer generated pseudo photographs promise to be the most saleable, and the company laboratories are assigned the task of inventing a film that will yield the desired results."[28]

The focus on routinized initiatives limits the direct applicability of much of business research to individual entrepreneurs who usually start their ventures in a much more ad hoc way. To illustrate, let us go back to 1938 to visit two young engineers in Palo Alto, California, who have pooled $538 to start their own business. They attempt to craft several electronic products in a rented garage, including a bowling alley foot-fault indicator and a harmonica tuner. Eventually they build an audio oscillator, which, without any market research, they price at $54.40, because according to one of the founders, it reminds them of "54°40' or Fight!," the 1844 slogan used in the campaign to establish the U.S. border in the Pacific Northwest. They soon discover that they cannot afford to build the machines at $54.40. Luckily, their nearest competitor is a $400 oscillator, which gives them room to raise prices.[29] Half a century later, their business has grown to a worldwide enterprise with more than $10 billion in revenues, called Hewlett-Packard (HP). HP continues its founders' interest in developing new products and lines of business. But in contrast to William Hewlett and David Packard's early efforts, executives at HP now undertake initiatives methodically: The features, prices, and marketing of new products are now tied to systematic analyses of customer needs, competitive offerings, long-term strategies, financial returns, and so on.

Although the research about the decisions faced by executives such as Lewis Platt, the current chairman and CEO of HP, does not tell us much about how individuals like Hewlett and Packard start and grow their businesses, it can be of considerable indirect help. The knowledge we have accumulated about large-scale enterprise provides reassurance about what a study of individual entrepreneurs could achieve. In contrast to many economic models that treat changes in technology and demand as exogenous, random events, business research suggests that we can analyze purposive change. Profitable initiatives aren't always based on chance discoveries. Even when chance provides the starting point for an initiative, it usually takes considerable purposive effort to turn it into a profitable enterprise. We cannot expect (per Baumol's "Heisenberg" principle) to derive a foolproof formula or a "complete" description for starting a profitable business; but, our accumulated knowledge of initiatives undertaken by large companies indicates a considerable gap between what we now know and what we could learn.

Knowledge developed about large companies provides an invaluable reference point for an empirical study of new businesses. Researchers cannot "just observe"; they also need a theory to guide the selection of significant facts. In lieu of a well-developed theory, we can start with the hypothesis that businesses started by individual entrepreneurs are just like the initiatives undertaken by large companies. The differences we actually observe can help us formulate more refined propositions. The comparative analysis leads us to examine the relationship between the improvised approach of individual entrepreneurs and the nature of the opportunities they pursue. It allows us to confront issues of luck and personality head on. We can ask whether and why luck plays a more important role in start-ups than in the initiatives undertaken by large corporations. We can examine the relevance of the innate traits that are popularly attributed to entrepreneurs: What distinctive problems and tasks make decisiveness, perseverance, willingness to take risk, and so on more important for the entrepreneur than for the large-company executive? Questions such as this can take us a long way toward demystifying the phenomena.

Besides illuminating an important hidden part of the economy, a comparative analysis provides a fresh perspective on the whole. We gain a broader understanding of the advantages and constraints of companies such as IBM and Procter & Gamble by comparing them to new and fledgling businesses than we might from just studying a sample of large companies. We can analyze the initiatives they specialize in and the degree to which they can—or should—adopt the freewheeling approach of the individual entrepreneur. And by examining the distinctive roles of new, transitional, and mature businesses, we can develop new insights about the process of economic change.

3. Studies Conducted

As mentioned in the Preface, I undertook a study of start-ups to help define the contents of a Harvard Business School elective course on new ventures. I sought to identify issues that the largest possible proportion of M.B.A. entrepreneurs would find useful. I could not, however, use *a priori* logic or a few in-depth case studies to select such issues. Ventures started by business school alumni are found in fields as diverse as dairy farming and launching satellites, and they range in size from niche "lifestyle" businesses to billion-dollar global companies such as Intuit. A large sample study was therefore necessary to systematically identify the issues most universally important to this heterogeneous set. But issues derived from the entire population of new ventures or small businesses might not hold much interest for my target audience.

Most start-ups derive from individuals seeking self-employment rather than the conduct of an entrepreneurial effort to develop new products, markets, technologies, and so on. In 1992, for example, about 21 million businesses filed tax returns in the United States. Seventy-one percent of these returns were from sole proprietors, and only 4 percent reported revenues of more than $1 million. The typical business apparently starts small and stays small. Although two-thirds of net new jobs in the private sector have originated among small firms in the past twenty-five years, only a few rapidly growing companies have created these jobs. Duncan and Handler found that only 24 percent of companies that started in 1985 and were surviving in 1994 reported *any* increase in employment. Birch and Medoff estimate that between 1988 and 1992, 4 percent of all firms—about 350,000 "gazelles"—generated 60 percent of all the new jobs in the U.S. economy.[30] Thus we may infer that a random sample drawn from the 700,000 or so businesses started each year would be swamped by hairdressers, laundries, and other such marginal businesses. It would not generate useful models for students with high opportunity costs who wanted to start companies. Nor would it advance our understanding of individual entrepreneurs.

Although Birch and others had gathered statistical data on gazelles, there was little reliable research on the hows and the whys of their success. In pursuit of breadth (compared to the individual case-study approach) and depth (as compared to an analysis of census or survey data), I undertook a far-reaching field study of start-ups. With the help of research associates Kevin Hinton and Laura Pochop, I interviewed founders of 100 companies from the 1989 *Inc.* 500 list, a compilation of the fastest-growing privately held companies in the United States. The average company on this list of 500 companies had 1988 revenues of about $15 million, 135 employees, and a five-year sales growth of 1,407 percent. (Appendix 1 contains further details including the list of companies and descriptive statistics of the sample.)

I narrowed my list of prospective interviewees to companies founded in the previous eight years, on the ground that the start-up history of older companies would be more difficult to obtain. The *Inc.* list's requirement of a five-year track record of rapid growth helped eliminate marginal ventures whose stories I believed would not contribute much to my objectives. At the same time, by sampling from a population of 500 companies, I avoided drawing inferences from a few billion-dollar "outliers" such as Microsoft or Federal Express, whose success might be attributed to the extraordinary talent or luck of the founders. The companies I studied—Software 2000, Gammalink, and Modular Instruments, to mention just a few—were successes but not household names.

The research was time-consuming. To get start-ups' stories in all their complexity, I conducted face-to-face interviews. Start-ups are characterized by close relationships among financing, marketing strategies, hiring, and control systems that would be hard to capture through a structured mail survey. Also, since executives of successful companies are inundated with mail surveys, response rates are generally low. Although we had some difficulty in contacting entrepreneurs and scheduling appointments, only a few declined to be interviewed. Each interview lasted from one to three hours.

Usually two researchers took handwritten notes, which were then compiled into a single transcript and returned to the interviewees for review.

To my knowledge, this is one of the broadest, most in-depth studies of start-ups ever conducted. Whereas other field studies have focused on limited geographic regions or industries, we visited more than twenty cities and towns in a dozen states to interview entrepreneurs in a wide range of businesses. Researchers who have undertaken similarly broad samples have relied on mail surveys.

I decided against trying to study an equivalent number of unsuccessful start-ups. I was, by design, comparing good apples and good oranges—using the "known" attributes of large, well-established corporations to tease out the distinguishing features of what I will call *promising* new businesses. I had to study successful cases because I could not know how to define a promising start-up until I had done the research. As we will see there are important differences between the origins of the *Inc.* companies and the common "marginal" start-up that I had to discover in the course of my study. I was not trying to explain variations in a predefined population of, say, high-technology start-ups or venture-capital-backed start-ups.

Moreover, although I do not discuss it in this book, my research also had a prescriptive purpose—I wanted to derive practical lessons about starting new businesses. To the extent that starting a business involves skills that are difficult to codify, I felt that in the first stage of developing a model of good practice, I ought to pay more attention to the "winners." A similar focus on successful practitioners informs studies of art, music, statecraft, surgery, and other fields involving a high level of skill. Eric Erikson's analysis of leadership, for instance, is derived from studying the lives of statesmen such as Gandhi, not of ward bosses.[31] When tennis players seek to improve their games, they turn to videos and observation of champions, not of weekend hackers. Of course, some knowledge of poor practice helps provide a cognitive backdrop for observing good practice. So although I could not identify in advance a suitable control group of failures, I did study and write cases on unsuccessful ventures. Indeed, the case studies in the course I taught had almost as many failures as successes.

I am aware that the research approach I have used can only generate plausible hypotheses. As mentioned, this is an exploratory work intended to provide propositions for modification or refutation through more research. My observations and analysis also reflect the theories with which I had prior familiarity. A researcher with different training—say, a sociologist—would likely have asked the *Inc.* company founders different questions and seen dimensions of the phenomena that I did not. Here, too, I hope that this work will encourage a broader inquiry that produces a more complete explanation.

After completing my *Inc.* company interviews I tested the findings, albeit crudely, through some other efforts. I conducted a mail survey of a hundred self-employed alumni of Harvard Business School to see whether the problems faced by the *Inc.* founders would be germane to M.B.A. entrepreneurs. One could reasonably infer that given their opportunity costs, the respondents would not pursue marginal ventures. In contrast to my *Inc.* sample, I did not select subjects on the basis of objective criteria for success. Nevertheless, as described in my note, "The Road Well Traveled,"[32] the experiences of the respondents to the survey turned out to be quite similar to those of the *Inc.* founders. Over several years I also had my students write more than two hundred papers on successful entrepreneurs. Instead of an examination, the students were required to write a "critical history" of a venture they considered successful: they had to describe the basic story and evaluate the strategies employed and the results obtained. Students were encouraged to interview their subjects rather than rely on secondary data sources; those who did (the great majority) were then required to have the entrepreneurs certify the accuracy of the narrative sections of their paper. Predictably, the papers covered more celebrities (Jann Wenner of *Rolling Stone*, Scott Cook of Intuit, and Calvin Klein) than I had found in the *Inc.* and HBS alumni lists. (See Appendix 2.) The experiences of this group, however, were remarkably similar to those of the other entrepreneurs I had studied and thus helped corroborate the findings of my interviews and mail surveys.

4. Contrasts and Questions

My research suggests that like Hewlett-Packard, most noteworthy businesses have unremarkable origins. Their founders face significant capital constraints. More than 80 percent of the *Inc.* founders I studied bootstrapped their ventures with modest funds derived from personal savings, credit cards, second mortgages, and so on; the median start-up capital was about $10,000. Only 5 percent raised their initial equity from professional venture capitalists. Their ventures were improvised—most *Inc.* company founders, like William Hewlett and David Packard, did not spend much time searching for opportunities, doing market research, or writing business plans; they merely replicated or modified an idea they encountered through previous employment or by accident. Lacking a strategy, and sometimes even a goal, for building a long-lived business, they adapted to unexpected opportunities and problems; many stumbles and detours characterized the evolution of their businesses. The *Inc.* companies did not have seasoned professional managers at their helm. Rather, they had enthusiastic but somewhat inexperienced founders who personally undertook most of the crucial functions of the business and recruited whomever they could for tasks they were too stretched to perform themselves.

The student papers on successful entrepreneurs and the mail survey of HBS alumni corroborated the widespread prevalence of bootstrapped, improvised start-ups. The founders of now celebrated companies such as *Rolling Stone,* Calvin Klein, Waste Management, and Wal-Mart started without much capital, research, industry experience, or top-notch employees. Their ventures did not attain success overnight—it took these companies decades to develop the assets and organizations that eventually made them the leading players in their fields.

New businesses financed by professional venture capitalists represent an exception to the general pattern of gradual evolution. As mentioned in the Preface, VC-backed start-ups such as Compaq represent an out-of-the-ordinary phenomenon. VCs provide capital to an elite group of entrepreneurs after careful, due diligence and research. The funds, counsel, and connections provided by the VCs, the quality and depth of the founding team, and a unique technology or concept allow these businesses to start out in the place that others take years to reach. They leapfrog into the middle of the investment-uncertainty-profit diagram (Fig. IN.1). Sam Walton built a distribution center in 1969 more than two decades after opening his first store. The VC-backed office products retailer Staples invested in such a facility in its second year. Microsoft took nine years to reach $50 million in annual revenues; the VC-backed Lotus Development Corporation shipped $53 million of its 1-2-3 spreadsheet in its first year.

The VC-backed start-up model does dominate in some fields, such as biotechnology and supercomputers, where start-ups have to invest significant capital before they realize any revenues. But in most other fields, the well-funded and carefully planned start-up represents the exception. Even the founders of companies such as Cisco Systems, who eventually turn to venture capitalists to secure the funds and managerial expertise they need to grow, start out on credit cards and sweat equity.

These findings raise several questions. Why do most entrepreneurs face such severe capital constraints? Does the small number of VC-backed start-ups indicate some kind of capital market failure? Why do decision-makers in large companies analyze initiatives much more extensively than do most individual entrepreneurs? Does the limited effort devoted by many entrepreneurs indicate an irrational "overconfidence"? Or, conversely, does the large corporation systematically overinvest in analysis? What distinctive problems does the improvised model entail, and to what degree are boldness, imagination, perseverance, and other such qualities important in solving them?

A second set of questions relates to the evolution of improvised start-ups. The transformation of successful VC-backed start-ups such as Compaq into large, established corporations involves relatively few discontinuities; their structures, strategies, and personnel have an inbuilt capacity for scaling up. The sharper contrasts between early efforts of entrepreneurs such as a Hewlett and Packard, Michael Dell, Bill Gates and Paul Allen and the "mature," multibillion-dollar HP, Dell Computers, and

Microsoft suggest that the transformation of the improvised start-up into an established company involves more radical and comprehensive changes. What are the underlying factors and mechanisms of these changes? What distinctive problems do entrepreneurs face building and growing their businesses that they don't face in the start-up phase? Does a different set of skills and traits come into play?

A third set of questions relates to social consequences and precursors. How is the economic effect of the improvised start-up different from that of the well-planned large company initiative? What environmental conditions influence the relative distribution of start-up and large-company activity? Similarly, what are the distinctive economic consequences of the transition from start-up to mature corporation? What are the factors that facilitate such changes?

5. Overview

The three parts of this book correspond to the three sets of questions mentioned above.

Part I examines the origins of new businesses. It discusses the following propositions (illustrated in Fig. IN.2) about promising start-ups:

Initial conditions ("endowments"). Most entrepreneurs start their businesses by copying or slightly modifying someone else's idea. They also usually don't have deep managerial or industry experience. This lack of proprietary ideas and "verifiable" human capital* (rather than the short-sightedness of investors or an "imperfection" of the financial market) precludes most entrepreneurs from raising much outside funding and forces them to "bootstrap" their start-ups with modest personal funds. The number of VC-backed start-ups is relatively small, I suggest, because of the limited supply of individuals who want to start their own businesses and who have the ideas and experience needed to secure outside funding.

Nature of businesses. Successful new ventures (like the *Inc.* 500 companies) started by entrepreneurs without novel ideas and significant funding tend to cluster in the upper left-hand region of the uncertainty-investment-profit diagram. (see Fig. IN.1). They cannot make the up-front investment usually required to undertake projects that hold the promise of large total returns. And although it may seem counterintuitive for some readers, high uncertainty (arising from technological change or deregulation, for instance) helps entrepreneurs who start businesses with limited endowments. Although their most likely profit is low, the unusually resourceful, hardworking, or lucky entrepreneurs who start businesses in an uncertain

---

* I limit the use of "human capital" here and in subsequent discussions to the skills, knowledge, reputation, and so on that an individual acquires and demonstrates through experience and education. I do not include the latent or innate talents for which there is no ex ante objective evidence.

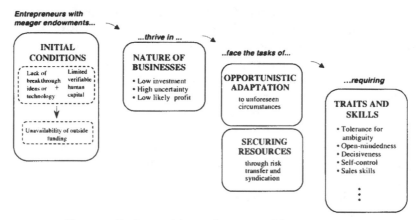

Figure IN.2. Propositions about Promising Start-ups

field have a small chance of securing a large payoff. And if they don't succeed, bootstrapped entrepreneurs have little to lose financially. In contrast, the founders of businesses with low uncertainty (in lawn mowing or hairdressing, for instance) all face a distribution of returns that is tightly clustered around a mediocre average.

Opportunistic adaptation. Entrepreneurs who start uncertain businesses with limited funds have little reason to devote much effort to prior planning and research. They cannot afford to spend much time or money on the research; the modest likely profit doesn't merit much; and the high uncertainty of the business limits its value.

Sketchy planning and high uncertainty require entrepreneurs to adapt to many unanticipated problems and opportunities. One entrepreneur likens the process of starting a new business to jumping from rock to rock up a stream rather than constructing the Golden Gate Bridge from a detailed blueprint. Often, to borrow a term from Elster's[33] discussion of biological evolution, entrepreneurs adapt to unexpected circumstances in an "opportunistic" fashion: Their response derives from a spur-of-the-moment calculation made to maximize immediate cash flow. Capital-constrained entrepreneurs cannot afford to sacrifice short-term cash for long-term profits. They have to play rapid-fire pinball rather than a strategic game of chess.

Securing resources. Entrepreneurs face a difficult problem in convincing customers, employees, credit, and other such resource providers to take a chance on their start-ups. They have no track record, and without a capital base, they cannot underwrite others' risks. Bootstrapped entrepreneurs cannot, for instance, offer credible money-back guarantees to customers, employment contracts to recruits, or collateral to banks. Instead, they syndicate or transfer risks to others. They undertake an extensive search for parties whose interests, values, and decision-making processes predispose them to take a chance on a start-up. They offer special deals to their first resource providers to compensate them for the risk of being the guinea pig. They frame the - trade-offs—usually through face-to-face selling—persuasively, by accentuating the positives and downplaying the risks others face.

Traits and skills. Starting an uncertain business requires a high *tolerance for ambiguity*. Entrepreneurs have to confront fluid, rapidly changing situations where they cannot anticipate the nature of the outcomes, let alone assess their probability distributions. A high tolerance for financial loss does not, however, significantly influence the propensity to start ventures where entrepreneurs do not invest much capital or face high opportunity costs for their time.

Chance events and serendipity naturally play important roles in uncertain, improvised start-ups, but so does the entrepreneur's capacity to overcome the challenges such ventures entail. Entrepreneurs who effectively adapt to unexpected problems and opportunities and who persuade resource providers to take a chance on their start-ups can influence their luck. In businesses that lack differentiating technologies or concepts, personal traits such as open-mindedness, the willingness to make decisions quickly, the ability to cope with setbacks and rejection, and skill in face-to-face selling help differentiate the winners from the also-rans. Overall, the reality of bootstrapped businesses does not bear out the popular image of an entrepreneur as an irrational, overconfident risk-seeker. Quite the contrary. Entrepreneurs can pursue "heads I win, tails I don't lose much" opportunities because they are less prone than average to irrational ambiguity aversion and they have a talent for exploiting the cognitive biases and defects of other individuals. They require exceptional self-control; they may have to tolerate difficult customers with unreasonable demands and focus on winning orders rather than arguments.

Large companies undertake different kinds of initiatives and follow a more systematic approach. Employees who initiate new projects have access to significant funds but are subject to extensive scrutiny by internal control systems. Initiatives whose payoffs are too small to cover the costs of evaluation and monitoring therefore get screened out. Advocates of new initiatives conduct extensive research and formulate detailed plans to secure approval. This creates a bias against projects whose uncertain nature makes it difficult to research the risks and returns. And prior planning and relatively low uncertainty reduce the need for opportunistic adaptation after the project has been launched.

Large companies can leverage their capital and reputations to secure customers, employees, and other resources for their initiatives. They can underwrite others' risks, and they can signal their commitment to the initiative by putting their capital and their reputations on the line.

Unlike the bootstrapped start-ups whose success depends on the innate skills and capabilities of one or two individuals, the success of an initiative undertaken by a large company turns on the joint efforts of many individuals and functions. The soundness of the initial idea also plays an important role; after-the-fact adaptation cannot make up for basic initial flaws.

The improvised start-ups of the capital-constrained individual and the carefully planned investments of companies such as IBM that run into hundreds of millions of dollars represent the bookends of entrepreneurial initiatives (see Table IN.1). Other firms and individuals have an in-between evaluation process and access to capital. As indicated in Figure IN.3, they usually fall along the diagonal space in the investment-uncertainty-profit diagram. Few individuals or companies have access to the resources needed to undertake projects, in the upper right region of the diagram, that are both large and highly uncertain. Projects in the bottom left-hand region, which are small and uncertain, have marginal returns and little economic significance.

Part II examines why only some new businesses grow into large, long-lived corporations. According to some models (e.g., in Nelson and Winter's theory), luck plays a central role in the evolution of firms—from many start-ups in an industry, the field gets successively narrowed to a few survivors through a more or less random process. Another theory, popular in the entrepreneurship field, seems to suggest that start-ups naturally pass through successive stages of growth, provided the entrepreneur is willing to delegate authority to subordinates.

Both explanations seem inadequate in view of the substantial differences between a typical start-up and a large corporation. Large companies derive their profits from many tangible and intangible assets such as their patents, know-how, production facilities, brand names, customer relationships, and access to distribution channels. They have deeply embedded mechanisms to coordinate their many assets and activities. They serve large markets. The profitability of many new businesses, in contrast, depends on

Table IN.1. Promising Start-ups vs. Initiatives of Large Corporations

	Promising Start-ups	Corporate Initiatives
Endowments and constraints	Lack of novel ideas and experience → severe capital constraints	Ample capital but subject to extensive checks and balances
Nature of opportunities	Low investment and likely profit; high uncertainty	High investment and likely profit; low uncertainty
Reliance on adaptation	Extensive adaptation, limited prior planning and research	Extensive prior planning and research, limited adaptation
Securing resources	Entrepreneur transfers or syndicates risk to resource providers	Firm (i.e., shareholders) underwrites risks, signals commitment
Differentiating factors	Entrepreneur's personal capacity to adapt, persuade resource providers	Joint effort of many personnel and functions; soundness of initial concept

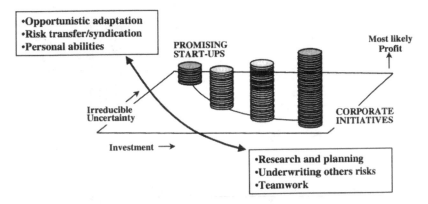

Figure IN.3. Distribution of Significant Initiatives

the personal efforts of the entrepreneur, or sometimes one or two products. The relatively narrow range of assets and activities limits the need for coordination mechanisms in start-ups. And they serve small, niche markets.

Bridging the gap between the fledgling enterprise and the large corporation requires more than just chance or the willingness to delegate tasks. As illustrated in Figure IN.4, entrepreneurs who build large and long-lived businesses make substantial changes in the types of initiatives they pursue and the tasks they perform. The small, "heads I win, tails I don't lose" opportunities used to launch the business give way to a multifaceted, multiperiod program to develop a portfolio of assets and coordination mechanisms and to enter larger markets. In other words, entrepreneurs migrate the initiatives they undertake from the upper left-hand corner of the uncertainty-investment-profit diagram toward the lower right-hand corner.

The effectiveness of a program of initiatives to build a large business depends on the degree to which the individual initiatives complement each other. To realize "complementarity" or "synergy" of investment and effort, entrepreneurs adopt a strategic approach instead of relying on opportunistic adaptation. They have to define and articulate ambitious long-term goals. They formulate general rules (a "strategy") to guide their firm's investments and efforts. And they translate the general rules into specific choices.

An entrepreneur's willingness and capacity to follow a strategic approach turn on a broader set of skills and traits than are necessary in the start-up stage. For instance, as previously mentioned, entrepreneurs usually have little to lose when they start a business; the willingness to bear personal risk often becomes a significant factor, however, in building and growing one. The small number of entrepreneurs who have this broader set of qualities and the desire to undertake a different set of tasks limits the number of start-ups that evolve into large corporations.

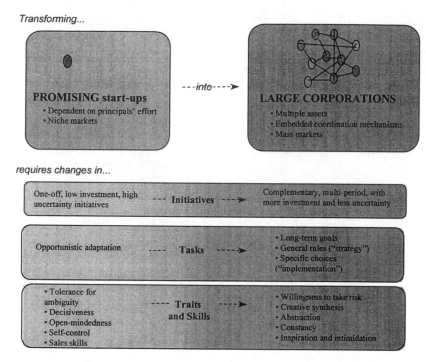

Figure IN.4. Propositions about Firm Evolution

Part III places the evolution of new business in its broader economic and social context. I discuss the economic significance of start-ups and the factors that determine the supply and demand for individual entrepreneurship. In the popular view, start-ups (or fast-growing, owner-managed companies) and large corporations represent competing forms of economic organization. I argue that entrepreneurs and large companies have a symbiotic relationship; in pursuing different kinds of opportunities for themselves, they play distinct and often complementary social roles. I also discuss the factors that determine the level of start-up activity. The recent popularity of individual entrepreneurs derives in part from a belated recognition of their role—they have always accounted for about half of economic activity. These changing perceptions aside, individual entrepreneurs have also increased their actual share of economic activity, as large corporations have withdrawn from activities they were unsuited to perform. Individual entrepreneurs also have benefited from changes in technology, public policies, and the social climate. We should, however, avoid making the error Schumpeter and Galbraith made of assuming that the current trajectory will continue forever. Small, virtual corporations aren't going to take over the world, causing the Justice Department to lay off its antitrust lawyers—witness Microsoft. Moreover, large corporations will eventually complete their retrenchment, and the underlying trends favoring start-ups may reverse themselves.

I conclude with a discussion of unanswered questions. My work has been, of necessity, exploratory. Although we are surrounded by entrepreneurs, their world remains a *terra incognita.* I have tried to provide rudimentary maps and outlines for this largely unexplored territory. Considerable refinement and detail need to be added to make our knowledge of individual entrepreneurs comparable to that of the world of large companies. Such an enterprise, I will suggest, requires realistic expectations about the evidence that can be marshaled to address the critical questions about starting and building new businesses and a careful synthesis of the analytical tools and knowledge derived from many disciplines.

I

The Nature of Promising Start-ups

The following chapters contrast "promising" start-ups, exemplified by the *Inc.* 500 companies, with the following types of ventures: *corporate* initiatives, undertaken by large, public companies, such as new-product launches or entry into new markets; *marginal* start-ups—the many small proprietorships that have little prospect of attaining significant size or profitability; *VC-backed* start-ups—businesses such as Compaq and Intel launched with funding from professional venture capitalists; and "revolutionary" ventures that incorporate a significant large-scale innovation, such as the launch of Federal Express and Motorola's Iridium project.

The categories represent noteworthy archetypes rather than a comprehensive taxonomy. They exclude, for instance, start-ups funded by ad hoc syndicates of wealthy individuals (the "angel" investors) and the initiatives undertaken by "transitional" businesses (sometimes with VC funding) or by large, privately held companies. I have chosen the archetypes with two goals in mind. Comparing promising start-ups to some clearly different types of initiatives highlights the attributes that distinguish an otherwise heterogeneous population of new businesses. The comparison also helps us build a comprehensive map of the "normal" features of entrepreneurial activity. For instance, the extraordinary features of revolutionary start-ups such as Federal Express—and the poor returns of marginal businesses—suggest (see Figure I.1) an inverse relationship between the initial investment and irreducible uncertainty of most economically noteworthy initiatives. Similarly, a comparison of promising, VC-backed and corporate initiatives indicates why prior planning increases and reliance on opportunistic adaptation decreases along the uncertainty-investment curve.

Terms and Assumptions

Following common usage, I call individuals who start their own businesses *entrepreneurs*. Theorists attribute a variety of functions to entrepreneurs, such as coordination, risk-taking, innovation, and arbitrage. I will examine whether and how their risk-taking, innovation, coordination, and so on actually affects their starting and nurturing businesses. I refrain from debating which of these roles are truly "entrepreneurial."

For brevity, I frequently refer to large, well-established companies as *corporations*, even if from a legal point of view a corporation may have only one employee and no fixed assets. To distinguish the decision-makers in corporations from entrepreneurs I refer to them as *executives* or *managers,* even though they play an important entrepreneurial role.

New *initiatives* refer to conscious efforts undertaken to generate new sources of profit that may or may not succeed. They do not include accidental discoveries of new technologies, oil deposits, or other such valuable assets.

My use of the terms in the investment-uncertainty-profit diagram involves the following nuances, whose significance will become clear through concrete examples in subsequent chapters.

Initial or up-front *investment* refers to the irreversible commitment of funds, time, reputation, or other resources that the individual or firm undertaking the initiative makes with the expectation of earning a return.

Uncertainty refers, per Frank Knight's 1921 definition, to unmeasurable and unquantifiable risk. Uncertainty, which may be contrasted with the precisely quantifiable risks of betting on a coin toss or roulette wheel, bears a close relationship to "ambiguity" and "fuzzy probabilities" discussed by Camerer in 1995.[1] Entrepreneurs who undertake uncertain initiatives face a wide spread between desirable and undesirable outcomes, but they cannot quantify the odds they face or even fully anticipate the possible results.* And the uncertainty is *irreducible* to the degree that it

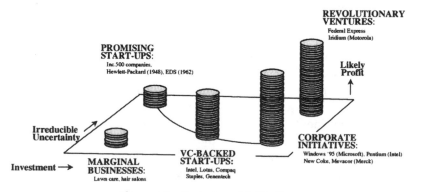

Figure I.1. Archetypal Initiatives

---

* George Wu suggests that "a decision under uncertainty is a situation in which many experts arrive at different subjective probability estimates of the outcomes." Pankaj Ghemawat offers a similar definition for "ambiguity" (Ghemawat [1991], pp. 129–30).

cannot be resolved without actually undertaking the initiative by prior testing or research.

Uncertain initiatives do not necessarily involve novel or pioneering efforts. NASA's meticulously planned *Apollo 11* mission in 1969, which first put a man on the moon, had less uncertainty, for instance, than a hitch-hiker's journey from New York to San Francisco. Similarly, the potential loss depends more on the initial investment in an initiative than on its uncertainty; we can have a large spread between good and bad outcomes without the "worst" outcome involving significant financial loss.

Likely *profit* refers to an objective best guess of the value of the cash flows expected from undertaking an initiative. The construct has three noteworthy features. It is not a "probability weighted" estimate and excludes feasible but unlikely outcomes. Bill Gates and Paul Allen may have been convinced that writing a BASIC for the Altair in 1975 was a stepping-stone to a multibillion-dollar software enterprise; but although this outcome was possible, an informed, objective observer would not have identified this as the most likely case.

Likely profit excludes the investment made; a project to develop an oil field in the North Sea may have large total expected cash flows but a very small "net" present value after capital outlays are taken into account, and it refers only to the value derived from undertaking the initiative. For instance, if an oil company owns reserves that it could sell for $X but chooses to develop the field itself, with the expectation of generating $Y, then we would attribute only $Y – $X to the development effort.

I will assume (following Knight's analysis) that profitable initiatives (in contrast to lucky discoveries) involve at least some irreducible uncertainty and that large likely profits also require large investments. Bootstrapped entrepreneurs, for instance, cannot objectively expect to make the billions of dollars that flow from a mega-oil field or a blockbuster drug after commensurately large prior outlays, so references to "large" or "small" opportunities include the initial investment as well as the likely profit.

Structure

Chapters 1 through 4 focus on promising ventures. Chapter 1 describes how the founders of promising ventures usually start with meager endowments and face significant capital constraints, and it draws the link between these unpromising initial conditions and the nature of the opportunities they can profitably pursue. In Chapter 2 we will see how and why entrepreneurs usually do not devote much effort to planning and instead rely on opportunistic adaptation. Chapter 3 explores the problem of securing resources (i.e., customers and inputs). Chapter 4 discusses the qualities and skills that attract certain individuals to promising businesses and help differentiate the winners from the losers. Chapter 5 contrasts promising start-ups with corporate initiatives in terms of the nature of opportunities pursued, prior planning, approaches to securing resources, and the key success factors. Chapters 6 and 7 extend this contrast to VC-backed start-ups and to revolutionary ventures.

1

Endowments and Opportunities

This chapter discusses the nature of the opportunities that entrepreneurs with meager endowments who start promising tend to exploit. Section 1 describes how entrepreneurs usually launch businesses with mundane ideas and often without much managerial or industry experience. In Section 2, we will see how this lack of valuable intellectual property or human capital leads to severe capital constraints. Sections 3 to 5 discuss the types of opportunities that entrepreneurs with limited capital and undifferentiated concepts can expect to profit from—the market niches most hospitable to start-ups.

Most new businesses lack any ideas or assets that differentiate them from their competitors. They don't really earn a profit; they merely provide a wage to their proprietors that is set by a competitive market for the proprietors' labor. For many individuals this wage turns out to be lower than what they could make working for someone else, so they have a powerful incentive to shut down.

Many founders of "promising" start-ups, such as the *Inc.* 500 companies, also start without novel ideas or scarce assets. Nevertheless, they earn attractive returns: Most of the entrepreneurs we interviewed said their businesses had generated a positive cash flow within months of launch. The profitability of their businesses is difficult to estimate—small firms often keep inaccurate financial records and commingle company and personal expenditures. But the capacity of the *Inc.* companies to finance high rates of growth through internally generated funds* suggest that their profit margins were significantly positive.

---

* Companies on the 1989 *Inc.* 500 list grew their sales, on average, at 169 percent *per year* from 1983 to 1988. The growth was financed primarily through retained earnings: Not only had most of the entrepreneurs I interviewed bootstrapped their ventures with modest personal funds, but also fewer than a fifth had raised follow-on equity financing in the five to eight years they had been in business. About half had raised bank financing but, reflecting the poor creditworthiness of most start-ups, this had usually been in the modest amounts that could be collateralized by the firm's assets three or more years after start-up. We may reasonably infer that if our interviewees hadn't reached profitability quickly they wouldn't have achieved the growth rates needed to make the *Inc.* lists.

How do the *Inc.* companies, about 90 percent of whom don't offer a unique product or service, grow so profitably and so quickly when most other start-ups struggle to survive? The unusual profitability of the *Inc.* companies, I will suggest, derives, to a significant degree, from the hospitable nature of the markets they compete in. On the surface, they seem broadly scattered across the economy. The *Inc.* 500 companies I studied operated in a variety of fields such as pizza chains, trucking, software, SAT preparation, graphic arts, and selling secondhand copiers. But a comparison with the overall population of start-ups suggests some fields contain more *Inc.* companies than others. For instance, County Data Corporation compiles a list of the twenty most popular fields for start-ups that account for about a quarter of all new businesses formed in the United States.[1] We find little overlap between these popular fields, shown in Table 1.1 below, and *Inc.* 500 businesses. None of the hundred *Inc.* founders we interviewed (and only two of the several hundred successful entrepreneurs my students wrote papers on) started ventures in cleaning services, beauty salons, arts and crafts, painting, lawn maintenance, and landscape contracting—businesses that all belong to the list of top twenty start-ups. Conversely, the top twenty list excludes computer software, which accounted for about 10 percent of the *Inc.* companies I studied.

Their limited overlap with popular businesses appears to be a recurring

Table 1.1. Most Popular Start-Ups, 1996

Type of business	Number of start-ups
Construction	24,787
Restaurant	22,781
Retail store	21,081
Cleaning services (residential, commercial)	19,642
Real estate	17,549
Automotive services and repair	16,158
Consultant	13,835
Beauty salon	11,762
Computer service and repair	11,111
Designer	10,676
Management and business consulting	9,665
Arts and crafts	9,412
Painter	9,156
Lawn maintenance	8,498
Marketing programs and services	8,314
Landscape contractor	8,268
Investment broker	8,206
General contractor	8,137
Communications consultant	8,022
Building contractor (remodeling, repairing)	7,998

Source: County Data Corporation

feature of *Inc.* 500 lists, and not just in the sample I happened to study. For instance, from the time that *Inc.* began compiling its lists in 1982, a quarter or more of the companies on the *Inc.* 500 lists have been in computer-related fields—a considerably greater proportion than found in the universe of start-ups. Apparently start-ups can more easily turn a profit in some fields than in others.

One obvious feature of promising businesses is the low scale needed for their profitable operation. The more subtle factor–and the one that most sharply distinguishes promising ventures from marginal ventures–is that of uncertainty. In particular, we will see, opportunities characterized by two types of uncertainty–deriving from market turbulence and from their dependence on their principals' effort–allow entrepreneurs who don't have novel ideas, exceptional training and qualifications, or access to significant funds, a chance to make a profit. The objective, best-guess payoff from starting a promising business typically has the same low value as the pay-off from starting a marginal business. But uncertainty introduces a skew into the distribution of profits and creates a small chance that the entre-preneur will earn a large return (see Fig. 1.1[2]).

1. Concepts and Prior Experience

Promising start-ups bear a remarkable resemblance to the popular new busi-nesses listed in Table 1.1, both in the ordinariness of their concepts and in the limited experience and credentials of their founders. As we might expect, the many new businesses started every year in cleaning services, real estate brokerage, lawn maintenance, and so on, do not involve any material innovations. The human capital needed to start such businesses is also lim-ited. Starting a beauty salon or acquiring a real estate broker's license may require a modest amount of prior training or apprenticeship; the skills

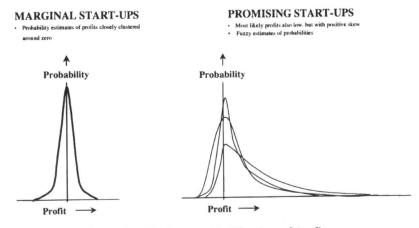

MARGINAL START-UPS
- Probability estimates of profits closely clustered around zero

PROMISING START-UPS
- Most likely profits also low, but with positive skew
- Fuzzy estimates of probabilities

Figure 1.1. Estimated Distribution of Profits

required for lawn maintenance, home cleaning, or painting can be acquired in days. The limited innovation and investment in human capital needed to start such popular but marginal businesses is only to be expected. The ease of entry makes the businesses popular—and limits their profitability. It *is* surprising, however, that most successful businesses, like the *Inc.* 500 companies, also do not start with innovative concepts or founders with much significant prior experience or training.

Concepts

The typical *Inc.* company starts with products or services that are quite similar, at least in their tangible attributes, to the products or services offered by other companies. Of the 100 *Inc.* founders we interviewed, only 6 percent even claimed to have started with unique products or services. As indicated in Figure 1.2, 58 percent said that identical or very close substitutes were available for their product or service, and the rest indicated slight to moderate differences between their offerings and those of their competitors. Another survey of all *Inc.* 500 founders, from 1982 to 1989, also suggests that most promising new ventures do not start with a unique or proprietary product. Only 12 percent of the founders attributed the success of their companies to "an unusual or extraordinary idea," and 88 percent reported their success was mainly due to the "exceptional execution of an ordinary idea."[3]

The *Inc.* founders we interviewed typically imitated someone else's ideas that they often encountered in the course of a previous job. Any innovations

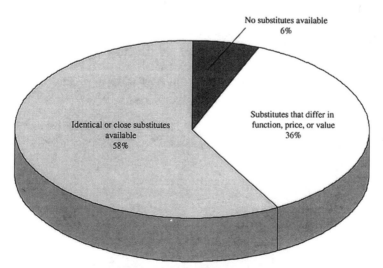

Figure 1.2. Availability of Substitutes
Percentage of 1989 *Inc.* 500 Founders Surveyed
Source: Author's survey.

were incremental or easily replicated; they were too obvious to qualify for a patent and were too visible to protect as a trade secret. To illustrate:

Sean Ropko and his wife founded Excel to sell used copier equipment to wholesalers. Ropko had previously performed the same function for Xerox but started his own firm after Xerox decided to shut down its in-house operation. "People have been buying and selling for years," Ropko told us. "We simply do it better than anyone else."

Carol Sosadian and Atul Tucker started Attronica Computers as a franchisee of Byte Computers, a retail chain. Byte went bankrupt two weeks later. The founders then became a World of Computers franchisee, which also folded. Attronica then became an independent dealer, primarily of AT&T's products, and grew their business by gaining more technical proficiency with the line than AT&T's own direct sales force.

Robert Grosshandler and two partners started the Softa Group because they saw opportunities for "a simple software product." Their first product, Total Recall, gave the partners "market knowledge" but was otherwise not a great success. On the side the Softa Group operated another mundane business—selling hardware and peripherals—to generate cash flow.

Ken Dougan, who had previously worked in the military and as a long-shoreman, started Unique Transportation Systems. Notwithstanding the name, its business was simply to provide trucking services with "one straight truck and two vans." Dougan drove one of the trucks. "I'd talk to people in shipping and I'd do anything they'd ask me to do."

Philip Cramer founded Compuclassics, a software mail order company, in 1984. In his previous job at a music company, Cramer had telephoned a mail order company to purchase a database package: "It took me about ten calls to get through, so I thought that either they can't handle the demand or they have a lousy phone system!" Cramer had a brother-in-law who was a software distributor. "I was tired of the music business, so I asked him about mail order. He thought it was a good idea, but he couldn't do it because he didn't want to compete against the people he was selling to." Cramer then decided to enter the business himself. "We weren't breaking new ground—we were in the second wave. But, we had examples that told us that if we did it right, we'd be okay. Our philosophy was that we'd charge a little more and go out of our way to service."

Karen Kirsch founded Best Mailing Lists, a broker of mailing lists for the direct mail industry, after working for another company in the same business. "My service and product were not unique, but I offered service to which no one could compare."

Mark Lavender and a partner founded Colter Bay to manufacture and sell sweaters and apparel under "private label" to retailers. He had previously been a senior executive with a sweater manufacturer. Lavender's experience and relationships helped Colter Bay "shave 12 to 15 percent off the cost factor" and offer "a quality product at a fair market price."

Stephanie DiMarco and her partner founded Advent Software to develop PC-based software for the investment services industry. Investment management software already existed for mainframes and minicomputers; like other start-ups in the early eighties, Advent attempted to deliver similar features at lower cost on personal computers.

Carol Russell and Rosalind Katz started Russell Personnel Services to provide temporary and full-time workers to employers in San Francisco—a business Russell had previously worked in for nineteen years. Asked what was special about their enterprise, Russell told us that the company gradually differentiated itself in three ways: "First, we introduced the idea of a spokesperson—Carol Russell. If you have a strong personality and credibility, people will buy from you. Second, we took a new approach to advertising—humor. In 1983, nobody did. Third, our counselors became salaried, not commissioned."

John Katzman started the Princeton Review, an SAT preparation service, by conducting classes at Hunter College in New York. Over time, Katzman differentiated his company's services by offering smaller classes, more computer support, and "clever teaching techniques" acquired by recruiting Adam Robinson, a highly regarded tutor.

My students' papers on successful entrepreneurs, too, indicate that imitation or mundane adaptation is the rule for start-ups that go on to become household names and blockbuster successes, not just for the average company on an *Inc.* 500 list. Of the two hundred or so entrepreneurs that my students wrote papers on, only a very small proportion started with a significant innovation. Like the *Inc.* 500 founders, most of the entrepreneurs started by imitating or slightly modifying someone else's idea and introduced breakthrough products or new ways of doing business many years later. To illustrate:

WordPerfect. Alan Ashton and Bruce Bastian started the company in 1978. They first tried to develop a word-processing software package for mini- and mainframe computers, but they couldn't raise the capital they needed: VCs turned them down because Wang and other competitors already offered such products. Ashton and Bastian then became contract programmers and secured a project to write a customized word-processing package for the city of Orem, Utah, on a Data General minicomputer. The Orem project helped fund a word-processing package for the IBM PC, which WordPerfect released in January 1983. Their product wasn't the first on the market, however; it was introduced almost one year after WordStar's program. WordStar continued to be the market leader until 1985, when it stumbled in its introduction of WordStar 2000. WordStar 2000 was more difficult to use than the previous-generation product WordStar 3.1 and did not easily read files created in the 3.1 version. At about this time WordPerfect released a new version of its software that was "easy to use, provided a seamless conversion from WordStar 3.1, and most of all, it was a technically superior product." More than six years after launch, Word-Perfect finally had its "first 'killer' application,"[4] which made it the number one vendor of word-processing software for several years thereafter. (In 1994 Novell acquired WordPerfect for $885 million.)

Rolling Stone. Jann S. Wenner's magazine followed several other publications that emphasized rock and roll. Paul Williams had previously started *Crawdaddy!*, which billed itself as "a magazine of rock and roll criticism." It "was the first to take rock seriously as a cultural phenomenon but failed to recognize the need to cater to a popular audience. *Crawdaddy!* was elitist in nature and could secure only limited readership. *Mojo Navigator R&R News* was the first to target a broader market and included celebrity interviews and industry gossip. It also was the first of its genre to secure advertising from the rock and roll industry. In England there were several popular rock and roll newspapers such as *Melody Maker*, which served as a model for *Rolling Stone*. Wenner's goal was simply to do "a more popular and commercial magazine" that would take rock and roll "seriously on the terms that it was then coming out."

The Virgin Group. Richard Branson, founder of the Virgin Group, started with a string of undistinguished businesses. In 1967 Branson launched a magazine called *Student*. The venture was unprofitable. Two other unprofitable, and not very original, ventures followed: a mail order record business and a record shop. In 1973 Branson started a music publishing business, Virgin Records. The company's first album, Mike Oldfield's *Tubular Bells*, was a hit and helped finance further growth. By 1984 Virgin Records' revenues approached £100 million, and its associated retail company had become the third-largest retailer in the United Kingdom. Branson also diversified into nightclubs, computer games software, and property development, and by 1993 had amassed a personal fortune of more than $1 billion.

Clayton Homes. Now the leading "manufactured" or "mobile" home company in the United States, with more than $1 billion in revenues in 1997, Clayton Homes started as a pure imitator. Its founder, Jim Clayton, started as a car dealer in 1957. Nine years later, while taking a customer on a test drive, Clayton saw a mobile home being pulled off into a lot and decided to start selling mobile homes. From 1968 to 1973 Clayton sold mobile homes at the unprecedented rate of seven hundred a year from a single lot. Clayton took advantage of not having a novel product. A national retailer, Taylor Homes, was located a few blocks away from Clayton's lot. "Taylor spent heavily on advertising," my students Anderson and Keller wrote. "Clayton succeeded at stealing many of Taylor's customers that stopped by his lot on their way to Taylor." Clayton's status as a local TV personality also helped: From 1960 to 1976 he served as part-time host of *Startime*, a weekly variety show, on which he played the guitar and sang with celebrities such as Dolly Parton. In 1970 Clayton began building some of the homes he sold in an auto body shop and in the following two years started two manufacturing lots. By 1997 the company was vertically integrated with more than a dozen manufacturing plants, more than five hundred retail centers, a subsidiary that provides financing to purchasers of homes, and sixty-seven mobile home communities in twenty-eight states with nearly twenty thousand homesites.

Prior Experience

Many individuals who have the initiative and the incentive to start their own business often lack deep business experience. R. X. Cringely describes the entrepreneurs who built the personal computer industry as "amateurs" who had "little previous work experience and no previous success." Steve Wozniak, who built the first Apple computer, "was an undistinguished engineer at Hewlett-Packard."[5] His partner, Steve Jobs, had just "worked part-time at a video game company," and neither had graduated from college. Bill Gates dropped out of Harvard in his sophomore year to start Microsoft, and Michael Dell quit the University of Texas in his freshman year to start Dell Computers. Substantial businesses have been started by inexperienced founders in other fields as well. Richard Branson, founder of the Virgin Group, was just sixteen when he started his first magazine. Jann S. Wenner, a dropout from the University of California at Berkeley, was a twenty-one-year-old when he started *Rolling Stone* in 1967. Wenner says he "knew nothing about the magazine business," so "the business aspects of how you created such an enterprise didn't even occur to me."[6]

I do not mean to suggest that Jobs, Gates, et al. were ordinary individuals who got lucky. In Chapter 4, I will in fact suggest that individuals who start promising ventures have an unusual tolerance for ambiguity and, compared to the founders of popular businesses, have more education and come from more well-to-do backgrounds. Certain intrinsic qualities of the founders, such as their tolerance for ambiguity and their capacity to adapt, are critical determinants of the success of their businesses. Here we simply note that a significant number of successful companies are started by individuals who don't have extensive prior business training and experience. They may have unusual talents that reveal themselves later, but they don't have verifiable human capital or objective business experience.

Besides lacking business or managerial experience, entrepreneurs often have limited knowledge of or contacts in the industry they enter. In some cases this is because the industry is so new that no one has deep prior knowledge. We also find individuals who want to leave the mature or declining fields in which they have previously worked to enter new fields that offer more opportunity but where they lack personal experience. About 40 percent of the *Inc.* founders I interviewed had no prior experience in the industry in which they launched their ventures, and among those who did, the experience often did not seem deep or well rounded. For instance, John Katzman had been a part-time tutor in college before he launched the Princeton Review, an SAT preparation service. Karen Kirsch, a recent college graduate, had worked as a list broker for just over a year before she started her own brokerage. Richard Schoenberg was enrolled at the American Film Institute, when he briefly worked for someone who was a broker for film stock, before he started his own business in the field. Jann Wenner describes himself as an "amateur journalist" when he started *Rolling Stone*: While a student at Berkeley, he had written a rock column for *The Daily Californian*. He left college to become the entertainment editor of *Sunday Ramparts* and began thinking about his own publication after that weekly folded and Wenner was out of a job. These prior experiences were invaluable in exposing entrepreneurs to opportunities and ideas they could imitate and adapt; such brief stints could not, however, allow the individuals to accumulate deep knowledge, personal reputations, or trusted relationships. They usually accumulated such human capital in the course of operating their business.

2. Capital Constraints

The widespread lack of innovative ideas, often accompanied by limited business or industry experience, preclude typical entrepreneurs from raising much capital from investors. To issue equity in a start-up that does not have an ongoing stream of cash flow, an entrepreneur has to convince investors that the enterprise has intangible assets that can generate cash flow in the future. To borrow terms from the VC industry, investors have to believe that the start-up merits a positive "premoney" valuation deriving from some intellectual property or human capital that the entrepreneur has contributed to the venture. Most start-ups, however, don't have the assets that an objective investor would consider valuable. The founders, therefore, have to rely on their own resources or raise funds from relatives or friends who are willing to overlook the founder's me-too strategies and inexperience.

Many entrepreneurs don't have significant personal means (or rich and trusting friends), so ventures that turn out to be out-of-the-ordinary successes often start with the same limited means as the typical lawn care or painting business. As we might expect, most of the hundreds of thousands of businesses launched in the United States every year start with little capital. The Census Bureau's 1987 survey of businesses showed that 30 percent of all companies were started with less than $5,000, and only a third had more than $50,000. Promising ventures like the *Inc.* 500 companies also start with similar amounts. As previously mentioned, most of the founders of companies on the 1989 *Inc.* 500 list that I interviewed bootstrapped their ventures with meager personal savings and borrowings or funds raised from families and friends; 26 percent started with less than $5,000; only

21 percent raised more than $50,000, and just two raised more than $1 million. Most founders did not even try to raise outside equity for their start-ups; about a quarter tried to raise venture capital funding and failed.

Inc.'s survey of all the companies on its *Inc.* 500 lists from 1982 to 1989 produced similar results. More than a third of respondents started their businesses with less than $10,000, and more than another third started with $10,000 to $50,000. Most reported "own resources," "personal loans," and the like as a significant or most important source of capital. Fewer than 5 percent relied on outside equity investors.[7] The funding sources for companies on the *Inc.* lists in the 1990s were similar to those who made the *Inc.* lists in the 1980s. Companies on the *Inc.* 1996 list (more than three quarters of these companies were launched after 1988) raised an average of $25,000 at the start-up stage. Only 4 percent reported raising any money from professional venture capitalists and 3 percent from the so-called venture angels.* As with the 1980s generation of *Inc.* start-ups, the main sources of funding were personal savings and borrowings. (See Fig. 1.3 for a further breakdown of funding sources.)[8]

The capital constraint problem faced by start-ups, we may note, goes beyond the usual information asymmetry and agency problems in going concerns that financial economists often focus on.[9] When an established firm sells stock, it has to overcome the suspicion of investors that the executives know that the stock is really worth less than its issue price

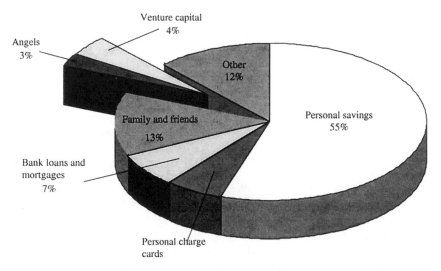

Figure 1.3. Primary Source of Initial Funding
Percentage of 1996 *Inc.* 500 Companies
Source: Inc. magazine.

* Venture angels are wealthy individuals who invest in new ventures on an ad hoc basis. Unlike professional venture capitalists, they do not form structured limited partnerships that invest others' funds.

because they are privy to confidential information about the company's prospects. According to the "pecking order hypothesis" this information asymmetry problem—the difficulty of persuading investors that they aren't being sold a "lemon"—leads companies to first rely on internally generated funds, then on debt, and to issue equity only as a last resort. Agency issues—for example, the fear that the decision-makers will slack off after they have sold all or part of their interest in a business—poses another problem in selling equity to investors.

In many start-ups the founders face a more intractable problem than the fear of lemons or conflicts of interest: They have little to offer investors besides their hopes and dreams. Mechanisms such as audits and contracts can mitigate lemon and agency problems: An investor can be offered the opportunity to exercise extensive due diligence or may rely on incentive schemes that to some degree motivate decision-makers to increase the value of the firm. However, these mechanisms cannot address the asymmetry of expectations that exists when entrepreneurs do not have an observable innovation, experience, or a record of past achievement. The entrepreneurs believe that they can somehow make a profit, but investors do not. Their capital constraint derives from the absence of objective information about their ability to make a profit, rather than their inability to accurately communicate this information.* Even with utterly honest entrepreneurs, investors can only discover after the fact who has the innate capacity to succeed. If the average entrepreneur cannot earn a profit, investors will not back any of them.

In a relatively small number of promising start-ups, information asymmetry and agency problems do constrain capital raising. As previously mentioned, about 10 percent of the founders of *Inc.* companies claimed they started with unique products or ideas. Here access to funding depends on whether the expected returns are large enough to cover the costs of investigation and ongoing oversight. As we will see in the chapter on VC-backed start-ups, these costs can be substantial compared to the magnitude of the expected payoffs. Therefore many entrepreneurs with novel ideas cannot raise outside capital and must bootstrap their ventures. Only rarely does the expected value of the intellectual property and human capital contributed by the entrepreneur cover investors' due-diligence and monitoring costs.

3. Niche Opportunities

Entrepreneurs who don't have a significant innovation or access to much capital cannot pursue opportunities likely to generate large profits. They cannot, for instance, contemplate high-volume production, where they would have to incur substantial costs in advance of the realization of revenues. They cannot make large up-front investments—to develop a

---

* In Camerer's terms this is a problem of uncertainty or ambiguity, which he defines as "known to be missing information" (Camerer [1995], 644).

major drug or oil field or to build a national brand, for instance. Nor can they easily withstand the competition from large, well-established companies that they would likely encounter if they tried to take a significant share of a large market. Instead, most entrepreneurs start in niche markets where they cannot realistically expect million-dollar profits but do not need much working capital or up-front investment in R&D, manufacturing plant, or marketing, and where they do not have to confront large rivals.

Most of the *Inc.* companies I studied started off by serving local markets or a small number of customers with specialized needs. For instance, Sosadian and Tucker's Attronica Computers served the Washington, D.C., market; Russell Personnel Services restricted itself to San Francisco clients; and Katzman started the Princeton Review offering SAT preparation classes using the premises of Hunter College, on the Upper East Side of Manhattan. More than 60 percent of *Inc.* companies I interviewed started out serving just local or regional markets; just over a third served national markets, and only two reported overseas customers. Moreover, many of the start-ups that ventured outside local or regional markets often provided specialized or even customized solutions to the problems of a few customers. For instance, Roxy Westphal and Bob Davis's Corporate Resource Associates designed and developed customized training programs (e.g., for sales staff, users of new accounting or bank teller systems) for large companies such as the Bank of America, Hewlett-Packard, and AT&T. Electrotek, started by Bud Miles and two partners, provided consulting studies and developed software systems for electric utilities around the country.

In some cases the *Inc.* companies served customers who were both local and had special needs. The first client for Inter-Ad, a manufacturer of public access computer information systems, was the city of Rochester. Inter-Ad's founder, James Odorczyk, recalled: "The city was about to celebrate its 150th birthday, and they needed a system to put in City Hall to talk about Rochester. We were offering touch screens and high-resolution graphics, which attracted a lot of people. And the city wanted someone local and they had budgets and timelines, which didn't allow them to do a lot of shopping. We were the only game in town then, and we did a complete system, with custom programming included, for $25,000."

By serving local or specialized customers, the *Inc.* start-ups avoided competition from large, well-established companies: As Figure 1.4 shows, fewer than 5 percent of the *Inc.* 500 start-ups I studied competed against large *Fortune* 500-type companies; 73 percent competed against small companies or other start-ups, 5 percent against midsize companies, and the rest reported no direct competitors.

In some cases entrepreneurs picked niche markets where they did not expect large profits because they wanted to establish a springboard or base for more ambitious subsequent initiatives.

For example, Raju Patel launched NAC with the goal of serving the

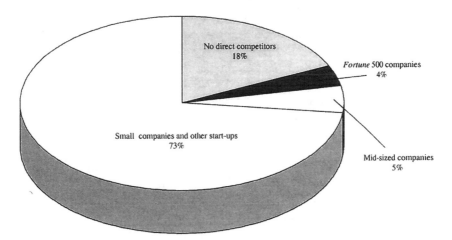

Figure 1.4. Competitors Faced by 1989 *Inc.* 500 Start-ups
Percentage of 1989 *Inc.* 500 Founders Surveyed
Source: Author's survey.

Baby Bells created by the AT&T breakup. NAC's first offering, however, targeted companies reselling long-distance services from carriers such as MCI. "We thought it would be appropriate to get a cash generator to make us known as a new entrant," Patel explained. After Patel happened to meet a reseller who mentioned his need for more accurate customer-billing capability, NAC rapidly developed and shipped a billing system. The system was later phased out as the customers themselves began to fold. But its quick, albeit short-lived, success helped NAC attract the engineers it needed to grow because it enabled Patel to offer security as well as the excitement of a start-up. "We weren't seen as a revolving-door company. We were able to offer health plans and other benefits comparable to those of large companies." More ambitious products, aimed at the Bell companies, followed. By 1989 NAC had become a supplier of intelligent network platforms to the Bell companies, with $26.7 million in revenues.

Robert Grosshandler's Softa Group also used the cash flow from one small-scale activity to fund a larger business. "Our property management software was funded by selling hardware and peripherals. It was low-margin, but it had fast turnaround. Goods arrived in the morning and left in the evening. Our software, on the other hand, took nearly a year to develop."

In other cases, the entrepreneurs overestimated the potential of their initial business but then stumbled into larger and more profitable opportunities. For instance, Robert Rodriguez started a business with Eddie Sarasola in 1982 to rent large, inflatable balloons festooned with advertisements to auto dealerships in Miami. "Eddie and I thought," recalls Rodriguez, "that eventually there would be one of those balloons in every corner of the country. We would be the next IBM." The business of renting balloons to auto dealers did not meet these lofty expectations, but it led Rodriguez and his partner to provide balloons for special events (such as the inauguration of a new location) and conventions to large companies such as Eastern Airlines and Burger King. In 1985 Natcom began organizing promotional programs for this clientele, and by 1989, balloon rentals accounted for less than 5 percent of revenues of $3.89 million.

Many members of today's blue-chip companies also started with niche opportunities that they could exploit without having much capital or having to face large competitors. Companies such as Compaq, which went head-to-head against IBM from the start and booked $100 million of sales in its first year, are unusual. Companies such as Microsoft, which started in a niche that was too small to interest the establishment, are more common. When Bill Gates and Paul Allen launched Microsoft in 1975, their first product, the 8080 BASIC computer language, ran just on the Altair, a rudimentary personal computer made by MITS, a tiny Albuquerque start-up. MITS sold the Altair in kit form to hobbyists at a rate of a few thousand units a year. Microsoft's competitors were, like Gates and Allen, other freelance programmers, not IBM or Digital.*

Similarly, Hewlett and Packard started with an audio oscillator for which there was limited demand—another entrepreneur, Walt Disney, was one of their first customers. HP developed products for broader markets such as printers and calculators decades later. Other companies, such as General Motors, Ford, and Eastman Kodak, started off in niches that they subsequently helped transform into mass markets. When William Durant formed General Motors in 1908, Buick, the leading automobile producer in the United States, sold 8,487 units. Ford, the second-largest (it had just introduced the Model T), sold 6,181 vehicles, and Cadillac was third with 2,380 units.[10] Wayne Huizenga, founder of Waste Management, started in Fort Lauderdale with one "beat-up open truck, one helper, and a few containers" and generated revenues of $500 a month. He then expanded to four trucks, bought another three-truck business in Pompano, and proceeded over the next decade to build a NYSE-listed company operating in thirty-two states.

Serving niche markets not only allows entrepreneurs to start a business with limited funds, it also limits the competition they face from well-capitalized entities. Established corporations and professional venture capital funds expend considerable resources on evaluating and monitoring their investments. They tend to avoid investments in niche opportunities

---

* Gates and Allen suggest that right from the start, their mission was to put "a computer on every desk and in every home, running Microsoft software." That apparently prescient goal would at the time have seemed as outlandish to industry executives as Natcom's vision of becoming the IBM of balloon rentals. It is also hard to imagine that Microsoft's founders foresaw that they would come to dominate large markets for PC operating systems, spreadsheets, and word processors that simply did not exist in 1975.

whose profit potential isn't large enough to cover their fixed evaluation and monitoring costs. Therefore the bootstrapped entrepreneur in a niche market faces direct competition mainly from other undercapitalized businesses.

4. Turbulent Markets

Capital and other constraints, we have seen, usually force the founders of promising ventures to pursue small-scale opportunities. But small-scale by itself cannot explain the unusual profitability of such start-ups; after all, the popular marginal ventures also operate in small, localized markets. The distinguishing characteristic of promising niches, we will see next, is uncertainty. Uncertainty does not, of course, assure attractive returns, but it does allow entrepreneurs with meager initial resources a better chance of making a profit than the typical popular business with predictably poor returns. Although promising businesses have the same low most likely payoff, they come with a valuable option or lottery ticket attached.

One important source of uncertainty derives from unsettled market conditions—about half the *Inc.* founders I studied started businesses in fields that were in a state of flux or turbulence because of a new technology, regulatory regime, fashion, or other such external change. Turbulence improves a start-up's prospects in several ways. Starting a profitable business in a stable market, where competitive forces have long shaken out weak technologies and firms, requires a significantly better approach or new "combination." In highly competitive fields such as house painting or lawn care, providing the same products or services as everyone else can yield only low industry average returns. In businesses where long-standing relationships, reputations, and other such barriers to entry generate high profits for the incumbents, imitation or small modification of existing products and technologies leads to returns that are *worse* than industry average.

In a new or changing market, however, entrepreneurs often do not require a significant innovation or insight to make a profit. Customers and suppliers lack information about their alternatives, so many firms, all offering the same products and using the same technologies, can make a profit. We commonly attribute such profits to "shortages" or an "excess of demand over supply"; in fact, entrepreneurs do not need the foresight or the luck to acquire a good that later becomes scarce. They can exploit the lack of *information,* buying inputs cheap from uninformed suppliers and selling them dear to uninformed customers. They do not even need to discover the opportunity themselves or realize they are engaging in a form of arbitrage. As long as buyers and sellers remain ill-informed, they can simply follow the example of others.

New markets have other attractive features for start-ups. Incentives to compete on price are limited, especially if demand is expanding, because all the players are profitable. Inexperience makes customers more tolerant and trusting. They don't have well-formed expectations about product quality and knowledge of what could go wrong. The playing field is level. The start-up does not have to displace rivals who have established reputations, and cost advantages deriving from their accumulated experience, and customers locked in because of inertia or switching costs. In mature markets entrants have to take their share away from entrenched incumbents.

The entrepreneur's inability to raise outside funding does not pose a serious handicap, because their competitors face the same problem. Even if the distribution of returns has a positive skew, investors often avoid nascent markets because the expected profit cannot cover their evaluation and monitoring costs. The irreducible uncertainty of new markets also discourages large-scale investment. As we will see in Chapters 5 and 6, decision-makers with discretion over significant amounts of capital usually require objective evidence about the prospects of new initiatives. They avoid markets where they cannot obtain critical data needed to evaluate the risks and returns and where the technologies, customer wants, and so on can evolve in innumerable ways. They tend to wait until the prospects about market size and structures have become clear enough to place bets with well-defined probabilities. Until then the bootstrapped entrepreneur faces rivals who are also capital-constrained, rather than well-funded corporate or venture-capital-backed entities.

The leverage provided by external change is illustrated by the success of numerous start-ups in the personal computer industry. For the past two decades the industry has been in a constant state of flux. Successive waves of change, such as the introduction of the Apple II, the IBM PC, the Macintosh, new generations of Intel microprocessors, and Windows 3.0 created opportunities for innumerable entrepreneurs who didn't have a breakthrough product, great managerial abilities, or much capital. The introduction of the IBM PC in 1980, which legitimized personal computers in the corporate world, created new markets for low-cost clones, add-on boards, applications software, training, and distribution. Start-ups did not have to be first or possess exceptional skill to make a profit. More than a quarter of the entrepreneurs I interviewed had started computer-related businesses; all of them had started at least two years after the introduction of the IBM PC and five years after the introduction of the Apple II. Their products were fairly mundane: training videotapes and software with features that were available on minicomputers and Apple IIs. Sales and service businesses needed technical knowledge that was probably easier to acquire than competence in automobile repair. But because buyers weren't very knowledgeable or demanding, the installation and servicing of computers generated sizable profits and growth. As one midwestern dealer told me: "We have a joke slogan around here: 'We aren't as incompetent as our competitors.'"

Changes in the basic hardware, operating systems, and networks continued to offer new openings for start-ups through the 1980s and 1990s.

Entrepreneurs who missed the opportunity to start dealerships for IBM PCs and clones later found chances to become dealers and systems integrators for Novell's networking products. The introduction of Windows 3.0 in 1990 created opportunities for software start-ups, just as the introduction of DOS had in 1980. The disproportionate number of promising start-ups in the computer area reflects the abundance of such opportunities. For instance, the proportion of computer-related businesses in the *Inc.* 500 lists has been consistently more than four times the proportion of overall economic activity accounted for by this sector. As indicated in Figure 1.5, computer-related businesses accounted for 20 percent or more of the companies appearing on the *Inc.* 500 lists between 1986 and 1988. By contrast, a broadly defined "Information Technology" sector, comprising all computing and telecommunications, represented only 5 to 6.4 percent of the Gross Domestic Product of the United States during that period.[11]

Changing customer tastes and regulatory regimes, like technological discontinuities, can create opportunities for entrepreneurs to profit from uninformed buyers and sellers. Bob Reiss, for instance, started a profitable

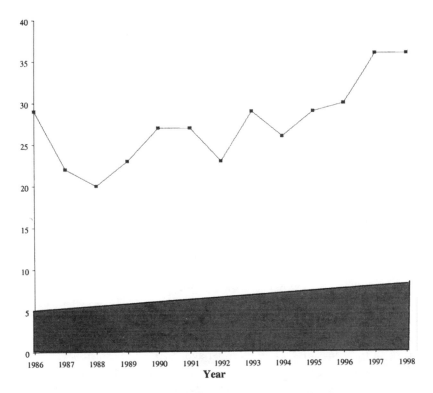

Figure 1.5. Percentage of Computer Companies in *Inc.* 500

Source: *Inc.* magazine.

US. Dept. of Commerce Economics and Statistics Administration (1998) report (estimates based on Bureau of Economic and Analysis and Census data)

watch business by taking advantage of the "fashion watch" trend. Until the 1980s, watches sold in the United States comprised three main categories: expensive, high-fashion such as Piaget and Rolex; conservative, moderately priced such as Seiko and Citizen; and "popular"-priced, functional such as Casio and Timex. Sales growth in this mature market was in line with GNP growth. In the 1980s the Swiss company Swatch stimulated an increase in watch ownership by introducing moderately priced watches marketed to consumers as fashion accessories. Unit sales more than doubled as consumers began to own several watches with artistic designs, licensed characters such as Mickey Mouse, the logos of professional sports teams, and Christmas motifs. Swatch, the innovator, was only one of several companies to profit. Entrepreneurs would use freelance artists to design watchfaces, secure a license from companies like Disney, or simply copy someone else's design. Factories in Hong Kong and China made the watches, and mail order catalog companies, home shopping TV networks, mass merchandisers such as Wal-Mart, and specialty watch chains handled the sales. Without any proprietary assets or technology, an entrepreneur could realize $10 or more for a watch that would cost about $5 to make and enjoy rapid growth. For instance, Bob Reiss launched Valdawn in 1988, several years after the trend toward fashion and fun watches had been in place. By 1994 Valdawn's annual revenues had grown to more than $7 million, with a pretax profit margin exceeding 15 percent. The company made the *Inc.* 500 list three years in a row.[12]

Changing tastes and sensibilities also created an opportunity for *Rolling Stone*. Founder Jann Wenner recalls that when he launched the magazine in 1967, "it was the beginning of a new era in rock and roll. The nature of what musicians and bands were doing was changing. They began to really take themselves seriously, and we wanted to write about these serious, meaningful things. There was a big cultural shift taking place. We were at the beginning of it. We caught it, we withstood it, and we rode it." As described in a previous insert, *Rolling Stone* was not the first or the only rock and roll magazine of the time. The twenty-one-year-old self-described "amateur journalist" had raised all of $7,500 from sympathetic individuals who, according to Wenner, "figured they weren't going to ever get any of it back." Wenner says that he had "no clue whatsoever about where the first issue was shipped: In fact, six months later, we found out that most of the boxes [containing the first issue] weren't even opened." The start-up missed four publishing dates in its first year. But because *Rolling Stone* was tapping into a new market, it didn't have to compete with a *Time* or a *Newsweek*; it simply had to deliver higher quality and reliability than only slightly older rivals who faced similar organizational problems. "As amateurish as some of the first issues were," Wenner says, *Rolling Stone* could "set itself apart" through "serious in-depth interviews and exclusive articles on major artists and issues."[13]

The low representation of "promising" start-ups from many prominent but mature markets also points to the important contribution of disequilibrium to the profitability of undifferentiated ventures. In my *Inc.* sample I did not encounter a single company in textiles, chemicals, fertilizers, footwear, and other such mainstays of U.S. industry. We interviewed only one entrepreneur who had started a business (in brake remanufacturing) connected with the automotive industry. Besides the Big Three—General Motors, Ford, and Chrysler—the automotive sector includes many small businesses. But lacking any significant technological upheavals, the field has apparently not provided easy profits or growth to entrepreneurs. If *Inc.* lists had been compiled in the 1900s and 1910s, it would probably have been as well populated with dealers and suppliers of ancillary goods and services for automobiles as contemporary lists have been with computer-related businesses.

Entering a turbulent and unsettled market does not, of course, ensure large profits. Notwithstanding the tailwind of a "new era in rock and roll," the objective best-guess return from starting *Rolling Stone* could not have been much greater than zero. Even where imbalances create opportunities for riskless arbitrage, the profits tend to be small and transitory. The main contribution of market turbulence is to create a small chance of noteworthy success. The entrepreneur who started a rock and roll magazine in the sixties had some hope of building a *Rolling Stone*. Taking advantage of transitory opportunities to assemble clones of IBM PCs in the early eighties provided a springboard for a college student such as Michael Dell to then build a more substantial enterprise.

5. Entrepreneurs' Value Added

The founders' capacity to differentiate their product or service through their personal effort seems to be an important reason for the profitability of many of the *Inc.* companies I studied. In about 40 percent of cases, start-ups had neither a unique product nor the benefit of a market in disequilibrium. Like Ken Dougan, founder of Unique Transportation Systems ("I'd talk to people in shipping and I'd do anything they'd ask me to do") or Karen Kirsch, who founded Best Mailing Lists ("I offered service to which no one could compare"), the entrepreneurs relied entirely on their personal capacity to provide services customers valued. The entrepreneur, rather than a product or technology, represented the principal source of the start-up's profits. As Carol Russell of Russell Personnel Services put it: "Our business is done on the cult of personality. You roll up your sleeves and say to the customer, "Hi, I'm Carol Russell, and I'm going to work overtime to get you employed or employees." In a people business, being a young company and visible is an advantage. In the large services, you won't meet the Mr. Olstens or the Mr. Kellys.

Some entrepreneurs claimed they secured customers by reading the true nature of their expectations. Clay Teramo, founder of Computer Media Technology, a computer supplies distributor, described the way he used the customer's perception of service to make up for the fact that his larger competitors carried more inventory. When someone called with a next-day order that Computer Media couldn't handle, Teramo would tell them that he didn't have the whole order in stock and would ask if he could fill part of it the next day and part later on. If the customer agreed, he'd follow up personally to make sure everything had gone smoothly and to say thanks. As Teramo pointed out, his competitors could probably have filled the whole order at once, but the customer wouldn't think he had received any special service.

The impact of an entrepreneur's ability and effort depends in part on the size and capital intensity of the business. The CEO's labor represents a relatively small proportion of the value added in a large, capital-intensive oil-refining company, where plant location, process technology, access to distribution channels, organizational cohesiveness and teamwork, and other such factors have a significant impact on profitability. But all small, labor-intensive businesses do not hold the same promise—few hardworking and resourceful proprietors of grocery stores and hair salons make it into the ranks of the *Inc.* 500. The potential for entrepreneurs like Clay Teramo or Carol Russell to earn high profits by dint of their diligence or "hustle" often seems to derive from the nature of the features or attributes that their customers value.

In markets for standardized goods and services, such as the delivery of newspapers, customers evaluate offerings along simple, concrete dimensions, such as whether the newspaper is delivered punctually and regularly and placed on the doorstep instead of in a puddle. Entrepreneurs who provide such goods and services cannot easily differentiate their offerings and have to accept prices set by a competitive market. An especially diligent, good-natured, or courteous individual may earn higher than average tips; but even generous tips in these businesses will not generate the profitability and cash flow of an *Inc.* 500-type company. The relatively low value that customers place on the intangible elements of the service they receive limits the difference in the profitability of the best and the worst providers.

In fields such as entertainment, fashion, professional services, and made-to-order construction, buyers don't have an obvious, well-ordered set of preferences. They place a high value on what Sabini and Silver call "fuzzy" attributes,[14] whose dimensions, such as trendiness, elegance, and responsiveness, they cannot easily measure or define. Their behavior may even contradict the purchasing criteria they espouse. For example, people who say they just want to maximize returns may nonetheless retain an investment adviser whose performance consistently lags market averages because the adviser caters to some inchoate desire for reassurance and attention.

The value that customers place on fuzzy or ill-defined attributes allows entrepreneurs to differentiate their offerings by tapping into the psyche of their customers or by responding to their unspoken wants. As we saw in the case of Teramo, because fuzzy attributes allow for multiple interpretations of quality, entrepreneurs can even put a positive spin on their weaknesses.

Entrepreneurs who have a superior innate capacity for (or a willingness to work at) satisfying fuzzy wants can realize high profit margins without proprietary technologies or assets. Rivals cannot imitate product or service offerings whose critical attributes are not easily observable and are embedded in the personal efforts of the suppliers' principals. They cannot lower prices to compensate for perceptions of inferior quality, because these market niches have a "winner take all" nature. Customers who don't fully understand what they want can't easily make price and quality trade-offs, and are willing to pay a considerable price premium to the "best" provider. And to the degree that products with fuzzy attributes cannot be produced through a standardized process, entrepreneurs with superior operational skills can also enjoy cost advantages over their rivals.

In other words, a venture's dependence on the personal efforts of its founders represents a desirable source of uncertainty that adds a positive skew to its prospects. The innate talent, motivation, and drive of an entrepreneur can make a significant difference in businesses when standardized processes and inputs do not produce the outputs that customers value. The objective prospects of all entrants may be low because of the limited capital or qualifications required to start such businesses; nevertheless, a few entrepreneurs can enjoy high profits. By contrast, in marginal businesses, standardized customer wants that any entrepreneurs can satisfy lock all firms into a narrow zone of low profitability. (For an illustration of how the attributes customers value affect the profit potential of start-ups, see the sidebar "Comparing Upscale Restaurants and Laundries.")

The leverage that the founders of *Inc.* companies derived from serving fuzzy wants shows up in the nature of their offerings. Most *Inc.* companies did not offer goods or services for which customers could easily do comparison shopping or would tend to reflexively buy the leading brand. Rather, they competed in markets where the purchasing decision involved subtle criteria and cognitively challenging trade-offs that the entrepreneurs could influence.

Three-quarters of the *Inc.* founders we interviewed served as their company's chief or only salesperson. Only 10 percent used brokers or distributors. The sales cycle in 75 percent of the cases ranged from days to months. Therefore, in contrast to a door-to-door vacuum cleaner sale, understanding and responding to the customer's situation and concerns were more important than closing the transaction quickly.

The median unit sale was $5,000, an amount high enough to support direct personal selling and to allow for customization of terms and features.

Comparing Upscale Restaurants and Laundries

In both fields, barriers to entry are low and competition is intense: Entrepreneurs can easily obtain the technology and equipment needed to open a new establishment. Average profitability and survival rates are notoriously low. But the range in the profitability of upscale restaurants seems to be greater than the range in the profitability of laundries. Although the financial prospects of the typical new restaurant are grim, every so often someone scores a hit. A city such as Boston contains several establishments such as Anthony's Pier 4 and the Hilltop Steakhouse that have generated significant wealth for their proprietors. Laundries, in contrast, do not seem to offer anyone a path to riches. A few hundred thousand dollars in profit seems to mark the limit of success.

The value that many customers place on the intangible aspects of their overall dining experience helps explain why some restaurants can make exceptional returns. Customers pay not just for the physical inputs and labor that goes into their meal, but also for the quality of the food, the choices on the menu, the decor and ambience, and whether the establishment is considered "in." Restaurateurs who can create the right atmosphere and "buzz" and provide a popular menu fill their establishments. Their gross profits considerably exceed their fixed costs, generating attractive profits. Rivals of a successful fine dining establishment cannot easily copy the elements that derive from the skill and personality of its owner. Nor can they draw away customers by lowering prices.

In the laundry business, customers may prefer well-lit, pleasant stores and courteous counter staff; they do not, however, go out of their way to patronize particular establishments because of the ambience or the personality of the owner. Many competitors can provide the concrete attributes that customers value—the hours the store is open, the turnaround time, the removal of stains, and so on. Moreover, they all incur similar costs. In a restaurant, costs vary with the proprietor's skill in purchasing, control of waste, menu design, management of the kitchen staff, and so on. In a laundry, all establishments use the same mature technology, the same raw materials, and a small, unskilled staff to produce more or less the same outputs. Competitive forces and imitation therefore lead to a uniformity of prices and service levels and low overall profitability: The typical laundry generates a 6 percent return on capital. This return—and the "wage income" the establishment often generates for family members—may be adequate for the owner, but it does not lead to the profits and growth of an *Inc.* 500 company.

The nature of competition in the low-budget or "value" fast-food market, however, is different. Customers value concrete (albeit intangible) attributes such as reliability, speed, convenience, and (often scripted) courtesy. Imitation and price competition are widespread. Profits depend on the firm's brand names, locations, systems, and other such proprietary assets rather than the personal touch of the principals.

Most *Inc.* start-ups sold to other businesses; only 14 percent offered consumer goods or services. The few consumer items we encountered also represented purchases that buyers would tend to think about and the entrepreneur could personally influence, such as a $20,000 recreational vehicle from Chariot Eagle. The companies did not sell $5 to $10 packaged goods for which the purchasing decision is based on habit or on impersonal factors such as advertising and shelf space. (Fig. 1.6 shows the distribution of unit sale prices for 1989 *Inc.* 500 companies.)

In the high-ticket items sold by the *Inc.* start-ups, entrepreneurs reported that their personal passion, persuasiveness, and willingness to satisfy special requirements were as important as the attributes of their products. As John Mineck, cofounder of Practice Management Systems, said, "People buy a salesperson. They bought me and I had no sales experience. But I truly believed our systems and software for automating doctors' offices would work—so the customers did, too. Also, we did an awful lot for our first clients; if they wanted something, we'd deliver. We were providing service and support long before that became a cliché."

As with the uncertainties that derive from turbulent market conditions, high dependence on the founders' personal value added ameliorates the disadvantage entrepreneurs might otherwise face because they cannot raise outside funding. Capital providers avoid businesses whose profitability

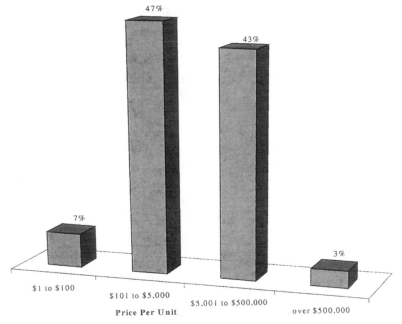

Figure 1.6. Dollar Value of Unit Sales
Percentage of 1989 *Inc.* 500 Founders Surveyed

Source: Author's survey.

depends just on the principals' "hustle." Most start-ups make low profits, and it is difficult for investors to predict which entrepreneur has the innate qualities to break from the pack. Investors also face difficult problems of motivation and appropriability of returns. To the extent that providers of capital bear the risks, they reduce the entrepreneur's incentive to make the critical but unobservable extra effort that separates the winners from the also-rans. And the value created by a successful "hustle" venture is closely attached to the founders rather than to the legal entity they operate in. The valuable assets of an advertising agency, for instance, lie in the reputations and know-how of the principals. Once these assets have been created, the principals can walk away to start a new agency, leaving little behind for the investors who provided the start-up capital. The reluctance of professional investors to back businesses whose value depends almost exclusively on the efforts and human capital of a few principals limits the bootstrapped entrepreneur's competition to other self-financed players.

6. Summary

The typical new venture confronts serious limitations. The founders of businesses usually start without an original idea, and they also often lack deep business or industry experience. These limited endowments preclude most entrepreneurs from raising much capital and force them to bootstrap their ventures with personal funds or small amounts raised from friends or relatives.

Entrepreneurs can more easily cope with their lack of original ideas, experience, and capital if they start niche businesses with high uncertainty due to unsettled market conditions or nearly total dependence on the entrepreneur's personal ability to satisfy fuzzy customer wants. Although the most likely payoff in such businesses isn't large, they provide the entrepreneur with a chance to make a significant return. By contrast, in popular fields for start-ups such as beauty care salons and lawn maintenance, competition between businesses of roughly equal capabilities forces all businesses to subsist at a very similar and low level of profitability. Competing in small, uncertain niches also allows the bootstrapped entrepreneur to avoid competing against well-capitalized rivals.

2

Planning vs. Opportunistic Adaptation

This chapter examines why the adaptation to unforeseen problems and opportunities represents an important task for the founders of promising businesses. Section 1 describes how most entrepreneurs start businesses without much prior planning. Section 2 suggests that the costs of extensive planning in a typical start-up exceed the benefits. Section 3 discusses the importance of adapting to unexpected problems and opportunities. Section 4 brings out the opportunistic nature of entrepreneurial adaptation by comparing it to other types of selection strategies, such as scientific experimentation and Darwinian processes of biological evolution.

When Paul Allen and Bill Gates developed Microsoft's first product, they did not do any market research or competitor analysis first. In December 1974 Allen visited his high school friend Gates, then a sophomore at Harvard. Allen spotted an issue of *Popular Electronics* featuring the Altair 8080 on the cover at a kiosk in Harvard Square. "I bought a copy, read it, and raced back to Bill's dorm to talk to him," Allen recalled. "I told Bill, 'Well here's our opportunity to do something with BASIC.'"[1] Allen and Gates did not write a business plan; they started working on a version of BASIC for the Altair right away. Gates writes that they "were like the characters in those Judy Garland and Mickey Rooney movies: "Let's put on a show in the barn!" We thought there was no time to waste, and we set right to it." Gates and Allen "didn't sleep much and lost track of night and day" to complete their BASIC in four weeks.[2]

Some theories suggest that such unplanned approaches to starting a business reflect entrepreneurial overconfidence. Whatever its psychological roots, I will suggest in this chapter that the lack of research and planning that we find in many promising start-ups has a sound economic basis. Capital-constrained entrepreneurs cannot afford to do much prior analysis and research. The limited profit potential and high uncertainty of the opportunities they usually pursue also make the benefits low compared to the costs. In lieu of extensive planning, we will also see, entrepreneurs have to rely on adaptation: They start with a sketchy idea of how they want to do business, which they alter and refine as they encounter unforeseen problems and opportunities. Moreover, the adaptation is often more opportunistic or myopic than scientific or strategic: The founders of promising start-ups experiment with course changes to maximize short-run cash flow rather than to verify a general theory or to make the best possible long-term choices.

1. Limited Research and Analysis

Few of the entrepreneurs I studied followed a systematic approach to identifying and evaluating opportunities. Only 4 percent of the *Inc.* founders we interviewed found their business ideas through a systematic search; 71 percent replicated or modified an idea encountered through previous employment, and another 20 percent discovered their ideas serendipitously (see Fig. 2.1). Having found an idea in an ad hoc fashion, the entrepreneurs did not spend much time on research or planning, either; 41 percent of the entrepreneurs had no business plan at all and 26 percent had just a rudimentary plan. Carol Russell, for instance, recalls that she and her partner "got together in the public library to plan, but we had no paper. We did our projections on the back of an envelope." Five percent worked up financial projections for investors. Only 28 percent wrote up a full-blown business plan.

Another survey of the founders of all *Inc.* 500 companies from 1982 to 1989 generated similar results. Only 7 percent had done a systematic search for business opportunities, and only 21 percent had developed a formal business plan. Having decided to pursue an opportunity, the entrepreneurs proceeded quickly, and apparently without much preparation.

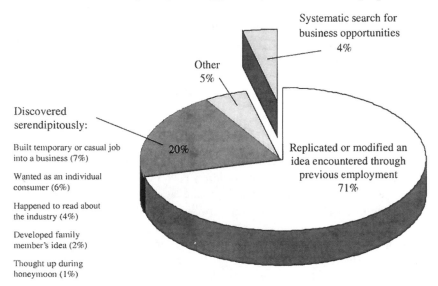

Figure 2.1. Sources of Start-up Ideas
Percentage of 1989 *Inc.* 500 Founders Surveyed

Source: Author's survey

More than half did not consult with a lawyer, for instance, and three-quarters did not develop any marketing materials. The period from the original idea to the beginning of operations was usually brief; as Figure 2.2 indicates, 63 percent took a few months or less, while only 9 percent took more than a year.[3]

My students' papers on successful entrepreneurs also record that the founders of many of today's well-established corporations also did not start their businesses in a planned, systematic way. Jann Wenner, founder of *Rolling Stone*, recalls that "the idea of making a business plan, finding out what other magazines were doing, studying the competition didn't even occur to me." Calvin Klein, too, started his fashion empire with his childhood friend Barry Schwartz without any planning: "We just sold as many coats as we could," Schwartz says, "and we worked seven days a week."

2. Costs and Benefits

Why didn't Gates and Allen conduct market research on the potential revenues or assess systematically their capabilities vis-à-vis other programmers who were also trying to develop a BASIC for the Altair? Why do so few *Inc.* founders compile even basic information on market size and

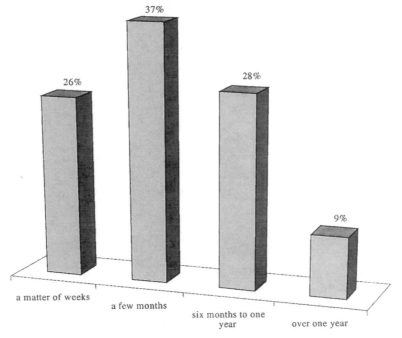

Figure 2.2. Time from Idea to Start-up
Percentage of *Inc.* 500 Founders Responding

Source: Case, John, "The Origins of Entrepreneurship," *Inc.* magazine, 1989.

competitive climate or draw up five-year financial projections? D. Lovallo and C. F. Camerer suggest that entrepreneurs have "blind spots" and fail to appreciate how much competition there will be in a market. Or they may know about the competition they face and "overconfidently think their firm will succeed while most others will fail."[4] Several studies from experimental psychology have shown that "most people rate themselves above the average on almost every positive personal trait—including driving ability, a sense of humor, managerial risk-taking and expected longevity."[5] Lovallo and Camerer's experiments suggest that expertise exacerbates rather than mitigates the propensity toward overconfidence: Experts are more likely to overrate their abilities vis-à-vis other experts than are novices against other novices. Their work also suggests that experts are more likely to overrate their prospects in games involving skill rather than chance.[6] Thus entrepreneurs like Gates and Allen might have such confidence in their programming skills that they do not bother with an objective evaluation of the abilities of their rivals and underinvest in research and planning.

It may well be true that entrepreneurs have a greater propensity toward overconfidence than the population at large. Their apparently cavalier attitude toward planning does not, however, reflect an irrational overestimate of relative ability or an underestimate of the value of analysis and research. Rather, their initial endowments and constraints as well as the type of opportunities they pursue dictate that entrepreneurs proceed quickly from idea to implementation.

Endowments and Constraints

The inability of many entrepreneurs to raise outside funding, their limited opportunity costs, and their prior knowledge discourage them from devoting much effort to prior research and planning.

Capital constraints. The entrepreneur's inability to raise much capital makes the opportunity cost of doing research prohibitive and precludes extensive investigation of an idea. Large corporations routinely spend, I can report from firsthand experience, hundreds of thousands of dollars to investigate new business opportunities. The typical entrepreneur who starts with $10,000 or $20,000 in initial capital obviously cannot afford such research: Scarce funds are much better spent on trying to make or sell a product than on conducting competitor analysis or focus groups. Therefore the line between "doing" and research is blurred. As one founder recalls, "My market research consisted of taking a prototype to a trade show and seeing if I could write orders." Mark Nickel, founder of Sampler Publications, spent $450 to see if "anyone would be interested in advertising in a crafts catalog." (See the sidebar "Researching by Doing.") This conflation of research and selling approach may not produce reliable information. The orders-at-a-trade-show test can generate false positives or false negatives—the entrepreneur may, for instance, secure an order by a lucky fluke. But most entrepreneurs do not have much of a choice: They simply cannot afford truly objective, statistically significant data.

Limited opportunity costs. Entrepreneurs do not have much to lose from an erroneous forecast of relative ability or market size. As we have seen, they usually do not put much capital at risk. The opportunity cost of their time is often low because, like Gates and Allen, they don't have the credentials and experience that could secure them highly paid employment. As Michael Dell, who dropped out of college to start Dell Computers, explained: "The opportunity looked so attractive, I couldn't stay in school. The risk was small. I could lose a year of college."[7] The individuals who face high opportunity costs, we will see in later chapters, usually do not start small, bootstrapped ventures. Like Jim Clark, who was an associate professor at Stanford before he started Silicon Graphics, they pursue opportunities with the large likely returns (and capital requirements) that are commensurate with their opportunity costs.

Many of the *Inc.* 500 founders I interviewed did not even have to incur the emotional costs of quitting a satisfactory job; more than a third had been fired or left after a serious disagreement. Others worked on another job to support themselves while they launched their businesses. John Mineck, for instance, started Practice Management Systems in 1982 while still employed by the Personal Care Division of Gillette, Inc. "You could do something on the side very easily," he recalls. "They seemed to discourage hard work." Thus, while entrepreneurs may lack an objective basis for believing they can outcompete their rivals, their overconfidence isn't particularly consequential.

Prior knowledge. The entrepreneur's previous experience, even if it is relatively brief, mitigates the risks of inadequate research. Entrepreneurs who start a business by imitating or modifying an idea they encountered in their jobs already have firsthand evidence of the viability of the concept and knowledge of the critical market facts. Steve Shevlin and his partner, Robert Wilken, for instance, were only about twenty when they started Compu-Link in 1984. Their business was simple: "We brought in great rolls of computer cable, cut them and sold them, usually within twenty-four hours." They confidently launched this business without market research. Shevlin, who had worked briefly for a company in the same business, knew one crucial fact: His previous employer was making a gross margin of about 90 percent. Shevlin and Wilken made up batches of IBM printer cables and secured orders on the very first day by cold-calling computer dealers listed in the Yellow Pages. The dealers didn't have many other suppliers calling them at the time—the business was new—and they could sell a printer cable for $60 that they paid Compu-Link $16 for and that cost Compu-Link only a couple of dollars.

Researching by Doing: Sampler Publications

Mark Nickel founded Sampler Publications in 1984. Prior to Sampler, Nickel had worked as a managing editor of a magazine in Chicago. He came up with the idea of a folk crafts ad quarterly while attempting to market craft work made by his wife: "My wife and a friend of hers made crafts out of her house. They bought crocks, painted them with country designs, and put lids on them. They sold well at craft shows. I was tired of working downtown and asked myself, 'Why not build a crafts business?' We then decided, 'Why don't we try to sell mail order?' We looked around for country-style magazines to advertise in—that is, *Country Living* and *Country Home*. They had black-and-white ad sections in the backs of the books. A sixth . . . cost $1,750! That's a lot of money for selling a $3 widget. There was no good medium to advertise in. So I said to myself, 'Why don't I start my own?' The result was *Country Sampler*.

"I decided to see if anyone would be interested in advertising in a crafts catalog. I ran ads to get ads. I figured that a guy could spend $450. I ran two ads in magazines that crafters read. I also mailed my ads to all the crafters listed in the classifieds of the two magazines. . . . I'd go to craft shows and mail ads back to the people I met there.

"I got a good response, so I started putting a prototype together—at this time, the people responding to my ad still had not seen anything to show them what the product would look like. I did a four-page 11 x 17 foldup. A bank gave me a personal signature loan of $3,500 for printing the piece. I shot pictures of the products with dummy captions, product descriptions, etc. I hand-addressed and stamped each one, sent them out to everyone who had responded to my ads, and waited to see what would happen. . . . The deadline for advertisements was February 15, 1984. I got orders from eighty-four people. They had to pay up front. At $450 each, they paid for the production of the catalog. If it had bombed, I would only have lost $3,500.

"The product was a five-color, high-quality piece, with no editorial content. I ran an ad in *Country Living*: 'Buy direct from America's craftsmen!'

"It was a one-time deal initially. I told the crafters that I'd run their ads for one year. They didn't care! It was a pretty book, and they wanted to be in it. I didn't know what I was going to do next, but crafters started seeing this and saying 'holy cow!' I quit my job when I knew that I had enough business for a second catalog. I was still employed at the time, but I'd go in early to my office at around seven-thirty, and have my stuff done by nine.

"For the second one, I reprinted the pages as they were and added more. I was getting between two thousand and twenty-five hundred responses per month. Anyone could sell these catalogs at booths, craft shops, etc. Crafters sold them. They sold like crazy. . . . The ads paid for the production, and I made $3 every time we sold a magazine. I never had to borrow anymore."

Nature of Opportunities

The low likely profit and investment requirements and the high uncertainty of promising start-up opportunities also have a significant impact on the costs and benefits of prior analysis and research.

Profit and investment. The magnitude of the expected profits in a niche market cannot justify much expenditure on research. When a company such as General Electric contemplates a global trading company or when Citicorp executives decide whether to build an investment banking business in Japan, the stakes are high enough to justify large outlays on the analysis of competitors and customers. The business of splicing up computer cables does not. Low capital requirements also ameliorate the false positive or the "fluky" order problem that arises where selling is combined with research. A small, bootstrapped business with low capital requirements—does not need to serve many customers; as we will discuss in the next chapter, entrepreneurs can make satisfactory profits just by serving the unusual needs of unusual customers.

In fact, in many niche businesses the specific information generated by doing is more valuable than research about the world at large. "Average" costs and prices may not be relevant to the specialized markets in which entrepreneurs often start their ventures, and the entrepreneur may only be able to assess the viability of the venture by taking the concrete steps necessary to launch it. The profitability of a new restaurant, for instance, may depend on the terms of the lease; low rents might change the venture from a mediocre proposition to a significant source of cash. But an entrepreneur's ability to negotiate a good lease cannot be easily determined from a general prior analysis; he or she must enter into a serious negotiation with a specific landlord for a specific property. (Conversely, a large corporation that contemplates opening a chain of restaurants has to first investigate "average" prices and costs in its target area before researching conditions in particular locations.)

Uncertainty. The uncertain nature of many promising opportunities also reduces the value of prior analysis. In new or changing markets, research can be costly because of the transient nature of the opportunity. By the time the entrepreneur has completed a thorough investigation, the imbalances and confusion that start-ups can profit from may disappear. The profit margins that Shevlin and his partner enjoyed on selling computer cable were both extraordinary and short-lived. Similarly, if Gates and Allen had spent the time to do a competitor or market analysis, they might have missed the boat, since several other programmers were trying to develop BASIC for MITS's Altair at the same time as Gates and Allen. Ed Roberts, the founder of MITS, says that "we had at least 50 people approach us saying they had a BASIC."[8]

Entrepreneurs cannot expect, in uncertain businesses, to gather reliable data on potential demand and competition. How could Gates and Allen have known which other programmers were working on a BASIC or how capable they were? They had to trust their abilities to produce a working BASIC first; if they had been wrong, they would have wasted just a few months of labor. Similarly, entrepreneurs cannot objectively evaluate their relative ability to serve amorphous customer wants. Karen Kirsch found, after the fact, that she could build a profitable mailing list brokerage business simply by providing better service. But apart from her prior experience at another broker, Kirsch could not collect data to support an objective prediction of such an outcome; she could only test this assumption by starting the business. Similarly, Warren Anderson had to make instructional videotapes to discover whether customers would buy them. In 1982 Anderson was offering training courses in microcomputers when he conceived of the idea of turning the service into a videotaped-based product. He discussed the idea with "a lot of people" who said "it sounds good, but it depends on how well it is done" or "I'd have to see it first." Anderson then "just went on gut" and spent $30,000 on producing a video for D-base software.

Evidence

We cannot prove, of course, that entrepreneurs who do not plan would not enjoy higher returns (or fewer losses) if they researched their opportunities more extensively. But we cannot find any correlation between start-up success and extensive planning, either. For instance, a 1990 National Federation of Independent Business study of 2,994 start-ups showed that founders who spent a long time in study, reflection, and planning were no more likely to survive their first three years than those who seized opportunities without planning. My interviews also suggested that the few entrepreneurs who conducted extensive market research and formulated detailed business plans did so mainly because of their prior education and experience in large corporations. While planning was consistent with their prior conditioning, it did not seem to protect the entrepreneurs from the vagaries of starting a business. The limited utility of planning, especially in fluid and unstable environments, was dramatically illustrated by two interviews we conducted in a single day in the Washington, D.C., area.

By coincidence, our interviewees, the founders of Attronica Computers and Bohdan Associates, had both started their businesses in 1983 about ten miles away from each other. Both evolved (see the sidebar "Does Planning Pay?") into companies that distributed computers to corporate customers. Attronica's founders, who had worked together in a large telecommunications company, had decided after extensive market research and planning to purchase a franchise from a computer retail chain for $150,000. After that and other attempts to serve the retail market failed, Attronica developed, through trial and error, into a company serving corporate and government accounts. In

1988 the company had revenues of about $8.1 million. Bohdan's founder, in contrast, started selling computers out of his home by accident—he placed an ad to sell his used computer and was surprised by the demand. Then, simply by "reacting" to customers, Bohdan grew to a $48 million revenue business by 1988.

3. The Importance of Adaptation

With high uncertainty and limited planning, entrepreneurs often encounter surprises and setbacks that require them to modify or completely revamp the original business idea. More than one-third of the *Inc.* 500 founders we interviewed significantly altered their initial concepts, and another third reported moderate changes. Apparently, instead of committing to technology, customer, product line, and other such basic choices, entrepreneurs start with a set of tentative hypotheses. Then, as the venture unfolds, entrepreneurs revise their hypotheses rapidly through a series of experiments and adaptive responses to unforeseen problems and opportunities.

Common events that trigger a change in strategy include:

Failure to generate sales. The entrepreneur runs into a wall because customers are unwilling to switch from their existing vendors or do not find adequate value in the product or service the start-up has to offer. This problem is common because the entrepreneur did not have the time or the money to do market research or because the willingness of customers to purchase was unknowable before the fact.

Declining profitability. The opportunities that entrepreneurs find in new or unsettled markets are often short-lived: The 80 percent profit margins that companies such as Compu-Link earned in the early 1980s from chopping up rolls of printer cable were obviously not sustainable. But even though the declining profits are predictable, entrepreneurs often do not plan for that eventuality. This apparently myopic behavior is not irrational, however, because the short-lived nature of the opportunity requires quick rather than deliberate action. Also, although declining profits may be predictable, the future of the industry may be too uncertain to allow for a useful ex-ante plan, and the entrepreneur may just have to wait to see how the market evolves. Finally, the entrepreneur can make satisfactory short-term profits even if the long-run prospects of business are poor. Exploiting a short-term opportunity without a long-term plan thus creates an attractive option; and, as the option begins to expire, the entrepreneur can stay in the game by finding new opportunities in the now-changed market, or can walk away. In either case the decision is made ex-post rather than ex-ante.

Stalled growth. The initial niche, even if profitable, may be too small to satisfy the entrepreneur's aspirations for growth. In some cases (as in Raju Patel of NAC) the entrepreneur may already have a plan to exploit a larger market;

Does Planning Pay?: Attronica vs. Bohdan

Attronica. Carol Sosdian and Atul Tucker, who had worked together in a large corporation, started Attronica in 1983 to retail personal computers in Washington, D.C. Carol recalls that Atul "wrote a one-paragraph business plan and brought it to me, and I turned it into a real business plan. It took about one month, and then we bantered back and forth over the next three months. We got to where we thought it might work, and then we showed it to some friends. It passed the 'friend's test.'"

Heartened, Carol and Atul conducted almost two years of market research, which led them to purchase a Byte franchise for $150,000. Soon after they open their first store, however, Byte folded. They then signed on as a franchisee of World of Computers, which also folded; and in 1985 Attronica began to operate as an independent, direct dealer for AT&T's computers. This partnership clicked, and Attronica soon became one of AT&T's best dealers. Attronica also changed its customer focus from people off the street to corporate and government clients. They found large clients much more profitable because they valued Attronica's technical expertise and service.

Bohdan. Peter Zacharkiw founded Bohdan Associates in a Washington, D.C., suburb in the same year that Atul and Carol launched Attronica. Zacharkiw did not conduct any research, however. He was employed by Bechtel and invested in tax shelters on the side. He bought a computer for his tax shelter calculations, expecting to deduct the cost of the machine from his income. When Zacharkiw discovered that he was overdeducted for the year, he placed an ad in the *Washington Post* to sell his computer. He got more than fifty responses and sold his machine for a profit. Zacharkiw figured that if he had had fifty machines, he could have sold them all, and he decided to begin selling computers from his home. "At first I just wanted to earn a little extra Christmas money," he recalls. "My wife put systems together during the day, and I delivered them at night. We grew up to $300,000 per month, and I was still working full-time. I made more than I would have made the entire year at Bechtel."

Like Attronica, Bohdan evolved into serving corporate clients. "First we sold to individuals responding to ads. But these people were working for companies, and they would tell their purchasing agents, 'Hey, I know where you can get these.' It was an all-referral business. I gave better service than anyone else. I knew the machines technically better than anyone else. I would deliver them, install them, and spend time teaching buyers how to use them. " In 1985, after customers started asking for Compaq machines, Bohdan became a computer dealer and the business really took off. "We're very reactive, not proactive," Zacharkiw observes. "Business comes to us, and we react. We have never had a business plan."

often, however, entrepreneurs will start in a niche simply because it is expedient and helps create an option. When the potential of that niche is exhausted the entrepreneur starts looking for new opportunities.

Unexpected opportunities. Sometimes entrepreneurs encounter opportunities to build a much larger and more profitable business than they had initially expected or even wished for. Several founders of the *Inc.* companies I interviewed had no intention of building a multimillion-dollar business. They started small ventures with relatively low expectations before stumbling into larger profit opportunities. These opportunities were not merely unplanned; they also were unforseeable at the start. Just as Alexander Fleming had to work in a lab to discover penicillin, so the entrepreneurs had to start a business to encounter opportunities that would be invisible to an outsider.

The unexpected problems and opportunities that entrepreneurs encounter after they have launched their businesses can trigger radical changes in the nature or the products of service offered, customers served, channels of distribution used, and so on. (See the sidebar "Adaptation: Illustrative Examples.") As discussed in Chapters 6 and 7, such changes are less likely to be found in corporate initiatives and in VC-backed start-ups.

4. Myopic Opportunism

So far I have distinguished between adaptation on the one hand, from planning and anticipation on the other hand, and suggested that the typical entrepreneur relies more on the former than on the latter. The importance of this distinction will become clearer in Chapter 5 where we will see that corporate initiatives have the opposite tendency. Now we will explore the distinctive features of entrepreneurial adaptation. Like natural selection—and unlike scientific experimentation—in many promising start-ups this adaptation has an opportunistic or a myopic nature. But in contrast to the random process of biological evolution, the effectiveness of adaptation in start-ups depends on the conscious and purposive choices made by the entrepreneur. Unlike a biological species, entrepreneurs also can make radical (as opposed to evolutionary) changes and can switch from a myopic to a strategic approach.

Unscientific Experimentation

Although we may speak in a broad way of an entrepreneur's "experiments," they have little in common with scientific experiments and empirical methods. Well-designed scientific experiments are informed by a general theory or paradigm. Researchers derive testable hypotheses from the general theory and collect data that support or refute the hypothesis. Accidental discoveries—of penicillin by Alexander Fleming and of X rays

Adaptation: Illustrative Examples

The founders of Factor-Fox changed the basic service they had started their company to offer. Rich Fox and his partner, Allen Factor, had both worked for nonprofit companies before they decided to start a company that would "raise money for the causes [they] believed in." Their original plan was to help their clients raise money through direct mail solicitation, but they found it difficult to secure any business. A direct-mail solicitation involves significant up-front expenditures on printing and mailing without any assurance of results. Factor-Fox's prospects were apparently unwilling to entrust such projects to a start-up. They were, Fox recalls, "not open to hearing our message. The risks were too high, and they'd say 'we're happy with what we have.'" The founders then decided to offer telemarketing services that did not require clients to make large up-front commitments. In telemarketing, Fox recalls, the responses were extraordinary. We apparently had a winning formula. So we gave up on direct mail."

Silton-Bookman Systems altered both its product and its target market. The founders initially planned to sell PC-based software for human resource development. But established competitors who already sold similar software on mainframes were beginning to develop products for PCs. So the company adopted a niche strategy and developed a training registration product. And although the founders had initially targeted small companies that couldn't afford mainframe solutions, their first customer was someone from IBM who happened to respond to an ad. Thereafter, Silton-Bookman concentrated its efforts on large companies.

Gammalink found a niche for its product only after a series of setbacks and frustrating experiments. In 1984 Gammalink announced its first product, an internal fax modem for PCs, in *PCWeek*. The announcement attracted attention from independent sales representatives in the terminal emulation business but no orders. The founders had initially believed that customers would use their product for PC-to-PC communication, but finding no takers, they redesigned it for PC-to-mainframe communication by adding a rack-mounted host modem chassis. The redesign led to a deal with Dialog, a provider of on-line information services. Dialog planned to set up a database of trademarks that its clients could download from their offices. Such a service required a modem (now commonplace, but novel in 1984) that could receive graphics images. But after purchasing three modems, Dialog decided to abandon its trademark project. Gammalink then sent out a mailing to the MIS managers of five thousand companies. The mailing led to a single customer, BMW of North America. The BMW order suggested that while Gammalink's fax modem did not appeal to customers who connected their mainframes to PCs through leased lines, it was "suitable for large companies with dispersed PCs but not enough demand to justify dedicated leased lines."

Philip Doganeiro, founder of National Data Products, started selling business forms in 1982. In 1985 he started selling printers. Doganeiro recalls that a customer, AT&T Paradyne, "came to me and said, 'Do you think you can handle printers? We plan on buying seven to eight hundred Epson printers.'" Doganeiro thereupon secured a line of credit from Epson and sold $1 million of their printers in one year. In 1986 the company moved into selling computer systems after hiring a new controller, Anthony Limbo. "I knew that he had a degree from Villanova and an M.B.A. from the University of South Florida," Doganeiro told us, "but I didn't know that he had a knowledge of computer systems that I didn't have. He had been at Arthur Andersen's consulting division, during which time he had worked with systems. At his urging we got into computer systems."

The founders of Eaglebrook Plastics similarly discovered opportunities to build a larger and more profitable businesses than they originally envisioned. Eaglebrook Plastics was founded in 1983 by Andrew Stephens and Bob Thompson, who had been chemical engineering students at Purdue. At first they bought plastic scrap, had it ground by someone else, then sold it, primarily to the pipe industry. One year later they bought a used $700 grinder, which they operated at night so they could sell during the day. Soon they moved up to a $25,000 grinder. In 1985 the company developed an innovative process for purifying paper-contaminated plastic scrap—and began to make a name for itself in the industry. In 1987, with the profitability of scrap declining, the partners turned to recycling plastic bottles, a novel idea at the time. Next came plastic from recycled materials and then a joint venture with the National Polyethylene Recycling Corporations to manage their Styrofoam recycling operations. By the early 1990s Eaglebrook Plastics was one of the largest high-density polyethylene recyclers in the United States.

by Wilhelm Roentgen—have, of course, played significant roles in our understanding of the physical world, but such events fall outside normal research methods. To secure funds (and subsequent recognition) for their work, modern scientists must demonstrate its likely contribution to the long-term development of their field. In contrast, entrepreneurs experiment to solve a problem. They have little interest in validating general truths or principles. Finding that the initial business idea is unviable (i.e., refuting the initial hypothesis) has less value than discovering a substitute that works. In the initial stage of a business the entrepreneur is well satisfied with an anomalous or fluky source of cash.

The scientific method, as we will see in Chapter 5, has more in common with the market research techniques used by large corporations: Before a Procter & Gamble (P&G) undertakes the national launch of a new product, decision-makers make an effort to confirm their hypothesis about its viability through large-scale tests. P&G may also use market research to choose between or among specific alternatives, such as using coupons to stimulate sales or in-store promotions; in contrast, capital constraints require entrepreneurs to rapidly generate positive cash flow rather than discover the best possible alternative. As suggested by several examples in

"Adaptation: Illustrative Examples," it is more important for the founders of promising businesses to secure a paying customer than to find the highest-value use for their product or service.

Opportunistic Selection

Entrepreneurial adaptation has some interesting parallels to biological evolution by chance variation and natural selection: Although entrepreneurs have the cognitive capacity to act in a strategic fashion, they often exhibit an opportunism and a myopia that Elster observes represents an essential feature of evolution.

Mutations occur randomly in nature, Elster notes, but the subsequent process of selection takes place in a simple, deterministic way—the evolutionary "machine" accepts a mutation if it endows the first organism in which it occurs with a superior reproductive capacity. Natural selection thus has an "impatient, myopic or opportunistic" character—it has "no memory of the past and no ability to act in terms of the future." The evolutionary machine cannot learn from past mistakes because "only success is carried over from the past." It cannot wait; nature does not forgo favorable mutations now to realize better ones later. And it does not "employ the kind of indirect strategies epitomized in the phrase 'one step backward, two steps forward.'"[9]

Humans can adapt and solve problems with more foresight. As Elster observes, humans can delay gratification or wait: They can "reject favorable options in order to gain access to even more favorable ones later on." They can also employ "indirect strategies" of accepting "unfavorable options in order to gain access to very favorable ones later on."[10] For instance, humans can consume less now in order to consume more in the future.[11]

Entrepreneurs, however, often do not exercise their "unique human capacity" for waiting or for sacrificing for the long term. Rather, like an evolutionary machine, they make seemingly opportunistic and myopic choices. This is in part due to the capital constraints faced by entrepreneurs, who may have no long term at all if they fail to seize whatever short-term opportunities happen to come their way. Furthermore, because many entrepreneurs stumble into their businesses without a long-term strategy in mind, they don't have any criteria or calculi that tell them when to wait or what sacrifices to make. A few entrepreneurs, such as Jann Wenner of *Rolling Stone*, do start out with a long-term vision for their business. Many entrepreneurs do not; consequently they have a propensity to pursue any option that yields them a short-term profit. (It is the well-established companies that have the resources that allow them to wait and the strategies for making trade-offs with the long view in mind. Indeed, as I will argue in Part II of this book, the development of such strategies is a critical step in the transformation of a start-up into a long-lived enterprise.)

Contrast with Natural Selection

To anticipate some arguments made in later chapters, we may also note some characteristics of entrepreneurial adaptation that distinguish it from natural selection.

Conscious choices. Entrepreneurs encounter many chance events; whether and how they respond often depends on the significance they attach to these events rather than on a mechanistic natural selection rule. Consider, for instance, Peter Zacharkiw's description of how he took on Compaq's line of computers after starting as a "gray market" (i.e., unofficial) dealer of IBM computers: "When we were in the gray market, some people would ask for Compaq. I was impressed with them from the engineering standpoint of how they are put together. I called them to see if I could become a dealer. They turned me down at first, but I had a friend there who recommended that they reconsider us. He pushed us through." The move to Compaq was thus triggered by a chance event—customers asking for Compaq—and by Zacharkiw's good fortune in having a friend at the company. But the start-up's "mutation" was certainly not automatic—another entrepreneur might have ignored customer requests or not pursued Compaq so persistently. Zacharkiw's claim—"We're very reactive, not proactive. Business comes to us, and we react"—seems overly modest and understates the critical role of choice and resolve.

Imaginative variations. Entrepreneurs can try out variations that initially exist only in their minds. As the geneticist François Jacob put it, "[M]en choose between unactualized possibilities, whereas natural selection can choose only among the actual alternatives."[12] Entrepreneurial adaptations result from *imaginative* responses to unforeseen events. Although exogenous events trigger entrepreneurial responses, the responses themselves are the products of the entrepreneur's imagination. For instance, as described in "Adaptation: Illustrative Examples," the unwillingness of potential clients to use Factor-Fox for direct-mail campaigns represented an unpleasant surprise for the founders. The founders' counterproposal—"Will you try us for telemarketing instead?"—was not a chance variation. It was an attempted mutation or experiment that arose from the entrepreneurs' goal-seeking imaginations. If that experiment had failed, the entrepreneurs would likely have thought of another angle.

Radical changes. In nature, mutations in an organism are usually of small magnitude—hence we speak of evolutionary rather than revolutionary change. Variations that arise out of an entrepreneur's mind can allow for much larger-scale changes from the status quo. This capacity for large-scale change offsets the tendency for opportunistic choices to lead to local maxima. The natural evolutionary machine, which adopts mutations without any regard to their cumulative effect, Elster writes, "may lead a species to climb along a fitness gradient until it reaches a point from which all further movement can be downward only, and there it comes to a halt."[13] Thus a species can fall into an evolutionary backwater because it happened to encounter a particular sequence of mutations. It cannot escape from this backwater because of the small magnitude of the typical random mutation. Opportunistic choices may similarly lead entrepreneurs toward enterprises that have limited long-term value. But entrepreneurs can break out of undesirable local maxima by reinventing their business in a radical way. For instance, after a few years of grinding plastic scrap, the founders of Eaglebrook Plastics could branch out into the recycling business by developing a proprietary technology. After more than a decade of struggling with manufacturing software, Mitchell Kertzman, founder of Powersoft, developed the successful PowerBuilder software aimed at users of client/server computing. Or, to take a celebrated older example, 3M grew out of a failed effort to develop a carborundum mine.

Adoption of strategies. Entrepreneurs who start by making purely opportunistic choices can subsequently adopt a long-term strategy that allows for waiting and the sacrifice of short-term profit. Natural selection, by contrast, is consistently myopic.

These distinctions will play an important role in subsequent chapters, when we will discuss the importance of entrepreneurial talents and skills. As we will see, some stochastic and evolutionary models (such as Nelson and Winter's) suggest that long-run outcomes depend entirely on the sequence of random events that a business encounters. I will argue that entrepreneurs' capacity to recognize important changes and to frame imaginative responses, to make radical changes if a dead end has been reached, and, eventually, to formulate a long-term strategy, have major influences on the development of a business.

5. Summary

In the previous chapter we found that promising businesses whose founders lack novel ideas, experience, and funds tend to cluster in small, uncertain market niches. In this chapter we have seen why the meager endowments and the types of opportunities that founders of promising start-ups pursue limit the resources they devote to prior planning, and research: Capital constraints and the small scale of expected profit preclude much investment in prior planning, and the uncertainty of the enterprise limits its utility. Apparently the "unmeasurable" and "unquantifiable" risks that promising start-ups face cannot be easily reduced by expenditures on research even if the entrepreneur has the means to incur them. The low level of prior planning and high uncertainty in turn requires entrepreneurs to adapt to unexpected problems and opportunities. Capital constraints and the lack of a long-term strategy for the business often give this adaptation, like the processes of natural selection, an opportunistic or myopic character.

3

Securing Resources

This chapter examines how founders of promising businesses persuade customers, employees, suppliers, and other resource providers to participate in their ventures. Section 1 analyzes the problems that entrepreneurs face, and Section 2 analyzes some offsetting or mitigating factors. Section 3 discusses the strategies entrepreneurs adopt to secure resources.

The meager endowments that make it virtually impossible for many entrepreneurs to raise significant capital also make it difficult for them to attract customers, employees, suppliers, and other such resource providers. But whereas investors may be dispensable, these other sources of revenue and inputs are not. Securing these resource providers thus represents a critical problem for start-ups, which we will explore in this chapter.

Resource providers can face considerable risks in doing business with a start-up. If a new business fails, for instance, customers may suffer serious disruptions, former employees may not be able to return to their old positions, and suppliers may not be able to collect on their receivables. Unlike well-capitalized corporations, entrepreneurs cannot, however, easily underwrite others' risks or provide credible signals of their competence or staying power. Therefore, rather than offer insurance, entrepreneurs often provide quick gratification of immediate needs to resource providers with limited alternatives, unusual preferences or a myopic disregard for long-term consequences.

Scope. I will focus primarily on customers and, to a lesser degree, on employees and suppliers. In most of the start-ups I studied, customers appeared to face the greatest risk. For example, clients who retained Factor-Fox to execute a direct-mail campaign were at risk not just for the fees they would pay Factor-Fox but also for the much larger costs of printing and mailing the materials. Similarly, the exposure of Advent Software's customers extended well beyond the purchase price of Advent's portfolio management software. If the software was flawed or if Advent went out of business and could no longer support its product, clients would face significant costs in switching to another system. Employees and suppliers faced fewer risks and often did not have much choice; the problem of signing them on, therefore, wasn't as difficult as the problem of securing customers. The basic principles I discuss, however, apply to all outside resource providers.

1. Problems

The "rational" calculus of resource providers—that is the choices that traditional economic models assume people typically make to maximize their utilities—pose special problems for the founders of promising businesses. "Behavioral" tendencies—that is, deviations from the usual assumptions of rational decision-making due to cognitive biases or automated responses to stimuli—also pose difficulties.

"Rational" Calculi

The objective concerns of resource providers derive from their prognosis of the start-up and from their own switching costs. We should expect that customers, employees, suppliers, and so on will, like potential investors, assess the chances of survival of a start-up before they make an irreversible commitment of time or money, or close off other options. As Tom Davis, founder of Modular Instruments, manufacturers of medical and research equipment, recalls, "When we first started selling, people would ask, 'When are you going to go out of business?'" The company's first product, launched in 1984, was built around a PC and sold for $6,000—one-fifth of the $30,000 price for existing minicomputer-based products. But customers worried that the costs they would incur if Modular Instruments wasn't around to service and maintain its products would be greater than their substantial initial savings.

The objective evidence about most start-ups does not provide much reassurance about their prospects. Modular Instruments, at least, had a unique product, whereas most ventures have no verifiable source of competitive advantage. As previously mentioned, the founders also often lack deep management or business experience; before launching Modular Instruments, Davis had been an assistant professor at the University of Pennsylvania's medical school, and his cofounder was one of his postdoctoral students. Some entrepreneurs may have an innate capability to outperform their rivals, acquire managerial skills, and thus build a flourishing business. But it is difficult for customers (and others) to identify founders with these innate capabilities. Entrepreneurs without much business experience also don't have deep prior relationships or reputations that might provide reassurance about their capabilities. For instance, fewer than 30 percent of the *Inc.* founders I studied used prior relationships to make their early sales;

more than 70 percent had to get orders from customers who were more or less strangers.

The undercapitalization of start-ups also raises concerns about their longevity. The lack of capital obviously increases the prospect of financial distress; it also provides some subtle negative signals. It raises the possibility that the entrepreneur lacks the business sense to understand the risks of running out of cash or, alternatively, has failed to attract capital because investors were skeptical about the prospects of the venture. Low initial capital can also create negative perceptions of the founder's commitment to the business; with not much to lose, the entrepreneur may walk away if the venture does not get off to a good start. Or the entrepreneur may so completely redefine the enterprise that from the perspective of a resource provider, the original business no longer exists.

Switching costs can discourage resource providers in several ways from doing business with a start-up. Contracting with a new supplier involves administrative costs—the customer may have to generate new vendor numbers and close an existing account. Similarly, an employee who changes jobs faces the bother of enrolling in a new health or pension plan. Switching can entail the loss of specialized "relation-specific" assets, such as the applications a customer has created using a particular vendor's software or the valuable knowledge an employee develops about how things work in a certain organization. And switching requires resource providers to incur search costs without any assurance that the search will yield a superior alternative to the status quo. Therefore resource providers who are satisfied with their current arrangements have no incentive to look farther afield. Although neoclassical economists do not fully embrace the principle of "satisficing"— don't look for a better solution if you are happy with what you have—it provides a powerful explanation for the stability we observe in commercial relationships.*

Search costs pose special problems for start-ups because they don't have a track record that resource providers can rely on. The first set of customers, employees, suppliers, and so on have to conduct their own tests and investigations instead of using references or making inquiries with credit bureaus or the Better Business Bureau. The rational approach is to let someone else go first. But if all resource providers try to take a free ride on someone else's experience, then a start-up will never get a chance.

---

* "Don't search if satisfied," we should note, represents a rational rule. As Simon and several others have stressed, search costs force satisficing. Winter puts it well: It does not pay to acquire "information on unchanging aspects of the environment" or to "review constantly decisions which require no review." But "without observing the environment, or reviewing the decision, there is no way of knowing whether the environment is changing or the decision requires review." Decision-makers therefore have to set "limits to the range of possibilities explored" that depend on their threshold of satisfaction. So, "at some level of analysis, all goal seeking behavior is satisficing behavior" (Winter [1964], 262–64, cited in Elster [1993], 140).

Start-ups thus face an expectations trap. Resource providers' concerns about a start-up's prospects discourage them from taking a chance on the start-up, and this hesitation hurts the prospects of the venture. In other words, start-ups can fail just because others expect them to fail.

Behavioral Factors

Cognitive biases (see the sidebar "Cognitive Biases") can amplify the rational predilections of resource providers to avoid start-ups. The objective concerns of customers about the survival of a new business get reinforced by their "loss aversion," or status quo bias particularly if the existing supplier frames the choice in a manner that plays up to the customer's fears. If resource providers are satisfied with current arrangements and face high switching costs, their tendency to avoid disconfirming data reinforces their tendency to stick with existing relationships. A few vivid personal experiences with failed start-ups may also lead resource providers to believe that such events happen more frequently (or have worse consequences) than they actually do.

The reflexive behavior (see the sidebar "Reflexive Behavior") of resource providers, like their cognitive biases, can reinforce the rational propensity to avoid start-ups. The reflexive tendency to rely on "social proofs" (to do what others are doing), for instance, reinforces the objective logic of letting someone else try out the start-up first: If no one else is buying, there must be something wrong with the product. Similarly, the principle of consistency reinforces the resources providers' switching costs. Robert Cialdini describes this principle as a "nearly obsessive desire to be (and to appear) consistent with what we have already done." Once people make a choice or take a stand, they tend to act in ways that justify that choice. Thus after customers have sunk resources into a vendor's products or simply made a difficult decision to go with a particular vendor, they will feel an internal pressure to stick with that choice that goes beyond the tangible costs of switching.

2. Mitigating Factors

Some rational factors and behavioral tendencies can offset or mitigate the problems start-ups face in securing customers and other resources.

Rational Offsets

Limited or poor alternatives. Resource providers sometimes don't have the option of dealing with stable, well-capitalized entities. As we have seen, promising start-ups tend to thrive in businesses that large companies avoid and in new markets in which there are no established players. As

Cognitive Biases

The work of psychologists and experimental economists has generated a "long list of human judgmental biases, deficiencies and cognitive errors."[1] Researchers like Kahneman and Tversky have found that, contrary to assumptions of rational decision-making models, the judgments and decisions of human subjects show "extreme sensitivity" to "subtle changes in problem format and response mode."[2] Differences in labels or the framing of choices, not just the actual payoffs, apparently lead to different preferences. For instance, asked to choose between a certain but small loss (say, $5) and a large but unlikely loss (say, $5,000 with 0.1 percent probability), most subjects will take their chances with the larger loss. Labeling the small loss as an "insurance premium" produces a significant change in preferences; a majority of subjects choose to pay the premium rather than risk a large loss. Similarly, Thaler indicates, it matters to customers whether a difference between two prices is labeled as a surcharge or a discount; customers will more willingly forgo a discount than accept a surcharge.[3] Kahneman and Tversky suggest that these framing effects derive in part from our greater aversion to losing what we have to our desire for a gain of the same magnitude. Thus customers will more readily give up the "gain" of a discount than accept the "loss" of paying a surcharge (over a price they believe is already "theirs"), even though the net effect is the same.

Camerer[4] provides a comprehensive overview of the evidence on such systematic violations of rational models. Besides the preference reversals due to loss aversion already mentioned, Camerer discusses several other "mistakes" in judgments and choices. These include the following: (1) *overconfidence* in judging the likelihood of events—for instance, events people say are certain to happen only 80 percent of the time; (2) *memory biases*—people remember the most and least pleasant memories more easily; overweigh personal and concrete experiences; and allow available theories and options to limit their consideration of other alternatives; (3) *confirmation bias*—people seek evidence to confirm their hypothesis and avoid data that might refute it; (4) *self-fulfilling prophecies*—people's prior beliefs evoke actions that generate more but biased evidence to support those beliefs—a waiter treats badly dressed customers poorly because he believes they give low tips and thus reinforces his theory; *myopia*—people show greater impatience about immediate delays than about equivalent future delays.

Reflexive Behavior

Robert Cialdini's book *Influence: Science and Practice* provides an engaging account derived from laboratory experiments and from field observations of how reflexive or automated responses to stimuli affect behavior. Reflexive responses, Cialdini notes, are a common feature of animal and human behavior. Ethnologists who study animals in their natural setting have shown that a particular trigger feature will set off the same response time after time. For instance, a male robin will seek to defend his territory by attacking a clump of robin-redbreast feathers placed there but will ignore a perfect stuffed replica of a robin without the feathers (p. 3). Similar "fixed action patterns" have been documented by psychologists in humans as well. For instance, Ellen Langer's experiments suggest that people are more likely to accede to a request if it is accompanied by a reason, but without necessarily paying attention to the reason. For instance, "Excuse me, I have five pages. May I use the Xerox machine, because I'm in a rush?" got a significantly higher favorable response (94 percent to 60 percent) than just "Excuse me, I have five pages. May I use the Xerox machine?" However, the non sequitur "Excuse me, I have five pages. May I use the Xerox machine, because I have to make some copies?" generated a 93 percent favorable response.

Automatic, stereotyped behavior, Cialdini writes, "is prevalent in much of human action because, in many cases, it is the most efficient form of behaving, and in other cases it is simply necessary."[5] It enables individuals to act quickly without gathering and processing much data, and it helps avoid cognitive overload. "We need shortcuts," Cialdini writes. We can't be expected to recognize and analyze all the aspects in each person, event and situation we encounter. . . . Instead we must very often use our stereotypes, our rules of thumb to classify a few things according to a few key features and then to respond mindlessly when one or another of them trigger features present." Reflexive responses can be particularly valuable when the outcome is of such little consequence that it does not merit much analysis, where a speedy response is essential, or where uncertainty limits the utility of decisions based on careful, causal predictions.

In some circumstances, however, fixed action patterns can lead to silly or even destructive behavior. Cialdini cites the case of an automobile company that erroneously printed and mailed out coupons offering no savings to customers. These coupons generated the same response from customers as correctly printed coupons offering substantial savings. Similarly, animal behaviorists have found several predators that mimic trigger features that cause their prey to reflexively lower their defenses. For example, the killer females of the Photuris genus of fireflies mimic the special code used by fireflies of the Photinus genus to signal their readiness to mate. The subterfuge leads Photinus males to fly toward rather than away from their Photuris hunters.

Cialdini discusses several "fundamental psychological principles" that humans reflexively adhere to. They usually promote desirable outcomes but can occasionally lead individuals to make self-damaging choices. For example, the principle of reciprocation causes us to automatically accept and subsequently repay favors and gifts. Rejecting the initial gift or then failing to reciprocate leads to external social disapproval as well as the internal discomfort of transgressing a rule we have been conditioned to believe in. The rule and the attendant "web of indebtedness," anthropologists argue, facilitate exchange and the specialization of labor; it can also be deployed to evoke responses that individuals would otherwise avoid. Cialdini describes how members of one Hare Krishna movement press flowers on business travelers at airports to elicit donations. The gift is unwanted and quickly discarded. Nevertheless, the traveler, who is not predisposed to like the solicitors, cannot refuse the flower and feels impelled to make a reciprocal donation whose value typically far exceeds the cost of the flower.

Similarly, the principle of social proof ("the tendency to see an action as appropriate when others are doing it") usually works quite well: People generally make "fewer mistakes by acting in accord with social evidence than by acting contrary to it."[6] But doing what others do—or merely responding to triggers that suggest what others are doing—can lead to choices that would not be consciously made. When questioned, TV viewers describe the canned laugh tracks on TV shows as "stupid, phony and obvious."[7] Nevertheless, experiments have shown that the disagreeable tracks cause audiences to laugh longer and more often at humorous material and to rate the material as funnier.

Robert Grosshandler, who started a PC-based software company in 1984, observed: "Everybody in the business was new then. There were not many choices, and we weren't any worse than anyone else." In such markets, buyers have to deal with a new company or forgo the product or service altogether. "We had no track record and no commercial office—I was running the company from my home," recalled Prabhu Goel, founder of Gateway Design Automation, which supplies CAE software tools. "So we went after the users who had a problem that needed to be solved. The risk of dealing with us was small compared with the risk of not solving the problem."

Similarly, experienced managers, large suppliers, or multinational banks might shy away from a risky start-up; however, unemployed or unqualified workers, small suppliers, local lending institutions, and so on have to take their chances with employers, purchasers, and borrowers who don't have excellent long-term prospects. For instance, George Brostoff, founder of Symplex Communications, says that early employees weren't "risk-concerned" because they had come from businesses that had failed.

Search costs. If resource providers believe that the quality of alternatives is likely to be poor, they have an incentive to go with the first available choice, particularly if their need is pressing. When MITS contracted with Microsoft to supply a BASIC for the Altair, they followed a simple rule: Pick the first supplier with at least a semifunctional product. MITS needed a BASIC quickly, and they knew that while many individual programmers were working on one, established companies, such as IBM, weren't. So the youth and inexperience of Microsoft's two partners did not represent a major stumbling block.

Psychic utilities. The pecuniary risks of doing business with a start-up may be offset by the psychic benefits. For instance, an employee may value the thrill of working for a new business. A customer may similarly enjoy the excitement and prestige of being an early adopter or the satisfaction of giving a struggling entrepreneur a break.* Philip Doganeiro, founder of National Data Products, says that some of his early clients "believed in me and wanted to see a young guy who was busting his tail succeed." John Mineck of Practice Management Systems, a provider of PC-based office automation systems for medical practices, looked back to the risks his customers faced when he started in 1983: "People must have been crazy to do business with us. We're talking about trusting one's livelihood on software with immature technology. No one really understood what it was about or whether it was reliable. And you had to kludge things together—you had to get your hard drive from one company, software from another." The first customers were "risk-takers" who "saw the value" and liked and believed in Mineck: "I never believed it wouldn't work. I truly believed—so the customers did, too."

Personal agendas. Start-ups may secure resources from employees of organizations whose interests conflict with their employer's interests. From a company's point of view, buying software from an untested vendor may represent an unwarranted risk. The same purchase, however, may help the Information Technology (IT) staff justify their jobs and budgets, gain experience in their field as leading-edge users, enhance personal learning, and provide the satisfaction of backing an underdog. Given the frequency with which IT personnel change jobs (and the legal barriers to getting reliable employee references), the employer, not the employee, bears the costs of the failure of the start-up.

The flexibility of newness. The lack of an existing customer base or employees provides some advantages that can help alleviate the "liability of newness." The entrepreneur can provide special deals that a going business cannot easily match because its existing customers or employees might demand the same terms. Start-ups also have an advantage because the founder interacts directly with the resource providers. An entrepreneur can make quick decisions and counteroffers to customers and potential employees, whereas a salesperson or human relations employee is bound by policies and must seek the approval of superiors to deviate from them. "We

---

* Moreover, the typical promising start-up doesn't need to secure many customers, employees, or suppliers. The "average" potential customer may be too risk-averse to do business with a start-up, preferring to let someone else go first. A promising start-up with low fixed costs can, however, often generate positive cash flow with just a few exceptional buyers who are not quite as risk-averse.

got customers because I was the owner/salesman," Richard Nopper, founder of Beckett Corporation told us. "I wouldn't allow the salespeople who work for me today to make the kind of crackpot promises that I used to make. They would tear this place down!"

Entrepreneurs can also give the resource providers the satisfaction of dealing with the owners of the business instead of low-level or midlevel employees. Robert Grosshandler of Softa Corporation said that because he was personally involved in the selling and many of the early clients were small, "it was an owner-to-owner sale. It gave my prospects a lot of confidence that I knew what I was talking about." In a large company the CEO can only call on a few important accounts or interview recruits for just the top-level positions.

Aligned interests. Once someone has signed on with a start-up he or she has an incentive to help the entrepreneur attract other resource providers. For instance, the purchaser of a new software package has a vested interest in the survival of the vendor and can therefore be expected to provide testimonials and leads that will help convert other customers.

Behavioral Offsets

Confirmations biases. When desperation or convenience creates an incentive to do business with a start-up, resource providers will often avoid disconfirming evidence. "Very few people checked us out," says Practice Management's Mineck. "A couple of clients visited our office once, but that was all." Another entrepreneur got a long-term lease on his office because the commercial real estate market was depressed and the landlord did not do a credit check. Apparently, as the sidebar "Natcom's Whopper" also indicates, resource providers who don't know how shaky the prospects of a start-up really are, often don't want to find out.

Myopia. Confirmation biases seem closely related to the timing of benefits received: Immediate benefits often lead resource providers to myopically disregard (and avoid investigating) the long-term costs. Customers of the *Inc.* founders I surveyed seemed willing to make risky purchases from a start-up if its products or services could provide immediate and sizable advantages. They would buy a new firm's microprocessor because it was five times as fast as other models. A data processing manager would place an order for an innovative fax board because it enabled him to set up a communications network without contracting for expensive leased lines. The tangible payback period for customers that were at risk rarely exceeded a year. Given these quick payoffs, customers would ask the entrepreneur, in a perfunctory way, about what would happen if the start-up failed—but then proceed to buy anyway.

Other resource providers also ignored (or heavily discounted) long-term outcomes when they realized immediate benefits. Employees escaped

---

Natcom's Whopper

Robert Rodriguez started Natcom in 1982 by renting balloons to used-car dealers but then moved to serving a corporate clientele (see Chapter 1) One of his early customers was Burger King. Rodriguez recalled: "We painted 'Burger King' on a balloon and flew it in front of their office. The hoopla it created gave us a foot in the door and, by early 1983, we were putting balloons at the grand openings of restaurants for Burger King.

"In 1984 I was invited to a meeting with the executive vice president of marketing. He said, 'I want to do something incredibly elaborate for our national convention in Nevada. I want to build a hot-air balloon in the shape of a Whopper sandwich.' I said, 'Wow! What an opportunity. This is for us.'

"We made a presentation that they really liked, but I was scared they would send somebody down to see our little operation. They would have been shocked if they had seen our office: We were in an office-sharing complex in North Miami. I said to my partner, 'Man, if they send anyone here to investigate us, do you think a major corporation like Burger King is going to let us manage and build a hot-air balloon if they see this place? In fact, Burger King was too busy to do due diligence. They just wanted someone who sounded like they knew what they were doing, and they gave us a $35,000 advance to build the Whopper. It worked perfectly. Once that convention was over, we signed a two-year management contract. Burger King would pay us $75,000 a year to take this hot-air balloon with its pilot all over the country."

---

from unrewarding jobs or even unemployment. Suppliers who provided goods and services in small volumes to start-ups realized higher profit margins than from larger, well-established customers. Any outside investors in the start-ups were repaid quickly—most of the firms in our *Inc.* sample achieved profitability in a year or two, if not in months. The short-term gains apparently eclipsed long-run concerns. Employees did not usually ask for—nor were they offered—equity or options; 76 percent of the *Inc.* founders interviewed did not make equity or equity options available to employees.* They overlooked, or could be persuaded by the entrepreneurs to disregard, the long-term risks, such as being let go if they could not grow with the company. The small banks that provided credit when the big banks would not apparently did not worry that, as the venture grew, it would naturally look for more prestigious lenders with higher credit limits.

---

* In contrast, start-ups backed by professional venture capitalists usually offer equity options to employees because they have higher opportunity costs than the employees of promising start-ups.

Conversely, long-term inducements generally did not seem to adequately compensate the resource providers for their perceived risks. As we have seen, entrepreneurs usually could not persuade VCs to make a long-term bet on their ventures. Entrepreneurs also had little success in convincing well-qualified or experienced personnel to give up current income in return for a share of the long-term upside and had to make do with employees with limited alternatives.

Reciprocity. Even a token or unwanted gift such as a restaurant recommendation or a tidbit of industry gossip from an entrepreneur (like the Hare Krishna solicitor's flower discussed in the sidebar "Reflexive Behavior") can evoke a reciprocal favor from a resource provider.

Consistency. The urge to justify a prior action can lead resource providers to escalate their commitment to a venture. Seemingly inconsequential initial concessions create internal pressures to act consistently and grant larger favors later. Thus a buyer's willingness to grant a five-minute hearing can lead to the placing of a small trial order and then a larger order; at each decision point the buyer does not want to believe that the previous decision was a mistake. Per Cialdini's discussion, the strength of the resource provider's subsequent support depends on whether the initial commitment was public, involved undergoing pain or trouble, and whether it was regarded as flowing out of an internal choice rather than made in response to external rewards or compulsions. The early converts to, say, the Mac computer who made a risky, nonconformist choice may be expected, therefore, to be especially fervent supporters of the enterprise.

Contrasts. The tendency to exaggerate differences between two things that are presented one after the other helps entrepreneurs whose competitors often do not appear to be particularly competent. "If we are talking to a very attractive individual of the opposite sex at a party and are then joined by an unattractive individual of the opposite sex," Cialdini observes, "the second will strike us as less attractive than he or she actually is."[8] Similarly, buyers may be expected to overrate the prospects and competence of a venture if they have recently encountered a somewhat less inspiring competitor.

Credibility triggers. An entrepreneur who mimics the appearance of a well-established business can trigger an impression of stability. As Frank Vanini, founder of Continental Financial Resources, an equipment leasing company, put it: "In a young business, perception is as important as reality. Take our name, for example. People didn't know if we were big or small. I only wear white shirts and dark suits when I'm doing business. If you make the proper presentation, people will make the proper assumptions about you. If you have a nice [company] name, a nice suit, if you speak well, etc., you must know the business. It was hard to get into the door, but folks assumed we knew the business once we got in."

3. Strategies Employed

Entrepreneurs utilize several strategies to contain the problems they face in securing resources and to take advantage of the mitigating factors. These, my research suggests, include:

Special Deals and Benefits

The entrepreneurs I studied often provided special incentives to overcome the reluctance of resource providers to go first. For instance, they offered extensive customization or free ancillary services and training to their early customers. "We did a lot of things for our first clients that we wouldn't do today," said Practice Management Systems' John Mineck. Stephanie DiMarco, cofounder of Advent Software, recalls that the company "spent hours on the telephone solving problems that didn't have anything to do with us. Some people had never worked on a PC before. We would do anything to get their systems to work." George Brostoff, founder of Symplex Communications, recalls that their first significant order, from Mead Data, took about four months of "consultative" selling: "As we demonstrated our products we helped Mead refine their existing data network, so whether or not they bought our component, they would have an improved system."

Another special benefit entrepreneurs provided was simply to serve customers (or give jobs to individuals) that other businesses would not. As I will discuss in a later section, start-ups often served customers with poor credit histories or difficult personalities and hired individuals who were unemployed and faced limited job opportunities.

The start-ups I studied, however, seldom offered price breaks that would lead to losses. First, they needed the cash flow. Bootstrapped start-ups couldn't afford to buy market share by giving away their products or services; usually only the ancillary services and support were free. Second, many entrepreneurs felt that the donation of their core offering would undermine their credibility and that users might not give a serious trial to a free sample. Third, the entrepreneurs believed that concerns of the users were not primarily related to price and that their cost benefit calculus could not be significantly altered by an introductory price discount.

Mimicry

Many entrepreneurs sought to create perceptions of stability and reliability by adopting the outward manifestations of larger, more well-established businesses. "You have to create an image that you exist," the founder of Wang Communications told us. "I learned to use 'we' instead of 'I' when talking about the company. I hired an answering service with a live person to take messages. We [!] couldn't risk having a machine; that would show we weren't committed." Bud Miles, founder of Electrotek Concepts, initially a provider of consulting and subsequently of software to electric utilities, said: "We used a lot of smoke and mirrors to get people to think we were bigger than we are. We used consultants all over the place. They were experienced in how to do business and how to project to companies. Our proposals were absolutely stellar. People would say, 'My God, you must be a 20-million-dollar company.'"

James Odorczyk, founder of Inter-Ad, "described the future of the company as if it were the present" and "maintained an air of being bigger than we were" by producing quality brochures and sales materials and a professionally designed logo. "With a lot of companies, you can tell that the logo was designed by the person running the business. The logo might not cost a lot, but most companies do without a professionally designed logo. There is a mentality that engineers have that the product will sell itself. I saw it in myself and tried to fight it." Although Odorczyk was on an "austerity budget," he moved into an office suite so that he could have an "'office-sounding' address." Marcia and Steve Plotkin, who started Real World Systems, operated out of their home for several years, but when customers called, Marcia would tell them that "'Steve is in the warehouse,' which meant that he was in the garage!"*

Bruce Neurohr, founder of Transamerica Energy Associates, spent $1,500 per month on travel expenses because "I had to let customers see that I could afford to call on them. In the early years I had to demonstrate that I was viable."

Richard Schoenberg, founder of Steadi-Systems, bought a computer with a dot matrix printer. At the time, he says, no one else used computers, so he could "give the impression of being a much larger company while still being in my living room."

Samir Barakat, cofounder of the consulting firm Barakat and Chamberlain, says they always "kept their capacity tight. . . . I'm a firm believer in telegraphing that you are a scarce commodity. If you can get your clients to believe that you don't need them, then you can get them. When clients get the perception that you are desperate for business, that's the worst thing. Of course, we say to the client that you're important, but there's a balance to be struck."

Stephanie DiMarco, whose company sold portfolio management software, had a "sober logo" theory. DiMarco was a woman in her twenties when she started Advent Software, while her customer base was "predominantly male" and "the average portfolio manager was fifty." Therefore

---

* At one stage, Real World sought a dealership from IBM. Marcia Plotkin recalls: "IBM was tough. IBM came to our house—we had told them ahead of time that we worked out of our house. IBM had a policy against dealers who worked out of their homes. You had to have a storefront. They said, 'We have to get approval about the house.' But, by then, we had six employees and they could see that we were a business."

DiMarco didn't want the company logo to be "splashy" and say 'We're a California software company.' Our letters to portfolio managers looked like the letters they would receive from a colleague."

Going back to 1939, David Packard writes that when he and William Hewlett designated their first product, they called it Model 200A "because we thought the name would make us look like we'd been around for a while. We were afraid that if people knew that we'd never actually developed, designed and built a finished product, they'd be scared off."9

These efforts by entrepreneurs to mimic the appearance of a more established business may be contrasted with an IBM campaign to advertise a new computer line. The latter represents, in standard economic terms, a true signal of commitment to the business because it is costly and irreversible. Mimicry, on the other hand, is intended to trigger an unthinking, automated belief in the start-up's stability without requiring the entrepreneur to incur a significant expense: A sober letterhead does not cost more than a flamboyant one. The thought that goes into adopting a reassuring appearance may, however, provide genuine evidence about the entrepreneur's long-term prospects: Entrepreneurs who have the foresight to think about how others will perceive them are more likely to survive than those who do not. Resource providers can expect such entrepreneurs to be more sensitive and responsive to their other needs as well.

Framing

The *Inc.* company founders we interviewed "framed" choices and trade-offs to minimize their resource providers' perceptions of risk: They "accentuated the positives," "provided customers with as pretty and glossy a picture as possible," and "provided the facts, but with lots of glitz." William Rizzo, founder of Rizzo Associates, an engineering and environmental services company, recalls with regret that "we promised employees substantial opportunities in terms of personal growth and sold them a future. But we did not tell them that they had to live up to that future. In time, we had to bring people in over them, and they felt their future was sealed off. Eventually they said, 'The hell with you.' Four of the first seven employees who could not grow with the company left. Today I would be more candid about the fact that our promises are contingent on their performance."

Some entrepreneurs emphasized the value of a "safe" complementary good that they bundled with their more risky product or service. For instance, ICT was a "systems integrator" of turnkey Computer Aided Design (CAD) systems: the company put together IBM PCs with a modified version of Autodesk's Autocad software. At the time, Autodesk was a small, seventeen-employee company; therefore cofounder Harman Cadis recalls: "We didn't tell people that the software was Autocad." Instead they emphasized that the system was "based on a standard IBM PC. If ICT went out of business, they could still keep the hardware. Of the $18,000 list price, $12,000 was hardware and $2,000 to $3,000 was for installation and training. The software was a small part of the whole sale." (According to Cadis, it also helped that although ICT was based in California's Silicon Valley, the customers were based in Michigan and Ohio: "We sold to computer-illiterate people who were more easily wowed by the technology. We sold very little to Silicon Valley.")

Entrepreneurs put the best face (or "spin") on their limitations. Clay Teramo started Computer Media Technology, as what he called "a non-stocking dealer": Vendors would not give the start-up distribution contracts, and with just $10,000 in initial capital Teramo couldn't afford to carry much inventory. "I anticipated customers would be concerned about this," said Teramo, "and I came up with an answer. I would say, 'I have unlimited inventory. I draw from all manufacturers. If I was a distributor and I ran out of inventory, then you would have to wait for me to get more product.'"

Bruce Singer, founder of RPM Rent-A-Car, who started selling used cars to pay for a J.D./M.B.A. program, describes the importance of framing of otherwise problematic facts:

"When I started in the used-car business, the Federal Trade Commission wanted to standardize used-car dealers. I thought it was a neat idea—I would be the most honest used-car dealer in the world. I would have an accurate description of each car in the windshield, and run a silent auction. It failed miserably! You need someone to make the sale. Cold facts by themselves are frightening if you just read them. Say you read on a form, 'XYZ part may need to be replaced.' You are scared away. But if there is a salesman who points out that if you are a student who is only going to drive around campus for six months, and therefore you are unlikely to have to replace the part, you are going to feel more secure. Customers need a human being to decipher how certain facts fit their needs."

Downplaying the risks or glossing over deficiencies does not necessarily mean exaggerating the benefits. Indeed, many of the entrepreneurs we interviewed claimed that they build credibility with customers and valuable references by not overpromising or overselling. As George Brostoff of Symplex Communications put it: "We set our customers' expectations below what we knew we could do and pleased our customers by exceeding them."

Broad Search

Entrepreneurs had to conduct an extensive search to identify the resource providers who would take a chance on their ventures. Only a few providers had the right combination of objective needs, the psychic desire to help the underdog, disregard for long-term returns risks, and so on. Entrepreneurs could not easily identify these unusual, high-potential prospects because their special characteristics often were invisible. So, to find resource providers with the best "fit," entrepreneurs had to cast a wide net and approach as many prospects as they could until they found the right one.

The problem of locating the right customers was especially acute. The best prospects for a start-up weren't the most obvious or visible. Unlike hungry suppliers or out-of-work job-seekers, customers generally did not proactively approach start-ups; and the best entrepreneurs, I found, often had more success securing customers with sporadic or offbeat needs than customers with recurring or mainstream needs. Frequent buyers have more choices because they represent a more obvious target for vendors. They have a greater incentive to establish systematic procedures for identifying and evaluating suppliers. (See the sidebar on Ken Dougan.) They are also more likely to have had some bad experiences with unreliable vendors; the "availability" or "vividness" of these memories can lead them to avoid untried start-ups. Conversely, infrequent purchasers face fewer choices. They are more likely to be flattered by the attention an entrepreneur gives them. Lacking prior experience with start-ups, they may be ignorant of the risks they face or have an unwarranted confidence in their capacity to identify good entrepreneurs. Similarly, customers were more likely to give a chance to start-ups when they had an urgent, unexpected need rather than when the need was well anticipated. A buyer in a rush has few options, and as was discussed in the sidebar on Natcom, may myopically disregard the risks of doing business with a new vendor.

Locating customers who are in a rush or not tightly bound to a regular supplier, however, is like trying to find a needle in a haystack. The sporadic or unexpected purchases of customers that create openings for start-ups also make finding them a difficult proposition. The entrepreneur has to use a shotgun rather than rifle shot approach, approaching a very large number of prospects to find a few situations that click. To illustrate, let us return to the Gammalink example that we discussed in a previous chapter. As previously described, Gammalink's founders mailed out five thousand brochures to locate one customer, BMW of North America. Recall also that BMW had an unusual requirement: it needed to transmit data to many locations, but the volume of data was too low to justify dedicated leased lines. If this problem had been critical, the data processing manager would have proactively searched for a solution instead of waiting for a brochure to arrive in the mail. If BMW had been a high-volume purchaser of data transmission services, its suppliers might have tried to provide a solution. As it was, BMW of North America was not a high-profile customer, and while Gammalink provided a valuable solution, the company could have carried on without it. The small, out-of-the-way need both created an opportunity for Gammalink to secure its first customer and also made the search difficult.

The role of individual preferences and traits adds to the difficulty of

How Light Users Can Make Easier Prospects:
Ken Dougan's Experience

When Ken Dougan started Unique Transportation systems, a provider of trucking services in Lewisville, Texas, his first interstate account was the local unit of Burroughs Computer (now Unisys). Burroughs had relatively low-volume needs—one shipment a week out to Pennsylvania, and two incoming shipments, from Massachusetts and Connecticut, respectively. Larger truckers weren't too keen on this business because of its low volume, but Dougan was able to make a profit by consolidating the Burroughs loads with other small loads that he found through a broker. High-volume shippers such as food processing companies balked, however: Sara Lee said Dougan's company was too small. Tri-Valley Growers said they wouldn't do business with Dougan unless he could provide twenty-five to thirty trailers a day. Unlike Burroughs, the high-volume shippers had a list of approved carriers and required their vendors to provide financial statements that would prove their stability.

finding the right prospects. Many of the entrepreneurs interviewed suggested that the attributes of particular decision-makers played an important role giving them their early breaks. A "courageous head of marketing" at MCI entrusted Devon Direct, a six-month-old direct-mail and advertising agency, with a campaign to get consumers to switch their long-distance telephone service providers after AT&T was broken up in 1984. According to founder Brostoff, "movers and shakers who were seeking to better themselves and their companies" gave Symplex Communications its early orders. "We didn't sell to the typical procurement people. You had to get people who saw the value and needed the service." Bruce Neurohr recalls that many of the prospects he called on "would ask for our financial statements. We relied on young managers at our clients who understood that you just don't have anything when you are starting out."

But unconventional individuals who have a taste for the untried and a soft spot for struggling entrepreneurs are not easy to locate. Indeed, if their propensity to experiment with new products or give entrepreneurs a chance conflicts with their employer's interests, they have an incentive to hide this tendency. Therefore entrepreneurs have to do a lot of digging to find such individuals.

Incremental Commitments

Entrepreneurs got resource providers to increase their risks in stages. For example, because portfolio managers would not readily purchase a complete portfolio management system from a new vendor, Advent Software initially just provided accounting functions. The company then added reporting and performance measurement functions and eventually "filled out the whole map of investment functions." Robert Grosshandler, cofounder of the Softa Group, recalls that that their first real-estate management software sold for $5,000. Five years later, an enhanced package was priced at $20,000. Customers often placed orders for multiple units, so one sale could generate $500,000 for Softa. "We have gone from low-ticket, low-risk to high-ticket, high-risk," said Grosshandler. "The buyer now consists of a committee of seventeen people who spend three days here kicking the tires."

Russell Personnel Services started off by helping clients find permanent secretaries. This was a simple, low-risk brokerage function because the client had full discretion over whom to employ. The brokerage activity then served as a springboard for providing temporary secretaries. The temp business required clients to trust Russell to screen the temps carefully; clients also saw themselves at some risk if Russell defaulted on its payments to the temporary workers.

According to cofounder Samir Barakat, his consulting firm, Barakat and Chamberlain, started with "behind the scenes" assignments for clients rather than "high visibility" studies: "When we started, we were willing to do the $50,000 studies which the bigger firms were unwilling to do. We started with more analytical work and then we moved up to more management stuff. We first did most of our work with supervisors, then managers, and now with vice presidents and presidents."

If the entrepreneurs had started with an "all or nothing" approach they likely would not have made much headway. The gradual approach allowed customers to step up their commitment as their information about the start-up improved and it built a credible track record. The gradualism also may have been effective because of the psychological need to make choices that are consistent with previous commitments. Cialdini describes the "foot in the door" technique that sales professionals sometimes employ to take advantage of this tendency. "For the salesperson," Cialdini writes, "the strategy is to obtain a large purchase by starting with a small one. Almost any small sale will do because the purpose of that small transaction is not profit, it is commitment. Further purchases, even much larger ones, are expected to flow naturally from that commitment."[10]

The utility of getting resource providers to make small commitments to get them emotionally hooked is illustrated by the following account of how Silton-Bookman secured credit from a bank. Banks rarely lend to start-ups that don't have a track record or collateral. Therefore, Phil Bookman and his partner did not even try to get a loan when they launched their software company. Instead, they opened an account with a bank and would periodically ask the branch manager for business advice. About three years later, Bookman went to the banker with the company's financial statements and projections. "He looked over the numbers," Bookman explained, "and said, 'It looks like you need a $50,000 term loan.' We knew that all along, but it was important that he suggested it. We got the loan and paid it back, then used the same method the next year to get a line of credit."

By first asking for the banker's advice, Bookman generated an initial commitment that then paved the way for the more difficult decision to approve a loan.

Second-Tier Resources

The inability to provide compelling short-term inducements (or credible long-term insurance or payoffs) to top-tier resource providers forced entrepreneurs to make do with the second tier. "When you are new and cold-calling customers," observed Fred Zak of Venture Graphics, "the business that comes your way is usually from customers who can't pay the bills or shop only on price. They form the worst customer base. They are the kiss of death—unless you are physically very big and ugly." About 40 percent of his early work, Zak recalls, came from "deadbeats." To collect on his bills he would show up unannounced and make it so "nerve-wracking," that they would "pay us off so they wouldn't see me again." Zak also had one big early customer, TSR Hobbies, who manufactured the game Dungeons and Dragons: "They were not in good financial shape and I gave them terms. But it was better to be doing something than nothing. I worked with them and serviced them really well. As they became stronger, they caught up with their payments."

Entrepreneurs took a similar approach to recruiting personnel. In the typical VC-backed start-up, the VCs will insist that the entrepreneur recruit a top-quality team quickly. Generous cash compensation and stock options are used to attract experienced and capable personnel. It is not unusual, for instance, for such start-ups to hire CFOs or marketing managers at more than $100,000 per year. Bootstrapped ventures cannot afford to pay such salaries; and the perceived value of equity in their companies also is low. In the early days, therefore, the founders I studied served as the "chief cook and bottle washers," who performed all critical tasks. Other employees, if any, performed routine or mechanical tasks for modest pay. They were rarely well educated or experienced, and many had been unemployed or dissatisfied with their previous jobs. Mark Nickel, founder of Sampler Publications, did everything himself for a year. Then he hired the sister of a friend who lived across the street. Her husband had just left her, and she needed to support her kids. His second employee was "a suicidal alcoholic neighbor. I thought I'd rehabilitate her. When she sobered up, I'd let her come over and type names." The third employee was a friend of the second employee.

John Greenwood's first employee at Micron Separations was a sixty-two-year-old machine shop worker who had just been laid off. His production manager was a Worcester Polytechnic Institute graduate who had been working as an accountant in a company he hated and was looking for another job. "We never attempted to lure anybody away from another company," Greenwood told us. "One, we were cheap. Two, we had moral reasons—if we went under and it didn't work out for them, we wouldn't feel so bad."

Natcom's early employees were, founder Robert Rodriguez recalls, "street fighters":

> To get hired in this organization was a joke. If you came in and we needed a warm body, you were hired. Literally for any position. Our turnover was high because we had to fire many employees—they had a bad attitude or were doing side deals. I had to fire several operations managers. One took some of our merchandise and started his own balloon rental business. I had to call the police to get our stolen merchandise back.
>
> In a small company, unfortunately, such problems are unavoidable. We could not afford the committed professionals who, by their nature, are less interested in side deals. The average salary here was $15,000 to $20,000. Large companies can hire by credentials and screen people carefully. We needed to have things happen quickly and took people on the basis of their initial presentation. But many didn't do what they said they could.

4. Summary and Conclusions

Entrepreneurs who start businesses without much capital or high personal opportunity costs in uncertain markets acquire, in effect, a cheap option to build a business. The value of the option depends in part on the entrepreneur's ability to get others to bear some of the risks. To do so, we saw in this chapter, entrepreneurs adopt a variety of strategies, which often involve the exploitation of others' cognitive biases and reflexive tendencies, and the locating of resource providers with unusual needs or willingness to bear the risks.

The material that we have covered so far also allows us to make some inferences about the economic function or value added of the typical entrepreneur and about the role luck plays in their ventures.

Functions. As we saw in the Introduction, economists have described the role of an entrepreneur (as distinct from other factors of production, such as capital and labor) in a variety of ways: innovation (Schumpeter), coordination and combination of other factors of production (Say), risk-bearing (Cantillon), responsibility for uncertainty (Knight), and arbitrage (Kirzner). From these many roles that entrepreneurs can in principle perform, we can now identify those that the founders of "promising" companies actually do perform. We have seen that most do not start out as innovators or risk-bearers to any significant degree; those roles, we will see in Part II of this book, become salient at a later stage of the enterprise. Their activities (in the start-up stage) seem to correspond more closely to the role of arbitrageur; as we saw in Chapter 2, they often take advantage of information gaps to buy cheap and sell dear. And to the extent that they combine multiple inputs (rather than arbitrage an already existing good) we can attribute the role of coordinator to them as well.

From the data and analysis of this chapter we may add to the entrepreneur's coordination function the role of risk syndication: As we saw, entrepreneurs persuade several resource providers to bear risks, and for their trouble, earn a claim to profits of the enterprise. We also found that, in addition to coordinating others' labor and inputs, entrepreneurs also make a significant contribution of their own effort and skill to the enterprise. Thus the "entrepreneurial" role of arbitrage and risk syndication is closely intertwined with the doing of the actual work (or their labor input).

Luck. The finding that promising businesses usually start in "uncertain" market niches, and our analysis of the difficulties entrepreneurs face in securing resource providers, help explain the common belief that luck plays an important role in the success of new ventures. For businesses with changing technologies and regulations or with amorphous consumer preferences, one should expect random events to have a greater effect than for a business operating in a stable environment. Similarly, chance will likely affect when and how entrepreneurs connect with the "right," out-of-the ordinary resource provider. The observation that chance plays an important role does not necessarily mean, however, that successful entrepreneurs are especially lucky individuals. Although this is difficult to prove or measure, everything did not go smoothly for the entrepreneurs I studied. More often than not they had to overcome many setbacks and disappointments. Differences in the capacities to adapt to chance events and to execute strategies for acquiring resources apparently play important roles in separating the winners from the losers. In the next chapter we will examine the traits and skills that these capacities derive from.

4

Distinctive Qualities

This chapter examines the traits and skills that predispose certain individuals to start promising businesses and affect their capacity to undertake the tasks to do so. Section 1 examines the factors that predispose individuals to start promising businesses. Section 2 discusses the qualities that affect an entrepreneur's capacity to adapt, and Section 3 looks at the qualities that influence the capacity to secure resources. Section 4 discusses attributes that do not significantly influence the success of entrepreneurs in promising fields.

The belief that entrepreneurs are special has widespread appeal, but we cannot easily specify their distinctive traits and skills. Folklore attributes many qualities to the entrepreneur—great energy, vision, leadership skills, and a never-say-die spirit, to name just a few. Some formal research on entrepreneurship, too, assumes individuals with distinctive traits and skills. At best, however, empirical studies provide weak support for the beliefs. As suggested in the sidebar "Profiling the Entrepreneur's Personality," the studies have suffered from some basic methodological problems. First, many researchers have tried to identify a universal entrepreneurial personality. They have implicitly assumed that the owners of car dealerships, self-employed accountants, and the founders of software companies share common traits that distinguish them from the population at large. This seems unlikely, given the wide variety of problems and tasks that these individuals face. A related problem derives from the arbitrary selection of traits. Researchers have studied whether entrepreneurs have "Type A" personalities or a high need for achievement, without specifying why these qualities matter.

I have followed a different approach. Instead of trying to identify a universal entrepreneurial type, I will focus only on the founders of promising businesses. As shown in Figure 4.1, I will make inferences about the traits and skills of these founders from the distinctive nature of the businesses they start and the tasks they face. Where possible, I will use existing research on human behavior and cognition to support these inferences.

We will address three questions: What characteristics predispose some

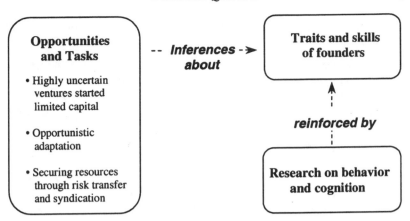

Figure 4.1. Inferring Distinctive Qualities

individuals to start promising businesses? Given the appropriate predisposition, what traits and skills determine an individual's capacity to adapt to new circumstances and to secure resources? (We previously identified these as the crucial problems of promising start-ups.) Conversely, what qualities do not have a material bearing on an individual's willingness and capacity to start a promising business?

1. Propensity to Start

Undeniably, chance events often provide the spark for starting a promising business. Entrepreneurs often encounter their opportunities by accident; Bohdan's founder, Peter Zacharkiw, it may be recalled, started selling computers after a classified ad he placed for his home machine drew a large number of buyers. Thus some individuals may not start promising businesses because they did not encounter such opportunities or because chance first inserted them into the larger arena of marginal businesses. In addition to these random events, we can also identify two factors that predispose some individuals to look for and take advantage of chance events: human capital and family backgrounds, and tolerance for ambiguity.

Human Capital and Family Backgrounds

The propensity to start a promising business can be thought of as an inverted U-shaped function of an individual's human capital. Too much prior training and experience raise the opportunity costs and risks of starting a small, uncertain enterprise, whereas too little human capital increases the chances of starting a marginal rather than a promising business (see Fig. 4.2). Similarly with backgrounds: Individuals from middle-class backgrounds are more likely to start promising businesses than individuals from either extremely wealthy or extremely deprived backgrounds.

Profiling the Entrepreneur's Personality

Following David McClelland's pioneering research, several studies have tried to identify the personality attributes that characterize the "entrepreneur." Such studies typically use survey questionnaires to assess whether certain attributes have a high incidence among entrepreneurs or association with the performance of a business. Researchers have tested a variety of attributes—Hornaday's survey lists forty-two attributes about which some claims have been made in one or several studies.[1] These attributes include:

- *Need for achievement (n Ach):* A person high in n Ach prefers personal responsibility for decisions; desires to attain high, self-defined standards; likes clear means of assessing goal accomplishment, and seeks to surpass others.
- *Risk-taking propensity:* Willingness to undertake a venture despite certain calculable probabilities of failure.
- *Internal locus of control:* The belief that personal effort is the primary determinant of outcomes; this belief is in turn associated with self-confidence, penchant for action, task orientation, and resilience.
- *Tolerance for ambiguity:* Willingness to act in an uncertain situation.
- *Type A behavior:* An incessant striving to achieve more and more in less and less time, and general competitiveness.

The studies have not yielded convincing results—Kelly Shaver and Linda Scott characterize the quest for a distinctive personality profile of the entrepreneur as largely "fruitless."[2] The support for unusual incidence of some traits among entrepreneurs has been weak or nonexistent. For instance, conflicting findings across studies led Brockhaus and Horwitz to conclude that risk-taking propensity "was not an accurate way of distinguishing entrepreneurs."[3] Similarly, whereas studies suggest that entrepreneurs have a stronger internal locus of control and a propensity toward Type A behavior than the population at large, these attributes do not distinguish them from managers and those in other such groups.

Some researchers attribute the inconclusive results of profiling studies to measurement problems; researchers don't have instruments designed to measure the traits entrepreneurs are supposed to posses and are forced to use measures intended for other purposes. Others attribute the conflicting results across studies to differences in the definition of an entrepreneur. Some studies define entrepreneurs as the founders of small, high-growth businesses. Other researchers study aspiring entrepreneurs, often students enrolled in business courses who express a strong intention to start their own business. Yet other studies count as entrepreneurs, the founders or owners of any kind of business that has survived for a specified period. According to Brockhaus,[4] these differences create "noise" that makes it difficult to identify a single clear profile.

These problems have led some researchers to abandon the search for a single entrepreneurial profile in favor of the identification of multiple types. One early example—Norman Smith's 1967 study—distinguished between the "craftsman entrepreneur" and the "opportunistic entrepreneur." Smith suggested that craftsman entrepreneurs had more limited cultural backgrounds and social involvement and a lower propensity for long-term planning and the likelihood of heading "adaptive" firms.[5] Subsequent researchers divided entrepreneurs into more categories—for instance, Karl Vesper identified eleven basic types and several subtypes.[6] This research, according to Hornaday, has led to a "bewildering" proliferation of "types" across studies, with findings that are as inconclusive as the results of studies that sought to identify a single entrepreneurial profile.[7]

Overqualification. We have already seen that founders of promising businesses usually face low risks because of their low opportunity costs. They do not have to give up high-paying jobs because they lack valuable experience and credentials. Some are unemployed, while others, like Zacharkiw, have jobs that allow them to start their businesses on the side. Small, uncertain ventures therefore provide high payoffs compared to the risks (at least in an objective financial sense). Individuals with secure, well-paying jobs obviously face different trade-offs and are much less likely to start small, uncertain businesses. Gates and Allen wrote BASIC for the Altair, and Hewlett and Packard tinkered with offbeat electronic devices in the hope that larger opportunities would materialize later. Few high-ranking employees at Microsoft and HP (or professors at Harvard and Stanford) would make that choice. They have an incentive to either stay on the corporate track or participate in the launch of the atypical ventures (to be discussed in Chapter 7) that have a concrete plan for securing large payoffs that match their greater opportunity costs.

The same considerations apply to individuals born into extreme wealth or who have become extremely wealthy. Except perhaps as a hobby, inheritors of large fortunes will generally not bother with niche businesses. To the extent that they have an interest in starting a business, they will tend to try something that is large enough to make a difference to their wealth or likely to provide a sense of accomplishment. Even entrepreneurs who

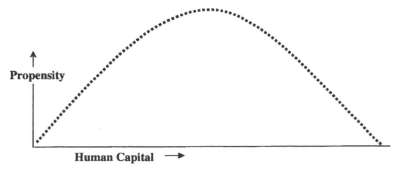

Figure 4.2. Propensity to Start Promising Businesses

have made a success of small bootstrapped businesses will often tend to start on a much larger scale the second time around. For instance, Jobs and Wozniak started Apple in their garage, making and selling computers for what was then a niche market. Jobs started his subsequent ventures, Next and Pixar, on a much larger scale.

Minimum thresholds. Too little human capital or truly deprived backgrounds can also reduce the odds of starting a promising business. The individuals who start such businesses usually lack deep business experience or great wealth. But they do have education and family background that gives them the confidence and ambition to undertake promising venture rather than open the marginal lawn care or beauty salon business. HP founders David Packard and William Hewlett received engineering degrees from Stanford. Packard's father was a lawyer, and Hewlett's father was a professor at Stanford Medical School. Bill Gates, a student at Harvard when he started Microsoft, was the son of a well-to-do lawyer. Gates and his partner, Allen, had previously attended Lakeside, a private school in Seattle, which "always drew on the city's big-money establishment."[8] Lakeside got Gates and Allen hooked on computers at an early age. In 1968, the school decided to expose its students to computers. The Lakeside Mothers Club held a rummage sale to help raise the funds needed to make Lakeside "one of the first schools in the country with computer capability."[9] Richard Branson, founder of the Virgin Group, did not have rich parents and did not attend college; his social background was by no means lower-class, however. Branson was "descended from a distinguished country family," and his mother "had grand ideas for her only son—including the dream that he would one day become Prime Minister" of the United Kingdom.[10]

Most of the *Inc.* company founders I interviewed were well educated— 81 percent had college degrees, and 10 percent had M.B.A.'s. Few had emerged from great poverty. According to *Inc.*'s own surveys, college education and a middle-class upbringing have been consistent features of the backgrounds of the founders of the companies that make its 500 list. For instance, as shown in Figure 4.3, more than 83 percent had at least a four-year college degree, and as Figure 4.4 indicates, only 5 percent reported that they came from poor backgrounds.

These backgrounds likely discouraged the entrepreneurs from pursuing marginal businesses and increased their likelihood of encountering promising opportunities. Gates and Allen would start a very small-scale software business but probably would not think about opening a laundry. Zacharkiw's chance encounter with computers came about because he was an early user. He was an employee of Bechtel, a well-known engineering company, and had bought a computer to track the tax shelters he invested in on the side. Conversely, many of the individuals who start marginal businesses have backgrounds and training that make it unlikely they will encounter or contemplate promising opportunities. The laundry business,

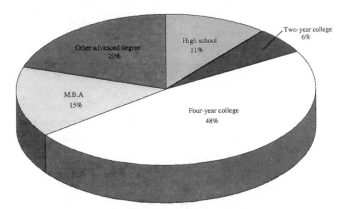

Figure 4.3. Educational Level of Founders
Percentage of 1998 *Inc.* 500 Companies

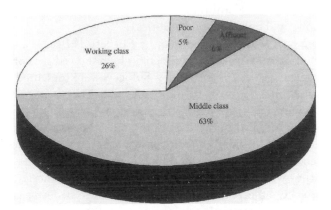

Figure 4.4. Origins of Founders
Percentage of 1998 *Inc.* 500 Companies
Source for both figures: Inc. magazine

for instance, represents a magnet for immigrants who have a poor command of English[11] and—unlike several foreign-born entrepreneurs who have successfully started computer businesses in the United States—who also lack technical skills.

Tolerance for Ambiguity

From a purely financial point of view, all individuals with low opportunity costs and adequate training should pursue "promising" opportunities where they have little to lose and something to gain. But, as we will see next, an innate or psychological unwillingness to act in the face of uncertainty can discourage many individuals from taking advantage of "heads I win, tails I don't lose" situations. Individuals who seek out such opportunities, or who jump on them quickly when they accidentally encounter them, have an unusual tolerance for ambiguity. In the section below, I will discuss the widespread prevalence of "ambiguity aversion," relying principally on Camerer's[12] review. I will further suggest that the low ambiguity aversion of entrepreneurs derives from their high self-confidence and the low weight they place on the social and psychological consequences of failure.

Ambiguity aversion. Camerer defines ambiguity broadly as "known-to-be-missing information." The definition, which includes missing information about probability distributions, is closely related to Knight's uncertainty and to the notion of fuzzy or vague probabilities. Ambiguity does not play a role in mainstream microeconomic theory, where decision-makers maximize their "subjective expected utilities"; the fuzziness of probability estimates doesn't matter because, by definition, the decision-makers can develop a subjective estimate of outcomes. But notwithstanding the assumptions of this theory, Camerer points to considerable experimental evidence suggesting that people do take ambiguity into account and make distinctions between known and unknown probabilities.

Following on a thought experiment by Ellsberg,[13] Becker and Brownson[14] conducted the following experiment, which showed the considerable aversion people have toward ambiguity. Subjects were presented with two urns each containing a mix of red and black balls. They were told the precise distribution of reds and blacks for one of the urns (say, fifty reds and fifty blacks) but not for the other. Subjects would choose a ball from one of the two urns, and if they drew a red they would receive $1. Subjects could choose which of the two urns they wanted to pick from and had to indicate how much they would pay for being able to make that choice.

Although the subjects did not have any reason to believe that the urn with the unknown distribution might contain fewer red balls, subjects always picked the urn with the known distribution. Moreover, they would pay high amounts for the privilege: For instance, subjects paid an average of 36 cents for the right to pick from an urn with fifty reds and fifty blacks. In other words, they would surrender 72 percent of the 50-cent ($1 × 0.5) expected value of a draw just to avoid ambiguity. Rational utility maximizers should, in theory, we may note, pay nothing unless they suspect that the experimenter had deliberately placed fewer red balls in the unknown urn.

Becker and Brownson's results, reported in a 1964 paper, led to several studies in the 1970s and 1980s that examined different variants and aspects of the urn problem. All the studies confirmed the original finding of ambiguity aversion and the willingness of subjects to surrender a significant portion of the expected value for the option of selecting from an urn with a known distribution. The studies also generated several other "stylized facts," such as Slovic and Tversky's[15] finding that ambiguity aversions are unmoved by written arguments against their paradoxical choices. Three such stylized facts seem particularly relevant to our discussion of start-ups.

First, increasing the range of possible probabilities (of the ambiguous urn) increases ambiguity aversion.[16] Thus the high uncertainty of promising opportunities may represent a significant deterrent for many individuals. Second, subjects are more averse to ambiguity when they know that the contents of the ambiguous urn will be revealed afterward to others.[17] Thus we might expect that many individuals will avoid objectively attractive opportunities because they are afraid of what others may think if they do not succeed, even if it costs them little to play. Third, and perhaps most significantly for our purposes, attitudes toward risk and attitudes toward ambiguity are uncorrelated;[18] risk-taking individuals who are prepared to bet heavily on structured gambles may be highly averse to ambiguity, and an ambiguity-tolerant individual may be exceptionally risk-averse. Entrepreneurs who have the high tolerance for ambiguity needed to start promising businesses, we may infer, may not have a risk-seeking disposition.

Offsetting factors. In contrast to the axioms of standard theories of choice, Camerer writes, ambiguity aversion implies "a gap between subjects' beliefs about an event's likelihood and their willingness to bet on that event."[19] Heath and Tversky[20] suggest that competence—knowledge, skill, and comprehension—may help close that gap. In their experiments, subjects were offered a choice between an ambiguous natural event and a structured draw with known probabilities. Knowledge apparently offset ambiguity aversion—subjects who had prior knowledge about the domain of the event, bet on the event. Those who knew little, bet on the unambiguous draw. Heath and Tversky suggested that knowledge influenced choices because of the subjects' asymmetric assignment of blame and credit. Experts could take credit, in their own minds and in the eyes of others, for winning in a way that less knowledgeable subjects could not. Moreover, those who lacked knowledge would also blame themselves more if they lost.

Heath and Tversky's conjecture is consistent with the results of experimental markets. Subjects apparently show considerable ambiguity aversion early in the experiment: They would rather do nothing and forgo profits than act in an environment they consider ambiguous. Later in the experiment, as the subjects learn and gain knowledge, they become less ambiguity-averse and conservative.

Knowledge and expertise do not, however, seem to provide a compelling explanation for why some individuals are willing to start uncertain businesses. Few of the *Inc.* founders I studied had deep experience in their fields; indeed, in a new market, few individuals have true expertise, except perhaps in their own minds. Moreover, as I have previously argued, high levels of expertise increase an individual's opportunity costs and thus reduce the propensity to start a small, uncertain business. More plausibly, the low ambiguity aversion of the individuals who start promising businesses derives from (or is a manifestation of) exceptionally high levels of self-confidence. Most individuals, we know, have a high opinion of their relative abilities for which they lack any objective basis. To hold such beliefs is one matter; to act on them is another. While many people believe that they drive cars better than the "average," this usually does not affect what they do when they get behind the steering wheel of an automobile. The self-confidence of entrepreneurs, however, appears so strong that they are prepared to start a business where they do not have any objective advantages over their rivals or even any knowledge of their relative abilities. As one entrepreneur put it, "Entrepreneurs are like gamblers in a casino who know they are good at craps and therefore are likely to win. They believe: 'I'm smarter, more creative, and harder working than most people.'" This is a different attitude, we should note, from a belief in one's luck: Entrepreneurs apparently have the confidence that they can make their own luck and can cope with some bad throws.

The high self-confidence of entrepreneurs may thus have different consequences than is sometimes believed. Even if objectively unwarranted, it does not necessarily lead to overinvestment in ventures with negative expected value. Rather, my analysis suggests, it can offset excessive ambiguity aversion and thus mitigate underinvestment in uncertain businesses. (Overconfidence may, however, lead to overinvestment in businesses that involve high initial commitments. The decision-maker's disregard for what others are doing can lead to boom-and-bust cycles in capital-intensive fields such as real estate, mining, and chemicals. But this very capital intensity puts such businesses outside the realm of the typical entrepreneur.)

We may further speculate that the unusual manner in which some individuals make attributions for success and failure may also influence their willingness to start uncertain businesses. Expertise, according to Heath and Tversky, increases the propensity to take credit for success and to avoid blame for failure. This tendency may be innate for entrepreneurs. Entrepreneurs may also be less concerned about avoiding regret or about what others will think if they fail—they don't avoid ambiguous urns whose contents will subsequently be made public. Thus in addition to low objective or financial risks, they may be less exposed than others to social or psychological costs.

To summarize: Promising opportunities have attractive risk returns, but only to those individuals with optimal skills and backgrounds and a high tolerance for ambiguity. Thus the number of entrants into such fields is likely to be smaller than in popular business, where the requirements for human capital, background, and ambiguity tolerance are not as great. But fewer entrants in these uncertain, offbeat fields does not imply the absence of competition or ensure profits. As we have seen, start-ups in promising fields have similar—and limited—initial resources and capabilities. They all usually lack distinguishing ideas, capital, or founders with deep experience and contacts. It is what entrepreneurs do after they start their business—how they adapt to unforeseen circumstances and secure resources—that separate the winners from the losers. In the next two sections we will explore the traits and skills that determine the performance of the post-start-up tasks.

2. Capacity for Adaptation

The following section discusses four traits that help determine an entrepreneur's ability to adapt to unforeseen problems and opportunities: decisiveness, open-mindedness, the capacity to manage inner conflict, and a talent for good attribution.

Decisiveness

The unexpected problems and opportunities that entrepreneurs encounter often require quick rather than well-thought-out or deliberated responses. For instance, the sidebar "Marcia Radosevich and the Health Payment Review" describes the case of an entrepreneur who must overcome the objections of an MIS manager at an insurance company. The MIS manager will not recommend the purchase of HPR's software because it is written in the C programming language. The entrepreneur has to make an on-the-spot decision about whether to offer to rewrite the software in COBOL. There is no time for further reflection, gathering data, and so on. If she hesitates, the moment is lost; it could be a long time before she gets to see the MIS manager again.

Decisiveness, in the context of a promising start-up, isn't simply the opposite of procrastination;[21] it involves quick choices under conditions of high uncertainty (or "ambiguity"). In the HPR case the entrepreneur actually made the commitment to rewrite the software without having crucial information about how much it would cost, how long it would take, or whether it was even technically feasible. (We may further note that this kind of decisiveness also represents one of the factors that predisposes individuals to enter uncertain businesses.)

Open-mindedness

Entrepreneurs need to be "open-minded" or willing to revise their mental models and forecasts because of the uncertain nature of their markets and their limited initial planning. In rapidly changing markets, unforeseeable developments can make previously sound assumptions obsolete. Snap initial judgments made without the benefit of much objective research may be wrong from the start. Even trained professionals who repeatedly make the same decisions show considerable inconsistency when they rely on intuition to make quick judgments.[22] Relatively inexperienced entrepreneurs, we might expect, would be prone to even greater error, especially with judgments that are not routinely and frequently made. To compensate, they have to be open to learning from their mistakes.

Marcia Radosevich and the Health Payment Review

Marcia Radosevich and several health care experts launched Health Payment Review (HPR) to develop and market software that would review reimbursement claims submitted by doctors, hospitals, and laboratories. HPR management believed that reviewing claims for overcharges and inconsistencies could result in significant savings for providers of health plans such as HMOs, insurance companies, and corporations. Payments for surgical procedures, for example, could be reduced by 5 percent to 15 percent. And using software would be far less costly than manually inspecting claims.

HPR developed its code in the C programming language. According to Radosevich:

> Our design was quite clever. Business applications on mainframes were traditionally written in a programming language called COBOL. Our software, written in a language called C, would run on several types of hardware "servers." These servers would be connected to but outside the mainframe, because we needed to update our knowledge bases frequently, and we didn't want to bring the whole system down while we did it. Besides, adding servers is much cheaper than adding more mainframe capacity.

Selling the software proved problematic, however:

> I tried to sell this concept all over the country, and I was just being laughed at. The industry was hooked on 1970s technology. When I used words like "servers," "C," and "Unix," they acted like I was a Communist, feminist radical from Boston.

The summer of 1989 found Radosevich in Fort Wayne, Indiana, trying to sell the product to an insurance company client. She recalled her conversation with the company's MIS manager:

> He was a great big guy, with a great big brass belt buckle. I was standing at a board, like a professor, doing price-performance charts, trying to convince him this is the cheapest way: You don't have to buy more iron, and you don't have to hire more people. This great big guy hitched up his belt buckle, slammed his hand down on the table, and said, "Little lady. I run me a COBOL shop and got me a bank of 3090 mainframes, and I got me an army of COBOL programmers. Don't give me this C s——t."
>
> It was summer. It was hot. I had had it. I looked at him and said, "If I give this to you in COBOL to reside on your mainframe, would you buy it?" He said, "Yes." I said, "Done."
>
> I now came home to Boston and wondered, "What are we going to do?" We had to architect an affordable, flexible, and maintainable COBOL product that would reside on a host without having to rewrite it for every different database manager and every different telecommunication system. It took a little while to get there, but we finally hit upon it, and then it all seemed easy and natural.

HPR, for instance, had developed its program in the C language, so it could run on cheap server computers instead of taking up expensive mainframe computing capacity. HPR's founders had never sold software to corporate users and lacked the means to conduct market research. Consequently they failed to anticipate that MIS personnel would have a vested interest in expanding their mainframe empires and would resist applications in C. HPR survived because instead of trying to overcome objections to C, the entrepreneur was willing to try rewriting the software.

Open-mindedness requires decision-makers to avoid some common cognitive errors. "Confirmation biases"—the tendency to look for and pay attention to only the evidence that confirms one's hypotheses and to ignore evidence that does not—represents an important source of close-mindedness. When negative outcomes are too obvious to be ignored, other biases can cause individuals to avoid correcting mistaken assumptions. A bias toward rationalization, for instance, leads to explanations that preserve one's positive self-image. "To avoid the pain of admitting mistakes," Russo and Schoemaker write, we may "distort our meaning of what we actually did or said" or "unrealistically blame the failure on others."[23] Conversely, people attribute to their skill successes that may have been entirely due to luck—for instance, winners of lotteries may provide elaborate explanations for how they picked their winning tickets. "Hindsight biases" can also hamper learning from experience. Several studies have demonstrated that people convince themselves, after an event has taken place, that they knew it would happen all along. In such studies, researchers ask subjects to make a prediction or provide a probability estimate of an event. Later, after the outcome is known, they are asked to recall their prediction or estimate. Subjects usually reconstruct their predictions to align them more closely with the outcomes. They will "remember," for instance, assigning a higher probability to whether Nixon would meet Mao in 1972 than they actually did before they knew what happened. Like the rationalization of mistakes, "the false clarity of hindsight creates the illusion that there is no lesson to be learned."[24]

Entrepreneurs who learn quickly may have an unusually low propensity to make these cognitive errors. Or they may have an especially strong preference for quick wins ("positive feedback") that encourages them to revise their models and assumptions. "Impatience" for profit (i.e., a high discount rate) may mitigate their confirmation biases and related cognitive errors—that is, entrepreneurs will be more willing to change their minds if they are anxious for a quick profit. Conversely, individuals who value being proven right over quick returns or actually derive positive utility from setbacks will be less likely to change their views. The tolerance for extended sacrifices in the pursuit of a deep inner conviction shown by a Galileo or a religious prophet does not serve most entrepreneurs.

Managing Internal Conflict

Adaptive entrepreneurs have to feel and communicate great confidence in the same theories and assumptions that they must be willing to reject. To start a business in an uncertain market requires a strong conviction in one's chosen course; getting others to put their resources at risk also often requires entrepreneurs to make convincing public declarations of their confidence. But even as they convince themselves and others of the soundness of their views, entrepreneurs have to be open to revising them. Moreover, when entrepreneurs change course, they have to feel and express the same belief in the new course as they did in the old. They cannot allow a previous error to undermine their self-confidence. Somehow they have to manage in their minds an ongoing conflict between the reservations of an objective skeptic and the faith of a believer.

Adaptation in an uncertain business requires a challenging kind of open-mindedness. Meteorologists have to be prepared to revise their forecasts and hypotheses as well, but they typically do not confront the risk of losing face or self-confidence to the same degree. The distinctive entrepreneurial open-mindedness is much closer to the mind-set that I have observed among bond and currency traders: To initiate a position, the traders have to believe their estimates are superior to the market's. If the position turns unprofitable, they will quickly revise their estimates, following the principle of "cut your losses and let your winners run." Sometimes they may even with great conviction entirely reverse their view, and go "long" if they were "short" or vice versa. But to continue in their jobs they cannot let setbacks undermine their confidence in their ability to "beat the market."

We may further note that the internal conflicts described above are especially sharp in the typical promising start-up because the entrepreneur does not face a boss or outside investors. In corporate or VC-backed initiatives, individuals who did not initiate the project provide external monitoring of progress against forecasts and assumptions. As we will see, such a separation brings its own problems; but they do not include the combination of believer or skeptic in one mind.*

An analysis of how entrepreneurs manage their internal conflict is beyond my scope here. We may speculate that a certain amount of "hindsight bias," "selective memory," or "self-serving explanations" may help preserve self-confidence. Entrepreneurs may justify erroneous forecasts on the grounds that "no one could have known" or that they lacked the resources to do much research. Such explanations can allow entrepreneurs to distinguish between confidence in their abilities and confidence in their ideas of the moment, so that they can drop the latter without affecting the former.

---

* The problem may be mitigated to a degree in partnerships where one individual provides the objective voice of reason that balances the other's enthusiasm.

Attribution Skill

Open-mindedness is a necessary but not sufficient condition for effective adaptation; the entrepreneur must also have an unusual capacity for attributing unexpected events to the right causes. The difficulty of deriving accurate explanations from the available facts may be illustrated by considering the predicament of an entrepreneur who has failed to generate sales. The entrepreneur faces several possibilities: a deeply flawed offering; deficiencies in certain features; weaknesses in the sales pitch; the wrong target market; or just bad luck in not being able to find the right customer. A number of factors make it difficult for entrepreneurs to distinguish among these possibilities and learn from their failure.

Missing information. Customers may simply say "no" or even refuse to see the entrepreneur without providing any reasons.

Noise. Customers may raise numerous objections, only some of which are critical. Or they may offer reasons intended to protect the entrepreneur's feelings ("we don't need your services right now, but call us in six months") rather than the real reasons for not placing an order. The failure to generate orders itself constitutes a noisy, difficult-to-interpret signal. As previously suggested, an entrepreneur should expect a low hit rate in getting early orders, and has no basis for knowing which rate indicates a significant problem: Do fifty or a hundred or a thousand failures suggest a fatal flaw?

Lack of repetition. Differences between or among successive attempts make generalizations difficult. Each prospect may have special needs or reasons for turning down the entrepreneur. Moreover, cash-constrained entrepreneurs tend to change their offering (or the sales pitch) continuously to incorporate the lessons learned in previous attempts. If the modifications don't work, entrepreneurs face a data set they cannot easily interpret because they have held little constant.

Wrong model. The entrepreneur's observations and learning are based on an implicit theory or model of the purchaser's incentives and behavior. Inexperienced entrepreneurs operating in new or changing markets may start with a model that focuses their attention on the wrong variables. For instance, they may focus on the prospect's concerns about price and features instead of vendor reliability. Or they may fail to recognize the influence individuals operating in the background have on the purchase decision. These faulty models cannot easily be corrected by "observation" if the wrong variables are being observed.*

To summarize: Entrepreneurial adaptation, unlike natural selection, is not automatic or deterministic. The effectiveness of entrepreneurs' responses

---

* As George Wu pointed out to me: "It is much easier to estimate the values of the parameters of a model than to change the parameters themselves."

to unexpected circumstances depends on their ability to act decisively, to be open-minded and yet confident, and to have a talent for assessing cause and effect from limited and confusing data.

3. Capacity for Securing Resources

In Chapter 3 we explored the strategies that entrepreneurs who start with meager resources employ to get others to take a chance on their ventures. We saw how entrepreneurs offer special deals and benefits to the early resource providers; mimic the superficial features of larger, well-established corporations; frame choices to minimize perceptions of risk; conduct a broad search; gain commitments incrementally, and make do with second-tier resources. Now we will examine four qualities that help determine an entrepreneur's ability to implement these strategies: tactical ingenuity, self-control, perceptiveness, and sales skills. I will also briefly discuss overlap between these qualities and the ones previously discussed in relation to an entrepreneur's capacity to adapt.

Tactical Ingenuity

Although most start-ups do not involve major innovations—entrepreneurs engage in businesses that several others are engaged in as well—we find considerable ingenuity in the details of how entrepreneurs overcome (and adapt to) the problems they face in attracting customers, suppliers, capital, and so on. For example:

Richard Fox, cofounder of Factor-Fox, a telemarketing firm that raises money for nonprofits, initially faced clients who were unwilling to let a new firm contact their contributors. Fox then proposed to WNET, a public television station in New York, a trial where his firm would telemarket just to inactive or "lapsed" contributors. This proposal vastly reduced the perceived risk and earned Factor-Fox a chance to prove its capabilities.

Bruce Singer, cofounder of RPM Rent-A-Car, generated customers from competitors who had taken more reservations than they had rental cars. He printed cards with "Overbooked?" written on them and RPM's number. This gave him prequalified (i.e., low credit-risk) customers, and he did not have to pay commissions to an agent. It was, as Singer says, "like the Motel 6 recruiting guests at a Hyatt!"

Entrepreneurs used creative ploys to get appointments with buyers. Buyers often resist seeing entrepreneurs, perhaps because they do not want to waste time or because they understand that if they agree to a visit they might feel an internal pressure to place an order (per the commitment principle). One gambit that entrepreneurs used to overcome this resistance was to claim that they "happened" to be visiting from out of town. Deaver Brown, for example, repeatedly called a buyer from a pay phone in a New

York airport, "saying I was in the Detroit area and could I stop by to see him. He said yes once and I immediately flew out to Detroit."

Steve Belkin used creative excuses to preserve a facade of stability. Belkin and his partner started Trans National Travel in Belkin's apartment, where they had no space for meeting with clients. So Belkin "always met people at the airport, said I was just leaving on a flight, then waited until they had gone before going back home."

Entrepreneurs coped with their capital constraints creatively. "We measured every penny," Carol Russell recalls. "We left out vowels in our classified ads. We used lots of i's and l's because you can fit more words into a line of type. O's take up a lot of space."

Jay Boberg and Miles Copeland, who launched International Record Syndicate (IRS) in 1979, used low-cost guerrilla marketing to promote their music label. Boberg and Copeland produced "alternative" music—undiscovered British groups such as the Buzzcocks and Skafish—that the major labels were ignoring because their potential sales were too small. But other small companies were also producing alternative music. IRS became one of the most successful new music labels in North America by coming up with alternative marketing methods to promote their alternative music. For instance, at the time, the major record labels had not yet realized that music videos on television could be used effectively to promote their products. Boberg, however, jumped at the opportunity to produce a rock show, "The Cutting Edge," for MTV. The show proved to be a hit with fans and an effective promotional tool for IRS. Before "The Cutting Edge," Boberg had to plead with radio stations to play his songs. Afterward, the MTV audience demanded that disc jockeys play the songs they had heard on the show.

Sampler Publications founder, Mark Nickel told us that when he started his company in 1984, "copier companies allowed you to use their copiers at no cost for a trial period. We would use a copier for a few weeks and then go to another brand. We went through about six of them!"

Self-Control

Securing orders for a new business requires great self-control and resilience. Entrepreneurs have to cope with considerable—and sometimes unpleasantly delivered—rejection and difficult demands. Doors do not open as easily for entrepreneurs as they do for, say, IBM sales representatives. The IBM representative has established personal connections, and customers presume that the rep has something distinctive and valuable to offer. Ongoing relationships and interdependencies also encourage customers to behave in a civil and polite manner. In contrast, most of the entrepreneurs I studied did not have prior relationships with customers, and many offered "me, too" products or services.

The capacity to deal with rejection is also important because the search for the right prospect involves many more misses than hits. Entrepreneurs cannot easily target the prospects who are likely to buy their products or services. As we saw in Chapter 2, the most receptive prospects have hidden our out-of-the-ordinary preferences and can be identified only after an extensive search. Similarly, entrepreneurs often get a break because they are "in the right place at the right time" when the customer has an unexpected need. But unless the entrepreneur is very lucky, getting such a break requires being in many places at many times. Plugging on with a low-yield search requires considerable resilience. "There was a point halfway through year two," Julie Wang, founder of Wang Communications, told us, "when I felt I would never get another client. I was taking antidepressants."

Rejections are not always gracious, and the entrepreneur has to deal stoically with gratuitous unpleasantness. The many entrepreneurs who lack a distinctive product or service face a great imbalance of power in bargaining with their customers. Some customers are sympathetic to the entrepreneurs' plight, whereas others are indifferent or may even derive pleasure in exercising their power. Unreturned phone calls, long waits in reception rooms, and canceled appointments are par for the course. The customer, however difficult or unpleasant, has to be served; as the sidebar on Philip Doganeiro suggests, entrepreneurs may have to put aside their pride and sometimes their dignity in order to secure an order.

Weak bargaining positions also expose entrepreneurs to difficult demands; getting an order can often require acceding to seemingly unreasonable conditions. Microsoft's breakthrough order to supply an operating system for IBM's PC required Gates and company to go along with IBM's numerous demands. For instance, they readily signed IBM's nondisclosure agreement, which Cringley describes as "the legal equivalent of a neutron bomb." Writes Cringley: "Nondisclosure agreements place limits on the ability of parties to reveal the secrets of organizations with which they are doing business. IBM's standard nondisclosure agreement goes even further. By signing the IBM agreement, would-be suppliers agree that whatever they tell IBM is not confidential, while whatever IBM tells them *is* confidential. . . . And if IBM takes legal action, the agreement prohibits the other party from even offering a defense."[25] Digital Research, which made CP/M, the then-dominant microcomputer operating system—and IBM's first choice—refused to sign this agreement, thus opening the door for Microsoft.

Many individuals also lack the self-control needed to handle rejection or to give in to difficult or capricious demands. What Thaler calls "bounded willpower"[26] is a common human trait. There is considerable evidence to show that even though people know what they need to do to achieve their goals, they lack the willpower to do it. A person on a diet may have the desire to lose weight but just cannot stay away from dessert. Similarly, at an intellectual level, entrepreneurs may understand the importance of tolerating rudeness or acceding to capricious demands, but in practice cannot

Doganeiro's Donuts

Philip Doganeiro started National Data Products in 1982, selling computer forms. Some early prospects were predisposed to giving the young entre-preneur a break, but one large account proved difficult. Doganeiro recalls:

"No matter what I'd do, they just wouldn't see me. I called on them for months, and no response. I found out from a secretary that the person I needed to see liked donuts, so I brought donuts every time I visited. He'd come out to the reception area, take the donuts, look at me, and go back into his office without saying a word to me. I did this for four weeks! Then, one day, he came out and got the donuts and turned to go back into his office. I was about to leave, and then he said, 'come on in—I've got a chance for you!'

"It was 1982, the day before Thanksgiving. He was having problems with a supplier who didn't have the forms he needed. I drove to a supplier, loaded as much paper as I could into my car, drove back to their dock, and started unloading the paper. He saw me, came out, and helped me unload. From that day, I've always done business with them."

avoid lashing back. As Argyris and Schon put it, their "theory-in-use" conflicts with their espoused theory.

Moreover, the capacity to endure rejection and slights can conflict with the traits that predispose individuals to start a business. Starting a business requires considerable self-confidence and a desire for control: The reasons that entrepreneurs typically offer for why they started their businesses often relate to a desire to have control over their destinies and avoid reporting to a boss. Such individuals are not naturally inclined to be compliant and willing to accede to others' demands; subjugating their egos requires an out-of-the-ordinary level of self-control and goal orientation. Bill Gates, for instance, has a reputation for a short temper and blunt expression of his opinions. In his classes at Harvard, a contemporary recalls, Gates "would look very bored, then a half hour into a proof on the blackboard, Bill would raise his hand and blurt out, 'You made a mistake; I'll show you.' He would stump the teacher. He seemed to take great joy in that."[27] In his dealings with IBM, however, Gates apparently kept these traits in check. He might excoriate or insult his programmers but not the employees of an important customer; the goal of getting the order governed all other impulses.

Perceptiveness

Entrepreneurs who win orders by satisfying psychic needs or providing an ancillary intangible service have to look through their customers' superficial requirements and objections and observe the unstated wants and inchoate fears. Perceptive entrepreneurs require an "allocentric" orientation: They must look at the world through others' eyes and see what others

value and how they "frame" their choices. They have to be skilled at elicit-
ing information, asking questions in an unthreatening way that encourages
others to open up. They have to listen without a confirmation bias and be
sensitive to the unspoken, to body language and other nonverbal cues. As
one entrepreneur observed:

> Clients will sometimes say, "Here's the language I want in the contract"
> and it will be totally unacceptable. You never say "No"; you say, "Let me
> understand what your concern is here. What's the problem you are trying
> to solve with this language?" Then you find out that they don't really want
> your firstborn child.

Perceptiveness does not, however, require unselfishness. Successful entrepreneurs don't identify with their customers in the same fashion that thera-
pists may with their patients or hostages with their abductors. They see the
world through others' eyes in order to advance their own interests.

Entrepreneurs also need the capacity to look through the superficial
qualifications, or lack thereof, of potential employees. As we have seen, the
typical start-up faces an adverse selection problem—it can only attract
employees who have poor job prospects. The entrepreneur faces the challenge of distinguishing between the individuals whose lack of credentials
and prior employment accurately reflects their inherent abilities from those
who have been unlucky.

"I never hired experienced people," said Bohdan Associates founder Peter
Zacharkiw, "and there are very few college graduates here. My vice president of sales was the best curb painter around—but that's the secret. He'll
always be the best at what he does. Personality and common sense are the
most important things that people here have." Similarly, John Greenwood,
cofounder of Micron Separations, believed that "people in the unemployment market are just as good if not better than the people in the employment market. And we have no prejudice against people who've been fired!
My partner and I started Micron after we were fired! In large companies,
people tend to get fired for lack of political skills."

But to identify individuals without experience who have "common sense,"
or employees who have been fired because of politics rather than for good
cause, entrepreneurs need unusual judgment or perceptiveness. Otherwise, as
we saw in the previous chapter, they can end up with slackers or thieves.

Sales Skills

Effective face-to-face selling is critical for entrepreneurs. They cannot afford
to advertise, and they have to secure orders by calling on prospects personally. In my *Inc.* 500 survey, for instance, only 12 percent of the founders
secured their early revenues through intermediaries. The other 88 percent
of founders sold directly to end users. And in all but a handful of cases, the

entrepreneur (rather than an employed salesperson) was principally responsible for making the sale (see Fig. 4.5, p. 110).

Unlike corporations that usually rely on a specialized sales staff, entrepreneurs cannot hire others to do the selling for them. An employee may
not have the same zeal and passion as the founder and cannot provide customers with the psychic benefits of dealing with a principal. Competent
sales personnel may be impossible to attract until the venture has established a track record. Good salespersons often tend to seek out "hot" items
where their skills will quickly generate high commissions; few have an
interest in the missionary selling necessary to sell the products or services
of a new company. Furthermore, in a start-up, obtaining an order can
involve more than just selling. As indicated by the earlier HPR example,
making a sale can require on-the-spot strategic choices, which entrepreneurs cannot easily entrust to subordinates.

Effective selling requires the intangible qualities discussed previously:
resilience, self-control, and perceptiveness. It also involves knowledge of
and skill in using concrete techniques, for objection handling, closing, and
so on. (See the sidebar "Sales Techniques.") Many individuals who start
businesses without prior experience or training in sales do not know these
techniques and have fundamental misconceptions about the mind-set
required for getting orders. "I had imagined salespeople to be slick, fast-
talking, amusing persons," recalls Marcia Radosevich, cofounder of HPR,
who had trained as a sociologist and taught at Yale. Then, before starting
with HPR, she worked for two entrepreneurs who taught her that:

> Selling is about building a relationship. It's about getting in early, defin-
> ing the playing ground and the rules of the game, creating a sense of
> urgency, and building toward a conclusion. It's about being nonthreaten-
> ing: "Go ahead and think I'm some nice girl from Iowa, and I'm a Ph.D.
> and I would never be threatening to anyone."
>
> These guys never raised their voices. They were smart, unassuming,
> and their egos didn't get in the way. They let somebody else take credit for
> their ideas. They spent all the time they needed to—morning, noon, and
> night—being available.

Unlike Radosevich, however, many individuals start businesses without
the benefit of an apprenticeship with effective salespeople; unless they have
great natural instincts, they face a considerable handicap.

4. Less Important Qualities

The success of promising ventures usually turns on a limited set of traits
and skills. These businesses do not require "superhuman" founders; in particular, the following attributes, common in entrepreneurship lore, do not

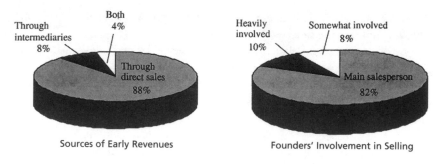

Figure 4.5. Importance of Founder's Sales Efforts
Percentage of *Inc.* 500 Companies Surveyed
Source: Author's Survey.

appear to play a significant role in an individual's propensity to embark on such ventures or to solve the problems involved in making them profitable:

Risk-taking. As we have seen, starting an uncertain business requires a low aversion to ambiguity, rather than to objective loss. Entrepreneurs often claim they have an exceptional willingness to take risk. For instance, in my survey of Harvard Business School's self-employed alumni, 87 percent "agreed" or "strongly agreed" with the statement "I am a greater risk-taker than most people." But this self-image may simply derive from a universal tendency to rate oneself as above-average on any desirable trait. Quite likely, most ambitious individuals today like to think of themselves as risk-takers. Thus the proportion of self-employed HBS alumni who saw themselves as above average risk-takers is virtually the same as the proportion of all HBS alumni.[28] Alternatively, entrepreneurs may equate risk-taking with an unusual willingness to deal with uncertainty and to tolerate the social and psychological consequences of failure.

Breakthrough creativity. Successful start-ups usually do not involve a blockbuster innovation. The entrepreneurs' ability to recognize the promise of someone else's idea, and to show resourcefulness and ingenuity in solving the problems of its implementation, provide sufficient bases for success.

Vision and foresight. The capacity to formulate a coherent, long-term view for the future of the business, or to make good forecasts and plans, does not appear to play a critical role. Given a fortuitous or deliberate choice of an adequately promising market niche, entrepreneurs can rely on "myopic" opportunism and adaptation.

Grand ambition. Schumpeter suggested that entrepreneurs are driven by the desire to build empires. This does not appear to be the case with the founders of most start-ups; only a few, such as Gates and Allen, start out with the goal of building a megacorporation or supplying software to every household in America. In fact, the desire to change (or capture) the world can be detrimental unless it is tempered by pragmatism about the here and now. Individuals captured by an *idée fixe* or who see themselves as the architects of

---

Sales Techniques

"Closing" the sale, or asking for the order: Although quite obvious, explicitly asking for the order is extremely important. Inexperienced salespeople do not ask for the order, expecting the customer to state a desire to buy. This does not often occur. The following are some techniques that I have found effective in asking for the order:

The straightforward or direct close: Summarize the benefits and ask for the order.

Subordinate-question close: Ask a minor question that implies yes to a major question. (Examples: What color would you like? or, Cash or charge?)

The window-of-opportunity close: Ask for the order based on the benefits of having the product/service before a particular event. (Example: Do you want the product delivered before the end-of-the-quarter budget closes?)

Puppy-dog close: Ask for a trial order over some time period, with no obligation.

Multiple-choice close: Give the customer alternative choices, both of which imply commitment. (Example: Do you want the twenty-inch or the twenty-five-inch TV?)

Objection handling: Asking for the order often brings out customers' objections, even when you think they have agreed in the previous phase that the product or service will meet their needs. There are a number of ways to handle objections. For example, suppose your customer objects to the weight of your computer.

Direct answer: Provide a direct answer to the objection. ("It weighs less than any other computer on the market." Or, "You stated a need for a computer weighing less than five pounds. This one weighs only four pounds.")

Outweigh objection: Play down the importance of the objection as compared with other benefits. ("For your needs, the ability to have a CD-ROM player and a portable color screen far outweigh the half pound of extra weight.")

Minimize objection: Reduce the importance of or restate the objection in more favorable terms. ("This is a desktop computer, and therefore the weight is not really important.")

Reverse objection: Turn the objection into a reason to buy. ("We have found that thieves avoid heavier computers.")

Source: Alter and Bhidé, *Selling as a Systematic Process* (1994).

---

a new paradigm cannot easily adapt to unforeseen circumstances or change erroneous forecasts. At least in the cases I have encountered, they tend to carry on relentlessly with the rationalization that they are ahead of their times rather than on the wrong track.

Charisma. Whereas the ability to read others' wants and fears and the capacity for low-key persuasion play significant roles in the success of most start-ups, the entrepreneur does not need to have exceptional charm, magnetism, or a capacity to inspire devotion. For instance, according to Cringley, the microcomputer industry has been built by "nerds." Cheatham, a computer science professor at Harvard, recalls that his former student Gates "had a bad personality and a great intellect. In a place like Harvard, where there are a lot of bright kids, when you are better than your peers, some tend to be nice and others obnoxious. He was the latter."[29] A fellow student who often found Gates asleep at the table after a night of programming in the Computer Center recalls thinking Gates was "not going to amount to anything. He seemed like a hacker, a nerd. I knew he was bright, but with those glasses, his dandruff, sleeping on tables, you sort of formed that impression. I obviously didn't see the future as clearly as he did."[30]

Using power. The ability to use one's position or control of resources to bend others to one's will has little importance in the early stages of an enterprise. Similarly, Machiavelli's advice that "it is better to be feared than loved" is more appropriate for a prince than for the founder of a new business. As we have seen, it is more important for entrepreneurs to control their own emotions than dictate others' actions and to appear nonthreatening rather than intimidating.

Administrative abilities. The efficient administration (or "management") of an organization does not represent a critical challenge in the early stages of most new businesses. As we have seen, founders often perform many of the important functions and do not have many employees to manage. The business tends to be simple, and with limited product lines and activities, entrepreneurs do not have to establish and oversee complex coordination and control routines. The competitors that start-ups face do not have deep managerial capabilities, and especially in new markets, customers expect delays and defects: Missing a publication date for *Rolling Stone* or the presence of bugs in Microsoft's software did not cause great consternation in the early days of these ventures. Therefore the lack of administrative ability is not as crucial as, say, the capacity to sell and to react quickly.

In fact, the experiences and training that enhance an individual's administrative abilities may impair the more crucial facilities. For instance, business school graduates and corporate executives are often conditioned to conduct extensive analyses before making a decision. Such efforts not only have limited utility in highly uncertain situations, they also may lead to emotional attachments to a plan and thus create a psychological barrier to responding to new information. Management education and experience also can impair an individual's capacity to secure resources. Corporate cultures often encourage executives to advocate their positions forcefully rather than to listen attentively or see things someone else's way. Successful executives have experience in selling themselves and their ideas, of course, but this is usually from a position of strength: Headhunters court recruits who have accumulated the human capital that many employers want. Selling is thus closely associated with negotiating the best possible deal. Experienced executives are similarly steeped in the exercise of power, of bending others to their will. Pleading for orders and caving in to others' demands—saying "yes"—isn't part of their usual repertoire. Inexperienced individuals who have never tasted much authority may thus have a greater capacity to subjugate their egos and not let pride stand in the way of getting business.

I do not mean to suggest, however, that qualities that are secondary in starting the typical promising venture are unimportant in all entrepreneurial endeavors. For instance, administrative abilities acquire considerable importance in starting larger and less-uncertain ventures: In Chapter 6 we will see that evidence of such abilities is essential in securing capital for venture capital-backed start-ups. Similarly, in Part II we will see how some qualities that do not have great importance in starting promising ventures become critical in their subsequent evolution and growth; entrepreneurs who cannot develop these new attitudes and skills cannot easily build large, long-lived businesses.

5. Summary and Conclusions

To conclude, let us take stock of the main features of promising start-ups that we have examined so far. In Chapter 1, we saw that most entrepreneurs start without a proprietary idea, exceptional training and qualifications, or significant amounts of capital. Given these limited endowments, profitable start-ups tend to cluster in small, uncertain market niches. In Chapter 2 we saw that capital constraints and small, uncertain opportunities preclude much planning and require rapid adaptation to unforeseen circumstances. In Chapter 3 we found that the meager endowments of entrepreneurs make it difficult for them to secure customers and other resource providers, and we examined the strategies they use to cope. In this chapter we have explored the distinctive qualities that predispose some individuals to start promising businesses and that affect their capacity to adapt and secure resources. We saw that although the individuals who successfully start small, uncertain businesses lack verifiable or observable human capital, they do need a willingness to tolerate uncertainty, openmindedness, and other such innate qualities.

These qualities do not overlap with the common image of the entrepreneur as an irrational, overoptimistic risk-taker. Successful entrepreneurs are more likely to conform to models of rational behavior than the population at large, along several dimensions; they have a lower aversion to ambiguity, a lower propensity toward information biases, and can exercise greater self-control, for instance. And they rely on exploiting others' cognitive defects and reflexive tendencies to secure the resources they need. We also saw that starting a promising business does not require "superhuman" qualities; long-term vision, foresight, charisma, and so on do not play a significant role in the success of most start-ups. The bundle of qualities that entrepreneurs require is unusual but not extraordinary.

5

Corporate Initiatives

This chapter contrasts initiatives undertaken by large, well-established corporations with promising businesses started by individual entrepreneurs. Section 1 examines how the endowments and constraints of corporate decision makers help determine the nature of the opportunities they usually pursue. Section 2 discusses why corporations rely more on prior research and planning than on ex-post adaptation. Section 3 covers the strategies they employ to attract customers and other resource providers, and Section 4 discusses how qualities that determine the success of corporate ventures are different from the qualities that are crucial to the success of promising start-ups.

Large corporations usually undertake initiatives that occupy the lower right-hand region of the investment-uncertainty-profit diagram. Corporate executives, as we will see in this chapter, start with different endowments and constraints than do individual entrepreneurs. Stockholders give executives control over large amounts of capital. In return, corporations institute processes to evaluate and monitor new initiatives that involve extensive checks and balances. As a result, corporations tend to concentrate their investments on a few initiatives with well-defined risks and returns and to avoid the small, uncertain opportunities that individual entrepreneurs often thrive on.

To illustrate: Scientists and engineers at the Xerox Palo Alto Research Center (PARC) developed innovative computer technologies such as the mouse pointing device and local area networks in the 1970s. Start-ups and small companies such as 3Com and Apple, not Xerox, commercialized these inventions. The unwillingness of Xerox's top executives to provide the attention and funding needed to turn the PARC inventions into profitable businesses, according to my analysis, reflects the small and uncertain likely profits from commercialization rather than flaws in the company's decision-making. The comparative advantage of large corporations lies in undertaking projects with low uncertainty and large capital requirements, such as the development of Intel's Pentium chip, Merck's cholesterol-reducing drugs, and Gillette's Mach3 razor.

The initial conditions and the types of initiatives corporations undertake also influence (see Fig. 5.1) the effort they devote to planning, the

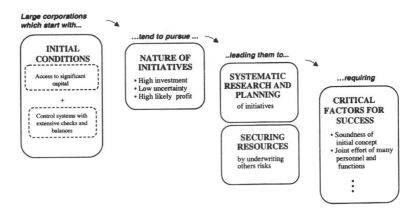

Figure 5.1. Propositions about Corporate Initiatives

strategies they adopt for securing resources, and the factors that determine the success of their endeavors. Corporations devote much greater efforts to planning and research than do most entrepreneurs; corporations underwrite resource providers' risks and play up to their loss-aversive tendencies. And the success of corporate initiatives depends more on the initial plans and assumptions than on ex-post adaptation, and on organizational capabilities more than the talents of a few individuals.

Scope. This discussion will focus on large public companies such as IBM, PepsiCo, Procter & Gamble, 3M, and the 1990s Microsoft. These corporations have complex operations (multiple product lines and worldwide presence), are well established (i.e., they have been in business for decades and do not face an immediate threat to their survival), and profitable. Closely held companies and partnerships (such as Fidelity Investments and most professional services firms), small family businesses, up-and-coming companies (such as Microsoft through the early 1980s), and large companies that face financial distress (such as Chrysler in the mid-1970s) lie outside the scope of this discussion. We will analyze risky initiatives (i.e., ones that have some chance of failure) that corporations consciously undertake to secure new profits. This excludes accidental discoveries, riskless profit improvements due to learning by doing, and investments to replace depreciated assets. For convenience, the initiatives discussed will refer mainly to new product introductions and entry into new markets, although the general argument can easily be extended to projects such as a cost-reducing process innovation.

1. Initial Conditions and Nature of Opportunities

Corporate decision-makers, we will see below, have access to significant amounts of capital and the incentive to invest in new initiatives. The checks and balances of internal control systems, however, limit their discretion over corporate funds. The combination of available capital and extensive internal controls leads corporations to undertake initiatives that require large initial investment and involve relatively low uncertainty.

Ample Capital

Established corporations have "sustainable competitive advantages" or "franchises" that generate significantly greater cash than they consumed in their normal course of business. Although companies could remit the surplus cash to stockholders via dividends or stock repurchases, they usually reinvest a significant portion of the funds. Explanations for this tendency often point to the conflict of interest between corporate executives and stockholders. Executives, it is claimed, retain funds for self-aggrandizement or because their compensation is linked to the size of the business rather than to returns to shareholders.

In Part II of this book I will argue that competition for capital, employees, and customers also creates powerful incentives to grow a firm. Corporate executives likely would not advertise their commitment to growth as widely as they do if it was entirely against the interests of their stockholders. A firm's growth prospects help determine its cost of capital. According to a common investment heuristic, the ratio of a firm's stock price to its profits should equal the expected rate of growth of its earnings; this means investors usually pay high prices for the stocks of firms with high expected rates of growth. High growth helps attract ambitious and talented recruits, whereas expectations of stagnation and decline can become a self-fulfilling prophecy that leads the best employees—and sometimes its customers—to leave. With the exception of firms that do not face much competition for customers, employees, and capital, long-run survival requires the capacity to undertake initiatives that will generate new sources of profit.*

Whatever the reason, corporate retained earnings and occasional new debt and equity issues result in investments of a formidable magnitude. For instance, Jensen compiled a data set of all 432 firms on COMPUSTAT with 1989 sales exceeding $250 million, for which complete data on R&D, capital expenditures, and some other measures were available for 1980

---

* A reviewer of the manuscript suggests that growth is not as important for the survival of large corporations as it was in the 1970s and 1980s. My observations suggest that labor and capital market pressures are, if anything, more intense: High-growth companies hold a powerful attraction for an increasingly mobile pool of technical and managerial talent and can secure seemingly outlandish valuations from the capital markets. What may have changed is the propensity of some large companies to satisfy stock market pressures for increased profit by reducing their costs. Profit growth through cost reduction cannot easily motivate rank-and-file employees, however. And once companies have exhausted the potential of cost reductions to increase profits, they face renewed pressure from capital markets to find new sources of revenue.

through 1990. Mean R&D expenditures for the 432 companies amounted to $1.3 billion in the 1980–90 period and net capital expenditures amounted to $1.4 billion. Some large companies had by themselves larger R&D and net capital expenditures than the total investments of the venture capital industry. For instance, GM spent a total of $67.2 billion on R&D and net capital expenditures, and IBM spent $62.2 billion. Total disbursements by venture capitalists in this period amounted to just $27.8 billion.[1]

Control Systems

On the surface, corporate decision-makers appear to have wide, open-ended discretion over investments. The evolution of common and statutory laws has given corporate executives and directors great leeway in the investments and the initiatives they can pursue. In the nineteenth century (and as recently as 1927 in Ohio, among other states), corporate charters were granted for a single, closely defined business, often after negotiations among the legislature, the promoters, and the investors.[2] Now there is no negotiation, and off-the-shelf charters allow a corporation to enter any legitimate business. Formerly major corporate decisions (such as those relating to dividend policies or diversification) had to be unanimously approved by stockholders; now, with the expanding "business judgment" rule, courts give the directors of corporations wide latitude in these matters. As R. Clark puts it: "As a matter of statutory law, stockholders' powers in a public corporation are extremely limited. . . . To influence corporate managers stockholders can vote for directors and approve or veto director-initiated organic changes, but cannot do much else."[3]

By way of contrast, we may note that in other forms of legal entities, decision-makers face more stringent contractual limits on their discretion. The limited partnership agreements used by venture capitalists often include provisions that preclude the general partner from making certain kinds of investments—for instance, an agreement may specify that the partnership will not make real estate investments or conduct business overseas. General partners are also usually bound to wind up the partnership after a specified number of years. Corporate executives, in contrast, do not have to return funds to stockholders.

Discretion over significant funds allows corporate decision-makers to make large, long-term investments without revealing sensitive information. General Motors can negotiate a $900 million sponsorship deal with the International Olympic Committee. Intel can invest $1.5 billion on a single fabrication facility. Gillette can invest $750 million to develop the triple-bladed Mach3 razor. Corporations can limit the risks of tipping off competitors prematurely because they do not seek approval from their stockholders before they undertake such initiatives. At the same time, giving corporate executives perpetual discretion over large sums of money exposes the stockholders of public corporations to the risk of abuse and self-dealing by the executives. As a safeguard, the large public corporation provides for more extensive checks and balances than we usually find in other forms of organization.

According to E. F. Fama and M. C. Jensen's analysis,[4] stockholders rely on the legal requirement of an independent board of directors for protection against the abuse of managerial discretion.* The separation of ownership and control, argue Fama and Jensen, requires a parallel separation between decision management (the initiation and implementation of decisions) and decision control (the ratification and monitoring of decisions). The combination of management and control in the hands of the same few individuals exists only in private or "closed" corporations where the senior executives also own most of the stock. In a public corporation these functions are separated: The board of directors wields control rights that hold the executives' management powers in check.

The diversity of activities in a large corporation requires the boards and top executives to delegate their control and management responsibilities to employees with the appropriate specific knowledge. Top executives do not initiate or implement many concrete proposals. Rather, they influence the initiatives undertaken by subordinates by formulating an overall corporate strategy and by shaping the organization's decision-making routines. The board similarly ratifies the strategy and the processes for evaluating new initiatives, not specific investment decisions. Rather than monitor the implementation of every project, the board evaluates aggregate performance and the control system. For instance, the board may evaluate whether the auditing function has sufficient independence from the operating managers.

The separation of "management" and "control" of broad policy thus leads to a corresponding separation of roles for specific decisions. By instituting monitoring devices and policies, boards and top executives can give decision-making rights to subordinates whom they cannot directly supervise, while protecting shareholders from abuse of these rights. For instance, a salesperson or brand manager who has direct knowledge of customer needs and

---

* Hostile takeovers, or the so-called market for corporate control, I have argued elsewhere, provide only modest protection for stockholders. Unsolicited tender offers, which A. Rappaport claims represent "the most effective check on management autonomy devised" can in fact protect stockholders only against flagrant incompetence or abuses. Acquirers who make unsolicited tender offers operate under significant informational constraints: They have to raise money deal by deal, making their case to financiers from publicly available data. Even at their peak in 1985–87, these acquirers posed a threat to only a small number of diversified firms, whose breakup values could be reliably determined from public data to be significantly higher than their market values. Similarly, incentive compensation schemes may also help align the interests of executives and stockholders, but only to a limited degree.

competitive offerings may initiate a proposal for a new product. A superior reviews the proposal and, if appropriate, forwards it up the corporate hierarchy with an endorsement. Higher-ups then decide whether to proceed, perhaps after seeking the advice of a specialized staff or outside consultants. Similarly, employees with the appropriate expertise may be given the discretion to implement the product launch, subject to monitoring and oversight by superiors and by an independent finance or control staff.

Objective Evaluations

Multilevel and multifunctional evaluations of new initiatives entail extensive documentation and evidence. Individuals who start businesses with their own limited funds may trust their intuition and their innate capacity to adapt to unforeseen circumstances. Corporation decision-makers require objective data on markets and the firm's capabilities vis-à-vis its competitors. The role of the evaluators of new initiatives is to play devil's advocate: to challenge assumptions and to try to poke holes in the case for proceeding. According to Heath, Larrick, and Klayman,[5] they provide an organizational remedy for the cognitive errors that individuals have a propensity to make, including avoiding disconfirming evidence, relying too much on vivid or available information, and so on.

The incentives of the staff who specialize in evaluating new initiatives encourage them to reject poorly documented proposals. Evaluators in staff positions do not receive bonuses for endorsing ventures that turn out well. If the venture fails and they did not follow proper procedures, they may be accused of dereliction of duty. Evaluators also may have limited personal contact with the initiators of proposals, who work at a different level of the hierarchy or in a different function. The organizational remoteness and anonymity of the evaluators that increases their objectivity limits their capacity to rely just on the personal abilities of the initiator.

The so-called line managers in a corporate hierarchy who also bear some responsibility for vetting projects proposed by their subordinates have somewhat different incentives from analysts in the staff function. Successful projects improve their prospects for promotion and their standing within the organization. They may also be influenced by their personal relationships with subordinates who advocate the initiative. The resulting tension between line and staff evaluators represents an important component of the distinctive checks and balances of the corporate form of organization. As we will see Chapter 6, the venture capital firms rely on mutual monitoring by the partners of each other's investments and do not provide for scrutiny by an independent staff.

I do not mean to suggest that corporate evaluations are totally objective and that personal relationships and reputations don't matter. Employees with good connections and standing within their organizations have an edge in securing funding for their projects, just as well-connected and well-regarded borrowers have an edge in securing bank loans. But corporate control systems (and bank credit approval procedures) help set minimum standards of objective evidence and analysis. Although they don't eliminate personal or political considerations, they protect stockholders from a system of pure cronyism.

Aversion to Uncertainty

The nature of the evidence required by corporate decision-makers leads them to favor initiatives where the risks and returns can be objectively assessed. Large corporations seek opportunities with the following characteristics: Demand has stabilized or has attained a predictable growth trajectory, allowing analysts to make reasonable projections of expected revenues. Consumer preferences are stable, measurable, and can be projected from an appropriately selected sample to the market at large. The company's known strengths (e.g., marketing and distribution) may be expected to provide competitive advantages over identifiable rivals. The need for objective and impersonal evaluation discourages investments where unpredictable or difficult-to-measure factors can lead to significant differences in outcomes.

A computer company like IBM will tend to avoid unformed markets (such as the PC business in 1975) where demand is difficult to predict or is subject to great technological or regulatory turbulence. Corporations will also avoid businesses whose profits depend on the superior abilities or skills of one or two individuals rather than on an already established, verifiable corporate capability. The fundamental nature of their evaluation process, in other words, leads corporations away from the uncertainty that individual entrepreneurs exploit, because the ambiguity or the "missing information" is too great.

Large corporations also lack the ability to monitor the implementation of uncertain initiatives. The successful implementation of uncertain initiatives we have seen involves tasks such as adapting to unexpected circumstances and responding to the unspoken wants of customers. An objective, multilevel monitoring system cannot easily evaluate the performance of such tasks and differentiate between bad luck and the lack of effort or talent.* And when corporations underwrite the risks of projects whose implementation they cannot effectively monitor, they face a moral hazard problem. The individuals responsible for undertaking the project have an incentive to slack off and attribute their slow progress to circumstances beyond their control.

---

* In the next chapter I will suggest that venture capital firms are better suited to making these subjective judgments.

Corporate decision-makers often wait until the uncertainty of a business has been reduced before they invest in it. IBM's Entry Systems Division lab director William Lowe secured funding from the Corporate Management Committee to build a personal computer in 1980, after some of the critical uncertainties about the market and technology had been resolved. Microsoft developed its web browser after Mosaic, Netscape, and others had established the market. We similarly find that large corporations invest in businesses after an entrepreneur has established a valuable technology or formula and the profits of the business do not depend just on the personal effort of the principals. After Rick Rosenfield and Larry Flax had developed California Pizza Kitchen's "formula" and proven its viability, PepsiCo bought a 50 percent stake in the company and financed its subsequent expansion.*

This is not to say that large companies avoid well-defined risk. Control systems that lead corporations to avoid irreducible uncertainty do not preclude them from taking calculated gambles. Indeed, according to Fama and Jensen's analysis, public companies are well suited to finance conventionally risky projects because their stockholders can diversify their portfolios. The owner-managers of private firms and partnerships are more risk-averse because much of their wealth is tied to their companies. They tend to "underinvest in assets with long-term payoffs."[6] Compared to private oil producers, public companies such as Exxon and Mobil place much larger exploration and development bets. Only one of the "majors" can put up the $2 billion to $3 billion it requires to develop a medium-sized heavy-oil field in Venezuela, for instance.

But the types of opportunities that public companies pursue have characteristics that allow decision-makers to measure, quantify, and objectively research the risks and returns. Before a large oil company makes a significant commitment to a new field, for instance, geologists and petroleum engineers can carefully examine seismic data and conduct preliminary drilling tests. Financial analysts can study multiyear cash flow projections to see whether successful development will provide an adequate return on investment. Corporations can also try to diversify away their "quantifiable and measurable" risks. Large oil companies, for instance, have a portfolio of exploration activities and will often develop fields jointly with competitors so that they spread their bets more widely. When the irreducible uncertainty is high, however, and the probability distribution of outcomes cannot be assessed, the risks cannot be reliably diversified away.

Similarly, control systems do not discourage corporations from developing or exploiting new technologies. Companies such as Intel and Merck spend more than $1 billion each year on R&D. The evidence suggests that

---

* Some businesses remain dependent on the inalienable human capital of their principals and therefore outside the domain of large corporations.

the R&D expenditures as percentage of sales are greater in large companies than in small companies.[7] If anything, aversion to uncertainty leads
large companies to favor investments in technologies and intellectual property they can control rather than in the human capital of individual
employees who can leave to join other firms. Decision-makers similarly
favor initiatives that exploit an innovative technology instead of relying
just on the hustle of a few individuals because they can more easily evaluate the risks and returns. New technologies, in other words, have desirable
uncertainty-limiting properties because they can reduce the firm's reliance
on difficult-to-control human agents.

A corporation's aversion to uncertainty does, however, affect the nature of
its R&D efforts. Objective evaluation criteria favor projects with well-defined
risks and payoffs. Significant outlays on speculative research projects that
have no prior path to commercial exploitation reflect a failure of a corporation's checks and balances and its managerial processes. Such projects tend to
contribute more to the public good than to the stockholders' interests.

To illustrate the nature of objective scrutiny, consider Intel cofounder
Gordon Moore's 1996 description of how the company allocates its annual
R&D budget of more than $1 billion. "Each product group," writes Moore,
"is required to submit a project list ordered in decreasing priority, explain
in sometimes excruciating detail why the list is ordered as it is, and indicate where the line ought to be drawn between projects to work on and
projects to put off." Only a "small group" tries to "stay abreast with what
is going on more broadly in the semiconductor industry," and even this
group avoids programs that will generate results only after ten years. The
company has learned to avoid technologies that are too far ahead of the
market—in the 1970s Intel developed and sold complete speech recognition systems at the rate of two per year.[8] Now Intel "limits internal basic
R&D to what is needed to solve immediate problems" and "looks to universities" for much of its basic research.[9] It does not "mount research efforts
aimed at truly understanding problems and producing publishable technological solutions."[10]

Moore contrasts Intel's strategy with the more exploratory approach traditionally adopted by "the large, central research laboratories of the premier
semiconductor firms." AT&T's Bell Labs and Fairchild Semiconductor's
large research organizations probably "contributed more to the common
good than they did to their corporations." Similarly, Xerox Corporation's
Palo Alto Research Center "made some tremendous contributions to the
community at large, notably in the area of local area networks and the
graphical user interface . . . Xerox itself, however, did not benefit nearly as
much."[11] These other organizations, Moore notes, have now changed their
approach: "While it used to be that each of the major [semiconductor]
players had a fairly important laboratory conducting basic research, much
of that has disappeared."[12] Arguably the firms have given up on blue-sky

R&D efforts because of the pressure top executives now face to provide higher returns to their stockholders.

The case of Merck, one of the world's leading pharmaceutical companies, also illustrates how management efforts to maximize the productivity of R&D help to curtail uncertainty. Merck's former CEO P. Roy Vagelos describes how he established the criteria for selecting research projects after he took over as the head of its research labs in 1975. Each research group he found was "working on as many as ten projects at once," which he believed "almost guarantee[d] that no single project would have the critical mass to succeed." The basic criteria Vagelos established to provide more focus helped limit the competitive and scientific uncertainties. "We would look for areas," reports Vagelos, "where there were no therapies or drugs available, where the science was advanced enough for us to believe that we could make a breakthrough, and where we had enough knowledge of the disease to have some idea about how to arrest it."[13] The criteria did not guarantee the success of Merck's projects. But by ensuring a market for successful developments ("no therapies or drugs [currently] available") and eliminating the more speculative efforts (through the requirement for existing advanced science), Merck made the risks and returns of its research portfolio more predictable.

This is not to suggest that large corporations *always* avoid projects with high uncertainty. Top executives who perceive an extreme threat or a once-in-a-lifetime opportunity (e.g., due to the Internet revolution) or who have an autocratic bent may override normal decision-making processes to take a great leap in the dark. Or they may establish a small slush fund to seed uncertain initiatives. My argument about the bias against large, irreducible uncertainty pertains to the normal pattern in healthy organizations. Intel may allocate some funds for uncertain investments in venture capital partnerships, but the bulk of its R&D, fixed-plant, and marketing expenditures will be devoted to investments with well-defined risks and returns.

Profit Requirements

The process corporations use to scrutinize new initiatives also leads them to concentrate their investments on a few initiatives that hold the promise of high total profit. Just as banks apply the same credit analysis to all loan applications, so corporate routines demand a minimum level of evaluation and monitoring for all new initiatives. But at least in the short run, corporations have a fixed staff available to provide such oversight, which limits the number of initiatives they can undertake. To meet their goals for growth, therefore, corporations allocate their limited evaluation capacity to a few projects that they expect will generate substantial total returns, even if smaller projects offer higher-percentage returns on investment.

By way of a simplified example (see Fig. 5.2), consider a corporation with total income of $2 billion that, to satisfy the expectations of its employees and the stock market, must undertake initiatives capable of generating $200 million in new profit each year. Assume further that the corporation has:

- A range of projects it can undertake, where each project requires an investment of $I and is likely to produce a profit of $P. As shown in the figure, larger projects produce proportionately lower profits—that is the return on investment (ROI, or the ratio of P to I) decreases with I.
- Checks and balances that require each project be subjected to six man-months of evaluation.
- A fixed annual capacity of forty-two man-months available to evaluate new projects. Therefore, it cannot undertake more than seven (42 divided by 6) projects per year, indicated by the horizontal line N_{max} in the figure.

To meet its profit goal of $200 million, the corporation can undertake many small projects or a few large projects—as shown in Figure 5.2, the required number of projects decreases with I. The corporation would prefer to undertake many small projects, because projects with smaller I have higher ROIs. But it cannot undertake more than seven projects. Each project must therefore generate a profit of at least $28.57 million ($P_{min}$) with an investment of I_{min} even though smaller projects have higher ROIs, and more projects would lead to greater diversification of the risks.

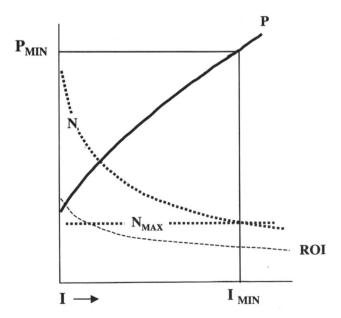

Figure 5.2. Size of Corporate Initiatives

Corporate decision-makers therefore require evidence not just for why a new initiative can be expected to make a profit but also for why the size of the opportunity is large enough to meet corporate requirements. Individuals like Bill Gates and Paul Allen may start a niche business with the hope of finding ways to subsequently build a substantial enterprise. The proponent of a new initiative at an IBM or a P&G must make a plausible case at the outset for how it will grow into a large business. Similarly, an independent wildcatter will be happy to exploit a small well, but Mobil will not invest in a project unless it has the potential to generate at least a $100 million after-tax profit. These minimum-profit requirements can frustrate employees who uncover small opportunities and create an incentive for them to start their own businesses or at least to complain about their employer's bias against entrepreneurship.

Competitive considerations often reinforce the tendency to focus on a few big investments: A corporation that introduces a new product for a large market, but does not back it with sufficient resources to establish first mover advantages, may fail to appropriate the full benefit of its innovation.

A former president of PepsiCo, Andrall Pearson, writes:

> Once an idea or concept is properly developed, it seems logical to assume that any sensible company would throw the book at it to make it a success. Yet I've found that reality is often quite different. Looking back, most of the new-product mistakes I've seen grew from the company's failure to back up the innovation with enough resources—not from overspending . . . many people fail to recognize that their competitors will retaliate— especially if their innovation takes customers away. . . . Second, people try to stretch their resources to finance too many projects at once [so] that none of the projects gets enough sustained support and effort to ensure its success. The only way around it is to be disciplined enough to say "next year" to most of the good ideas available. . . .
>
> In contrast, the big winners make careful plans to throw everything needed at new products to ensure their success. . . . They've learned that doing it right the first time is lots more effective (and usually far less costly) than doing the job on a shoestring and then scrambling to fix things when what happens doesn't meet expectation. They also know they're never going to have the first-blood advantage again, and that the best way to pre-empt or block out competition is to do it right the first time.[14]

To summarize: Large public corporations have an extensive capability for evaluating and monitoring initiatives, which helps determine their area of comparative advantage. The capability gives corporations access to substantial amounts of capital. This allows decision-makers to undertake projects that require large amounts of up-front investment but discourages them from pursuing small opportunities. The evaluation and monitoring capability also leads corporations to avoid uncertainty; or, put more positively, it encourages corporations to pursue projects where their distinctive capacity to evaluate and manage objective risk has the most value.

2. A Well-Planned Process

Most start-ups, as we saw in Chapter 2, are improvised—entrepreneurs often find new business ideas by accident rather than through a systematic search, they do not devote much effort to prior planning and research, and they make extensive changes in response to unforeseen circumstances. In contrast corporations follow a much more rule-based and structured approach. They are more likely than individual entrepreneurs to find opportunities after a systematic search, to conduct extensive research and formulate careful plans, and to stick to their plans once an initiative has been launched. This seemingly regimented approach does not reflect the incompetence or the bureaucratic tendencies of corporate executives, as their critics sometimes claim. Rather, it is a necessary consequence of the resources they control and the constraints they face.

Systematic Search

Top managers of large corporations, as we have seen, institute general policies to control the activities of employees whom they cannot directly supervise. These policies (or long-term "strategies") guide the search for new corporate initiatives. IBM and Hewlett-Packard, for instance, did not start making PCs (which accounted for 14 percent and 16 percent of their respective 1997 revenues) by accident. They made a strategic commitment to enter the market to defend and build on their minicomputer and mainframe businesses. There are exceptions, of course: 3M's now ubiquitous Post-it notes started with a failed attempt by scientist Spencer Silver to develop a strong glue. Later, another 3M scientist, Art Fry, was inspired to develop bookmarks using the glue while singing in a church choir. He scribbled a note to his boss on a prototype bookmark and thus invented Post-it.[15] The appeal of the Post-it story, however, lies in its unusualness: The norm is an orderly pursuit of strategy. Corporate decision-makers evaluate business ideas not just in terms of their stand-alone returns but also in terms of their conformance to long-term goals and interactions with existing activities.

Andrall Pearson's *Harvard Business Review* article "Tough-Minded Ways to Get Innovative" reflects the perspective of a successful corporate executive and consultant. Pearson, who had served as president of PepsiCo for fifteen years and was a director of McKinsey & Co. before that, writes that a "systematic effort to institutionalize innovation is what gives market leaders their competitive edges."[16] Pearson advises companies to make conscious choices about where to direct their innovative efforts. An unfocused approach—"put smart people to work and pray that they'll come up with something great"—usually produces "lots of small ideas that don't lead anywhere, big costs and embarrassing write-offs, and a great deal of frustration and stop-and-go activity." In contrast, successful innovators have "a pretty clear idea of the kind of creative competitive edges they're seeking," and "because their directions are so clearly set, their people can channel their efforts toward things that will work against competitors." Similarly, Pearson argues, "good concrete ideas" do not come out of techniques such as brainstorming; rather, they "most often flow from the process of taking a hard look at your customers, and your business."[17]

Merck's Vagelos, former CEO of Merck, one of the world's leading pharmaceutical companies, describes how he introduced a systematic research process to complement a "focus on the big projects that could result in breakthrough drugs." In 1975 Merck's labs

> were engaging in random screening of compounds, which meant that scientists were testing microorganisms, soil samples, or plant extracts, as well as chemicals made in our own laboratories to see if they caused any pharmacological activity. If they did, the scientists tried to create a drug. If they didn't, the scientists tested more compounds. We introduced a more targeted method that focused on creating specific molecules to attack specific molecular targets, an approach now known as rational drug discovery.[18]

Under the new approach, Merck relied extensively on "enzyme inhibition"—"blocking the action of particular enzymes involved in the disease process." For instance, when scientists looked for a drug to lower high cholesterol, they focused on blocking the enzyme that controls the overproduction of cholesterol and eventually developed two drugs, Mevacor and Zocor. Enzyme inhibition also led to Vasotec, used to treat high blood pressure, and Proscar for prostate disease. Merck's approach was widely adopted by its competitors. "Today the entire industry uses the rational-drug-discovery process,"[19] Vagelos notes, making serendipitous development of new therapies an exception to the systematic rule.

Research

Corporations conduct extensive research to generate objective data for evaluating initiatives. A policy of investing in a few, large initiatives reinforces (as well as derives from) the requirement for extensive research and analysis. With substantial investments at stake, top decision-makers have to ensure that overconfident subordinates do not make inappropriate commitments to new ventures. Before approving the launch of a new product they require their staff to collect information on competitive offerings and plans, examine demographic factors and trends, study customer preferences (through focus groups, open-ended interviews, structured surveys, and so on), and conduct market tests and trials. According to one estimate, in 1995, each *Fortune* 500 company employed, on average, nine full-time market research professionals and had a research budget of $4.2 million.[20] Packaged goods companies (which spend about 20 percent more on average than nonpackaged goods companies) have developed a culture of extensive research and testing. A former assistant brand manager at Procter & Gamble recalls:

> Every brand at P&G has a research person supporting them. Research people have maybe three to five brands each. There are always multiple research projects going on—a quantitative survey, focus groups . . . something.
>
> We could not do anything without testing it. For example, I worked on a line extension of a base product, which was a blue pill. We planned to make the line extension blue, too. Unfortunately, product development told us that we could not make it blue—in testing, it started to turn purple over time. Our second choice was yellow (mostly because a lot of other colors were associated with the competition). I went to the general manager for the category—a senior manager at a level right below VP—and recommended this yellow pill. He was quite disturbed at the thought of changing the color and insisted that I run a test (at a cost of more than $10,000) to see whether consumers liked the yellow or the blue. I wasn't sure how the research would be useful—even if consumers liked the blue, we could not make it blue—but I was forced to run the test. As it happened, consumers preferred the yellow, so we made the decision to use yellow. Even though it did not feel right to my GM in his gut, he accepted the results of the research like the truth from God.

David Ogilvy, cofounder of the advertising agency Ogilvy and Mather, describes the importance of testing for companies who serve mass markets:

> The most important word in the vocabulary of advertising is TEST. If you pretest your product with consumers, and pretest your advertising, you will do well in the marketplace. Twenty-four out of 25 new products never get out of test markets. The manufacturers who don't test market their products incur the colossal cost (and disgrace) of having their products fail on a national scale, instead of dying inconspicuously and economically in test markets. Test your promise. Test your media. Test your headlines and illustrations. Test your level of expenditure. Test your commercials. Never stop testing and your advertising will never stop improving.[21]

Even a company such as 3M, which has a reputation for serendipitous development for products such as Post-it, conducts extensive tests. The color of Post-it—yellow—was guided by market research. Before a national launch in 1980, the product was tested in Richmond, Virginia, and three other cities through office-supply stationers. The "turning point" was "an intense sampling and marketing campaign in Boise, Idaho."[22] According to Post-it's inventor, Art Fry, the market research quelled doubts in 3M: "In the office supply business, an intent-to-reorder rate of 40% or 50% is considered a miracle. In our test market, we achieved a 90% intent-to-reorder rate. That was the end of the skepticism."[23] Research also led to further product extensions. For instance, in 1981, 3M introduced the Post-it Note Tray after research showed the pads were getting lost on customers' desks. By 1984, 3M had added twenty-two other such follow-on products to the Post-it line.[24]

The experiments and trials that corporations conduct before making a commitment to a full-scale launch have a different purpose and structure than the opportunistic adaptation practiced by capital-constrained entrepreneurs. The founders of companies such as Factor-Fox and Silton-Bookman modify their offerings to make a sale. Their adaptation has a short-term, satisficing objective: They want to generate cash flow rather than choose among multiple projects or find the optimal way of proceeding. The information their efforts generate represents a by-product. Their experiments are like those of a miner panning for gold at different places in a riverbed. The primary goal of corporate research, by contrast, is to reduce uncertainty and verify prior beliefs. Is there enough gold in a particular field to justify a large-scale mining operation? What is the optimal price point for the Mach3 razor? Corporate research represents an investment in information rather than an effort to generate short-term cash. The cost of extracting a sample core far exceeds the value of the gold it might contain.

Corporate research is correspondingly more scientific. Sometimes without much aforethought, capital-constrained entrepreneurs respond to the preferences of individual prospects to make a sale. Their adaptation to the specific local circumstances impairs their capacity to draw general inferences and test hypotheses. Corporations try to factor out idiosyncratic factors and select large and representative samples for their experiments. When Gillette conducts market research or when mining companies drill test holes, they want to make sure they can draw reliable inferences about the preferences of the typical customer or of the richness of the overall deposit. Corporate decision-makers who use research to place large bets have to be wary of encouraging but false positive results. They cannot rely on the ad hoc improvisation of bootstrapped entrepreneurs who can cover low fixed costs with fluky sales made to unusual customers. They have to undertake well-designed and well-controlled experiments.

Adhering to Plans

In addition to evidence on why a new initiative is likely to succeed, corporate decision-makers also require extensive plans on how it will unfold. While a self-financed entrepreneur may draw up a plan on the back of an envelope, proposals for new corporate initiatives contain detailed milestones, staffing requirements, financial projections, and so on, which facilitate objective evaluations and monitoring of new projects. The complexity of corporate ventures also requires more planning. Promising ventures started on a small scale usually involve straightforward tasks and simple functions. For instance, to start Compu-Link, Steve Shevlin and his partner bought a large roll of printer cable, cut it into smaller pieces, and sold them over the telephone to dealers listed in the Yellow Pages. Starting Microsoft required Gates and Allen to write a version of BASIC for MITS's Altair and then strike a deal with MITS's owner, Roberts. Planning was neither possible nor necessary. In contrast, the large projects that corporations undertake tend to be complex: The development and launch of New Coke or Microsoft's Windows NT involved numerous activities and functions located within and outside the firm.* Such initiatives require detailed plans to coordinate these functions and activities. To revert to the analogy used earlier, an individual skipping across the stones in a stream has little use for planning. The Golden Gate Bridge, on the other hand, cannot be built without extensive planning and preparation.

Cypress Semiconductor's "goal system" illustrates how established companies use plans to coordinate complex initiatives. According to CEO T. J. Rodgers, most of the work at Cypress is organized by project rather than by function. Each project has numerous long-term and short-term goals. For example, to design and ship the company's third generation of PROM chips, a team of circuit designers, product engineers and test engineers completed 3,278 goals over roughly two years.[25] Cypress management reviews project goals more or less continuously. After project teams meet on Monday, goals are fed into a central computer. On Tuesday mornings functional managers receive printouts on the status of their direct reports' new goals. On Wednesday mornings the vice presidents of the company receive goal printouts for the people below them. On Wednesday afternoons the CEO reviews reports with the vice presidents.[26]

Just as construction of the Golden Gate Bridge follows the basic initial blueprint, once corporations have decided on a plan, they tend to stick to its basic elements. Several factors keep corporate initiatives on their planned course. Corporations don't need or expect to generate positive cash flow as quickly as the bootstrapped entrepreneur. In many large projects, such as PepsiCo's entry into India, or IBM's launch of its OS/2 operating system, top decision-makers expect to lose money for quite a long period. Slower-than-expected progress does not therefore automatically force a change in direction, as it often does with capital-constrained entrepreneurs. The choice of low-uncertainty initiatives and extensive prior analysis also reduces the chances of major surprises and hence the need for significant changes in direction.

---

* In Part II I will argue that the capacity to coordinate many resources and activities represents an important *raison de être* of the large corporation.

Large, complex projects that require the coordination of many individuals and tasks cannot be easily reoriented. Intel, for instance, cannot institute significant changes in the direction of its Pentium development effort in midstream. The many levels of approval required to make changes also encourages companies to stick with a plan that has been agreed on in spite of the subsequent discovery of some shortcomings. Moreover, if a plan has been internally or externally publicized, a major change in direction may damage the reputations and credibility of powerful individuals. An organization may go into a state of denial about the need for changes if subordinates are fearful of carrying bad news to their bosses.*

Criticism of the Corporate Approach

Critics of large companies sometimes claim that their structured approach to new initiatives is overly bureaucratic and that executives should become "more entrepreneurial." Such claims overlook basic differences between corporate and individual initiatives. Although corporate checks and balances slow down decision-making and can sometimes become dysfunctional, they are inextricably linked to the specialization of risk-bearing and management and to their capacity to undertake large and complex projects.

Careful research, planning, and testing can significantly extend the time it takes to launch new initiatives. Corporations take considerably longer than the weeks or months it takes for many individual entrepreneurs to go from having an idea to becoming operational. For instance, 3M patented the adhesive behind Post-it in 1974 and launched the product in 1980. Intel began work on its Pentium microprocessor in 1989, and using a development process that is much admired in the industry for its speed and efficiency was able to launch the product in 1993. Gillette took more than a decade to launch its Mach3 razor (see the sidebar "Mach3 Milestones").

Sometimes the decision-making process can become dysfunctional. Chris Argyris describes an organization where "the completion of the paperwork became an end in itself. Seventy-one percent of the middle managers reported that the maintenance of the product planning and program review paper flow became as crucial as accomplishing the line responsibility assigned to each group. . . . Still another frequently reported problem was the immobilization of the group with countless small decisions."[27] A normal corporate aversion to high uncertainty can become a pathological unwillingness to tolerate any at all, and protracted due processes can make it impossible to undertake new initiatives in a timely fashion. The failure to undertake new initiatives ultimately leads to the

---

* The difficulty of making changes also reinforces incentives to plan carefully and prepare for all contingencies and to avoid turbulent or uncertain environments that make quick adjustments unavoidable.

Mach3 Milestones

1985:	Research begins on developing the first new edge for Gillette's blades since 1969.
1988:	Researchers arrange three blades in a progressive alignment, meaning the first blade sticks out less than the second and third blades.
1992:	An advanced prototype, Manx, beats SensorExcel, Gillette's most advanced razor, in shave tests.
1995:	Gillette's board approves Manx development.
Mid-1996:	Gillette engineers develop a method of assembling Manx's cartridge that is three times as fast as SensorExcel production.
Fall 1997:	Board approves final stage of the $750 million investment. Production begins.
Apr. 14, 1998:	Mach3 unveiled.

Source: William C. Symonds, "Would You Spend $1.50 for a Razor Blade?" *Business Week* (April 27, 1998), p. 46.

---

demise of the organization; as mentioned, corporations have to keep finding new profit opportunities to survive.

Corporations cannot, however, adopt the freewheeling ways of bootstrapped entrepreneurs. Without careful, objective review and oversight, investors would not readily give boards and top managers of large companies broad discretion over large sums. Adherence to due process and factbased decision-making can also promote teamwork and preserve organizational morale in large organizations. Large companies have many employees generating new initiatives. Employees who secure corporate backing for their initiatives have the satisfaction of seeing their ideas implemented and increase their chances of receiving promotions or bonuses. An organization that selects ideas capriciously or because of personal pull will discourage talented employees from displaying initiative and reduce its chances of long-term survival. Conversely, companies that make fair, by-the-book choices secure more loyalty. Thus the general manager at Procter & Gamble who puts aside his personal misgivings about yellow pills reinforces the company's reputation for fairness and respect for the facts.

Moreover, large companies usually compete in oligopolistic markets against other firms subject to the same pressure to institute checks and balances. Provided they don't take due process to extremes, the benefits of careful research and planning exceed the costs that large companies incur. According to Pearson, PepsiCo's disciplined approach "led to $2 billion to $3 billion worth of successful innovations."[28] The "rational drug discovery process" that didn't stray too far from the existing science instituted by Vagelos at Merck led to a series of drugs with total annual sales of $6.1 billion.[29] The "excruciating detail" required to justify projects and a focus on solving "immediate problems," Moore suggests, has given Intel a much higher "R&D capture ratio" than did Fairchild Semiconductor's ad hoc approach. Intel has generated few spin-offs or technologies of greater value to society than to its stockholders.[30] Its approach, concedes Moore, "might at some point cause Intel to miss a revolutionary idea that has the potential to wipe out established positions." He argues, however, that the alternative, of having large R&D organizations conducting basic research, "has not been shown to be protection against change in a basic business paradigm."[31]

Procter & Gamble's "testing fetish," Peters and Waterman suggest, has played a valuable role in the success of its new product introductions. They cite comments made by an employee of Crown Zellerbach, a competitor of P&G in some paper product markets:

> P&G tests and tests and tests. You can see them coming for months, often years. But you know that when they get there, it is probably time for you to move to another niche, not to be in their way. They leave no stone unturned, no variable untested.[32]

Companies, of course, vary in their scrutiny of new initiatives and requirements for planning and research. "Flat" organizations with lean staff may evaluate initiatives relatively expeditiously. Similarly, differences in administrative skill, culture, and internal trust may lead some companies to have less stringent demands for objective evidence than others. But even the most freewheeling large companies, such as 3M, have more stringent procedures and criteria and devote more resources to evaluation and monitoring their projects than the typical bootstrapped entrepreneur. And as the sidebar, "Routinized Innovation: The 3M Case" illustrates, growth in size and complexity leads to increasing pressures to systematize its decision-making. 3M may never become as disciplined or focused as PepsiCo or P&G. However, neither will 3M's management processes allow two engineers to buy a grinder and start a plastic scrap brokering business, as Eaglebrook's founders did in 1983. It is telling that 3M has participated in the PC revolution mainly through high-volume, relatively stable products such as diskettes and other storage media. No matter how entrepreneurial a large company might be, the threshold requirements for total profit, verifiable advantages, budgets, milestones, and so on significantly exceed those of bootstrapped start-ups.

3. Securing Resources

In Chapter 3 we saw that start-ups face significant problems in securing customers, employees, suppliers, and so on. Entrepreneurs have to over-

Routinized Innovation: The 3M Case

C. A. Bartlett and A. Mohammed's "3M: Profile of an Innovating Company" illustrates how the pressures to adopt systematic processes for finding and evaluating new business opportunities escalate over time. In 1902 five businessmen from Minnesota formed 3M to mine corundum, an abrasive mineral. When the mine failed, 3M began to manufacture sandpaper. The sandpaper business, too, generated losses until a young bookkeeper, William McKnight, took over the sales manager's job. McKnight subsequently served as the company's president from 1929 to 1949 and then as its chairman from 1949 to 1969.

McKnight, who was the company's "spiritual leader," Bartlett and Mohammed write, "developed an unshakable belief in the power of individual entrepreneurship."[33] 3M encouraged researchers to pursue projects of personal interest. As a result, 3M "stumbled onto literally scores of new products and technologies." Management adopted a philosophy of "make a little, sell a little," not only because 3M could make a profit in niche markets but also because "many products and technologies subsequently found applications never [originally] dreamed of." For instance, a material first introduced as a decorative ribbon "spawned scores of other products" from "protective face masks, to surgical tape, to Scotch Brite cleaning pads."

Eventually, however, questions about the effectiveness of the new product development process led McKnight's successors to change 3M's freewheeling approach. When Lou Lehr, a thirty-five-year 3M veteran, became CEO in 1980, he expressed concerns about "fragmentation" of the company's efforts. Under Lehr the company adopted "a new organization structure, planning process and funding policies" that "had an enduring impact on 3M's product and process development." Bartlett and Mohammed quote a division vice president:

> Previously innovation was driven by management asking researchers, "What rabbit can you pull out of the hat to meet our targets?" We relied on a pool of technology, some talented people, and a supportive culture to create innovations by spontaneous combustion. The individuals who came up with the new products were heroes, no matter what the fit with existing businesses or market access. So there were hundreds of initiatives—you could do anything. But as development became more expensive and riskier, we needed the focus and discipline of the new structure and processes.[34]

3M did not reduce its commitment to innovation, however; during Lehr's six-year term as CEO, spending on R&D more than doubled, from $238 million in 1979 to $507 million in 1985. Allen Jacobson, who took over as CEO in 1986, wanted 3M to become even "more focused in its choice of project development." Under his tenure the company began to develop "a more disciplined approach" to funding projects. According to a vice president of the Dental Products Division:

> Previously a scientist could work on a project for years, with money just dribbling out to support it and management not really knowing how much had been invested or what the potential was. Today we try to do a lot more sorting out early. We ask for a product positioning statement right up front, and if it's not clear, it won't be funded. . . . So now, instead of running 100 programs as we did before, our division is focused on 12.[35]

Another vice president observed that "the day of the individual entrepreneur is over at 3M," although "we still like to talk about the brilliant inventor who converts his innovation into a new business."[36]

come the liability of newness: Resource providers are reluctant to take chances on start-ups that may not survive. Doing business with a newly formed business also involves high switching costs. Below we will see how established corporations have several advantages over bootstrapped start-ups in securing resources, as well as some distinctive challenges. We will also examine how the strategies corporations pursue are different from the approaches individual entrepreneurs use to secure resources.

Corporate Advantages and Problems

Several factors mitigate the concerns of resource providers about the survival of corporate initiatives. The extensive scrutiny and analysis that corporations perform on new initiatives provide some reassurance about the soundness of the enterprise. The cash flows generated by existing businesses, financial reserves, and unused borrowing capacity similarly provide comfort about a corporation's staying power.

Corporations, having made large up-front investments and wishing to protect their reputations, have greater incentives to stick to the initiatives they have chosen to pursue. Resource providers can expect that IBM will not quickly abandon a floundering initiative (such as the PC Jr. computer or the OS/2 operating system) after it has spent significant resources on planning and market research, product development, and advertising, and has put its credibility at stake. A small-scale assembler of PC clones, in contrast, is much more likely to shut down quickly or embark on a different business—as many entrepreneurs in fact did when profits from assembling clones declined in the mid-1980s.

A corporation's resource providers also face lower switching and search costs. When Hewlett-Packard introduces a new product, potential customers know what they can expect in terms of quality, value for money, ongoing support, and so on. Similarly, potential recruits can easily investigate the working conditions and organizational climate at HP. Existing relationships can also reduce costs: Buying an additional, new item from HP is less burdensome than adding another vendor to the company's list of approved vendors. A popular business heuristic suggests that selling to existing customers is more profitable than cultivating new customers, and maintaining customer loyalty is less costly than adding new customers. Similarly, companies with an existing pool of employees have an advantage in staffing up new initiatives because internal transfers of personnel involve less disruption and loss of specific knowledge than switching across firms.

Well-established companies can benefit from the unwillingness of other organizations' employees to take personal risks when benefits accrue mainly to their employers. For instance, employees in other organizations may order expensive laptops because they see no advantage in buying a cheaper no-name clone. With a clone, the employer reaps the savings while the employee receives little benefit; if the cheaper computer malfunctions, the employee gets faulted for having made a poor choice. Buying IBM is safe; "no one ever gets fired buying from IBM." The large scale of new corporate initiatives provides psychologically reassuring "social proofs": The buyer knows that lots of others will be buying IBM's new computers and does not have to fear being alone. Further reassurance is provided by the perception of expertise: Just as people will unthinkingly follow the orders of doctors and other such figures of authority, they may defer to the credentials of an IBM "systems engineer" or "networking specialist" who tells them what they should buy.

Against these advantages, however, corporations also face the problems of securing larger quantities and higher quality of customers and employees than do start-ups. For instance, bootstrapped start-ups can make attractive profits serving a very small number of customers because their fixed costs are low. The typical large corporation has to secure significantly more customers to earn an attractive return. New Coke generated more sales in its first year than did Nantucket Nectars' entire line of drinks five years after the company was started. And as Christensen points out, Apple sold three times as many Newtons as it had Apple IIs in the first two years after their respective launches: By 1994 Newton had sold 140,000 units, and by 1979 the Apple II had sold 43,000 units.[37] But because Coca-Cola and Apple dedicated vast resources to launching New Coke and the Newton, both products represented major flops. Whereas a start-up can make do by identifying a few offbeat customers and adapting their offerings to their customers' needs, the products and services of large corporations must have mass appeal.

The size of corporate initiatives and the competition they typically encounter require top-quality resources. In a small start-up that faces undistinguished rivals, the founder's personal drive and skills can compensate for "second-tier" resources. When Coca-Cola launches a new soft drink on a national scale and attempts to take a market share away from Pepsi, or when 3M goes head-to-head against Iomega's popular Jaz line with a new high-density drive, they need stellar resources: Employees, suppliers, distributors, ad agencies, and so on must be of a high caliber. Marginal providers of labor and services who are eager to do the job because they lack better alternatives are often not good enough.

Securing top-quality (rather than merely adequate) resources involves special challenges. Although credentials may provide good signals of quality, they are not foolproof. Whereas bootstrapped start-ups struggle to find the false positives—employees who are inherently better than their qualifications would indicate—large companies face the problem of avoiding the false negatives—personnel who pass objective screens, but are not as talented as their résumés would indicate. The joint effort involved in corporate initiatives also makes it difficult to detect mediocre hires quickly. In a large and complex project involving many personnel, the performance of individuals is difficult to evaluate. Also, many talented personnel do not like to work for large corporations; the security and other such inducements that corporations are uniquely positioned to offer may not appeal to them.

Corporate Strategies

Existing reputations, relationships, and access to capital allow large companies to pursue strategies for attracting resources that capital-constrained start-ups cannot. Entrepreneurs, we have seen, struggle to get others to bear the risks of their ventures, whereas companies like IBM can underwrite the risks for resource providers through explicit or implicit guarantees. For instance, they can offer customers money-back guarantees or contracts with penalty clauses. They can mitigate the career risks of the employees who participate in new initiatives by making an implicit promise to retain them if the initiative fails; thus we often find corporate policies that say "we do not punish failure."

They can publicly stake their reputations to a new initiative. The irreversible up-front investments that corporations make to launch a new initiative in R&D, market research, new capacity, and so on, provide a signal of commitment that "speaks for itself." Corporations often amplify the signal by undertaking extensive advertising and public relations campaigns. For instance, IBM's recent ads in the mass media seem like an inefficient way for the company to communicate the launch of its "e-business" line of web servers and software; at most a few thousand of the millions of readers who will see the advertisements have any role in purchasing such offerings. But the ads provide a credible signal of IBM's commitment: If the company weren't determined to make the venture a success, it wouldn't stake its reputation so visibly to the new line of business.*

Companies also advertise their overall stability and prosperity. Usually this is done indirectly. Investment banks, lawyers, and other professional firms receive clients in well-appointed offices, high-tech firms maintain verdant campuses, and firms such as Mobil sponsor programs on public television. Sometimes the message is explicit. In a recent full-page ad in the *Wall Street Journal*, insurance company Conceco declared: "We are unapologetically profitable. Profitability is the ultimate security for our policyholders. And it's also the most important factor in our agents' long-term success. We are driven to perform for our customers, agents, and shareholders."[38]

Corporations can take advantage of existing relationships with customers, suppliers, banks, and other resource providers. A competent salesperson at IBM can identify the customers who will derive the most value from a new

---

* In the early 1990s IBM undertook a similar media blitz to reassure customers about its continued commitment to its AS1400 line of midsize computers.

product, understands how the purchasing processes work, and knows the influential decision-makers and what they respond to. Furthermore, the salesperson's personal relationships, trust, and past favors (personal and professional) done for the client can help secure orders. Similarly, existing relationships with suppliers can be used to get them to tool up for a new line.

Corporations often reduce the risks to consumers by offering new products or services at substantially discounted prices or even free. Packaged-goods companies such as Procter & Gamble, for instance, often distribute coupons or free samples of new products through the mail or at supermarkets. AT&T offered a "no fee for life" deal to anyone who signed up for its Universal Credit Card in its introductory year. Microsoft captured a 25 percent share of the Internet browser market in two years simply by giving away its product, the Explorer.

On the cognitive and psychological side, corporations can frame choices that play up to the resource providers' tendency to loss aversion. Their sales forces, for instance, may sow FUD (fear, uncertainty, and doubt) in their customers' minds to dissuade them from considering new or less well established vendors. They take advantage of the reflexive tendency of customers to follow the lead of authority figures and experts. Shoe companies such as Nike, for instance, sign multimillion-dollar contracts with top athletes to wear and endorse their products. Such endorsements have helped Nike redefine what consumers look for and the prices they are willing to pay for shoes. Colgate grew the sales of its premium-priced designer pet foods from $40 million in 1982 to $900 million in 1996. The company spent very little on traditional advertising; rather, it concentrated its marketing and promotion budgets on persuading veterinarians to recommend its brands.

In some extreme cases, a company that dominates its field may be able to force resource providers to sign on. For instance, when Microsoft introduces a new version of its word processing or spreadsheet software (and stops supporting the old version), many customers feel compelled to switch. Similarly, independent software producers have to rewrite their applications when Microsoft introduces a new operating system.

The strategies do not, of course, ensure the success of corporate ventures. The capital and other advantages corporations enjoy more or less ensure the availability of *some* customers and employees. They cannot, however, guarantee that the volume of sales will be high enough or that employees will be talented enough to provide a large enough return to meet the corporate standards of success.

4. Requirements for Success

The success of corporate initiatives depends on factors that are quite different from those that pertain to bootstrapped start-ups. First, the initial or prelaunch conditions and concepts matter a great deal more in corporate ventures. Entrepreneurs can start with an undistinguished product or business concept but still may make a worthwhile profit by dint of what they do after they get started: They can generate orders if they knock on enough doors, modify their offering in response to what customers tell them they really want, work hard to satisfy their first clients, and so on. Corporate initiatives such as the IBM PC Jr. or New Coke may be doomed from the start. Corporations cannot easily make major midcourse corrections because of the scale and complexity of their initiatives and because of the number of players involved. It can be difficult, and sometimes impossible, to recover from inappropriate choices of product design, advertising, distribution channels, and so on that were made before launch. (I do not at all mean to suggest that good plans are a sufficient condition. As I will argue at length in Part II, good execution is as important in a large enterprise as it is in a start-up—a sound design and blueprints alone did not assure the successful completion of the Golden Gate Bridge.)

Second, broad-based organizational capabilities, rather than the talents of a few individuals, play a more important role in determining the success of corporate initiatives. Compared to bootstrapped start-ups, corporate initiatives depend more on the joint efforts of many individuals and on specialized functions. As we have seen, individual entrepreneurs (or a small team of founders) bear considerable responsibility for the success or failure of bootstrapped ventures. The entrepreneur secures—or fails to secure—orders. The entrepreneur is responsible for the quality of services provided. Employees, if any, play a secondary role. The entrepreneur also personally makes important trade-offs, such as what additional features or services to offer to make a sale. This concentration of responsibility and decision-making results from the small scale of the enterprise.

In a large corporate initiative, critical responsibilities for evaluation, planning, and execution are diffused across many employees in several specialized functions. The introduction of Coca-Cola's new soft drink or IBM's new computer requires the joint efforts of many product design, marketing, financial control, production, logistics, and other such personnel rather than the talents of a few versatile individuals. As we will see in Part II, the quality of the joint efforts in turn, depends on the caliber of individual contributors as well as on the organizational mechanisms and routines used to coordinate their work and to resolve conflicts. Reporting relationships, incentives, control systems, formal policies, tacit norms and other such factors that affect how diverse functions with different knowledge, outlooks, and interests work together have a significant influence on results. They determine whether the organization can strike the right balance between objective criticism and the repair of cognitive defects on the one hand, and the elimination of all initiative on the other. They also determine whether plans to take advantage of existing reputations, sources of capital, and other such assets can be realized or whether they crumble during execution.

5. Summary

Corporate decision-makers have access to significantly more capital than individual entrepreneurs, but control systems intended to protect stockholders place limits on their discretion. These initial conditions lead corporations to favor large, low-uncertainty initiatives and to plan their ventures carefully instead of relying on opportunistic adaptation. The cash flows, relationships, and reputations provided by existing businesses help corporations secure customers, employees, and other resources for their new initiatives; corporations do, however, face tougher quality and quantity requirements than most new start-ups.

The factors that determine the success of corporate initiatives also are different. The soundness of the original concept and the joint efforts of several players are much more important for corporate ventures than they are for promising start-ups.

6

VC-Backed Start-ups

This chapter examines the unusual nature of venture capital (VC)-backed start-ups in order to put the characteristics of the more common promising ventures into sharper relief. Section 1 examines the endowments and constraints of the founders of VC-backed start-ups. Section 2 shows how the initial conditions affect the scale and uncertainty, degree of prior plans, strategies for securing resources, and key success requirements. Section 3 discusses whether the small number of VC-backed start-ups is a temporary phase that reflects the immaturity of the field.

Venture capital (VC)-backed start-ups have had a powerful influence in shaping popular beliefs (and formal research) about new ventures for several reasons. They have made significantly greater contributions than bootstrapped ventures to certain high-technology fields such as semiconductors and genetic engineering. Their geographic concentration (notably in California and Massachusetts) raises intriguing questions for policymakers, economists, and sociologists. Researchers can more easily document their strategies and performance. They make more of a splash—the successful VC-backed start-up grows at a much faster rate than the average *Inc.* 500 company, going public or getting acquired in about five years, as opposed to the *Inc.* companies, which remain privately owned for an average of about eight years.

We should not, however, confuse vividness with representativeness. Only 5 percent or so of *Inc.* 500 companies start with VC funding and, overall, VCs fund a few hundred new businesses per year. As we will see, VC-backed start-ups have several out-of-the-ordinary features. Their founders have exceptional qualifications and ideas, which allow them to raise much more capital than the founders of the typical promising start-up. The typical *Inc.* 500 company, we have seen, starts off with less than $30,000, whereas VC-backed ventures raise between $2 million to $5 million dollars. The capital has strings attached, however. In contrast to the founders of self-financed businesses, VC-backed entrepreneurs face extensive scrutiny of their plans and ongoing monitoring of their performance by their capital providers. These distinctive initial conditions lead them to pursue opportunities with greater investment and less uncertainty, rely more on anticipation and planning and less on improvisation and adaptation, use different strategies for securing resources, and face different requirements for success.

Scope. This chapter contrasts VC-backed and promising start-ups. Some promising start-ups do subsequently raise financing from VCs, and the VC industry typically disburses about two-thirds of its funds to post-start-up, or "later stage" companies. But this reinforces my claim that few entrepreneurs starting new businesses fit the VC investment model. The high proportion of later-stage investments reveal a strong preference for funding businesses after entrepreneurs have reduced the high uncertainties of the start-up stage and demonstrated the potential for large payoffs.*

1. Initial Conditions

In the section below, I will offer an explanation for the large amounts of capital available to VC-funded entrepreneurs, the unusual ideas and human capital they must have, and the scrutiny and monitoring they face. Investing in start-ups (as opposed to, say, publicly traded stocks) requires careful evaluation and monitoring. Time constraints limit the number of investments VCs can make and encourage them to concentrate on a few start-ups they expect will produce large payoffs. Furthermore, only a few individuals have the ideas and human capital VCs consider necessary to generate large returns. I will also briefly contrast some of the initial conditions found in a VC-backed start-up with those of corporate initiatives; as we will see, VC-backed start-ups don't have access to as much capital as corporate initiatives but are usually subject to less scrutiny and monitoring.

Evaluation and Monitoring

Investors in start-ups have an incentive to conduct more due diligence than investors in the stock of well-established public companies. Modern finance theory suggests that investors in publicly traded stocks do not get rewarded for assuming company-specific risk. These risks can be diversified away by holding a portfolio of stocks. The "market" or "systematic" risk of the portfolio, rather than astuteness in the choice of individual securities, determines the investors' long-run return. Efforts to analyze a company's prospects carry little reward because the market price already reflects all available information. Investing in start-ups represents a qualitatively different game. Discrimination among opportunities is crucial, because investors cannot take a free ride off the research and due diligence incor-

---

* In Part II we will study the evolutionary process that changes the uncertainty and size characteristics of businesses and makes them eligible for substantial outside funding.

porated in "market prices." While prudence demands some diversification, diversification is not an adequate substitute for choosing individual investments carefully.

Buying twenty randomly selected stocks listed on the New York Stock Exchange eliminates most company-specific risk and provides returns that track those of the overall stock market. Historically, this has amounted to about 10 percent per year. Providing venture capital to twenty random entrepreneurs (out of more than half a million start-ups per year) will likely provide, given the dubious prospects of most new businesses, a return of close to zero. Moreover, backing randomly selected ventures without doing any screening makes investors vulnerable to opportunistic or self-dealing founders. Dispersed investors in start-ups do not enjoy the protections available to minority shareholders in public companies through the SEC, stock exchange rules, the scrutiny of analysts, and the threat of takeovers. Therefore we should expect investors to analyze each venture they back carefully. We should also expect investors to expend resources in negotiating prices and terms; investors in start-ups cannot count on the trading and arbitrage in public markets that equilibrate the expected risks and returns of individual securities.

Investors in start-ups also have an incentive to provide considerable monitoring and oversight of the venture's ongoing performance. In public markets, the diversified investor's ability to monitor and to intervene is low. Firms cannot engage in meaningful dialogue about strategy and performance with widely dispersed public investors; consequently stockholders lack the confidential information to monitor managers and distinguish between their luck and skill. Free-rider problems also undermine incentives for stockholders to intervene; the stockholder who incurs the costs of inducing a firm to change its strategy or management must share the benefits with the other stockholders who did not make the effort.[1] Investors (such as index funds) therefore take a passive approach and make no effort to evaluate firm management; others follow the so-called Wall Street rule of selling a stock if they are unhappy. In small, private firms, however, investors can demand access to the information they need to evaluate performance. Free-rider problems are mitigated by smaller investment groups and the lack of liquidity precludes investors from avoiding intervention by selling their holdings. The extent and quality of monitoring, therefore, influence investors' returns.

Partnership Terms

VCs, who invest others' funds rather than their own capital, face additional incentives to institute systematic procedures and criteria for evaluating and monitoring investments.

Wealthy individuals, pension funds, and other entities who have the capital to invest in start-ups often lack the resources (or the confidence) to evaluate and monitor such ventures. Instead, they invest in limited partnerships organized by professional VC firms. Under the terms of such partnerships, VCs have broad discretion over the funds under management. At or before the expiration of the life of the partnership, usually within ten years, VCs sell the illiquid holdings of the partnership for cash or convert them into marketable securities and return the proceeds to their clients. For the services they provide, VCs receive a flat annual fee (usually 1 to 2 percent of assets managed) as well as a "carried interest" or share (on the order of 20 percent) of profits generated for clients.[2]

These terms may be contrasted with the arrangements that investors have with "investment advisers" for publicly traded securities. Investment advisory activity that does not involve as much due diligence and oversight can easily be scaled up—it does not take much more effort to invest $1 billion in liquid securities than it does $100 million. The typical investment adviser, therefore, handles substantially greater funds than a VC. An adviser serving institutional clients with fewer than a few billion dollars under management is considered small, and many advisers manage tens of billions of dollars. The average VC partnership, in contrast, is well under $100 million. Investment advisers also usually receive a smaller annual fee (ranging from 0.1 to 0.6 percent of assets) from institutional clients and do not share in the profits of the portfolio. And because holdings are liquid, clients can withdraw funds from or terminate the services of an investment adviser at any time.

The terms of their deals with clients encourage VCs to formalize their investment processes and criteria. Limited partnership structures allow VCs to avoid the delays and leakage of sensitive information that might result from having to raise funds for individual investments; but they also require clients to cede full control over investment decisions to VCs for an extended period. The "carried interest," which gives VCs a share of the profits but not of the losses, creates an incentive to invest in excessively risky projects. VCs therefore institute—and advertise—procedures to reassure clients that they will not abuse their discretion by making reckless investments. And when successful VCs seek to raise new funds, they try to convince potential investors that their past records are the result of a systematic investment process rather than, say, intuition or luck.

The evidence seems to bear out the claims VCs make to market their services. Professional VCs do seem to devote considerable effort to performing due diligence, structuring deals, and providing ongoing counsel and oversight. Partners in VC firms, Sahlman reports, usually have responsibility for just under nine investments and sit on five boards of directors. They visit each company they have invested in about nineteen times per year and spend a hundred hours in direct contact (either on site or by phone) with the company. They "help recruit and compensate key individuals, work with suppliers and customers, help establish tactics and strategy, play a major role in raising capital, and help structure transactions such as mergers and acquisitions. They often assume more direct control by changing management and are sometimes willing to take over day-to-day operations themselves."[3] Lerner's study of VCs who serve on the boards of the companies in their portfolios suggests that their involvement becomes more intense around events such as the turnover of the chief executive and that they tend to serve on the boards of companies that are located close by.[4]

Typical Criteria and Process

As with corporate initiatives, the limit to the number of deals VCs can effectively manage establishes a high threshold to the total return they require from each deal. Instead of fragmenting their time across many small opportunities, VCs prefer to concentrate on a few ventures that have the potential—based on objective or verifiable data—to make substantial absolute returns. Significant failure rates and limited time horizons reinforce this preference. Even after extensive due diligence and monitoring, many VC investments yield disappointing returns: One study of venture capital portfolios by *Venture Economics, Inc.,* reported that about 7 percent of investments accounted for more than 60 percent of the profits, while fully one-third resulted in a partial or total loss. VCs therefore avoid small opportunities where even substantial returns on a percentage basis will not cover the opportunity costs of their time or compensate for the other failures in their portfolios. Every venture they invest in must hold the promise to provide returns in the tens of millions of dollars, rather than in the tens or even hundreds of thousands of dollars.

The attractiveness of a venture also depends on how long VCs expect it will take them to "harvest" or cash out of their investment. VCs have to cash out before the life of their partnership expires. In a ten-year fund, a venture that does not fold typically is taken public or sold to another company within five years. This consideration also leads VCs to favor investments with the potential for large payoffs: Small companies cannot afford the fixed costs of going public and then conforming to regulatory and reporting requirements.

A brochure produced by Primus Venture Partners describing the firm's investment criteria and process illustrates how VCs try to identify ventures that have the potential to generate high absolute returns. The first "core requirement" listed in the brochure is "competent management with deep experience in the industry or markets they address." The second core requirement is the company's potential to become "a leader in its chosen market" by providing "distinctive products with a proprietary edge" or "unique services with strong customer appeal." The brochure also indicates that Primus expects to realize a return in a span of three to five years, has an "optimum investment size" of $1 million to $5 million, and has some industry preferences, but is "more attracted to outstanding management teams" than to specific industries.

Primus's evaluation process, according to the brochure, begins with the review of a business plan developed by the entrepreneur seeking funding. The minimum information these plans must contain, according to the brochure, includes:

- a statement of the strategic direction the business is to follow and why that direction makes sense within the company's market or industry environment;
- a detailed description of the products or services to be provided, with special emphasis on their proprietary nature;
- profiles or résumés of the key managers;
- a brief analysis of the markets served and their outlook (e.g., the competitive climate, trends influencing projected changes in market size, the role of foreign competitors);
- financial projections on where the business can be taken in sales and profits over three to five years.

According to the brochure, if the business fits Primus's investment criteria and if management has the necessary experience profile, Primus professionals then have extensive discussions with management and conduct a complete check of their references. They also independently investigate the company's products, markets, and competition, conducting "as thorough a review as time permits in order to verify that management has a high probability of making their plan work."

Other VC firms have somewhat different criteria. Some have a stronger industry focus—Hummer Winblad, for instance, will only invest in software deals. John Doerr, of Kleiner Perkins, says he looks for "technical excellence; outstanding management; strategic focus on a large, rapidly growing market [and] a tremendous sense of urgency." Kleiner Perkins seeks to "back ventures that are the first or second entrants in their markets, so speeding the product to market in advance of competition is absolutely critical."[5] But the core elements of Primus's approach—the need for proprietary products, experienced managers, minimum investment thresholds, and extensive due diligence—are fairly uniform across VC firms because they derive from a universal incentive to identify big winners. A small firm, for instance, can be profitable simply as a result of an entrepreneur's personal drive, energy, relationships, and so on; but a significant payoff, realized through the sale of the company or a public issue of its stock, generally requires something inherently proprietary in its products or processes.* Similarly,

---

* There are, of course, exceptions to this general pattern. A renowned individual with exceptional skills or know-how may receive funding to find an opportunity and develop a business plan; this is not how VCs usually operate or advertise their value added to their clients.

experienced founders significantly increase a venture's chances of attaining large scale quickly. Some untrained or inexperienced individuals may be able to learn how to manage rapidly growing firms, but it is difficult, before the fact, for VCs to identify entrepreneurs with this latent capacity.

Unusual Founders

Few individuals start with the ideas and human capital necessary to secure VC funding. Mitch Kapor had adequate endowments to secure VC funding when he started Lotus in 1982; when Gates and Allen started Microsoft in 1975, they did not. (See the sidebar "Meeting VC Criteria: Kapor vs. Gates.") But most founders of new ventures are like Gates and Allen rather

---

Meeting VC Criteria: Kapor vs. Gates

Mitch Kapor could obtain VC funding to start Lotus Development Corporation because he had the necessary endowments. Gates and his partner, Allen, who didn't, were forced to bootstrap. Although Kapor was not a corporate type—he had previously worked as a disc jockey and transcendental meditation instructor—he had a degree in cybernetics from Yale and had completed three-fourths of an accelerated masters in business program from MIT. Before launching Lotus, Kapor had successfully developed Tiny Troll, VisiPlot, and Visitrend software and had been the product manager for Visicalc, the first electronic spreadsheet. Kapor made a significant personal investment to fund the early development of Lotus's software—he had earned more than $1 million from Tiny Troll, VisiPlot, and Visitrend—and hired Jonathan Sachs, who had fifteen years of programming experience. Sachs had already designed and implemented spreadsheet software for minicomputers. By 1982 the market potential for personal computers was well established. In 1981, a total of 836,000 personal computers had been shipped, and the Yankee Group was forecasting annual growth rates of about 66 percent per year. Visicalc had established spreadsheets as a viable product category—about one in three personal computer owners at the time used the software. In his business plan, therefore, Kapor could project revenue of $24.9 million by the third year of operation, with conservative estimates of market share.[6] Additionally, according to Ben Rosen, the VC who backed Kapor, Lotus's first product, 1-2-3, was "significantly superior" to Visicalc.[7] IBM had just introduced the personal computer (PC), and 1-2-3 took advantage of the new sixteen-bit architecture of the PC to provide more functions and sharper graphics than could the then dominant spreadsheet, Visicalc, on Apple's 8-bit machines.

In contrast, when Gates and Allen launched Microsoft in 1975, only a small number of hobbyists even knew about personal computers. Microsoft's first product did not have the potential to generate significant revenues. Steve Jobs had not yet conceived of the Apple. Kapor's 1982 business plan contained objective industry data on competitors, customer segments, the installed base of computers, and so on. Given the nascent state of the PC industry in 1975, Microsoft's founders could not have drawn up such a plan. By objective standards Microsoft lacked the "outstanding management" required by VCs like Primus. Gates was still a teenager, and Allen was only two years older than Gates. Both had dropped out of college. Compared to Kapor in 1982, they had limited business or industry experience or the capacity to attract seasoned personnel.

Microsoft, unlike Lotus, could not have productively utilized much start-up capital either. VC funding of $4.7 million allowed Lotus to accelerate its product introduction and launch 1-2-3 with the software industry's first serious advertising campaign. 1-2-3 quickly dominated the market for spreadsheets for the new sixteen-bit generation of personal computers. A slower rollout or less aggressive marketing expenditures to lock in customers might have allowed the makers of Visicalc to catch up. The tiny hobbyists' market for Microsoft's BASIC for the Altair, in contrast, could not justify much investment in promotion, distribution, or marketing. For Gates and Allen, therefore, start-up financing from VCs was neither feasible nor useful.

Moreover, even though Microsoft eventually overshadowed Lotus, it is not obvious that an investment in Microsoft would have produced a more attractive return for a VC over the usual three-to-five-year investment horizon. Lotus exceeded its sales projections by a wide margin, shipping $53 million in its first year.[8] In October 1983, fewer than two years after receiving VC funding of $4.7 million,[9] Lotus went public at a valuation in excess of $200 million. In contrast, five years after launch in 1980, Microsoft was booking about $5 million dollars in sales from several niche products, without any imminent prospect of a public stock offering. By the standard of an average start-up, Microsoft made spectacular progress in its first five years and made the 1984 *Inc.* 500 list. But compared to VC-backed successes such as Lotus and Compaq, the absolute increase in firm value in its early years was undistinguished—it took about nine years for Microsoft to book the same revenues that Lotus did in its first year, and ten years for it to go public.

than Kapor; they do not meet VC criteria. This holds true even if one looks only at ex-post successes, such as the founders of the *Inc.* 500 companies.

Initial business ideas. Most entrepreneurs do not have a proprietary product or service capable of generating significant revenues. They are often not the first or the second entrants in their markets. As we have seen, they often copy the products of other firms. In other cases they develop an idea independently but at the same time as many other entrepreneurs. In yet other cases an entrepreneur's idea is easily imitated.

Usually the revenue potential of an initial concept is limited. Most entrepreneurs start off in small niches that cannot justify the million-dollar investment thresholds of most VCs. Their immediate goal is to generate enough sales to cover their low fixed costs. Those who go on to make the *Inc.* 500 list subsequently add new customers or products but, as we have seen, this expansion is usually more opportunistic than planned. Investors cannot count on such an expansion at the outset. Entrepreneurs might be confident that they will find growth opportunities, but they cannot provide much objective data.

Moreover, even the exceptional, after-the-fact growth that the founders of the *Inc.* 500 companies manage to generate often falls short of the magnitudes necessary to meet VC standards of success. Most companies on the *Inc.* 500 list are five to eight years old; a five-year track record is a requirement for inclusion, and fewer than 30 percent are older than nine years. Thus their typical age is somewhat greater than the three-to-five-year VC investment horizon. But their revenues tend to be considerably less, even after eight years, than the revenues booked by VC-backed successes such as Compaq and Lotus in their first couple of years. As Figure 6.1 shows, companies on the *Inc.* 500 lists have median revenues below $10 million. In contrast, the typical VC-backed company that goes public does so just five years after formation[10] (see Table 6.1), with revenues in the prior year (i.e., four years after formation) of about $37 million.[11]

Human capital. Most entrepreneurs don't have the experience that VCs believe is necessary to rapidly build and manage large companies. And the entrepreneurs themselves may lack the confidence to pursue the growth rates dictated by the economics of the VC business. Some entrepreneurs we interviewed said that self-doubt about their management capabilities led them to avoid rapid expansion. Stephanie DiMarco, who cofounded Advent Software in 1983, had previously worked as a financial analyst and portfolio manager at the Bank of America, Summit Investments, and Cole

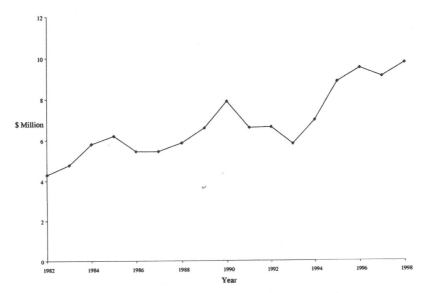

Figure 6.1. Median Revenues of *Inc.* 500 Companies

Source: *Inc.* magazine.

Table 6.1. Venture-Backed IPOs, 1984–1994

Year	No. of IPOS	Average Offering Valuation ($ million)	Median Age of Company at IPO (years)
1984	53	65.9	5
1985	47	69.7	3
1986	98	86.7	5
1987	81	85.1	5
1988	36	91.8	5
1989	39	100.0	5
1990	42	109.3	6
1991	122	118.5	6
1992	157	101.7	6
1993	165	100.5	7
1994	136	86.8	7
Totals/average	976	92.4	5

Source: Venture Capital Journal (February 1995), p. 45.

Financial Group. These experiences exposed her to the opportunity for developing portfolio management software for PCs, but did not prepare her to run and manage a business. DiMarco recalls holding back on hiring a marketing manager because "it was important for me to learn the business myself before I hired someone else. I had never managed anybody before. Instead of trying to create an organization, I was trying to prove myself first."* As Advent's founders gained experience and confidence, revenues grew, from $167,000 in 1983 to $2.3 million in 1988. From 1988 to 1996 revenues grew nearly twentyfold, reaching about $40 million in 1996. In 1995 Advent completed a public offering of its stock at a valuation of just over $125 million. But a rate of growth that satisfied DiMarco likely would not have been optimal from the point of view of a VC. Annual revenue of $2.3 million five years after start-up would likely not represent a stellar success to a VC whose initial investments are of that magnitude. Similarly, waiting twelve years for a public offering does not suit a limited partnership that is set to terminate after ten.

In exceptional cases, an inexperienced founder may team up with a seasoned manager; and in fact, VCs can help entrepreneurs create such teams. This requires, however, a high-potential idea or technology. If, as is often the case, entrepreneurs start off with a me-too concept or a differentiated product for a small market, they cannot initially recruit partners or employees with the experience profile that a firm like Primus Ventures would consider necessary to fund the venture.

---

* Asked what she might do differently if she had to start Advent over again, DiMarco said that she and her partner would "have grown the company faster" because they would "know how to run a company."

Contrast with Corporations

VCs have fewer resources to devote to scrutinizing and monitoring initiatives than do large corporations. VC firms have flat organizations comprising a small number of general partners and associates (who serve as apprentices to the partners). For instance, Institutional Venture Partners, a relatively large and prominent firm, Sahlman found, had just six partners and two associates managing funds of several hundred million dollars. Thus the total pool of labor available to evaluate and monitor investments is low. In contrast, large companies like IBM have several layers of hierarchy, staffs at divisional and corporate levels, and large budgets for consultants available to scrutinize and monitor investments.*

The VC process also involves fewer checks and balances. As in any partnership form of organization, a general partner's decision to proceed with a project is subject to some "mutual monitoring" by the other partners who have a financial interest in the returns. But as a matter of practice, while the other partners may express concerns, they usually will not override one another's decisions. Unlike credit committees in some banks, which vote on loan applications, peer reviews in VC firms generally involve "advice and consent." In contrast, a decision to launch a new product at a company such as IBM or P&G has to be reviewed and ratified at several levels, with the input of various staff functions. And (unlike partners in VC firms) the individuals who evaluate and ratify the initiative usually do not have a financial stake in the project. They do not, therefore, have much of an incentive to say "yes" without a thorough analysis.

Corporations also have significantly more capital available for investment than VCs, perhaps (per the Fama and Jensen analysis) because of the more extensive safeguards that their control systems provide investors.** As Sahlman points out, IBM spent three times as much on capital outlays and R&D in 1988 as the amounts disbursed by all professional VCs that year.[12] Similarly, Merck's budget for developing and marketing a drug or Intel's outlays on a single semiconductor fabrication facility are larger than the total capital of many VC funds.

To summarize: The initial conditions in a VC-backed start-up are quite different from those found in a typical promising start-up. The founders of VC-backed firms have unique ideas and deeper managerial experience. They can therefore raise significant amounts of capital from VCs, who also

---

* Note that my comments here apply only to the "quantity" of resources devoted to evaluating new initiatives, not their quality or effectiveness.
** U.S. regulations that encourage institutional investors to own the stocks of publicly traded corporations (Bhidé [1993b]) may also limit the funds such investors will supply to private partnerships. Large, established corporations may also have advantages in exploiting large-scale opportunities. For instance, as we saw in the previous chapter, they can use existing relationships and reputations to quickly secure customers, employees, credit, and so on.

provide more oversight and monitoring. The less qualified founders of promising ventures who copy or slightly modify others' concepts cannot raise much capital and are also not answerable to their investors. VC-backed start-ups do not have access to as much capital and do not face as much scrutiny and monitoring as corporate initiatives, however. The configuration of initial conditions in a VC-backed start-up thus falls between those of promising new ventures and corporate initiatives.

Implications of the Initial Conditions

In the section below we will discuss how initial conditions affect the opportunities VC-backed start-ups pursue, their approach to planning and to securing resources, and to their requirements for success. Reflecting the "in-between" nature of the initial conditions, we will find that VC-backed start-ups have hybrid features (in terms of opportunities, planning, and so on) that fall between those of promising and of corporate ventures.

Opportunities

VC-backed start-ups seek to exploit larger and less uncertain opportunities than the typical promising venture; compared to corporate initiatives, however, the size is smaller and the uncertainty is greater.

Uncertainty. The due diligence processes of VCs and their requirement for objective evidence lead them to avoid the types of uncertainty that the founders of promising ventures often exploit. VC-backed start-ups (like many promising new businesses) do seek to take advantage of exogenous change, but with two important differences that reduce the uncertainty of expected profits. First, VCs do not generally back ventures unless there is evidence, to use John Doerr's words, of a "large and rapidly growing" market. Thus most VCs did not fund start-ups in the PC industry in the 1970s, when there was great uncertainty about what large-scale needs, if any, PCs could satisfy. Second, VC-backed start-ups do not rely only on market turbulence. They start with some unique asset that the founders and VCs expect will distinguish the start-up from other players in the market and will afford some protection from adverse external developments. Proprietary products and technologies are thus expected to mitigate uncontrollable market uncertainties.

Similarly, VCs usually will not fund businesses when profits depend primarily on an entrepreneur's personal ability to satisfy fuzzy customer wants. VCs expect their firms to enjoy high profit margins because of a differentiated product or technology. The entrepreneur has the responsibility to effectively exploit this asset—a critical role that leads VCs to say that the quality of the founders is the most important determinant of the success of a start-up. But VCs generally do not fund ventures whose expected competitive advantages are more or less entirely embedded in the capabilities of the entrepreneur. The uncertain and unverifiable prospects of such businesses do not meet VC requirements for due diligence.

VCs do, however, have a greater tolerance for uncertainty and "missing information" than corporations because VC decisions do not involve as much multiparty scrutiny. The greater discretion available to VC general partners allows them to rely on judgments about the entrepreneur and the opportunity to fill in gaps left by missing information. VCs who are in close personal touch with entrepreneurs can monitor the subjective quality of their ongoing effort instead of having to rely just on the numbers. Their carried interest or share of partnership profits also gives VCs a greater incentive than corporate employees to approve uncertain projects. Consequently VCs may be more willing to take a chance on new markets and technologies sooner than large corporations will.

Size. VCs require, we have seen, their ventures to have the potential to generate much larger profits than the typical *Inc.* 500 start-up. Conversely, the availability of VC funding enables entrepreneurs to undertake larger ventures than they could through bootstrapping. At the same time, VCs do not control as much capital as corporate executives do, and the new businesses VCs create do not have to be as large. A multibillion-dollar corporation has to create much larger profit streams to satisfy the growth expectations of its investors and employees than does a $100 million venture capital fund. Therefore the typical VC pursues smaller opportunities (in terms investment and total expected return) that does the large corporation. (See the sidebar "Why VCs Pursue Smaller Projects.")

These differences in initiatives call into question claims about the inherent superiority of the decision-making processes of VC firms. Some commentators suggest that the flatter structures and financial incentives of VC firms make their decision-making processes more efficient than those of hierarchical corporations. That is, VCs get more bang for their evaluation and monitoring buck. Such claims, however, overlook the relationship between due diligence and access to capital. The more costly and deliberate due diligence of large corporations gives them more access to capital and encourages them to undertake initiatives that require greater up-front investment. The more streamlined decision-making of VC firms isn't better or worse—it is simply appropriate to a different kind of opportunity. Legendary venture capitalist Arthur Rock and other investors could provide Robert Noyce and Gordon E. Moore with the $2.5 million needed to launch Intel in 1968. VCs cannot, however, fund projects like Intel's 1993 Pentium chip which required an estimated up-front investment exceeding $750 million.* Access to capital on this scale requires the more elaborate checks and balances that the hierarchies of large corporations provide.

---

* Intel's total investment in the Pentium over the life of the chip reportedly exceeded $2 billion.

Why VCs Pursue Smaller Projects

By way of a simple illustration, let us compare the hypothetical corporation that we discussed in the previous chapter. Recall that this corporation has to generate $200 million in new profits with a VC fund whose goal is $100 million.

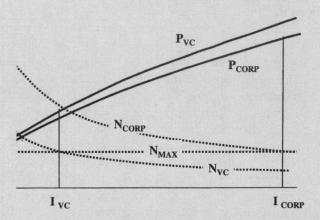

Figure 6.2. VC and Corporate Initiatives

Note: N_{CORP} = number of projects the corporation must undertake to meet its $200 m profit goals

N_{VC} = number of projects the VC firm must undertake to meet its $100 m profit goals

As shown in Figure 6.2, the corporation faces a range of projects, each of which requires an investment of I and is expected to produce profits of P_{corp}. The VC fund faces a slightly better distribution—investment I leads to profits of P_{vc},—because it is willing to tolerate more uncertainty. As before, the corporation has a minimum requirement of six man-months for evaluation and monitoring, for which it has a total of forty-two man-months available. The VC firm has both lower minimum requirements and available capacity, but in the same ratio, so that, like the corporation, it cannot undertake more than seven projects (N_{max}). The minimum profit per project required by the corporation is then twice that required by the VC firm ($28.57 million vs. $14.29 million). And to the degree that the ratio of profits to capital per project declines with the size of the investment, the corporation's minimum investment per project (I_{corp}) is more than twice as large as the VC's minimum investment (I_{vc}).

Planning vs. Adaptation

VC-backed ventures rely more on prior planning and research and less on adaptation than do promising start-ups for many of the same reasons that we discussed in the chapter on corporate initiatives. With few exceptions, securing funds from VCs requires an entrepreneur to write up a business plan and to do some research on customers and potential competitors. The due diligence that VCs conduct before making an investment supplements the entrepreneur's research efforts. More planning is also merited by the greater complexity and investment requirements of VC-backed start-ups. Businesses like Compaq or Lotus, which are started on a much more ambitious scale than promising start-ups, involve the coordination of many more employees and functions and therefore require more planning.

Similarly, although some adaptation to unforeseen circumstances is inevitable, VC-backed start-ups face less pressure to change their plans than do promising start-ups. The lower inherent uncertainty of the businesses and the greater initial research reduce the likelihood of surprises. The availability of capital reduces the incentive to deviate from initial plans. In contrast, the bootstrapped venture faces great pressure to generate cash; if the initial concept doesn't show positive cash flow, the entrepreneur has to change course quickly or wind up the business. The financial projections of VC-backed firms usually anticipate negative cash flows for several years, and VCs expect that the projections themselves will be overly optimistic. "Everything takes twice as long and thrice as much money or thrice as long and twice as much money" is an often-repeated adage in the business. Therefore, the failure to generate cash for a few years does not, by itself, force a change in strategy. In fact, to avoid diluting the focus on building long-run advantages, VCs often discourage entrepreneurs from pursuing short-term opportunities just to generate cash.

The nature of the entrepreneur's relationship with VCs also fosters adherence to the original plan. VCs and entrepreneurs often negotiate equity-sharing arrangements based on the achievement of certain milestones. According to Gompers and Lerner, VCs can "significantly dilute the entrepreneur's stake in subsequent financings" if they fail to meet these targets.[13] Worse yet, admitting to an erroneous forecast can jeopardize the entrepreneur's job. VCs who have selected a venture from many proposals, conducted due diligence, and advocated making the investment to their partners, we may expect, develop a personal commitment to the concept. If the entrepreneur subsequently proposes a radical change in course, VCs have to decide whether their initial assessment of the idea was erroneous or whether the entrepreneur lacks competence. The entrepreneur's claims about a new strategy rekindle memories of the confidence expressed in the original proposal. The investors have to wonder, "Are we being fooled twice?" Endorsing the proposed new strategy, rather than changing management, requires VCs to discard what seems like hard evidence of the entrepreneur's poor planning, bad judgment, or overselling, and to admit the inadequacy of their own research.

The risk of being removed for proposing a radical change can, in turn, encourage entrepreneurs to try to make their initial plans work even when they lose faith in them. The former CEO of an advanced materials company described the pressures to stick with untenable strategies that outside investors can generate.

> When we started, well-defined markets for our materials did not exist. My first job as CEO was to figure out what product market we would go after, so I hit the road for about three months. I identified a product—aluminum oxide substrates—but by the time we got to market, the competition had improved and our substrates never really took off. I realized that, given our size, we should have been manufacturing to order rather than for the market at large. But by that time we were already stumbling and I was losing credibility with the investors. They weren't interested in a new strategy. They just wanted the substrates to be profitable. I wish I had stood my ground and said, "I'm turning off the furnace tomorrow." But I didn't quite have the guts to do that.

Conversely, a VC's incentive to stick with a strategy, if not a specific founder, can lead to the eventual fruition of business ideas that self-financed entrepreneurs would have to abandon. For instance, National Demographics and Lifestyles (NDL) took four rounds of financing (see the sidebar "Sticking to Plan: The Case of NDL") before it achieved economic viability. Cofounder Jock Bickert says that he and his partner seriously underestimated the capital and time it would take to reach the critical mass needed to become profitable. Without the support of VCs who were used to overly optimistic projections, the founders of NDL would not have been able to make a fundamentally sound concept work, although they might have successfully redirected their energies to a less capital-intensive enterprise. Whereas capital constraints may require bootstrapped entrepreneurs to quickly reorient their businesses, VC-backed entrepreneurs have the incentive and the option to stick to their basic concept.

This is not to suggest that VC-backed start-ups rigidly adhere to plans, merely that the nature of the entrepreneur-investor relationship makes the degree and the occurrence of deviations less than in self-financed businesses. And when compared to corporate initiatives, VC-backed start-ups rely more on adaptation and less on planning. This is because the irreducible initial uncertainty is greater, the administrative costs of changing course are lower, and the availability of capital and the capacity to sustain losses are not as great.

Securing Resources: Problems and Strategies

Problems. The problems VC-backed start-ups face in securing resources fall between those of bootstrapped ventures and those of corporate initiatives. Like any de novo business, VC-backed start-ups face "a liability of newness." They have neither an existing source of profits that can sustain ongoing losses nor an established track record. Their customers and potential

Sticking to Plan: The Case of NDL

Jock Bickert and Rob Johnson started NDL in 1976. They planned to collect data contained in the product registration cards that purchasers of items such as refrigerators and stereos submit to manufacturers. The data would enable NDL to compile better marketing lists than those traditionally derived from motor vehicle registrations, telephone listings, and so on. According to Tom Claflin, a VC who invested in the company, NDL "looked like a money-making business. The potential operating leverage was tremendous, even allowing for a certain degree of optimism on their part."[14]

In December 1979, NDL raised $1.2 million from VCs. But by mid-1980 the need for more funding became apparent. Purchases of mailing lists required a minimum number of names, and it was taking longer than expected to secure them from the manufacturers who controlled the product registration cards. Bickert and Johnson raised an additional $1.6 million, which they estimated would be sufficient to generate positive cash flow. Again, however, NDL failed to meet its projection, forcing it to raise another round of financing. The VC, Claflin, commented:

> All the venture capitalists believe in the company, and in Jock and Rob. Yet this is their fourth time back to the well for capital, when the money raised in each of the previous rounds was supposed to have been sufficient. The company has consistently fallen short of its revenue projections. Although there has been definite progress, the company is once again coming back to the well, at a time when we are a long way from turning the corner. Before the venture group puts in another $1 or $1.5 million, we must address the key issue: Is it just taking longer to prime the pump than we expected or is there something fundamentally wrong with the concept?[15]

The VCs ultimately did provide more money, which enabled NDL to turn the corner. A few years later, NDL was acquired for approximately $80 million, to the great satisfaction and relief of the founders and the VCs.

recruits face high switching costs. Some factors mitigate these problems, however. Proprietary technologies or other sources of competitive advantage increase the expected likelihood of survival; they can also provide a benefit large enough to offset the resource providers' fixed switching costs. The credentials, personal reputations, and prior relationships of the founders provide reassurance to resource providers. Founders who are generally more qualified than bootstrapped entrepreneurs and who have given up higher-paying jobs may also be expected to be more committed to the enterprise. Greater commitment may also be inferred from the larger initial capital that is sunk.

Venture capitalists contribute to the credibility of the start-up through their scrutiny and certification. Their financial reserves may not be of the same magnitude as those of a company like IBM, but they can certainly keep a business afloat longer than can a bootstrapped entrepreneur. Venture capitalists can also draw on their own reputations and contracts to help the start-up secure customers, employees, suppliers, and so on.

As with corporate ventures, however, the greater expected scale of success poses quantity and quality problems for VC-based start-ups. A VC-backed start-up cannot earn a satisfactory return by securing a few customers, and it cannot rely for its growth on the labor of the founders or inexperienced employees.

Strategies. Although VC-backed start-ups have more capital than promising ventures, they do not have the capacity of a corporation to underwrite others' risks, or (with some exceptions, such as Netscape) to "buy" market share. So they have to use, at least to some degree, strategies that exploit others' cognitive biases that we have seen the founders of promising businesses rely on extensively. There are, however, two notable differences between the strategies of VC-backed start-ups and promising start-ups. First, the founders of promising businesses often have to undertake an exhaustive, hit-or-miss search to find the right customers. VC-backed start-ups, which typically serve more defined markets and have conducted more extensive prior research, can target their customers more easily. Second, promising start-ups often rely on employees whose alternative employment prospects are poor, because they cannot afford the salaries required to attract individuals with better qualifications and because a share of their equity has little perceived value. VC-backed start-ups cannot only pay higher salaries, they also can use stock or stock options as a recruiting tool because experienced outside investors have ascribed a high value to their equity. Thus whereas promising start-ups rely on offering an immediate benefit, VC-backed start-ups can hold out a credible prospect of significant long-term returns.

Requirements for Success

In the previous chapter we saw that the quality of the initial plans plays a more important role in the success of corporate initiatives than it does in promising start-ups and that organizational capabilities matter more than the talents of one or two individuals. In VC-backed start-ups we find that the soundness of the initial plan is more important than in promising start-ups but that the capacity to refine and adapt the initial plan is more important than in corporate initiatives. Similarly, the joint efforts of a team play more of a role in VC-backed start-ups than in promising start-ups. But compared to corporate initiatives, this team is not as large or as heterogeneous, and the role of the top decision-makers is more critical.

Initial plans and conditions. Having the right plan or concept from the outset has greater importance in a VC-backed start-up than in a promising start-up. Promising start-ups are "defined" mainly by their founders rather than by some initial idea or technology; consequently the entrepreneur can radically change a flawed idea without terminating the "business." More-

over, with few employees or investors involved, the obstacles to change are
not severe. A VC-backed start-up has, from the beginning, an identity and
a life that goes beyond just its founders—it is "defined" by its core idea or
technology and by the VCs and employees enlisted by the entrepreneur to
exploit the idea. And as we have seen, the participation of these multiple
players makes changing the core concept difficult. Few VC-backed ventures, therefore, can survive major flaws in their initial plans and assumptions. When Momenta Corporation could not develop a pen-based
computer with accurate handwriting recognition, or when Stardent stumbled in its launch of superfast workstations, the ventures folded. In such
cases, little remains except perhaps the legal shell. Therefore getting the
initial conditions and plans right is crucial.*

At the same time, the greater uncertainty makes it difficult for the decision-makers in a VC-backed start-up to anticipate contingencies to the
same degree as in a corporate initiative. Therefore the capacity to adapt
(within the framework of the original concept or plan) to unforeseen circumstances plays a greater role in the success of VC-backed start-ups.

Team and founder contributions. In the typical promising venture, the
entrepreneur's personal contribution has critical importance. The greater
size and complexity of VC-backed ventures require a larger team of
employees, whose joint efforts have a significant influence on the success of
the enterprise. According to the folk wisdom of the VC industry, a great
founder cannot compensate for a mediocre team. At the same time, the
numbers of individuals and functions involved in a VC-backed start-up are
often smaller than in a significant corporate initiative. Therefore the quality of these individuals (including the founders) and their interpersonal
chemistry have more significant roles than the "organizational" routines
and cultures discussed in the chapter on corporate initiatives.

We may further note that the set of traits and skills that determine the
effectiveness of the founders of VC-backed start-ups is broader than the set
that the founders of promising start-ups need. Tolerance for objective risk
(or low aversion to loss) can have a major impact on an individual's propensity to start a VC-backed business. Whereas the founders of promising
businesses have little to lose, the founders of VC-backed start-ups can face
significant opportunity costs. Direct financial exposure can also be high
because VCs often encourage entrepreneurs to invest their personal savings
(or sometimes the proceeds from second mortgages on their homes) in their
ventures to demonstrate their commitment to the enterprise.

A long-term vision and the ability to communicate it to others also play
more important roles in VC-backed start-ups. To secure funding and to

---

* To emphasize the point that there are no second chances, one entrepreneur distributed T-shirts emblazoned with a saber-toothed tiger to his employees. In attacking a
mammoth, the entrepreneur told his employees, the tiger had one chance to kill. If the
first attack failed, the intended prey would usually destroy its predator.

recruit a top-quality team, entrepreneurs have to envision and articulate a long-term path that leads to the creation of significant new value in which others can share. The founder of a promising business, in contrast, can make do, at least initially, with opportunistic adaptation. Similarly, to launch a larger and more complex venture, VC-backed entrepreneurs also require administrative or managerial talents and experience, qualities that the founders of promising ventures, who do it all themselves, need not have.

3. A Temporary Phase?

In the sections above I suggested that the relatively small number of VC-backed start-ups reflects a scarcity of entrepreneurs who have the ideas and qualifications to qualify for significant funding. Alternatively, it could be argued that the VC industry is in a transitional state (see the sidebar, "A New Industry") and has not yet attracted its equilibrium level of funds; that is, the VC industry faces a capital shortage. As its funding pool increases, VCs will back more entrepreneurs, and VC-backed start-ups will become much less unusual. Below I will argue that whereas professional VC firms represent a relatively new form of financial intermediation, the notion of shortages of venture capital does not seem consistent with the distribution and returns of VC investments.

Starting from a virtually nonexistent base, the number of VC-backed start-ups has grown exponentially, but their proportion of the overall population of start-ups remains extremely small. In the record year of 1987, for instance, VCs invested in just 344 seed and start-up investments. The proportion of venture-backed firms in the *Inc.* 500 lists of the 1980s and 1990s remained between 5 and 10 percent. Most of the *Inc.* 500 founders I interviewed were aware of VCs but chose not to approach them or tried to raise VC funding and failed.

It could be argued that VCs have gained visibility but not sufficient funds. This reasoning suggests that if VCs had more capital they would relax the criteria they use and fund more start-ups. But if in fact capital

A New Industry

The VC industry has gained prominence and significant capital in just the past two decades. In the 1950s, with the exception of a couple of firms such as American Research and Development (founded in 1946), professional firms that specialized in funding new ventures did not exist. The authors of a Federal Reserve study on venture capital note that in the 1950s many ventures were financed on "an ad hoc, deal by deal basis" by syndicates of wealthy individuals and institutional investors organized by investment banks.[16] The Small Business Investment Act of 1958 provided for the establishment of Small Business Investment Companies or SBICs. SBICs, forerunners of modern VC firms, were intended to "provide professionally managed capital to risky companies" and could supplement their capital with Small Business Administration (SBA) loans. But many SBICs "concentrated on providing debt financing to small companies that had positive cash flows" to "take advantage of the leverage provided by SBA loans." And as an SBA administrator told Congress in June 1968, the SBA faced losses of about $18 million in the program because of "the wrong people who operate[d] SBICs." About a third of SBICs were "problem companies" because of "dubious practices and self-dealing." With tightened supervision, the number of SBICs fell from about 700 in 1968 to 276 in 1977.[17]

A "hot new issues market" in 1968–69 engendered a spurt in the formation of limited partnerships organized by professional VCs. In 1969 such partnerships raised a record $171 million. By modern standards, the partnerships were small, with funds between $2.5 million and $10 million, raised mainly from individuals. The next eight years saw modest growth, with about $100 million of new commitments to limited partnerships annually. "Numerous favorable regulatory and tax changes" between 1977 and 1980 led to "explosive growth" in the early 1980s. Commitments to limited partnerships in 1980–82 were two and a half times the commitments during the entire decade of the 1970s. Following this surge, commitments to VC partnerships fluctuated between $2 billion and $3 billion for the rest of the 1980s. Commitments fell in the 1990–91 recession, but then rebounded to reach a new high of $4.2 billion.[18] As shown in Table 6.2, overall the outstanding stock of venture capital rose almost eightfold, from $4.5 billion in 1980 to $34 billion in 1994.

Table 6.2. Venture Capital Partnerships

Year	New Commitments to VC Partnerships	Number of New Partnerships Formed	Average Partnership Size (millions of dollars)	Venture Capital Stock Outstanding (billions of dollars)
1980	.62	26	28.0	4.5
1981	.83	40	24.3	5.8
1982	1.21	40	27.4	7.6
1983	2.49	76	39.1	12.1
1984	3.02	83	38.4	16.3
1985	1.77	59	32.8	19.6
1986	2.01	59	51.6	24.1
1987	3.11	78	43.7	29.0
1988	2.06	54	44.3	31.1
1989	2.76	64	47.6	34.4
1990	1.65	21	52.0	35.9
1991	1.37	21	50.8	32.9
1992	2.57	33	64.7	31.1
1993	2.89	37	78.9	34.8
1994	4.20			34.1
1980–94	32.56			

Source: Fenn, Liang, and Prowse (1995), pp. 12–13.

shortages had led VCs to adopt overly stringent criteria, we should expect
to see exceptionally high returns and low failure rates. In fact, as Figure 6.3
shows, we do not find statistically significant differences between the average returns of VC funds and publicly traded stocks (which also offer
investors greater liquidity). And notwithstanding a careful selection
process, a high proportion of VC-backed projects have failed to yield attractive returns. Even in the pre-1980 period, when we might expect the small
number of VC firms to have been even more selective than they are today,
the proportion of successful investments does not seem to have been especially high. For instance, the first modern, professionally managed VC firm,
American Research and Development (ARD), generated a 15.8 percent
annualized rate of return over its twenty-five-year existence as an independent entity from 1946 to 1971. But excluding a single $70,000 invest-
ment in Digital Equipment (out of total investments of $48 million),
ARD's annual returns were only 7.4 percent, compared to 12.8 percent on
the Dow Jones Industrial average over the same period.[19]

VC returns in the past two decades seem to have followed a boom-to-
bust pattern, suggesting capital "shortages" have been cyclical and temporary rather than chronic. Moreover, in periods of ample availability of funds,
VCs seem to pay higher prices for the stock of businesses that fit their profile rather than to materially alter their criteria in the direction of the *Inc.*
500-type start-ups. Gompers and Lerner estimate that a doubling of capital
available to venture funds leads to a 7 percent to 21 percent increase in the
prices they pay for their stakes.[20] The "over investment" in favored companies and sectors, Sahlman's and Stevenson's paper[21] on the disk-drive industry suggests, then leads to low returns and a temporary "bust."

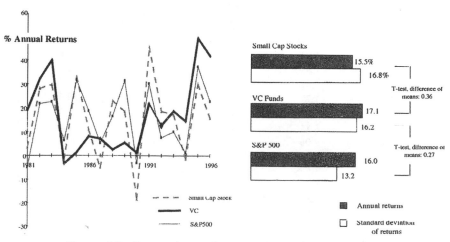

Figure 6.3. Comparison of Annual Investment Returns
Note: Small Cap stocks refers to the *Wilshire Next 1750 Stock* index.
Source: Venture Economics and Datastream.

The distribution of VC investments also suggests that more capital would not necessarily lead to a large increase in the number of VC-backed start-ups. A significant and increasing portion of the funds raised in the so-called private equity market has been used for leveraged buyouts and other such investments in established companies. Fenn, Liang, and Prowse, authors of a Federal Reserve study of the industry, argue that the shift away from "traditional" venture capital investments has been "due principally to an abundance of profitable opportunities" in established companies rather than greater risk aversion or change in the culture of VC firms. Venture investing in the 1980s, they note, produced lower returns than nonventure investing, suggesting that "private equity capital has flowed to its most productive uses."[22]

Even in their "traditional" venture investments, VCs seem to favor "later stage" companies over de novo ventures. The National Venture Capital Association's annual report shows that in 1996, 77 percent of companies receiving venture capital funding were three years old or older. Over 80 percent had more than twenty-five employees. Similarly, data collected by Fenn, Liang, and Prowse from the *Venture Capital Journal* shows that only about a third of investments are "early-stage." Two-thirds are "later-stage" investments (see Table 6.3) in companies that Fenn, Liang, and Prowse write "have a proven technology and a proven market for their product. They are typically growing fast and generating profits." Such investments are "larger than early-stage investments, ranging from $2 million to $5 million, and are held for a shorter term, simply because the firm is closer to being sold publicly or to another firm."[23]

I do not mean to downplay the role of later-stage investments. VCs, for instance, helped turn Cisco from a small, struggling enterprise into the world's leading supplier of the "routers" that link computer networks in different locations. Sandy Lerner and Len Bosack started Cisco in 1984. They put a used mainframe in their garage and persuaded friends and relatives to work for deferred pay.[24] They financed the venture by running up bills on their credit cards, and at one point in 1986 Lerner took a job as a corporate data processing manager to provide more cash. In 1987 Cisco received funding from Sequoia Capital. Cisco's founders and Sequoia agreed, according to partner Donald Valentine, that besides providing financing, "Sequoia would find and recruit management, and we would help create a management process. None of which existed in the company when we arrived." Valentine hired an experienced manager, John Morgridge, to run Cisco in 1989; he duly installed a professional management process and paved the way for an IPO in February 1990. As of November 30, 1998, the market value of Cisco's stock exceeded $118 billion. It booked revenues of $8.45 billion in 1988.

McAfee Associates founder John McAfee credits VCs for the transformation of his bootstrapped business into a large, publicly traded company. John McAfee started selling software to combat computer viruses in 1989. The company was entirely self-financed, and the founder represented the

Table 6.3. Investments by Venture Capital Partnerships, 1980–94

Year	Total Amount Invested (billions of dollars)	Number of Companies Invested in	Average Investment Per Company (millions of dollars)	Early-stage Investments as a Percentage of Total
1980	.61	504	1.21	—
1981	1.16	797	1.46	—
1982	1.45	918	1.58	
1983	2.58	1,320	1.95	35
1984	2.73	1,410	1.96	34
1985	2.67	1,388	1.92	30
1986	3.22	1,512	2.13	35
1987	3.97	1,740	2.26	29
1988	3.85	1,530	2.52	29
1989	3.38	1,465	2.31	21
1990	2.30	1,176	1.96	30
1991	1.36	792	1.72	31
1992	2.54	1,093	2.33	24
1993	3.07	969	3.13	24
1994	2.74	1,011	2.71	37

Source: Fenn, Liang, and Prowse (1995), p. 14.

company's entire management team until 1991, when he sold shares to two venture capital firms. The VCs recruited William Larson to become CEO. Larson, a veteran of Apple Computers and Sun Microsystems, and the VCs recruited other experienced managers, focused on the growing network management industry, made acquisitions to expand the product line, and helped establish basic controls. In 1992 McAfee went public. On November 30, 1998, the company (renamed as Network Associates) had a market value of $6.6 billion and annual sales of about $900 million.*

The preference of many VCs for later-stage investments has significance for my argument in what it reveals about their area of comparative advantage. The VC model best suits initiatives in the middle of the investment-uncertainty-profit diagram. VC funding allows only some exceptional ventures, such as Compaq and Lotus, to start out in that space. These exceptions apart, firms receive VC funding *after* the high initial uncertainties about the size of the market and the profitability of the business have been reduced (see Fig. 6.4). John McAfee had a profitable product and $15 mil-

* VCs have played a less active role in other later-stage investments. Microsoft apparently sold a small number of shares to VCs shortly before its IPO, mainly for the reassurance that VCs could provide to prospective public purchasers of its stock. Moreover a majority of companies, including Wal-Mart, HP, Oracle, and Dell, make the transition to public ownership without ever raising venture capital. Between 1978 and 1997, according to data compiled by Gompers and Lerner (1999), the number of venture-backed IPOs as a percent of all IPOs ranged from a low of 3.74 percent in 1979 to a high of 36.22 percent in 1995.

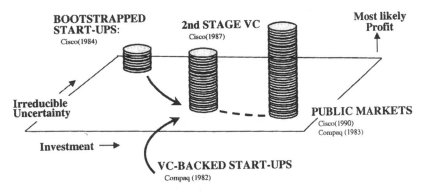

BOOTSTRAPPED START-UPS:
Cisco(1984)

2nd STAGE VC
Cisco(1987)

Most likely Profit

Irreducible Uncertainty

PUBLIC MARKETS
Cisco(1990)
Compaq (1983)

Investment →

VC-BACKED START-UPS
Compaq (1982)

Figure 6.4. Stages of Funding

lion in cash in the bank when he sold stock in his company to VCs. When Cisco secured VC financing in 1987, it faced a serious shortage of cash, but it was making profits. According to cofounder Bosack, the company was booking $250,000 to $350,000 in monthly sales "without a professional sales staff and without an official conventionally recognized marketing campaign. So it wasn't a bad business just right then." Up to that point Bosack and Lerner had failed to get any funding—Sequoia was the seventy-seventh venture capital firm the founders approached. The low likely profit and the high uncertainty associated with most start-ups seem incompatible with the structure and decision-making process of the typical VC firm.

To summarize: The availability of appropriate investment opportunities rather than of capital limits the number of VC-backed start-ups. Perhaps Hewlett and Packard bootstrapped their company because there were not many sources of professional financing available for start-ups at the time. But capital shortages cannot explain the high proportion of bootstrapped *Inc.* 500 companies in the midst of a VC boom. An increase in the funds available will not make VC-backed start-ups a common phenomenon unless there is a corresponding increase in the number of appropriately endowed individuals with proprietary ideas who want to start businesses.

4. Summary and Conclusions

VCs provide start-up funding to an élite group of entrepreneurs who have innovative ideas or technologies and a verifiable record of business or technical achievement. The capital, ideas, and expertise enable the start-ups to leapfrog into the middle region of the investment-uncertainty-profit diagram—a place that takes promising businesses many years to reach. Compared to promising businesses, VC-backed start-ups also rely more on prior planning and research and less on opportunistic adaptation. They can secure resources more easily but also face more stringent quality and quantity requirements. And the talent and drive of the founders of VC-backed start-ups represent two of several factors that determine the success of the venture.

7

Revolutionary Ventures

This chapter looks at ventures that offer a revolutionary new product or service. It represents the last stop in our tour of the investment-uncertainty-profit diagram. Section 1 summarizes the differentiating features of the archetype. Sections 2, 3, and 4 illustrate these features with three examples of revolutionary ventures.

In the popular imagination, Frederick Smith's launch of Federal Express represents the epitome of entrepreneurship. Smith had a bold vision for a company that would operate a national network of jets, trucks, and personnel to provide reliable overnight delivery of letters and small packages. The charismatic former Marine Corps pilot risked his personal wealth, raised about $70 million—a substantial amount for an individual entrepreneur in the early 1970s—from outside investors and lenders, built a fiercely loyal workforce, lobbied regulators and politicians, and after many brushes with bankruptcy made his company's service a ubiquitous verb ("to FedEx").

Although such stories are captivating, ventures such as Federal Express that provide a revolutionary product or service lie far outside the normal pattern. Whereas VC-backed start-ups are unusual, revolutionary ventures are extremely rare. Moreover, many transitional businesses pursue opportunities with the same investment, uncertainty, and profit profile as VC-backed start-ups. In contrast, the region on the investment-uncertainty-profit diagram that revolutionary ventures occupy is sparsely populated. Only larger-than-life entrepreneurs can undertake initiatives that require large investment *and* involve high uncertainty.

Examining these outliers reinforces our understanding of more typical new initiatives. Given the small population of the revolutionary ventures, we cannot, however, illustrate their features with many examples. I will therefore use just three cases: Frederick Smith's Federal Express, Daniel Ludwig's attempt to develop a timber, pulp, and farming enterprise in the jungles of the Jari region of Brazil; and Motorola's ongoing Iridium project to provide a global, satellite-based, cellular phone service.*

1. Features

Below I discuss the features of revolutionary ventures started by individual entrepreneurs; as we will see in the section "Motorola's Iridium Project," however, many of these features also apply to revolutionary corporate ventures.

Initial conditions. A revolutionary venture requires major new insight about customer needs; often these needs are latent or not well articulated. Revolutionary ventures also typically involve creative new processes or technologies; opportunities to provide valuable products or services are rarely overlooked unless there are serious technological problems in providing them. For instance, the recognition of an untapped market for a reliable overnight delivery service was a necessary but not sufficient condition for starting Federal Express. To serve a large network of cities reliably with a relatively small fleet of planes, Smith and his associates also had to design a nonlinear hub-and-spoke logistics system.

Founders of revolutionary ventures require considerable personal wealth, contacts, and credibility to fund their ventures. Revolutionary ventures require substantial capital to develop and refine new technologies; to acquire dedicated assets or infrastructure (radical innovations often preclude the use of standardized or off-the-shelf inputs); to educate consumers and distributors about the benefits of the offering; and to cover losses until the venture attains critical mass. As one example, Smith had to raise substantial amounts of capital because Federal Express could not use commercial flights. To provide its unique service of overnight delivery, the company acquired a dedicated fleet of jets. The jets, a central hub, operations in twenty-five states, and several hundred trained employees had to be in place before the company could open for business. The venture also had to absorb losses (amounting to more than $29 million in its first twenty-six months of operations) before revenues became large enough to cover the high fixed costs of the enterprise.

Type of opportunity. Revolutionary ventures have to hold the promise of very large profits to justify the substantial initial investments. For instance, to raise capital for launching Federal Express, Frederick Smith had to demonstrate the potential for securing a significant share of an untapped $1 billion market. Billionaire Daniel Ludwig started on his Jari forestry venture anticipating a worldwide shortage of wood that would yield him profits on the scale of the fortune he had already accumulated in shipping.[1]

---

* The descriptions include more detail and color than I provided in previous examples in order to highlight the distinctive features of the archetype. I hope readers find the stories interesting; those who do not may skim sections 2, 3, and 4.

Revolutionary ventures also involve significant uncertainty vis-à-vis customer preferences, whether the new technologies and processes developed will work, and sometimes, because of the size of the project, regulatory issues. In the case of Federal Express, for instance, the customers surveyed by market researchers said they wanted the option of reliable overnight delivery; but it was impossible to determine how many would actually pay a premium for the service and whether the hub-and-spoke transportation system would provide the reliability that was central to the idea. The willingness of the Civil Aeronautics Board (CAB) to grant the regulatory waivers Federal Express needed to fly its jets was also a source of uncertainty.*

Planning and adaptation. Revolutionary ventures require extensive prior research and planning to attract capital on a large scale and to coordinate the deployment of heterogeneous resources; as we will see, Frederick Smith commissioned two consulting firms to undertake independent studies of the feasibility of the Federal Express concept. Unlike the founders of promising businesses who launch their business in weeks or months of getting their idea, it took Smith about eight years from the time he conceived of a business that would provide overnight delivery to the time it became operational.

The scope for adapting or changing the basic concept (for the reasons that we discussed in connection with corporate and VC-backed ventures) is very limited after the business is launched. If the core assumptions of the Federal Express plan had been mistaken, the start-up would have failed. But given the high irreducible uncertainty that cannot be eliminated through prior research, the entrepreneur often has to change important elements of the plan; for instance, Federal Express had to adopt a new marketing approach to generate adequate revenues.

Securing resources. Revolutionary ventures face significant hurdles in securing resources of sufficient quantity and quality. They have to attract a large number of customers to cover fixed costs. The large size and high uncertainty also demand highly talented and motivated employees. To secure such employees, the entrepreneur has to rely on the potential of large long-term financial payoffs, as well as on the psychic benefits of participating in a revolutionary enterprise.

Requirements for success. To succeed, a revolutionary venture must fulfill requirements much more demanding than those met by the other types of start-ups we have discussed. The founder of a revolutionary venture must start with the right basic concept *and* cope with serious unexpected problems. Success requires highly skilled and cohesive teams as well as entrepreneurs with exceptional qualities and talents. The entrepreneur must have a

---

* Unlike many promising or VC-backed start-ups, revolutionary ventures usually do not, however, seek to capitalize on exogenous turbulence. In fact, with great external uncertainty, customers and investors may be hesitant to back a radical product and technology until the environment settles down.

high tolerance for uncertainty and for risk. As we will see in the Frederick Smith and Daniel Ludwig examples, entrepreneurs who dedicate themselves to a grand plan face huge personal losses if they fail.

Vision, tenacity, and charisma also are critical qualities for revolutionary entrepreneurs. Founders of promising businesses, we have seen, often start with a short-term opportunity rather than a long-term plan. Persistence with a failing concept can impair their chances of success. And as long as they can make a few critical sales, they do not need great charisma. In contrast, the revolutionary entrepreneur has to have an audacious vision and the fortitude to stay the course through serious crises and setbacks. The entrepreneur also needs an evangelical ability and personal magnetism to attract and retain investors, employees, customers and other resource providers.

2. Frederick Smith's Federal Express

Frederick Smith's launch of Federal Express illustrates most of the features of revolutionary ventures outlined above. Below I will describe Smith's background (or "endowments") and how he developed and researched the concept, secured the resources needed to launch the company, and coped with numerous crises before Federal Express finally turned a profit. The facts and quotes I will use are drawn from *Absolutely, Positively Overnight* by Robert Sigafoos.

Background

Frederick ("Fred") Wallace Smith was the son of a wealthy Memphis businessman (also Frederick Smith) and his fourth wife, Sally. His father had made his fortune in fast-food restaurants and a bus line: The elder Smith invested in a struggling restaurant chain called the Toddle House in 1934 and expanded its operations throughout the United States. He also built one of the largest bus lines in the South, which Greyhound Corp. subsequently purchased. When Smith was born in 1944, his father was forty-nine and his mother, twenty-three. His father died when Smith was just four, and young Frederick was raised by his mother in Memphis.

Smith was born with a bone-socket hip disorder called Calvé-Perthes disease, which required him to wear braces and use crutches throughout grammar school. He grew out of the hip disorder and distinguished himself as a student leader and as an athlete at the prep school he attended.[2] He entered Yale in 1962. Unlike Gates, who did well in the graduate-level math courses he took as a freshman at Harvard, Smith did not shine academically in college. He graduated with a B minus average and says he was a "crummy student."[3] Smith was also more sociable than Gates, however, and organized the Yale Flying Club, was elected to the prestigious Skull and Bones Society, and enrolled in the U.S. Marine Corps platoon leaders' program.

At graduation Smith was commissioned as a second lieutenant in the Marine Corps and sent to active duty in Vietnam. By the time he was discharged in July 1969, he had attained the rank of captain and had been awarded the Silver Star, Bronze Star, two Purple Hearts, the Navy Commendation Medal, and the Vietnamese Cross of Gallantry. According to Sigafoos, Vietnam was "an awakening" for Smith, exposing him to a much less privileged world than that to which he had become accustomed in Memphis and at Yale.*

In August 1969, shortly after his return from Vietnam, Smith purchased a controlling interest in a struggling Little Rock company called Arkansas Aviation Sales. His stepfather, a former general in the air force, had taken over the company, which provided maintenance services for turboprop aircraft and corporate jets, in 1967. Upon taking control, Smith turned Arkansas Aviation into an "aggressive business buying and selling used corporate jets."[4] Smith also began investing in real estate.

Smith's purchase of Arkansas Aviation and his real estate investments were financed through an inheritance he had received when he turned twenty-one. Sigafoos does not provide the size of this inheritance, but we may infer from subsequent events that it was on the order of several million dollars. Smith was also the beneficiary of a trust called the Frederick Smith Enterprise Company ("Enterprise Company"), whose assets included real estate in Memphis and Squibb-Beechnut stock worth about $13 million in 1971. Smith was the 38.5 percent beneficiary of the Enterprise Company; two half sisters, Fredette and Laura, had slightly smaller shares. The National Bank of Commerce in Memphis acted as trustee. In 1965 Smith had joined the board of directors of the Enterprise Company, and in 1971 he became president of the board. Enterprise and his personal inheritance would provide substantial funds for starting Federal Express.

By 1971 Smith had also established "a good credit relationship with the local banks." The bankers saw "a financial golden boy, bright, handsome, wealthy, self-confident, a battle-decorated leader possessing a proven business record—even though that record was less than 36 months old."[5] Thus when he started Federal Express, Smith had access to both debt and equity capital.

Developing the Concept

Smith had conceived of the original idea for Federal Express in the course of writing a term paper at Yale in 1965. The paper had suggested that there

---

* Sigafoos (1983), p. 26. Quite possibly the Vietnam experience helped mold a charismatic personality who evoked great loyalty. In the colorful words of an employee Sigafoos interviewed: "If Fred Smith lined up all 13,000 Federal Express employees on the Hernando de Soto Bridge in Memphis and said, 'Jump!' 99 percent of them would leap into the Mississippi River below. That's how much faith they've got in this guy" (Sigafoos [1983], p. 23).

was "a huge market" for "an efficient service for moving high-priority, time-sensitive mail shipments like medicines, computer parts, and electronics."[6] This market was not being well served by air freight shippers who relied on the passenger route systems: "Air freight would only work in a system designed specifically for it, not as a simple add on to passenger service."[7] Under the existing system, packages were "hippety-hopping around the country from city to city and from airline to airline before reaching their destination."[8] The paper did not provide much detail about an alternative system; it was a last-minute effort for which Smith famously received a grade of C.

Smith returned to the idea after he began running Arkansas Aviation. Its first incarnation was a scheme to contract with the Federal Reserve System "to move cash letters within the system on an overnight basis."[9] The check-clearing process at the time was "cumbersome and inefficient. It often took two or more days to get checks sorted and distributed back through the system to the correct Fed district."[10] Smith proposed a scheme whereby "planes would pick up cash letters from 36 points in the United States, fly them to a central sorting hub, and, overnight, fly the sorted items to an appropriate drop-off point."[11] In May 1971 Smith asked the Enterprise board to provide $250,000 of seed capital to a company that would provide such a service. Smith promised to match the Enterprise investment with his personal funds. Upon receiving approval from the board, Smith incorporated Federal Express in Delaware on June 18, 1971.

On June 29, Smith persuaded the Enterprise board to guarantee a $3.6 million loan to purchase two Dassault Falcon 20 fan-jets from Pan American World Airways. Purchasing the two jets, Smith claimed, would convince the Federal Reserve that the new venture was serious and would lead to the grant of a five-year contract for transporting checks. With such a contract in hand, Federal Express could secure credit for buying more jets. Smith's half sisters and the other board members agreed to put up $4 million of Squibb-Beechnut stock as collateral for the Falcon fan-jet loan. Shortly after the planes had been acquired, however, the Federal Reserve project collapsed—the Federal Reserve district banks "could not reach a consensus on Smith's proposal. Each wanted to arrange for its own transportation network."[12] Thus, by the summer of 1971, Federal Express was merely "a shell organization" with two jets, Smith, and two employees.[13]

Smith continued to pursue the idea of starting an air cargo company. An investment banker suggested that Smith commission a research study that would "verify what you think the status of the domestic air freight industry is like."[14] In December 1971 Smith retained national consulting firm A. T. Kearney (for a $75,000 fee) to estimate the market size, capital requirements, and profitability of a business that would serve "businesses shipping priority items"—a clientele that would include banks, brokerage houses, department stores, and petrochemical companies. Shortly after commissioning the A. T. Kearney study, Smith visited a much smaller outfit—the Aerospace Advance Planning Group (AAPG)—a New York-based consulting firm started by Art Bass, Vincent Fagan, and Tucker Taylor, men who had previously sold corporate airplanes for Pan American Business Jets. According to Sigafoos, "Smith felt a special rapport with Bass, Fagan, and Taylor and hired them to duplicate the market study A. T. Kearney had just been hired to do," for the same $75,000 fee.[15] Neither group was told, however, that the other was at work on the same assignment.

According to Roger Frock, the New York-based consultant who led the A. T. Kearney study, Smith "really wanted to know if his concept was practical." Sigafoos suggests two other possible reasons that Smith paid $150,000 for two feasibility studies. He felt it "would require two independent studies to convince investors" and he "wanted statistical data on the market for priority air freight to take to the Civil Aeronautics Board."[16] Federal Express would require a special regulatory dispensation from the Civil Aeronautics Board (CAB) to use Falcon fan-jets to haul air freight.

A. T. Kearney and AAPG took about six months to complete their studies—both consultants independently concluded that there was "a large untapped air freight market" for priority cargo which "represented over a $1 billion annual business." Overnight service was not available "within a network of at least 100 major cities." The consultants estimated that start-up costs would range from $6.5 million to $15.9 million and that the business would be profitable within six to twelve months after launch.[17] Smith and the consultants also mapped out the following strategy for the business that would continue to operate under the Federal Express name:

The company would focus on small packages. According to Smith, Federal Express would not "carry mice and elephants on the same plane like a lot of [competing] cargo outfits."[18] Unlike other shippers, it would have its own jets and trucks to provide a high level of reliability.* Federal Express would provide overnight service "between most American cities, not just the major metropolitan markets."[19] To serve these many locations, the company would use the hub-and-spoke logistics that had been planned for the Federal Reserve business. The company would have twenty-three jets in service, with three backup planes. To maximize the use of the planes during the day, Federal Express would offer a same-day charter service to customers with extremely urgent needs.

Securing Resources

Smith had to secure a wide variety of resources to implement the plan to launch the venture. Below we will see how he acquired the aircraft, waivers

---

* Responding to criticism that trucks and airlines were distinct businesses, Smith observed: "A plane and a truck are both vehicles. One has a pilot, and one has a driver. What's the difference?" (Sigafoos [1983], p. 43.)

from the CAB, personnel, infrastructure, customers, and capital that Federal Express needed for its overnight delivery business.

Aircraft. As previously mentioned, Smith had acquired two Falcon fanjets for a Federal Reserve Board contract that fell through. He quickly took steps to acquire more Falcons well before his consultants completed their feasibility studies.* In December 1971—the same month that Smith was commissioning the A. T. Kearney and AAPG studies—Federal Express signed an option to purchase twenty-three Falcons from Pan Am's Business Jets division. Apparently the market for the Falcons had been depressed, and Pan Am had stored these jets in the desert near Roswell, New Mexico, hoping for prices to rise. But a desperate need for cash forced Pan Am to enter into the following deal with Smith: Federal Express would pay approximately $1.26 million for each jet and would begin taking delivery about nine months later, in September 1972. Federal Express paid $1.15 million to Pan Am for this option—money that it borrowed from a local bank against a guarantee extended by Enterprise, the Smith family trust company. In February 1972, two months after securing the Pan Am option, Federal Express purchased eight secondhand Falcons, financed with short-term demand notes mainly from the Worthen Bank in Little Rock. With this purchase, Sigafoos writes, "Smith was elated. He felt he had cornered the market for Falcons and had purchased the planes at bargain rates."[20]

CAB waivers. Federal Express had to secure a special regulatory dispensation to use the Falcons. Air transportation was then closely regulated by the CAB. Smith planned to operate Federal Express as an "air taxi operator" to avoid restrictions on routes and schedules faced by "certified carriers." But the Falcons that Federal Express planned to use violated the Part II98 regulations governing air taxis. Part 298 forbade air taxis from using airplanes whose takeoff weight exceeded 12,500 pounds. Citing an unserved public need for overnight delivery, Federal Express proposed amending the regulation to limit payload capacity instead of take off weight.

The CAB held hearings in January 1972. Smith's proposal to expand the capacity of planes flying under Part 298 authority drew strong opposition from certified carriers, especially local service airlines. The certified carriers claimed that the change would lead to unfair competition from air taxis operating outside the regulated structure. Nevertheless, Smith— assisted by respected Washington attorney Ramsey Potts—prevailed, and on July 18, 1972, the CAB amended Part 298. Later that year Hughes Air Corporation, North Central Airlines, and the Air Line Pilots Association petitioned the U.S. Court of Appeals for a review of the CAB order. On

---

* Sigafoos suggests that Smith "had his emergency exit covered": If the air freight operation did not materialize, the Falcons could be sold at a profit (Sigafoos [1983], p. 49). This seems implausible: Smith modified the twelve-seat corporate passenger jets for cargo use, at considerable expense, as quickly as he could. More likely Smith had prejudged the results of the consulting studies.

December 5, 1972, the Court of Appeals ruled that the CAB had acted properly in liberalizing Part 298. A Federal Express lawyer later observed that "if the court had ruled in favor of Hughes and the others, there wouldn't have been a Federal Express." An adverse ruling would have forced the company to go through a certification process, which would have had a "crushing effect" on the company's ability to obtain financing.[21]

Personnel. In 1983, after Federal Express had become a billion-dollar corporation, Sigafoos wrote that "Smith *is* Federal Express. He is as well known as the company. Most of the rank and file employees believe it; security analysts believe it; the competition believe it; and certainly Fred Smith appears to believe it."[22] But in spite of this close identification with his company, the success of Federal Express has been due, Sigafoos suggests, "to the huge contributions of a loyal and talented group of senior officers and managers" who "willingly accepted a secondary role when the publicity started flooding the media about Fred Smith and *his* Federal Express."[23]

Unlike Bill Gates and Paul Allen (as well as most of the *Inc.* 500 founders I interviewed), who "did it all" in the early years, Smith relied heavily on others from the start. He retained two consulting firms to plan the venture, and in his frequent visits to New York to review their progress, Smith would arrive with an entourage from Arkansas. Smith would bring with him a close aide, Irby Tedder; attorneys Frank L. Watson, Jr., and William N. Carter of Little Rock; and Robert L. Cox, his personal attorney who was also secretary of the Enterprise Company."[24] In May 1972, even before the final A. T. Kearney report had been submitted, Smith began an extensive recruiting effort. Like many *Inc.* 500 founders, Smith hired some people he knew, or people referred by friends or relatives. But he also went well beyond this ad hoc recruiting to secure high-powered talent.

Roger Frock, who had led the A. T. Kearney study, was one of the first recruits. Frock was hired as general manager for $36,000 per year. While this was $1,000 per year more than Smith's own salary, it represented "a big pay cut" for Frock, who had worked at A. T. Kearney for ten years. Smith was "very persuasive," Frock recalls, offering an oral commitment that Frock would get stock if Federal Express became successful. Some months later, Art Bass, who had led the AAPG study, joined Federal Express to develop a marketing plan and handle industrial relations. Bass's partners, Taylor and Fagan, remained at AAPG but did considerable work for Federal Express. In 1974 they closed their consulting firm and joined Bass at the company.

Smith used executive search firms to recruit many key technical personnel.[25] His persuasive powers also played an important role. As Bass recalls:

> If anyone he wanted showed a reluctance to accept his offer, he'd really go to work on them. Fred's face would light, and he'd paint this glowing portrait of how Federal Express was to be a giant *Fortune* 500 corporation, and

that they ought to be part of this adventure. Of course, Little Rock was the end of the Earth to some of these fellows and their families, but Fred Smith successfully overcame most of their concerns.[26]

The first pilots were either from the military or had experience flying Falcons as corporate jets. Smith also established a Veterans Administration–supported Flight Training School in October 1972 to train pilots for the Falcons. The government paid most of the tuition for the trainees, producing "a double benefit"—a source of revenue and a pool of trained pilots.[27] The company closed the school a year later, after it had satisfied its need for pilots.

Infrastructure. Federal Express contracted with Little Rock Automotive (LRA) to modify the Falcons. LRA installed large doors (which were seventy-four inches high instead of the original thirty-one inches), revamped the interiors, installed avionics, and painted the company name on the planes' exteriors. In early 1973 Federal Express purchased LRA outright.* The LRA acquisition provided Federal Express with a fully equipped hangar, a flight school, and office space.

In January 1973 Federal Express moved its base of flight operations from Little Rock to Memphis. The Memphis and Shelby County Authority had "an aggressive management interested in promoting additional revenue generating activities."[28] Smith knew the key people heading the Authority, and they agreed to lease Federal Express hangar facilities and issue bonds that would finance improvements of these facilities as well as the construction of administrative and cargo-handling buildings. The public agencies in Little Rock would not match the Memphis package. "The favorable lease terms provided by the Airport Authority," writes Sigafoos, "were a stroke of good fortune. . . . It is doubtful that any other major metropolitan airport would have made such a generous deal to an unproven company run by a 28-year-old with limited business experience."[29] Construction work began immediately, and by March a relatively primitive "hub" capable of handling ten thousand packages per hour was in place. On March 12, 1973, Federal Express began offering its service to a network of eleven cities.

Customers. While Federal Express was building the infrastructure for its package delivery system, it sought other uses for its Falcons. The U.S. Postal Service was the company's first customer. Federal Express won a three-year contract to fly six mail routes starting on July 10, 1972. The company "low-balled" its bids "because Smith really wanted these contracts."[30] During that summer Federal Express also sought to sell charter services to large industrial shippers. Ford Motor Company, for instance,

---

* LRA was on the verge of bankruptcy because its main customer, Federal Express, had not paid its bills. Smith perusaded the Worthen bank to lend Federal Express $2.5 million for the purchase of LRA.

contracted with Federal Express to fly a shipment of auto parts from Ypsi-
lanti to Kansas City. Overall, however, this effort was not a great success.
Smith tried to use his Arkansas corporate jet sales force to sell charter services; but "this flamboyant, unruly group," which was "used to selling-
million dollar aircraft and living it up on expense accounts,"[31] did not
readily adapt to their new assignment.

Finding customers for the company's core overnight package-delivery
business also proved extremely difficult. The first night of service—March
12, 1973—was, according to Mike Fitzgerald, head of the sales force, "a
bust." The Falcons that flew into Memphis carried a total of six packages,
one of which was a birthday present for Smith from one of his aides. This
failure led to the realization, according to Fitzgerald, "that we didn't have
enough cities and people hadn't heard of us."[32]

Federal Express expanded its network to twenty-five cities for a second
try, on April 17, 1973. This time the Falcons flew in a total of 186 packages.
Sigafoos writes that "getting Federal Express known to the business public,
and converting prospects into sales, was a hard struggle during the summer
and early fall of 1973."[33] The nightly package count averaged 473 in May,
1,000 in late July, and 2,517 in October. The facility, however, was constructed to handle 10,000 packages *per hour*. With potential recruits, airport
authorities, local bankers, and so on, Smith could rely on his contacts, persuasiveness, and vision. But to reach a critical mass of customers dispersed
throughout the country required mass marketing. As we will see, the cash
and time it took to refine and implement an effective marketing strategy
would keep Federal Express on the brink of bankruptcy for several years. It
took more than twenty-seven months—not the six to twelve originally estimated—to build the volume of business needed to cover fixed costs.

Capital. In the early stages, Smith raised capital with relative ease. The
initial requirements, although large by the standards of an *Inc.* 500 type
start-up, were commensurate with Smith's personal wealth and credit
capacity. The need for funds, however, quickly escalated: For instance,
whereas the consultants had estimated that the initial start-up costs would
range between $6.5 million and $15.9 million, Sigafoos calculates that
Federal Express paid $56.1 million just for the purchase of the Falcon fan-
jets and their conversion from passenger to cargo use. Consequently,
"Smith's enormous energy was almost totally consumed trying to get commitments from groups of venture capitalists and lenders. At the same time,
Smith had at bay a legion of creditors demanding payment and threaten-
ing foreclosure, or its equivalent—confiscating the Falcons."[34]

As previously mentioned, Federal Express purchased two Falcons from
Pan Am in the summer of 1971 with loans guaranteed by Enterprise, the
family trust company. Local banks provided the loans to purchase another
eight used jets in February 1972. In May 1972, with the preliminary results
of the A. T. Kearney and AAPG studies in hand, Smith sought long-term

financing from Commercial Credit Equipment Corporation (CECC), a subsidiary of Control Data Corporation.* On July 8, 1972, CECC entered into a loan agreement with Federal Express to provide a ten-year, $13.8 million loan. The loan was secured by a mortgage on the ten Falcons Federal Express owned. Sigafoos's account suggests (although he is not clear on this point) that the local banks that had provided the short-term credit to finance the purchase of the planes had not secured their loans with a first lien on the asset. In addition to the security of the planes, CECC relied on a personal guarantee from Smith and a $2 million guarantee provided by Enterprise. The Enterprise board also agreed to purchase $2 million of Federal Express common stock.

We cannot tell from the Sigafoos history how the $13.8 million was used. His account of the Arkansas banks' subsequent efforts to recover their loans suggests that Federal Express did not retire its short-term obligations.** Presumably the CECC loan was used to buy and convert more jets, establish the hub-and-spoke infrastructure, and pay for operating expenses. In any event, the $13.8 million loan and the $2 million Enterprise equity investment were not enough to pay for the twenty-three Falcons that Federal Express had under option. Smith would need to raise much more capital.

Smith had initiated discussions for financing Federal Express with the old-line investment banking firm of White, Weld & Co. in November 1971. It had been a White, Weld partner who had advised him to commission a feasibility study. Smith was told that "third-party opinions greatly soothe the trepidations of venture capitalists." Smith had kept the White, Weld investment bankers informed of the progress of the A. T. Kearney and AAPG studies; and they were, according to Smith, "extremely enthusiastic" about the prospects for Federal Express. In September 1972, White, Weld outlined a rough plan to raise venture capital for Federal Express. A few months later the firm "sent Homer Rees, one of its key people, to Little Rock for an extended period so he could assemble the operational and financial details of the company and examine Federal's corporate plan."[35]

White, Weld's timetable and due diligence prevented Federal Express from purchasing the Falcons from Pan Am before its option expired. The twenty-seven-year-old Smith had either underestimated or simply not considered the time it would take to raise capital when he purchased the option in December 1971; when it expired in September 1972, he had to agree to

* Smith had prior connections with CECC. While serving in Vietnam, Smith had used his inheritance to help his stepfather acquire a controlling interest in Arkansas Aviation. Later, when Arkansas Aviation ran into financial difficulties and Smith had returned from Vietnam, he took control of the company from his stepfather, and contributed equity to pay down some of the company debts. CECC had been one of the creditors helped by Smith's intervention.

** Sigafoos also notes that at the end of 1972, Federal Express's debt stood at $21.7 million. This number suggests that the company continued to owe about $8 million to its banks.

pay a higher price to extend the option for another month. At this juncture Smith was probably maneuvering for time—White, Weld had not even proposed a detailed financing plan, so there was no realistic possibility of paying for the Falcons. But according to Sigafoos, if Pan Am had sold the planes to someone else, it would have "sealed the company's doom. Replacement Falcons could neither have been found quickly, nor on such favorable terms as had been granted by Pan Am."[36]

Federal Express negotiated a second delay in November 1972, and then asked for a third, in January 1973. The January negotiations were "bitter" because "Pan Am desperately needed the cash." Frank Watson, an attorney for Federal Express, says the company was dealing with "unyielding and unpleasant" negotiators. Watson spent twenty-three days in New York working on a deal "to keep Pan Am from selling the Falcons out from under us. . . . We had to play real hard ball to keep the agreement alive . . . Federal Express almost died at the bitter meetings." Under the terms of the agreement that was eventually signed, Federal Express gave Pan Am warrants on its common stock. Federal Express could buy the Falcons until May 15, 1973, but every day it delayed after March 31, it would incur a price increase of $1,500 per plane. May 15 thus became, according to Sigafoos, a "do-or-die target date."[37]

While Federal Express was negotiating with Pan Am, White, Weld was completing its financing plan. On February 2, 1973, it offered a proposal to raise $6 million in equity and $4 million in subordinated notes (with attached warrants) for Federal Express. The $10 million would provide working capital for Federal Express and also would enable the company to raise an equivalent amount of bank debt. White, Weld did not guarantee it would succeed in raising the funds; rather it promised to use its "best efforts."

White, Weld also asked Smith to contribute an additional $1.5 million of equity to Federal Express. By then, Smith and Enterprise had already invested $3.25 million in the company's equity. Apparently, because relations with his half sisters had become strained, Smith did not want to ask them to authorize a further Enterprise investment. Instead he submitted a fabricated copy of a resolution of the Enterprise board to the Union Bank in Little Rock to obtain a $2 million loan. The resolution purported to secure the loan through the assignment of a stock repurchase agreement between Smith and the Enterprise company. Smith forged the signature of the board secretary, Robert Cox, on the resolution. Later, when the forgery came to light, Smith would face serious legal consequences. But in February 1973, argues Sigafoos, "there can be no doubt that without the Union Bank loan, Federal Express would have collapsed."[38]

Although Smith may have averted a "collapse," he and White, Weld were unable to raise the $20 million. By the end of April 1973 Federal Express had accumulated losses of more than $4.4 million. "Most of what

Fred Smith had personally invested, as well as what Enterprise Company had invested, was gone," writes Sigafoos. "Once again, the end appeared imminent."[39] And once again, Smith raised a $1 million short-term loan using a fictitious Enterprise board resolution.[40]

On May 4, just eleven days before the Pan Am option was scheduled to expire, a White, Weld partner arranged for Smith to meet Henry Crown. Crown, an industrialist and financier, was the controlling stockholder of General Dynamics, an industrial conglomerate.* Crown was impressed with Smith's presentation, and the following week organized several meetings between Smith and General Dynamics executives. On May 12, General Dynamics signed an agreement guaranteeing loans to Federal Express totaling $23.7 million in return for an option to buy 80.1 percent of Federal Express for $16 million. The agreement gave General Dynamics three months to decide whether to exercise its option; if it did, Federal Express would effectively become a subsidiary, but if General Dynamics decided against investing in Federal Express, its loan guarantee would terminate. (General Dynamics would still receive 6% of Federal Express stock for having provided a three-month loan guarantee.)

The solution was short-term, but it did enable Federal Express to exercise its option to purchase eighteen Falcons from Pan Am.** Chase Manhattan, General Dynamics's corporate bank, provided a four-month loan, secured by the eighteen Falcon fan-jets. To protect the value of Chase's security, the loan agreement prohibited Federal Express from converting the fanjets to cargo use. Federal Express personnel ignored these prohibitions.[41]

General Dynamics sent a fifteen-person technical team to investigate Federal Express's business—as we have seen, Federal Express had already begun operations. The team "interviewed all of Smith's key people, examined the company's plans, and prepared 'best case,' 'middle road,' and 'worst case' forecasts."[42] Engineers on the team tested the landing gear, cargo handling capabilities and the operational characteristics of the Falcons. On July 12, the team submitted a favorable report on the "excellent results" that Federal Express had already achieved and anticipated that it would operate profitably in the fiscal year of 1974.[43] Nevertheless, on July 19, 1973, the General Dynamics board decided against exercising its option to purchase Federal Express stock. The board was concerned about CAB regulations that might block its investment, as well as the possibility that the Federal Express investment would distract managerial efforts from more urgent problems that General Dynamics faced.

General Dynamics did, however, agree to extend its guarantee on the Chase loan. It also indicated a willingness to invest $5 million to purchase

---

* Crown, whose personal wealth exceeded a billion dollars, also had large real estate investments and owned a significant portion of Hilton Hotels stock.

** Apparently, Federal Express had already purchased five of the twenty-three jets it had under option.

a minority interest in Federal Express—a noncontrolling stake would not expose General Dynamics to regulatory issues with the CAB.*

On July 23, 1973, White, Weld, now joined by New Court Securities, resumed its efforts to raise capital for Federal Express. Again the goal was to raise $20 million in venture capital and a similar amount in long-term bank loans. In addition to the $5 million General Dynamics had said it would probably invest, Prudential Insurance Company had indicated it would invest $5 million. Prudential did not normally invest such large amounts in start-ups, and earlier in the year it had written to Smith indicating that it would not invest in Federal Express. Apparently the intercession of Arkansas congressman Wilbur Mills, Chairman of the House Ways and Means Committee, caused a change of view at the Prudential. (Mills had also called Henry Crown earlier to recommend Smith.)[44]

To raise the remaining $10 million, White, Weld and New Court called the venture capital groups at Citicorp, Bank of America, First National Bank of Chicago, and Allstate Insurance, as well as several private limited partnerships. Those who showed interest were invited to Memphis for presentations by Federal Express and by the General Dynamics team that had just completed its feasibility study. In October 1973 the investment bankers had lined up 23 investors, who pledged a total of $23 million.

Bank loans were secured after extended negotiations. Chase Manhattan, First National Bank of Chicago, and a group of regional banks agreed to provide a $20 million revolving line of credit, and a second tranche of $5 million if Federal Express reached certain financial targets. To secure this credit the Enterprise Company had to invest an additional $4 million. On November 6, 1973, Smith got the Enterprise board to make an equity contribution of $1.5 million and a subordinated loan of $2.5 million to Federal Express. A board member representing the trustee bank commented that they had little choice: "Enterprise stood to lose $5.4 million if Federal Express closed its doors. We had a tiger by the tail and we could not let go at this point."[45] With the additional investment Enterprise's exposure stood at $6.25 million. Smith had already invested $2.5 million of his own funds, so the family had put in a total of $8.75 million. Finally, on November 13, 1973, the closing of the financial package, amounting to $52 million, took place.

As the investment banks put together the financing between July and November, Federal Express faced "mounting vendor suits"[46] for failing to pay its bills. The State of Arkansas pressured the company for unpaid sales and use taxes. On September 14, 1973, Smith sent a memo to employees asking them to delay cashing or depositing their payroll checks. The Worthen Bank of Little Rock had lent Federal Express amounts far in

---

* General Dynamics also helped Federal Express by purchasing one Falcon from Federal Express for $1.55 million and leasing it back. The transaction helped mollify the Worthen Bank of Little Rock, which had provided the financing in 1972 and was now threatening to call its loan.

excess of its loan limit for borrowers and had also syndicated some loans to several small Arkansas banks. Worthen Bank's staff visited Federal Express every week to press for repayment. According to an old-time employee, "Every time Worthen's people came around, word was passed to keep the Falcons from landing. If they had chained the planes, that would have been the end of Federal Express."[47].

It might be argued that Smith acted imprudently in buying the options on the Falcons and launching the operation in March 1973 before securing the capital he needed. This financial brinkmanship, however, may have been necessary: Crown, General Dynamics, and the VCs might not have funded Federal simply on the basis of a paper plan drawn up by a twenty-eight-year-old.

Reaching Profitability

The November 1973 financing enabled Federal Express to pay off existing creditors but did not leave much of a cash cushion. The company was still operating well below its break-even point. Federal Express and Smith would have to overcome several more difficult years before its financial situation finally stabilized.

Fuel shortages represented one unexpected problem. As a result of the oil crisis of 1973, the federal government started rationing fuel to airlines on November 1, 1973. Allotments were to be based on 1972 consumption levels, but because Federal Express had not started operation until April 1973, there was no benchmark available to determine its quota. According to Sigafoos, "Smith and his assistants swarmed on the newly created Energy Policy Office of the Department of the Interior in Washington to plead for special consideration."[48] The Energy Policy Office agreed to give the company an allotment of 40.9 million gallons. The amount "turned out to be far in excess of its actual need"; Federal Express would not reach this level of consumption until the late 1970s. The "generous allotment," Sigafoos writes, "raised the eyebrows of many in the airline industry. Here, they said, was a company getting special consideration which after eight months of operation had taken in only $2.4 million in revenues."[49]

In the fall of 1973 the company adopted new approaches to sales and marketing. In September Ted Sartoian, a former UPS salesman, was made head of sales. He replaced Bill Lackey, whose previous experience had been in selling corporate jets. Sartoian implemented the "team selling" approach used at UPS. He led, Sigafoos writes, "sales teams of eight persons into different cities to contact in a one- or two-week period all the big shippers in those cities. It was a quick-hitting, saturation campaign designed to get immediate results."[50]

Federal Express also reoriented its customer focus in late 1973. After "much experimentation," according to Sigafoos:

Company planners realized perhaps they should have been trying to attract the same type of customers as Emery Air Freight instead of those using UPS. Emery had traditionally done a heavy volume of business with industrial customers. UPS served a much different clientele and carried primarily consumer-oriented, non-priority-type parcels.[51]

The arrival of Vince Fagan as senior vice president for marketing led to yet another shift. Unlike the former UPS employees, who had hitherto shaped the marketing approach at Federal Express, Fagan believed that calling on prospects in person was "costly and non-productive."[52] Resources devoted to the field sales force, he argued, should be used on advertising instead. Moreover, Fagan stressed the use of television ads, which other companies, such as UPS and Emery, had never used. Another innovation introduced by Fagan was attention to the "front door" market, comprising professionals working in fields such as law firms, financial services, consultants, and so on. Previously Federal Express (and other freight companies) had focused on shipping departments, mailrooms, and loading docks—the "back door" market. Front-door customers had rarely shipped packages by air; but if Federal Express could get their attention, Fagan believed, these customers would provide large revenues.

Fagan's approach, according to Sigafoos, helped Federal Express recover from its disappointing start, but it did not produce immediate results. The company continued to struggle with cash flow problems in early 1974. Federal Express did not have the systems to collect on its receivables in a timely fashion; on average, customers were paying their bills nearly two months after their receipt. Some employees complained about delayed payroll checks; a disgruntled courier in Kansas City took the station manager hostage and threatened to "blow his head off" unless he was paid the $300 Federal Express owed him. (After some scrambling the $300 was paid and the station manager freed.)[53]

On February 12, 1974, the venture capital group and the lenders met to review the company's situation. Federal Express had failed to meet the revenue and profit projections that had been made in November, and to avoid (yet another) "financial collapse," the investors and lenders agreed to infuse another $6.4 million in equity and $5.1 million in debt.[54] This round of financing was scheduled to close on March nineteenth.

Thirteen days before the closing, however, Union Bank's attempts to collect on an overdue loan to Enterprise led to the exposure of the forgery Smith had committed the previous year. As mentioned, Smith had forged an Enterprise Board resolution to secure a loan from Union in February 1973. Now, when the bank sought to enforce the agreement contained in the resolution, the board informed the bank's officers that there was no such resolution. Smith then had to inform all the investors in the forthcoming financing about his misrepresentation. Smith claimed that he had intended to repay the Union Bank loan and had been forced into his deception because he had been having a "recurring battle" with the Enterprise board about its continued support for Federal Express.[55]

On March 12, the investor and lender group met in Chicago to consider Smith's future at Federal Express. The majority decided he should stay, writes Sigafoos, because "they realized he had a real power base": He had "the loyalty and dedication of his employees," and to outsiders "he *was* Federal Express."[56] The group did decide to recruit, however, an experienced chief financial officer and an experienced chief executive. After this meeting, the second round of financing was completed as planned on March 19.[57] Peter Willmott started as the new chief financial officer on May 6. Willmott came from the position of treasurer of the Continental Baking Company and had previously worked as a management consultant at Booz, Allen, & Hamilton and as an analyst for American Airlines. General Howell M. Estes, who had been serving as president of World Airways, a military and commercial charter airline, after his retirement from the air force, was recruited to be CEO. When he joined on June 1, 1974, Smith became president of the company.

Federal Express's survival remained doubtful through the summer of 1974. Shippers were "highly complimentary of the service Federal Express was providing," but "earnings were nonexistent and there was no cash flow to pay off bank debt."[58] The company "faced a multitude of creditors ranging from the City of Detroit to their own employees. Airport officials in Detroit parked a fire truck in front of a Falcon one day because Federal had not paid the landing fee. Couriers often used their credit cards to buy gasoline for their delivery vans and sought reimbursement from the company later."[59]

After considerable effort, New Court Securities was able to complete a third round of financing, in September 1974. Seventeen of the initial twenty-four investors subscribed to this round, which raised $3.876 million. The low price of the new securities made it "very painful for those who chose not to take part." The Enterprise Company, for instance, which did not invest, saw its share of Federal Express reduced to 0.4 percent, even though it had put up 11 percent of the equity capital to date.*

Willmott, who had found a "financial administrative mess" when he arrived, took about three months "to get financial numbers that investors could believe in." He also pushed for price increases; "contrary to the thinking of Smith and his staff, Willmott felt that "if the company offered a quality service, customers would pay for it."[60] Willmott's views prevailed, and the company instituted several price increases in 1974. The inaction of

---

* Smith apparently managed to avoid significant dilution of his personal stake. Before the financing he held a 9.8 percent voting interest, which was similar to the Enterprise Company's 9.25 percent. Presumably because Smith had the willingness and the resources to participate, his share after the third round dipped only slightly, to 8.5 percent.

competitors apparently limited the repercussions: If Emery or Airborne Express had competed aggressively for the priority small-package market, Sigafoos suggests, Federal would not have survived.[61]

General Estes lasted nine months. Smith was "always respectful" and did not have "open disagreements" with Estes but did not carry out his suggestions.[62] The "arm's length" relationship between the two men ended in January 1975. On the twenty-first of that month Smith informed the Federal Express Board that a federal grand jury was investigating his submission of forged documents to secure the Union Bank loan; his half sisters had apparently taken up the matter with the federal authorities. On January 31, Smith was indicted for using false documents to obtain funds from Union Bank. That very night, Smith hit and killed a pedestrian. He was charged with leaving the scene of the accident and for driving with an expired license. (Smith claimed that he had failed to stop because he did not realize he had hit someone.[63])

On February 25, the directors of Federal Express met to consider Smith's future with the company. General Estes and several others urged the board to terminate Smith. Other senior executives, however, told the directors that they would resign if Smith was fired, and that Federal Express would probably "cease operations the following Monday morning because of a mass walkout." That afternoon the board announced that it had "accepted with regret the resignation of General Estes" and had decided to reinstate Smith as chairman.[64] Art Bass would take over Smith's position as president and would also serve as acting CEO until a new individual could be found for that position.

In December 1975 Smith was tried for submitting forged documents to Union Bank. According to Sigafoos, "Smith's defense was based on the theme, "I am Frederick Smith Enterprise Company." Smith testified that:

> Almost 50 percent of the Enterprise Company is Fred Smith, either personally or in trust for me. And I felt at the time that I was the Enterprise Company. It's as simple as that. And I felt that both of the [half] sisters felt the same way. Both of them had written letters to the bankers that sat on the board saying, "We support Fred Smith in whatever he wants to do."[65]

Smith's counsel also had Smith "elaborate extensively on his Marine Corps combat experience in Vietnam and on his development of the concept which led ultimately to the formation of Federal Express."[66] After ten hours of deliberation, the jury acquitted Smith. Smith had faced a five-year prison term if he had been found guilty.*

---

* Smith continued to face a civil charge filed by his half sisters that he had acted imprudently in investing Enterprise funds in Federal Express. Eventually in 1978, Smith agreed to buy his half sisters' interests in Enterprise at a price that reflected their 1971 value. Thus, from Fredette and Laura's point of view at least, the venture was not a great economic success.

The company's finances also began to improve in 1975. In July 1975 Federal Express recorded its first monthly profit: $55,000. Almost a year later, the company announced its first yearly profit, reporting a net income of $3.6 million for the fiscal year ending May 31, 1976. In 1976 Federal Express also became the leading company in the small shipment market. Federal Express handled 19 percent of all priority air shipments under one hundred pounds in the United States, whereas the next largest player, Emery, had a 10 percent share, and Airborne Express had 5 percent.[67]

Two problems limited the company's profitability, however. First, Federal Express was reaching the capacity limit of its aircraft, while some of its "ground" capacity was underutilized. Federal Express asked the CAB to allow it to use DC-9s, which had a larger payload as well as lower operating costs than the company's aging Falcons. The certified carriers opposed Federal's request, which the CAB denied. Smith lobbied Congress for legislative relief but failed to get it.

Second, Federal Express faced a heavy debt load, and through 1975 and 1976 had to seek rescheduling of its loan payments. The directors had decided to proceed with the preliminary steps for a public equity offering to reduce the company's debt burden in June 1975. The public offering had been held up, however, by a dispute over warrants that the company had previously granted to its banks. Smith claimed that he had "a right of first refusal" to purchase these warrants in consideration of the dilution he had suffered through successive rounds of financing. Smith "reminded the lenders that the Smith family had put over $8 million into Federal Express, and as of 1976, he held only an 8.5 percent interest, and the family-owned Enterprise Company only 0.4 percent."[68] The banks, however, refused to sell their warrants to Smith. As an alternative, the Federal Express board initiated merger talks with the Purolator Courier Corporation, but Purolator's management decided not to proceed.

Both problems were resolved after the passage of the Air Cargo Deregulation Act in November 1977. The act, which allowed Federal Express to fly larger aircraft, considerably brightened the company's prospects and "triggered a positive attitude of all parties."[69] On April 12, 1978, Federal Express raised $17.5 million in a public issue of stock priced at $24 per share. The company also made a loan to Smith that enabled him to purchase warrants held by the banks at a price of $5.25 per warrant. (Each warrant gave the holder the right to purchase a share for $2.50.) Sales and profits grew rapidly thereafter. Federal Express received $1 billion in revenues for the fiscal year ending May 31, 1983 (up from $160 million in 1978), and $89 million in profits (compared to $19.5 million in 1978). Smith "emerged as one the new glamour symbols of the entrepreneurial world" and Federal Express became a "darling" of Wall Street.[70]

3. Daniel Ludwig's Jari Development

Daniel Ludwig's forestry venture, located at the confluence of the Jari and Amazon Rivers in Brazil, was, in 1981, the "largest individually owned tract" and the "largest tropical forestry company in the world" as well as "the largest project ever embarked upon by a private citizen without recourse to the capital markets."[71] It then comprised 252,000 acres of tree plantations; 2,600 miles of roads; 45 miles of railroad; a Kaolin mine; a pulping complex; and cattle, water buffalo, and rice farms, all "cloaked in secrecy and off limits to Brazilians."[72] The headquarters town of Monte Dourado, which had been built from scratch, accommodated a population of 30,000. Jari was also a colossal failure: Ludwig lost between $500 million to $1 billion of his personal wealth on the project.

The stories of Daniel Ludwig and Frederick Smith differ in several ways. Smith was twenty-seven years old when he incorporated Federal Express in 1971; Ludwig was sixty-nine when he bought Jari. Smith inherited a small fortune; Ludwig had amassed wealth that put him in the ranks of the superrich. Smith was a well-known public figure; Ludwig was "obsessed with privacy" and "almost unknown."*[73] Smith relied extensively from the beginning on the advice of consultants and associates, and evoked great loyalty from rank-and-file associates; Ludwig's methods were governed by "impulse" and "a supreme confidence in his intuition." He went through two dozen project directors at Jari, replacing them on average once every six months.

In the sections below I will discuss Ludwig's background, how he developed the Jari idea and secured the resources needed to launch it, and, finally, how the enterprise collapsed.

Background

Accurate details about Ludwig's background are difficult to come by, such was his penchant for secrecy. In 1957, when Ludwig granted his first—and last—in-depth press interview, to Dan Saunders of *Fortune* magazine, Ludwig was already the second-largest ship owner in the world and had accumulated a $500 million fortune. Ludwig provided the following account of his life to Saunders. He had started on his own as a shipowner and operator at age twenty. He had struggled through the shipping slump after World War I, started making some money hauling oil in the 1920s, and then had been almost wiped out during the Depression. In the mid-1930s he developed the ship-financing scheme through which he would earn his

---

* When J. Paul Getty died in 1976, the *Sunday Times* of London wrote that "according to the experts, the man upon whose elderly and seemingly reluctant shoulders the mantle of 'Richest Man in the Word' must fall is the almost completely unknown American tycoon, Daniel K. Ludwig" (Blundy [1976]).

fortune: He would secure a long-term charter from an oil company to haul its oil, and use the charter as collateral for a bank loan to finance the ship. The charter contracts would produce a small, steady income, and when they expired, Ludwig would own fully paid-up ships.

Initially Ludwig acquired old ships that he renovated; then, in 1939, he started his own shipbuilding operation in Norfolk, Virginia. During World War II Ludwig secured government contracts to build tankers for hauling oil to Europe and the Far East. After the war, when the government did not need the tankers, it sold them back to Ludwig. Ludwig, now the fifth-largest shipowner in America, had the fleet to take advantage of the post-war shipping boom.

In 1951 Ludwig secured a lease from the Occupation government in Japan on the former Imperial Navy Shipyard at Kure and moved most of his shipbuilding operations there. Over the years, Ludwig told Saunders, he had introduced design and structural modifications in shipbuilding techniques that reduced nonessentials and increased cargo-carrying capacity. He also believed in economies of scale: He had started the race to build larger and larger supertankers with the 30,000-ton *Bulkpetrol* in 1948, and the Kure shipyard had enabled him to stay in the lead. In 1956, for instance, Kure had turned out the 84,730-ton *Universe Leader*, then the world's largest tanker.

Ludwig had also experimented with building self-unloading vessels for dry cargo (such as iron ore and coal) and versatile bulk carriers that could haul petroleum as well as dry cargo. To help fill his ship, Ludwig had diversified into activities such as mining, ranching, oil refining, and salt production in South America, Australia, and a variety of other locations. After the Saunders story appeared, Ludwig continued to diversify, into real estate, hotels, banking, and financial services. When he started Jari, therefore, Ludwig had a variety of business interests that spanned the globe.

Jerry Shields, who wrote an unauthorized biography, *The Invisible Billionaire*, provides a more critical account of Ludwig's background. According to Shields, Ludwig was not quite self-made: He was the grandson of a well-to-do Midwesterner who had banking, lumber, and shipbuilding interests. Ludwig's father, Shields suggests, was closely involved in his early forays into shipping. He started off hauling molasses to Canada for a major bootlegging operation. In 1922, at the height of the Prohibition, Customs officials seized and impounded the *Mosher*, a ship co-owned by his father, with Ludwig on board as engineer. The *Mosher* was carrying a large shipment of rum; Ludwig and his fellow crew were arrested, while his father absconded. But according to Shields, the father's connections in Washington forced the New York district attorney to drop charges.[74]

In the 1930s and 1940s, according to Shields, Ludwig likely profited from his connections with public officials. For instance, during the war years, Shields suggests, Ludwig sold old ships to the government for "sums in excess of their market price"; chartered tankers for hauling oil at per annum rates that were "far in excess of their market price"; and collected in claims for lost tankers amounts that were considerably greater than their value.[75] He secured the fifteen-year lease of the Kure shipyard for $275 per month through the intercession of the State Department.[76] Shields does concede, however, that "much of Ludwig's success was due to his willingness to venture where more timid entrepreneurs dared not go."[77]

Developing the Concept

In the early 1950s, according to Shields, Ludwig conceived of a scheme to grow trees on a mass scale on or near the equator, where large tracts of land could be acquired cheaply. If he started planting in the 1960s, Ludwig felt, the trees would be ready for harvesting in the early 1980s, by which time Ludwig expected a worldwide shortage of wood. In the early 1960s Ludwig began a search for a hardwood tree that would grow rapidly in a tropical climate. Most existing forestry operations involved softwood trees such as pines and firs which grew about twice as fast as hardwood trees; hardwoods would, therefore, continually be in shorter supply. Ludwig commissioned botanists and other scientists knowledgeable in silviculture to look for hardwood species that would grow as fast as a softwood in a hot, wet climate and would be versatile enough to provide the raw material for paper, pulp, lumber, and furniture operations.

Chemical engineer Everett Wynkoop located the gmelina tree in Nigeria while he was conducting mining surveys for Ludwig. Wynkoop found the Nigerians using hard gmelina parts as props in the mines. The British colonial office had originally imported the tree from India and Burma; it was strong, durable, and grew at the extraordinary rate of one foot per month. Six years after a seedling was planted, the tree would be used for pulpwood; when it was ten years old, it could be harvested for lumber.

Ludwig then experimented with different locations to see where the gmelinas could be successfully grown. He found the seedlings did not thrive in Mexico but did exceedingly well in Costa Rica, Panama, Honduras, and Venezuela. Other timber company executives who examined the "miracle tree" were skeptical: Unlike other commercially grown trees, the gmelina grew somewhat crookedly and branched down to the ground and thus could not be used for long, straight, knot-free lumber. Ludwig, however, was undeterred: He had grown rich by "flying in the face of conventional wisdom and accomplished what lesser men deemed impossible or too risky."[78]

Another novel element of Ludwig's vision was to build "floating factories" in an industrialized country and tow them by water to the locations where the gmelinas would be grown. Ludwig initially planned to build two such factories: a pulp plant, and an associated power plant, which would generate the electricity for the pulping operation. Later Ludwig would add a newsprint plant and a plywood factory.

The operation would be highly mechanized—Ludwig's experiences with building supertankers had convinced him of the benefits of substituting capital for labor (and the importance of economies of scale). Ludwig anticipated investing $300 million to $500 million, on which he expected to earn a 30 percent return. Annual revenues were estimated at more than $300 million.

Assembling the Resources

In the early 1960s Ludwig started looking for a location for his project. According to Shields, he was looking for a several-million-acre tract of cheap land near the equator, with access to a deepwater plant, and located in a country whose government would grant attractive tax incentives and "keep its nose out of his business."[79] Ludwig had almost settled on Nigeria when Biafran separatists started an uprising there. Ludwig turned his attention to Brazil when the military overthrew the João Goulart government in the spring of 1964. The new ruler, General Humberto Castelo Branco, reversed the previous government's "Brazil for Brazilians" program and sought to attract foreign capital.

In December 1964 Ludwig met the Brazilian minister for planning, Roberto Campos, in New York. Campos was especially interested in developing farms, mines, and lumber operations in the Amazon basin. One obstacle, according to Shields, was the "Amazon Factor"—the belief that investments in the region were bound to fail.* Ludwig's interest was, therefore, unusual and welcome. Ludwig was still testing the gmelina seedlings, however, and it was not until two years later, in 1966, that he met with President Castelo Branco to discuss his project. Branco promised a ten-year tax holiday; the right to import equipment and materials without the payment of the usual duties; and, according to Shields, the assurance that Ludwig "could run his project in any way he saw fit without interference from the Brazilian government."[80]

In 1967 Ludwig purchased between 3.5 and 4 million acres lying on both sides of the Jari River (a tributary of the Amazon) for an estimated $3 million, or about 75 cents an acre. He opened bank accounts that initially would provide $600,000 per month of operating funds. He also hired an engineer, Rodolfo Dourado, to begin clearing the jungle.[81]

---

* Henry Ford's attempt to develop a rubber plantation was part of the Amazon legend. Rubber trees grew in a widely scattered fashion in the Amazonian wilderness which made it expensive to collect their sap. In 1927 Ford purchased a 4,000-square-mile trace (which he called Fordlandia), cleared it, and planted it with rubber trees. Ford apparently did not anticipate the risks that the spread of bugs and blight posed to trees that were planted close together. By the late 1930s, millions of his trees were afflicted with leaf blight, and in 1945 he folded the operation.

Ludwig did not attempt to determine whether gmelinas would adapt to the conditions at Jari before he concluded the purchase. Two of his employees, Kinkead reports, had surveyed the property on muleback and in dugout canoes but "made no effort to test the soil."[82] The region had "no history of commercial forestry."[83] Outside of Antarctica and the Sahara, no place on earth was "as empty or underdeveloped." The climate was "merciless," with 100 inches of rainfall each year. It was infested with insect pests that could "destroy crops and supplies overnight."[84] Malaria, yellow fever, and dysentery were rampant.

Ludwig did not seek to involve outside investors or debt because he wanted complete control. Similarly, everything within Jari—all the housing, transportation services, retail trade, and so on—would be owned by Ludwig. No other private business would operate within an area the size of Connecticut.

Unfolding of the Enterprise

The Jari project, as we will see next, was beset by a number of problems due to faulty initial assumptions, unforeseeable circumstances, and Ludwig's approach to management.

In the 1950s Ludwig had used giant bulldozers to raze a jungle in Venezuela to make way for a cattle ranch. Ludwig's attempt to use the same mechanized approach to clearing the Jari jungle failed because he had not properly investigated the ecology and soil conditions. In 1967 Ludwig had shipped eighteen bulldozers (Caterpillar "jungle crushers") to Jari. Construction crews knocked down and burned "trees up to 150 years old, some with trunks 12 to 15 feet across."[85] In two years this operation cleared about 250,000 acres, but the gmelina seedlings planted there "promptly died." The abundance of national vegetation had apparently led Ludwig to an erroneous inference about the richness of the soil; in fact, the Amazon jungle has "a mere scrim of topsoil, and the heavy machinery so compacted this fragile medium, that even weeds couldn't grow."[86]

Ludwig then brought in 2,000 seasonal laborers to clear the jungle through traditional "slash and burn" techniques that were less damaging to the soil. Independent contractors called *gatos* ("jungle cats") recruited the laborers from remote, impoverished regions of Brazil. "The cats skinned the workers," according to Kinkead, "sometimes feeding them cheap monkey and bird meat to cut costs." Stories about "inhuman conditions" led to demands from the Brazilian government that Jari provide "decent housing and wages."[87] Ludwig then began constructing the town of Monte Duardo, on which he would eventually incur a $6 million annual expense for social services.[88]

In 1970, heavy floods washed out nearly all of the four million seedlings that had been planted. Two years later, foresters discovered that the soil in about one-third of the plantation was too sandy to support the healthy growth of gmelinas. The underdeveloped gmelinas were removed and that tract was replanted with Caribbean pines. The pines were better adapted to growing in sandy soil but would take about two to three times as long as the gmelinas to mature.

On the positive side, Ludwig's staff also unexpectedly discovered one of the world's largest deposits of kaolin, a fine clay used in the manufacture of ceramics. Ludwig quickly started a mining operation and constructed a $25 million plant capable of processing 500 metric tons per day. Ludwig also embarked on a large-scale project (that was not part of the original plan) to grow rice in the southern part of his estate where the soil was too wet to grow trees. By 1980, 30,000 acres of rice paddy were expected to yield 100,000 tons of grain per year.

Ludwig's management style contributed to the problems at Jari. The budget "changed monthly," writes Kinkead:

> One visit from Ludwig, and there'd go another $50 million in another direction. He'd say, "Build 500 workers' houses here, put a road in there." If Jari's director complained about the cost of Ludwig's sudden switching of plans, the boss would reply, "You worry about getting the place built. I'll worry about the money." . . . Suggestions that he economize by opening his company town to private developers and entrepreneurs met with, "As long as I'm alive, no one will own a piece of Jari but myself." Since there were no penalties for exceeding budgets, people got to thinking Ludwig had money to burn. They ordered unnecessary equipment and didn't try to shave costs. . . .
>
> Ludwig's capricious changes of managers worsened the confusion. The project's division heads, knowing directors lived on borrowed time, went their own way. When Ludwig asked five people to do the same job, as he often did, the confusion became chaos.[89]

Large, unexpected outlays forced Ludwig to seek outside financing. In 1972 Chase Manhattan led a group of banks that made a $150 million loan. In the mid-1970s Ludwig tried to get oil and pulp and paper companies to invest in Jari, but they all demurred. Ludwig thereupon borrowed another $400 million—"one of the largest loans ever made to a private investor," according to Shields[90]—from a consortium of banks led by Chase.

By 1976 Ludwig had spent nearly twice as much as he had initially budgeted, and his tree farm was several years behind schedule.[91] Nevertheless, encouraged by a doubling of world pulp prices between 1973 and 1975, on February 18, 1976, he placed an order for his "floating" pulping and power plants. The Kure Shipyard in Japan, which had previously built Ludwig's supertankers, would build the plants. The plants, each of which would weigh 30,000 metric tons, would be 250 yards long and nearly 20 stories tall. The pulp plant was designed to convert 4,000 cubic meters of pulpwood a day into 750 metric tons of cellulose. The power plant would burn

2,000 tons of wood per day and generate sufficient electricity to run the pulping plant as well as to meet all of the power needs of the Jari project. Both plants were to be built on a hollow steel hull so they could be floated to their destination in Brazil.

The Japanese Export-Import Bank lent Ludwig $240 million for construction of the plants, $175 million of which was guaranteed by the National Development Bank of Brazil. (Cost overruns on the project were financed by a $29 million loan from Lloyd's Bank of London.)

In January 1978 the plants were completed, and a month later began their journey to Brazil. In about three months, tugboats towed the plants around the Cape of Good Hope, across the South Atlantic, 250 miles up the Amazon, and then another 80 miles northwest, up the Jari. Meanwhile, in Jari, workers had constructed a lagoon with a platform of wooden pilings at the bottom for the plants to rest on. Upon their arrival, the plants were towed into the lagoon. Water was pumped into the steel hulls, gradually sinking the plants until they came to rest on the platform at the bottom of the lagoon. The lagoon was then emptied, and the plants bolted to the platform.

"These were the largest industrial plants ever to be moved across water," Shields writes. Ludwig had once again "flown in the face of the doubters and obstacles and done the seemingly impossible."[92] A team of Brazilian engineers who would operate the plants, Japanese engineers who had designed and constructed them in Kure, and Finnish experts in pulp manufacture worked for about six months to get the pulping operation on stream.

Although the pulping plant was successfully commissioned, it soon became apparent that the tree plantation would not yield enough pulpwood to keep it operating at full capacity. According to Shields, Ludwig's foresters, who were trying to protect their jobs, had misled Ludwig about the rate of the gmelina growth: "They were taking the best yields on the plantation and passing them off as averages."[93] Wood production in 1979 was half of what it was expected to be, and its cost twice as high.[94]

In 1979 Ludwig faced loan repayments of $60 million on the Jari project, on top of an operating loss of $40 million and $50 million in construction costs. At the insistence of his lenders, Ludwig retained the consulting firm of Cresep, McCormick, & Paget to "get things back on track."[95] Following the Cresep report, Ludwig sold off the rice plantation, which had been losing $8 million to $10 million per year, sanctioned a variety of cost-cutting measures, and allowed Brazilian merchants to open stores and run taxi services to Jari.[96] An executive council was formed to review policy and act as a "buffer between Ludwig and Jari's managers."[97]

These measures led to a reduction of the operating deficit from $40 million in 1979 to $10 million in 1980. But the venture remained "deeply in the red," with $20 million of construction outlays and debt service of $64 million.[98] Moreover, after an "acrimonious meeting" with the Jari forestry department, the executive council discovered that average yields of gmelina were 40 percent to 75 percent off target.[99] Jari did not have an adequate supply of wood to maintain the pulping plant at a profitable level of capacity utilization. Meanwhile, pulp prices had begun to decline.

In August 1980 Ludwig demanded that the Brazilian government pay for the $6 million per year cost of providing social services at Jari. Otherwise he would "stop the forestry project and throw several thousand people out of work."[100] In May 1981 Ludwig put the Jari project up for sale, and later that year threatened to default on a $40 million loan installment; the Jari debts now amounted to more than $260 million. Eventually the Brazilian government formed a consortium that would assume Ludwig's debts (in return for his interest in Jari) and keep things running on a shoestring. According to Shields, Ludwig had sunk more than $800 million in Jari and it was a "safe bet that he had lost a large part of his investment."[101]

4. Motorola's Iridium Project

Motorola's $5 billion Iridium project to create a global cellular phone system provides a third example of a revolutionary venture. In Chapter 5, I argued that corporations usually invest in large initiatives with measurable and controllable risk. The Iridium case shows how, once in a very rare while, a visionary CEO may push through a revolutionary, highly uncertain initiative.

According to Hardy,[102] Barry Bertiger, a Motorola employee, conceived of a worldwide phone system in 1985 after his wife could not use her cellular phone in a remote location in the Bahamas. Bertiger conferred with his colleagues Raymond Leopold and Ken Peterson. In their spare time they formulated a plan that involved a network of seventy-seven low-orbit satellites that would communicate with each other and with "gateway" ground stations connecting to earth's telephone systems. The network would thus let users make a telephone call from anywhere to anywhere in the world.

The project's "technological, regulatory, and political complexity," Hardy writes, was "numbing": Iridium's engineers had to mesh more than 25,000 complex design elements. They had to hook 3.5 million lines of communications software into ground stations in at least 11 countries and make it work flawlessly with an additional 14 million lines of code that controlled navigation and call switching in the skies. The satellite manufacturing process had to be shrunk from the usual two or more years to five days, and the cost of a satellite—normally about $200 million—cut by 80 percent. Iridium had to secure spectrum rights from the World Administrative Radio Conference, a 140-nation body, and from regulators in 200 countries.

There was also great uncertainty about the demand for a worldwide cellular system. According to Hardy, no one could estimate the size of the market for high-priced, universal mobile phones. At $3 per minute Iridium calls would be more expensive than land-based cellular calls. A technology consultant at Arthur D. Little noted that "there was no good head-count of international businessmen who need this. There may be a market in developing countries, but not in big cities."[103]

Not surprisingly, when Bertiger and his colleagues first proposed the idea, Motorola's senior managers showed little interest. Then Robert Galvin, the chairman, heard about it on his "annual tour" of the company. After two meetings with Bertiger, Galvin told Motorola's president, John Mitchell, "If you don't write a check for this, John, I will. Out of my own pocket." Subsequently, Motorola formed a separate company, Iridium LLC, in which it took a 25 percent equity interest. Motorola also guaranteed nearly $1 billion of Iridium's debt.

The unusual position and background of Motorola's chairman help explain why the company invested in Iridium. Robert Galvin was the son of Motorola's founder and would accompany his father on business trips from the time he was ten. He joined the army in 1942 after two years at Notre Dame, and after completing his military service joined Motorola instead of finishing college. He progressed through the ranks and became president and effective head. At the time the company was a $227 million-a-year manufacturer of car radios and phonographs. Under Galvin, Motorola became an $11 billion-a-year company, the world's leading manufacturer of two-way radios and cellular telephones and the fourth-largest-semiconductor manufacturer.[104] As of 1997 his share of Motorola stock was worth more than $1 billion. Few CEOs of large companies have the self-confidence and the reputation for good judgment that Galvin had accumulated when he backed the Iridium project. The more typical CEO shies away from uncertain commitments. As a rule, top executives will only endorse large bets with known, well-researched risks.

5. Summary and Conclusions

Revolutionary ventures provide a sharp contrast to promising start-ups. The almost epic sagas of Federal Express and the Jari project have little in common with Natcom's balloon rentals, Country Sampler's craft catalogs, Advent's portfolio management systems, and various other *Inc.* 500 businesses reviewed in previous chapters. Promising start-ups often engage in small-time quasi-arbitrage, discovering and correcting, as Kirzner puts it, "earlier errors made in the course of market exchanges."[105] Revolutionary start-ups have, at their core, a Schumpeterian big idea. Whereas promising start-ups try to find a profitable niche, revolutionary entrepreneurs seek to transform—in the case of Ludwig, quite literally—the existing landscape. Or to adapt a distinction from Loasby, rather than merely respond to changing data, revolutionaries cause the data to change.[106] Promising start-ups can make a profit at low levels of output; in a revolutionary venture, size and profitability are inextricably linked. Founders of promising ventures syndicate the risks to others, often by downplaying their significance. Revolutionary entrepreneurs confront and assume visible and public risks. Additionally, whereas the founders of promising businesses have some unusual qualities, the revolutionaries are extraordinary.

We should note, however, that revolutionary ventures are rare not only in comparison to the universe of new initiatives but also compared to businesses that have a lasting impact on the economic landscape. Federal Express and Iridium are unusual in that they could not have been started on a smaller scale or in incremental stages. More typically, companies such as Microsoft and Wal-Mart and industries such as the personal computer industry start in a far more modest fashion. Although they also have revolutionary long-term consequences, they are not "Schumpeterian" at the outset. Ludwig's shipping empire did not start with a big bet on innovative supertankers. Initially he bought and fixed up old ships without risking much of his own money. As with most other entrepreneurs, it took Ludwig decades rather than years to achieve significant scale and scope. In Part II of this book we will examine how this transformation, from promising start-up to a long-lived institution, usually occurs.

8

Summary and Generalizations

The sections below summarize the propositions we have discussed about promising new businesses and other archetypal new ventures and discuss the generalizations we can draw.

Summary of Propositions

Individuals and companies who undertake new initiatives start out with different initial conditions or endowments, including capital, ideas, credentials, and control systems. These differences in endowments affect the

- nature of the opportunities they pursue;
- degree to which they rely on prior analysis and planning rather than adaptation to unforeseen circumstances;
- strategies they employ to secure customers, employees, credit, supplies, and other inputs;
- factors that differentiate the successful initiatives from the unsuccessful ones.

Initial Conditions

Most individuals who start a new business have meager endowments—they usually lack novel ideas, deep experience, and credentials. They also face significant capital constraints. Their personal financial means are limited, and because they don't have any "verifiable" intellectual property or human capital to contribute to their ventures, they cannot raise funds from outside investors either.

The employees of large companies who undertake new initiatives have access to considerable funds and to corporate reputations and relationships. Internal control systems, however, limit the discretion of corporate entre-

196

preneurs. Corporate initiatives face extensive, multilevel scrutiny. This is not an avoidable symptom of a bureaucratic malaise that afflicts large corporations; rather, per agency theory, it is the inevitable consequence of the separation of ownership and management.

Founders of VC-backed start-ups have unusual endowments. Unlike most other individual entrepreneurs, they start with an innovative concept for making significant profits and valuable human capital. They can, therefore, raise significant funds from investors; but, in doing so, subject themselves to outside monitoring and oversight.

Founders of revolutionary ventures (such as Frederick Smith's Federal Express) start with truly extraordinary endowments: a blockbuster idea, significant personal wealth or an exceptional capacity to raise capital, and resources for a visionary scheme. Similarly, corporations such as Motorola who launch projects like Iridium have executives with exceptional boldness, as well as a track record that gives them great credibility with investors, bankers, suppliers, employees, and so on.

Nature of Opportunities

The entrepreneurs' endowments and constraints influence the types of opportunities they can profitably exploit. Individuals who start without a novel idea or access to capital are most likely to make a profit in businesses with low initial investment requirements and high uncertainty. The lack of capital limits the entrepreneur's capacity to pursue opportunities that require large up-front investment but also makes uncertainty a desirable attribute: The entrepreneur has little to lose if the venture does badly but can earn sizable profits if circumstances are favorable. Uncertainty also allows entrepreneurs who simply copy others' ideas and concepts to make a profit by dint of their hard work and innate talent or by participating in a temporarily rewarding game. Conversely, entrepreneurs who pursue low-uncertainty opportunities find that talent or hard work cannot make up for the lack of a differentiating concept or technology.

Large corporations tend to pursue initiatives with large initial investment requirements and low uncertainty. They have the financial wherewithal to pursue projects that require large initial investment, and stringent evaluation and monitoring requirements encourage them to pursue a few large projects rather than many small ones. Multilevel evaluations of new initiatives also limit the uncertainty that corporations can tolerate by increasing the requirements for objective evidence. This does not mean that corporations avoid well-defined risks and only undertake projects that decision-makers are sure will succeed. In fact, their large profit goals usually entail large, irreversible commitments, which makes the potential losses significantly greater than in most de novo start-ups. But corporate control systems generally do require proponents of new initiatives to document the case for why the expected returns exceed the expected risks. High uncertainty (due, for instance, to fickle consumer taste; changing regulations, technologies, or standards; and the lack of a verifiable advantage such as a proprietary technology) makes it difficult for proponents to provide objective evidence about the risks and returns.

Businesses launched by the select group of individuals who can raise capital from VCs occupy the middle ground in terms of their investment and uncertainty. Access to VC funding allows—and requires—the pursuit of larger projects than the typical individual entrepreneur can undertake. At the same time, the scrutiny and due diligence of the VCs weed out the highly uncertain projects that self-financed entrepreneurs often undertake, or in some cases, reduces uncertainty by uncovering new facts. Compared to corporate ventures, however, the uncertainty is greater and the investment is lower. VCs don't have access to as much capital as corporate executives so they cannot fund the megaprojects an Intel, a Merck, or an IBM might undertake. And their more streamlined processes can accommodate more uncertainty than corporations will usually tolerate.

Entrepreneurs with radical ideas and exceptional capacity to secure capital and other resources pursue initiatives that require high initial investment and involve great uncertainty. Given the very scarce supply of such entrepreneurs, such ventures are rare.

Planning vs. Adaptation

Initial endowments and constraints, especially the terms and availability of capital, influence the degree of analysis and planning that entrepreneurs undertake before they launch their ventures. The severe capital constraints most individual entrepreneurs face preclude much analysis and planning. These constraints also indirectly influence the economics of prior planning by limiting the kinds of opportunities entrepreneurs can profitably pursue. In small and highly uncertain ventures the benefits of prior planning quickly fall below the costs: Small businesses cannot cover significant up-front research and planning expenditures. High uncertainty limits the value of prior planning. In lieu of prior planning and research, the founders of promising start-ups rely on their capacity to adapt to unforeseen problems and opportunities.

Corporate control systems require extensive planning and research of new ventures. Indeed, corporations favor large projects because the magnitude of expected profits can pay for extensive up-front research and analysis. Corporations also favor low uncertainty initiatives, where decision-makers can verify the expected risks and returns through objective research and analysis. But compared to promising start-ups, corporations tend to make fewer changes after they have launched their initiatives. The low uncertainty of their projects and the prior research they conduct make surprises less likely. Corporations cannot change course easily because significant deviations from plan can require many sign-offs and approvals. And the size and complexity of corporate projects also discourage opportunistic adaptation.

VC-backed start-ups fall between corporate and promising ventures in their degree of prior planning and research. Entrepreneurs who raise venture capital to fund their start-ups have to provide business plans to VCs; and usually VCs conduct due diligence and independent research to verify the claims made in the plans. The effort devoted, although greater than in the typical promising start-up, usually is less than in large corporations: The funds available for research are scarcer, the checks and balances are not quite as elaborate, and the inherent uncertainty of the opportunity is greater. Similarly, the incentive and the need for VC-backed start-ups to adapt to new circumstances and to modify strategies in the poststart phase also fall between those of promising start-ups and corporate start-ups.

In revolutionary ventures, the high levels of uncertainty make it difficult for the entrepreneur to draw up reliable plans. At the same time, given the scale of the enterprise, extensive research and contingency planning are necessary to raise capital and coordinate resources: Ventures such as the Iridium project or Federal Express involve many "moving parts" that have to be integrated in a planned way. Postlaunch we find that decision-makers change many elements of their approach, but in contrast to small, promising start-ups, they cannot alter their core concept in midstream.

Securing Resources

Promising start-ups cannot easily secure customers, employees, supplies, and other such "resource providers" because of their meager endowments. The lack of capital, track records, and objective competitive advantages discourages resource providers from taking a chance on the venture. Entrepreneurs therefore seek out "atypical" individuals and companies who have limited alternatives, unusual requirements and preferences, or who do not properly evaluate the risks they face. Entrepreneurs provide special benefits such as customization and free ancillary services to their first resource providers to offset the providers' incentive to let someone else try out the start-up first. Entrepreneurs also use psychological ploys. For instance, they mimic the superficial features of well-established companies to create the perception of permanence, and they frame choices to downplay the risks that the resource providers face.

Established corporations can rely on their capital, reputations, and prior relationships to secure resources. Resource providers derive comfort from the corporation's financial resources and the irreversible commitments it makes to an enterprise. Corporations can underwrite the risks of resource providers by offering free trials and long-term contracts. They can publicly stake their reputations to their initiatives. And in contrast to promising start-ups, corporations will often emphasize rather than downplay the risks faced by the resource providers to encourage them to make the safe choice of going with an established company.

The lack of a track record and a diversified source of ongoing profit poses a problem for VC-backed start-ups, as it does for any new business. They have some advantages, however: Access to capital, the reputation and relationships of well-regarded founders and VCs, and the irreversible investments made at the start provide reassurance about the prospects of the venture. The valuable intellectual property these start-ups are based on also allows them to attract resource providers by giving them a share of the upside. For instance, VC-backed firms can attract talented employees by offering stock options. (For most other start-ups, the low expected value of the equity makes it difficult to attract high-quality talent with a share of the upside, so such ventures often have to utilize staff who have limited employment alternatives.)

Revolutionary ventures, which start with more innovative ideas and access to capital than other types of start-ups, also face greater problems in securing resources. Their ambitious plans call for high-quality talent— unlike promising start-ups, they cannot make do with personnel who have limited alternatives. Nor can they rely on providing exceptional services and benefits to just a few customers. They cannot easily underwrite others' risks, even with access to significant capital, because the uncertainty of the enterprise is so great. They can, however, hold out the promise of larger financial rewards, unique and compelling benefits to customers (the only guaranteed overnight delivery service in the case of Federal Express), and the excitement of participating in a pioneering adventure.

The problem of securing resources is of secondary importance in marginal ventures. They have few or no employees. Suppliers do not make irreversible investments or extend credit. Customers have low switching costs and do not face significant losses if the venture fails.

Differentiating Factors

The success of promising start-ups that lack much capital or a proprietary technology depends on the skills and innate abilities of its founders. These include a high tolerance for ambiguity, adaptability to new circumstances and information, resilience, perceptiveness about the wants and needs of others, ingenuity and resourcefulness in solving problems and coping with capital constraints, and face-to-face selling skills. Attributes of lesser importance include tolerance for risk or loss, significant creativity and capacity to innovate, prescience or foresight, and leadership and managerial abilities. Successful promising ventures, in other words, require entrepreneurs with some special qualities and talents but not all-round super humans.

Requirements for successful corporate initiatives are different in two ways. First, good foresight is more critical; a flawed concept cannot be redeemed through opportunistic adaptation. Second, because of the large size of corporate initiatives, the quality and effectiveness of a team matter more than the caliber of just one or two individuals. Thus the success of a new corporate business depends on the talents of the personnel in a variety of functions in marketing, production, and finance, and on an organizational capacity to coordinate the specialized functions.

VC-backed start-ups fall between promising and corporate initiatives on both these two dimensions. Success requires more foresight than in promising start-ups and more adaptability than in corporate initiatives. Similarly, the role of teamwork is greater than in promising start-ups because of the larger scale of the venture, but the quality and talents of the founders also have a significant influence on outcomes. These talents also are somewhat different—for instance, the capacity to manage a sizable team of employees is more important for the founders of VC-backed start-ups than for promising start-ups.

The individuals who (or the companies that) start revolutionary ventures require the "superhuman" qualities that are sometimes attributed to entrepreneurs. In addition to the qualities that a successful founder of a promising start-up requires (such as adaptability and resilience), revolutionary entrepreneurs also require great foresight, an unusual willingness to take risk, an evangelical ability to inspire others, and the capacity to build quickly and manage complex organizational units.

Starting marginal ventures does not involve exceptional talent or skill; or, put differently, a highly talented founder of a laundry or lawn care business does not earn much higher returns than an individual of mediocre talents.

General Propositions

Our analysis of archetypal initiatives suggests a general hypothesis that relates the nature of the initiatives organizations tend to undertake to their decision-making processes. Different types of organizations use different routines for evaluating and monitoring new investments. For instance, in large, publicly traded corporations, we find extensive scrutiny of new initiatives by an organizational hierarchy and a specialized staff. In the partnership form of organization we have fewer checks and balances and a greater reliance on what Fama and Jensen call mutual monitoring by the partners. In the small soleproprietorship, the decision to undertake a new initiative lies entirely in the hands of a single owner. We can also find differences within a given form of organization. Some publicly traded companies have fewer levels of hierarchy and smaller staffs than do others. Similarly, some partnerships vest considerable discretion in the hands of a small executive group, while others rely on broadly based committees to evaluate and ratify new initiatives.

Organizations cannot easily adapt their routines to the idiosyncrasies of individual opportunities. In the normal course, all new initiatives undertaken by a particular organization face a minimum level of scrutiny and ongoing oversight. Organizations also have, in the short run, a fixed capacity for evaluating and monitoring new projects. A firm may hire consultants for special projects, but it cannot quickly increase the time its core decision-makers have available. The combination of a minimum level of scrutiny and a fixed capacity to provide it limits the total number of initiatives an organization can undertake.

The nature of an organization's routines helps determine its access to capital. Companies such as IBM, Intel, and Merck can more easily mobilize funds from public markets than young companies with less stringent and well-proven evaluation and monitoring capabilities. And because firms must apportion their available capital to a limited number of projects, they also have a target for the minimum capital they try to invest in each initiative. (For instance, a company with access to $1 billion in total capital, and the capacity to evaluate and monitor ten initiatives, will search for projects that require an investment of at least $100 million.)

Routines also affect the uncertainty of initiatives. The more rigorous the checks and balances an organization has in place, the lower the unmeasurable and unquantifiable risks it can tolerate. Put alternatively, the highest valued use of an expensive evaluation and monitoring capability lies in undertaking initiatives whose risks and returns can be objectively assessed.

We therefore find the following specialization: Organizations with rigorous checks and balances undertake projects with relatively low irreducible uncertainty, large investment requirements, and large likely profits (assuming that large likely profits require large investments). Organizations with less rigorous checks and balances undertake projects with high uncertainty, low investment, and low likely profits. The specialization affects the conscious search for new initiatives that organizations undertake as well as their exploitation of accidental discoveries. Well-established corporations encourage (or explicitly instruct) their employees to look for new business opportunities that have well-defined risks and hold the promise of large profits. They also avoid committing resources to small or highly uncertain investment opportunities that their employees discover as a result of accident or personal interest. Instead, large corporations sell (or cede) the rights to these opportunities to smaller companies or start-ups. Conversely, small companies that develop or accidentally find investment opportunities that require substantial capital sell the rights to exploit these opportunities to large corporations or form joint ventures with them.

Opportunities with high uncertainty and high initial investment requirements (the "revolutionary" archetype discussed in Chapter 7) fall outside the domain of normal business activity. Individuals who or organizations that confront such opportunities will try decomposing them into a sequence of projects that involve less uncertainty or require less capital. In some cases, however (as in Frederick Smith's scheme to provide national overnight delivery of small packages), the nature of the opportunity requires an all-or-nothing project. Only extraordinarily influential or wealthy individuals, large corporations acting out of character, or not-for-profit government agencies and universities undertake such projects. Similarly, opportunities with low investment and uncertainty that do not hold even an outside chance of much profit also fall outside the domain of normal business activity; individuals undertake such projects as a substitute for low-paid employment.

The sidebar "Organizational Specialization: An Illustrative Analysis" provides a simple mathematical demonstration of the hypothesis that different organizations specialize in different regions of the uncertainty-investment-profit diagram. Extensions to the other dimensions, such as the reliance on adaptation vs. planning, strategies employed for securing resources, and differentiating factors, are fairly obvious.

Organizational Specialization: An Illustrative Analysis

To illustrate how different firms specialized in different types of initiatives, we will make the following simplifying assumption about the universe of available opportunities:

- All initiatives require a single initial investment of I. Each such investment is expected to produce a single slug of cash flow or "profit" P, with (Knightian) uncertainty U. I can be any positive number. U ranges from a maximum value of 1 (when the probability distribution of returns is fully known) to 0.
- P increases with both I and U (i.e., the greater the investment and uncertainty, the larger the total profit). The increase is not proportionate, however; rather both I and U have diminishing returns.
- The returns from uncertainty diminish faster than the returns from increasing investment. Therefore, large uncertainty and low investment produce lower likely profits than large investment and low uncertainty. The plausibility of this assumption derives from the expected (rather than the after-the-fact) profits that can be attributed to the initiatives. Low investment projects in the real world produce large subsequent profits very unexpectedly or because the project starts with a valuable asset such as a patent.

The relationship $P = K_p I^\alpha U^\beta$, where $K_p > 1$ and $0 < \beta < \alpha < 1$ conforms to these assumptions. Note that profit maximizers will only undertake initiatives when $P > I$ (i.e., when $K_p I^\alpha U^\beta > I$ or $K_p I^{\alpha-1} U^\beta > 1$).

The firms that seek to exploit these opportunities have different evaluation and monitoring routines and capabilities such that:

- Each firm has a fixed staff or managerial capacity for evaluating and monitoring profits, which corresponds to total expenditure of $E.
- Each firm has to devote at least e_{min} to every project it undertakes, where $e_{min} = k_n E$ (i.e., firms with large E have greater minimum evaluation and monitoring requirements). These requirements determine the maximum number of projects (N) a firm can undertake:

$$N_{max} e_{min} < E$$
Or substituting for $e_{min} = k_n E$,
$$N_{max} < 1/K_n$$

- Each firm's evaluation and monitoring capabilities determine the total capital it has available to undertake initiatives (C) as well as the maximum uncertainty it can tolerate in any initiative (U_{max}). Larger E's imply a larger C and a lower U_{max}, such that

$$C = K_c E \text{ and } U_{max} = K_u / C$$

Implying that $$U_{max} = \frac{K_u}{K_c} \times \frac{1}{C}$$

- Firms undertake identical projects (i.e., they cannot undertake projects involving different U's and I's).

Given these assumptions, we infer that:

- Firms have an incentive to invest their available capital on many small projects instead of one large project because of the declining returns on investment. But they cannot undertake any more than $1/K_n$ projects. So they undertake this maximum number, in which they invest $I = $C/1/k_n = K_n C$, so $C = I/K_n$.
- Because P increases with U (and there is no limit to the total U across investments), each initiative that a firm invests in, has a $U = U_{max} = K_u/C$.

Substituting for $C = I/K_n$, we get

$$U = K_u/(I/K_n) = \frac{K_u \, K_n}{I}$$

In other words, the U and the I of the projects are inversely related.

We can also substitute $I = \frac{K_u \, K_n}{I}$ into the relationship $P = K_p \, I^\alpha \, U^\beta$

$$P = K_p \, \frac{(K_u \, K_n)^\alpha}{U^\alpha} \, U^\beta$$

$$P = K_p \, (K_u K_n)^\alpha \, U^{\beta - \alpha}$$

P is also, according to this equation, inversely related to U as long as $\beta-\alpha < 0$ — that is, $\alpha > \beta$.

The relationships among U, I, and P conform to our basic uncertainty-investment-profit diagram: Firms with large E invest in projects with low uncertainty and large required investment and likely profit. Firms with smaller E's specialize in more uncertain projects with less required investment and likely profit (their return on investment [P/I] is however, greater because they bear more uncertainty). Large U and large I projects cannot be funded by small E firms and lie outside the uncertainty tolerance of large E firms. Small U and small I projects are "uneconomical" (i.e., P < I).

II

The Evolution of Fledgling Businesses

In Part I we compared promising start-ups with initiatives undertaken by large corporations. The next four chapters examine how businesses change—how some fledgling businesses evolve into large, long-lived corporations. The sections below provide an overview of these chapters. I will summarize the approach and scope, the data used, the propositions developed, and the structure of the chapters.

Most start-ups do not evolve into large and long-lived firms. Bruce Phillip's and Bruce Kirchoff's estimates from the U.S. government's small-business database suggest that about 60 percent of start-ups fail in the first six years and more than 70 percent in the first eight.[1] Moreover, the evidence suggests that of the start-ups that survive, most remain small. *Inc.* 500 companies—winners from the category of promising start-ups—appear to have higher survival and growth rates. In 1995, *Inc.* checked back on all the 500 companies in the "class of 1985" and found that only 19 percent were no longer in business or could not be located. Another 27 percent had been sold to new owners, and 6 percent had gone public. Forty-eight percent had survived ten years under the same ownership—nearly twice the proportion, according to *Inc.*, of the typical new business. Moreover, the survivors had continued to grow. In 1984, all 500 companies on the *Inc.* list accounted for sales of $7.4 billion and employed 64,800 workers. By 1995 just the 233 known survivors recorded more than $29 billion in revenues and had 127,000 employees. Even so, only three of the 1985 *Inc.* 500 companies—Microsoft, Merisel, and TechData—made *Fortune* magazine's 1995 list of the 500 largest corporations in America.[2]

The evolution of young businesses has more economic significance than that small number that eventually join the ranks of well-established corporations might suggest. Building a business involves some Schumpeterian innovation; rather than capitalize on disequilibriums or provide customized services to a few customers, entrepreneurs create new combinations and shape the structures of their industries and markets. And as we have already seen, the few businesses that attain significant size and longevity play a distinctive economic role: They can undertake much larger initiatives than individual entrepreneurs; their accumulated reputations and perceived staying power have significant influence on the nature of their relationships with customers, employees, lenders, and other such resource providers.

Although common wisdom and academic research concur that only a few start-ups evolve into long-lived corporations, the underlying factors have not been well identified. We can find considerable historical data about specific cases, but little by way of a general explanation for why certain firms survive and grow. My analysis suggests that most new businesses aren't just large businesses in miniature and that their trajectories do not point to noteworthy size and longevity. Extrapolation of the initial approach leads businesses to fail or get stuck in a rut—what Elster would call evolutionary "local maxima." Building a long-lived firm requires comprehensive changes. Instead of relying on opportunistic adaptation to exploit niche opportunities, they have to formulate and implement ambitious long-term strategies.

Only exceptional entrepreneurs have the capacity and the will to make such changes. The passage from a fledgling business to a large corporation requires entrepreneurs to develop new skills and to perform new roles. Entrepreneurs must also have unusual ambition and tolerance for loss. Starting a heads-I-win-tails-I-don't-lose-much enterprise has a compelling financial logic. Once an entrepreneur has navigated a venture through its uncertain initial period, however, selling out to a competitor or large corporation often provides better risk-adjusted returns than efforts to grow the business. Entrepreneurs who forgo these exit options *may* eventually amass very large fortunes, but they can also lose it all. Their drive to build a large corporation transcends goals of maximizing risk-adjusted financial returns.

Approach and Scope

The problem of identifying the common features of the evolution of long-lived corporations primarily derives from the lack of a general framework or theory rather than a lack of data. We can find ample information on the growth of most large corporations in the United States in memoirs, popular biographies, and scholarly histories. Such writings tend to focus, however, on specific events in particular companies—how and why HP entered the printer business, for instance—rather than on a general theory of firm evolution. Looking across histories of long-lived companies reveals few recurring patterns; on the surface, at least, their evolution seems highly idiosyncratic. To provide any general explanation for the data, we need some way to filter the common elements from the contextual noise. Collecting more data on long-lived corporations (or on a matched sample of short-lived businesses) without such a filter cannot provide much additional insight.

The approach I will use extends the comparative analysis of Part I. In Part I we identified the features common to an otherwise heterogeneous set of promising start-ups through a comparison with the known features of established corporations. Now we will use the features of start-ups on the one side and established companies on the other to frame our inquiry of the transition between the two states. In other words, our knowledge of the origins and destinations of the typical long-lived corporation will help us identify the important common elements of their evolution.

As in Part I, this analysis emphasizes the contribution of individual entrepreneurs. We will contrast the role they play and the problems they face in building a business with those of starting a new venture, and with the roles and problems of executives who manage an established corporation. We will also examine the qualities that affect an entrepreneur's willingness and capacity to build a long-lived corporation. The focus on the roles and qualities of individual entrepreneurs represents a departure from existing economic analyses. As we will see, theories of firm evolution often assume that as industries mature, the number of competitors converges to a number determined by factors such as the economies of scale, and that chance determines which firms survive. I will argue that the ambition and capability of individual entrepreneurs have a significant impact on firm longevity and growth and by extension on the long-run structure of markets. McDonald's likely dwarfs Oscar Mayer (the leading vendor of hot dogs in the United States) because of the unique abilities of Ray Kroc—I know of no intrinsically larger economies of scale in making or selling hamburgers vs. hot dogs. Industries do not naturally converge to a predetermined structure, nor is their evolution a matter of pure chance. The entrepreneur's efforts shape the structures of industries. I do not mean to suggest that exogenous factors such as technology or product characteristics do not play any role. My emphasis on the entrepreneurial factor is to redress its prior neglect.

In contrast to the earlier chapters, however, I will no longer use the term "entrepreneurs" synonymously with the individuals who start the business. By "entrepreneurs" I will now refer to the top decision-makers—typically one or two individuals—who control the enterprise and who have a significant economic stake in its fortunes. They need not be the initial founders or even hold the official title of CEO or president of the company. For instance, George Eastman, who started and built Eastman Kodak, officially served as the treasurer of the company. Marvin Bower urged two older colleagues at the failing McKinsey, Wellington & Co. to join him to start McKinsey & Co. in 1939 and was the principal architect of its subsequent transformation into a worldwide enterprise. Bower did not, however, assume the position of managing partner until 1950; from 1939 to 1950 he served as the deputy to a much older cofounder, Guy Crockett.

The scope of this inquiry is limited to the transition from the fledgling to the mature enterprise and does not address the issue of immortality. We will not examine why only some firms survive beyond the multidecade life span of the *Fortune* 500-type company.* Our goal is to explain how a few entrepreneurs like Sam Walton, turn a small chain of franchised discount stores in Arkansas into the multibillion-dollar retailing enterprise Wal-Mart. An analysis of the problems that the executives of Wal-Mart now face of sustaining an already well-established corporation is relevant to this discussion mainly because it helps us identify the different challenges that Walton faced in the transitional phase.

The normal emphasis of business research on the problems of large, established corporations makes it particularly important to keep in mind my focus on transitional businesses. For instance, research and popular wisdom often ascribe the poor performance of companies to their lack of focus and cumbersome administrative procedures—and indeed, a comparison of large companies may show that firms with more diverse lines of business and greater administrative overhead earn lower returns. Looking at the evolution of fledgling businesses, however, provides a different perspective: We find that the transition to a large enterprise requires greater heterogeneity of assets and functions and investment in administrative infrastructure.

Data

In formulating hypotheses on firm survival and growth I have relied on a somewhat different set of data and ventures than I used for drawing inferences on the origins of new businesses. My primary sources of information comprised the critical histories of successful entrepreneurs written by my students (as described in the Introduction); detailed case studies that I wrote on some prominent, long-lived companies (as well as some that failed to survive); books and articles on companies like Microsoft; and the memoirs of entrepreneurs like Walton. I relied somewhat less on the *Inc.* 500 interviews. I had interviewed the *Inc.* founders when their companies

---

* Arie de Geus reports that the typical large company in North America, Europe, and Japan that survives the difficult early years has a life span of about four to five decades. De Geus notes some exceptions, however: The Japanese conglomerate Sumitomo started as a copper casting shop in 1590. Stora, a major paper pulp and chemicals company based in Sweden, had its roots in a copper mining operation more than seven centuries ago. These examples suggest to de Geus that "the natural life span of a corporation could be two or three centuries—or more." By de Geus's standard, most commercial corporations are "underachievers" that "exist at an early stage of evolution."

were about seven years old and their future prospects were far from assured. In contrast, the critical histories (listed in Appendix 2) and case studies (listed in the References) covered more than a hundred "tried and tested" companies that had survived and grown through at least a decade, and in many cases for much longer. These companies were also significantly larger than the *Inc.* ventures, with revenues in the hundreds of millions or billions of dollars, compared to the $20 million median in some of the *Inc.* companies.

The varied fields from which I drew my companies (e.g., Wal-Mart in discount retailing; McKinsey & Co. in management consulting; Sun Microsystems in engineering workstations; and Physicians Sales and Service [PSS] in medical products distribution), and the diversity of their experiences limit the number of generalizations we can draw. The many stories do not, for instance, conform to a simple script such as a life-cycle model. But the repeated occurrence of a few key patterns—particularly with respect to the role of the entrepreneur—across such a varied sample offers reassurance about the robustness of the generalizations. Virtually all the data I used, incidentally, are in the public domain, so the hypotheses I have drawn are open to verification and challenge by others.

Propositions

As we will see, some life-cycle models suggest that businesses have a natural tendency to grow and mature, provided that the entrepreneur is willing to "let go." Evolutionary theories, in contrast, assume that random events lead to differences in the growth of firms. I argue that the long-term growth and survival of a business are not simply matters of preordination or luck; rather, I suggest that:

- A substantial gap exists between improvised start-ups and well-established firms in terms of their assets, coordinating mechanisms, and capacity for growth.
- Closing the gap requires entrepreneurs to make larger, longer-term investments than are required to start a promising business; in other words, they have to undertake initiatives in the middle region of the investment-uncertainty-profit diagram. And to achieve complementarity across initiatives, entrepreneurs have to formulate and implement long-term strategies instead of relying on opportunistic adaptation.
- The willingness and the capacity to pursue a strategic rather than an opportunistic approach require traits and skills that do not play a significant role in the start-up stage and that very few entrepreneurs have.

Structure

Chapters 9 and 10 lay the groundwork. Chapter 9 examines the require- ments for longevity and growth that fledgling businesses usually do not satisfy; this analysis will help us specify the gap between fledgling busi- nesses and established corporations. Chapter 10 reviews existing theories and models on firm evolution. Although they provide some useful con- cepts, we will find that they seriously underplay the entrepreneur's contri- bution to bridging the gap between fledgling and long-lived businesses. Chapters 11 and 12 connect the transition from a fledgling to a well- established enterprise to the entrepreneurs' ability and willingness to pur- sue a strategic rather than an opportunistic approach. Chapter 11 examines three crucial tasks entrepreneurs must undertake to build a long-lived busi- ness. First, they have to adopt and articulate an ambitious long-term goal or "purpose" for the enterprise that goes beyond survival and generating positive cash flows. Second, they have to formulate a strategy for attaining the long-term goal. Finally, they have to implement the strategy—that is, translate the general rules and objectives that comprise the "strategy" into specific decisions and actions. Chapter 12 identifies the qualities and skills that affect an entrepreneur's predisposition and capacity to undertake these tasks.

9

Missing Attributes

This chapter identifies the basic differences between fledgling businesses and large corporations. Section 1 provides the necessary definitions. Section 2 discusses why large and long-lived businesses comprise a broad portfolio of assets. Section 3 then moves on to examine the mechanisms necessary to coordinate these assets. Section 4 examines the relationship between longevity and growth. The concluding section shows how most fledgling firms don't satisfy the requirements for longevity and growth.

The transition of a fledgling business into a large, well-established corporation requires a fundamental transformation rather than a simple scaling up, because of some basic differences in their attributes (see Fig. 9.1). The profits of fledgling businesses derive from a few (and often transient) factors. Fledgling businesses also face serious growth constraints due to factors such as the small size of the markets they serve. In contrast, large, long-lived corporations have a broad and well-coordinated portfolio of products, relationships, know-how and other such assets that allow them to profitably compete in large markets. Building a large and long-lived corporation therefore requires a considerable broadening of the fledgling firm's assets, establishing effective mechanisms to coordinate the assets and developing the capacity to compete in large markets.

The discussion will require us to grapple with elusive definitions: To analyze longevity, we must first specify what we mean by the life of a business. Similarly, an analysis of growth requires us to define the size and boundaries of firms. The inquiry will also lead us to reevaluate common beliefs about the rationale for diversification, horizontal and vertical integration, and growth. But although we confront basic issues about the nature of businesses, I do not attempt to develop a new "theory of the firm." We examine the requirements for longevity and growth that fledgling businesses don't satisfy in order to identify the distinctive problems that entrepreneurs face in building a large and long-lived business.

213

1. Definitions

Defining the "longevity" and the "size" of a business (or to use the common technical term, "firm") is not straightforward. Unlike a living being who has a tangible, physical form, a "firm" is an economic and legal abstraction whose boundaries and life span, by extension, also represent intangible constructs. Different theories use different definitions depending on the problems they seek to analyze. For instance, standard microeconomic analysis of perfectly competitive markets assumes that all firms competing in a market transform the same inputs—capital and labor—using the same technology or production function. The theory makes questions about the growth or survival of individual firms moot.

I have adopted the so-called resource-based view (RBV) that has evolved from the efforts of some economists to develop a theory that would permit a meaningful analysis of firm growth. In 1959 Edith Penrose proposed a model that treated the firm as an "administrative unit" that wasn't tied to a particular market or technology; it could, given appropriate resources, "produce anything for which a demand can be found or created." Different firms had different administrative attributes, expanded into different markets and thus developed distinct identities. As we will see in the section "Longevity and Growth" later in this chapter, Penrose's model helped explain the tendency of firms to grow—that is, to expand the boundaries that delineated their "area of coordination." Other theorists, such as Nelson and Winter, have adopted and extended the view of a firm as an entity with distinctive attributes. Their work has led to the resource-based view of firms with distinct decision-making routines, memories, reputations and other such intangible, and almost human, attributes.

Following the RBV approach, I define firms as comprising a distinctive bundle of "assets." I use the term assets in a broad fashion: They encompass a firm's properties (e.g., its plants or patents), reputations (e.g., for fair dealing and reliability), relationships with customers and providers of

FLEDGLING BUSINESSES   **LARGE CORPORATIONS**

• Profitability based on a few factors
• Niche markets

                                 • Multiple assets
                                 • Embedded coordination mechanisms
                                 • Mass markets

Figure 9.1. Differences in Firm Attributes

inputs, and competencies or capabilities (e.g., marketing know-how).* For convenience, I will refer to a "firm's" assets when they actually belong to its "resource providers" such as stockholders, employees, suppliers, or even the providers of complementary goods. Although it seems natural to think of a firm as an integrated, living entity, we should remember that the firm merely uses the assets that one or more of its constituents own and may redeploy. For instance, employees with valuable skills can join another firm or worse yet, withdraw their services while staying on the payroll. Similarly, stockholders can (acting through the board of directors) cause the sale of all or part of the "firm's" assets.

Defining a firm as a distinctive bundle of assets leads to the following specifications of its longevity and size.

Longevity. This analysis associates the "life" of a firm with the continuity of its asset portfolio. The composition of a firm's portfolio of assets tends to change for a variety of reasons. Some assets become worthless or disappear: Patents expire, relationships with customers sour, and valued employees retire or leave. At the same time, the pursuit of new initiatives creates new assets. The significance of firm longevity that we discussed in Part I (e.g., the capacity to secure unsecured credit from banks and irreversible commitments from customers) derives from its continuity rather than its sameness. A long-lived firm may be compared to the proverbial Japanese temple. Although its every beam has been replaced over the centuries, devotees still regard it as the same temple because the changes have been gradual. As Penrose wrote "[T]he name of a firm may change, its managing personnel may change, its geographic location may change, its legal form may change, and still in the ordinary course of events we would consider it to be the same firm and could write the story of its life. Whether the continuity was maintained by bankers in times of crisis or by the ingenuity of a clever promoter is irrelevant, providing that the firm neither suffered such complete disruption that it lost the 'hard core' of its operating personnel, nor lost its identity in that of another firm."[1]

Firm longevity is closely associated with its capacity to provide its stockholders (or other residual claimants) a satisfactory return. Chronic losses will lead stockholders to shut down or liquidate a firm. Stockholders also have an incentive to liquidate if the price they can realize for the assets exceeds the returns they expect to receive by maintaining it as a going concern. An analysis of firm longevity is therefore virtually indistinguishable from an analysis of long-run profitability. (This does not mean, however, that building a large, long-lived firm necessarily provides attractive returns; a firm may be worth less than the costs incurred to create it but more than the liquidation value.)

---

* Modern RBV theorists make finer distinctions among competences, resources, static, and dynamic capabilities and so on. My argument does not require these distinctions, so I will stick with the broad category of "assets."

Size. I will treat the size of the firm as the area of influence of its unique assets. In economic terms, this corresponds to the markets where the firm affects prices. This definition is somewhat broader than Penrose's, who delineated firms by the area of their direct administrative control. It contrasts even more sharply with theories that use the criterion of ownership or employment as the basis for setting firm boundaries—any asset owned or person employed by the firm is "inside," and the rest is outside. My definition corresponds to constructs in the management literature that refer to a firm's "business system," "value chain," and "differentiated network": Any asset, regardless of its legal ownership, that is partially or fully specialized for the use of a firm is part of that firm.

This definition involves trade-offs. It makes firm size difficult to measure. It leads to overlapping boundaries when firms share assets (such as a close supplier-customer relationship). And readers who are used to defining firms in terms of their assets or employees may misinterpret some of the arguments that will follow. But I believe my definition will help us identify some critical conditions of firm longevity and growth that the sharper ownership and employment approach to delineating firms may obscure.

2. Diverse Assets

Large, well-established firms comprise a more heterogeneous bundle of assets and activities than most fledgling businesses. As Hewlett and Packard noted in their first year in business, "a single product rarely [makes] a successful company."[2] Mature corporations typically offer many lines of products and services, often through autonomous business units. Even the relatively few long-lived firms that stick to narrow product lines, such as Wedgwood (fine china) and Cartier (jewelry), have many assets, including brand names, distributor relationships, skilled craftsmanship and design, and marketing capabilities. This is not to suggest that long-lived firms necessarily own a very broad range of assets or have employees who perform many functions, just that their overall business system encompasses many distinctive elements. Microsoft is a more complex entity now than it was in the 1970s both because its sells more products, owns more technologies, and has employees who perform more functions, and because more customers, subcontractors, and suppliers of ancillary goods and services have developed resources tied to the Microsoft system.

Increased heterogeneity naturally follows increases in the volume of a firm's business. As firms grow they add customers, employees, locations, and suppliers that are to some degree different. And more volume permits the specialization that increases the heterogeneity of their activities: For instance, larger firms can afford to separate bookkeeping from their financial control function. Heterogeneity also can contribute in subtle ways to a firm's survival. A broad base of assets, as we will see next, fosters longevity because of "complementarities" (or "synergies") and insurance effects. They do, however, create some offsetting problems, which require long-lived firms to have effective coordination mechanisms.

Complementarity

The distinctive assets that give a firm its identity (such as its unique products, know-how, and relationships) have limited value on their own. Their optimal use requires other distinctive assets to complement their function. Failure to develop effective complements encourages stockholders and other resource providers to withdraw the asset from the firm.

To illustrate, consider a pharmaceutical company that owns a patented drug. Unlike the undifferentiated commodity producer assumed in models of perfect competition, the pharmaceutical company cannot sell its unique product in an anonymous auction market. To realize the value of its patent, the pharmaceutical company must secure the use of a complementary sales and marketing capability; through its own personnel, a joint venture, or third-party distributors, it must persuade doctors to prescribe the drug. Failure to train and deploy knowledgeable sales and marketing staff limits profits from the drug and encourages stockholders to liquidate the firm to realize the value of the patent—that is, redeploy the asset in a higher-valued use.* Complementary downstream sales capabilities also help the firm retain valuable upstream research personnel—a researcher cannot derive much psychic or financial reward working for a firm that does not effectively market the products its R&D staff develop. The argument can be extended to any asset that differentiates a firm's products or services: To the extent that the firm's output is unique, its value will depend on the firm's ability to locate customers who will derive the most utility, educate these customers about the benefits, and analyze their willingness to pay and bargain over terms.

Insurance

A broad base of assets also provides insurance against the loss of value of any one asset because of imitation by rivals, shifts in demand, and so on. For instance, in a firm with strong marketing capabilities and customer relationships, the loss or diminution of the superiority of its product will reduce but not necessarily eliminate its profits. Stockholders don't have to close operations; the marketing assets buy time for the firm to recoup the loss of its product advantages.** Multiple product lines, technologies, and organizational capabilities, we should note, afford far greater protection

---

* I am not suggesting that returns to investing in the complementary asset will always be positive, merely that once the investment has been made, ongoing profits will be greater and that the incentives to liquidate will be lower.

** The long-run failure to do so will, however, encourage stockholders to try to realize the value of the marketing asset through sale or liquidation of the firm.

than simply having a lot of cash on hand or having access to financial markets. Maintaining large cash balances as insurance reduces profitability. These reserves earn low returns and can make a firm a target for takeovers. And whereas a single-product firm may have easy access to equity and debt markets in good times, these sources of funds can become prohibitively costly when changes in demand or competition threaten the firm's profitability

A broad base of assets seems particularly crucial for protecting firms against being leapfrogged by new generations of technologies. In some high-technology industries, the life spans of companies that rely solely on their product development capabilities tend to coincide with the life cycles of their products. Henderson's study of the photolithography industry, Christensen's study of disk drives, and other such research suggest that winners often do not repeat in successive rounds of technological races. One explanation is that winning a round leads to myopia or incompetence— the winner does not recognize the threat from the next generation of technology or does not manage the development process efficiently. Given several keen competitors, chance may also play a significant role in determining who succeeds in developing the next technology first. Therefore, just as the random walk hypothesis tells us that the top stock picker in one period has no edge in winning in the next, we should not expect the winner of the $5^{1}/_{4}$-inch disk drive race to also be the first to market with $3^{1}/_{2}$-inch disk drives.

Multiple assets apparently provide some protection to the laggards. Long-lived companies usually are not the first in every new generation of technology or market. In fact, given our discussion in Part I, we should expect large corporations to be laggards in the development of what Christensen calls "disruptive technologies" such as personal computers that "are first commercialized in emerging or insignificant markets."[3] Such technologies "underperform established products in mainstream markets" and their distinctive features appeal only to "a few fringe (and generally new) customers."[4] And, as discussed in Part I, the decision-making processes of large corporations discourage them from pursuing small opportunities whose long-term potential is highly uncertain.

Their broad base of assets gives companies such as IBM, HP, and Microsoft an opportunity to catch up with and surpass the pioneers. (See the sidebar "Catching Up.") New entrants using the next generation of technology may wipe out a business whose profits depend primarily on its capacity to manufacture one generation of disk drives. Companies with a broad line of profitable products, brand names, close client relationships, sound engineering capabilities, financial reserves, and other such assets have greater staying power. Diverse assets provide what Dixit and Pindyck[5] call a valuable "option to wait" until uncertainties about market size and product attributes have been reduced to the point where the corporate decision-making process can endorse a substantial commitment of resources. They do not, of course, ensure success, but they give late entrants more of a chance to catch up. IBM and HP, for instance, could more easily cope with the threat microprocessor-based workstations posed to their minicomputer businesses than could companies such as Digital, Data General, Wang, and Prime, which focused on minicomputers.

The perceived stability of firms with multiple assets can create positive feedback effects that help them expand their portfolio of assets. As discussed in Chapter 4, firms that are expected to survive have an advantage in persuading resource providers to invest in assets that are of value to the firm. For instance, firms often make implicit promises to provide long-term rewards to employees for developing human capital (such as the sales personnel's knowledge of the firm's product line) that has value to the firm but is of limited use to other employers. These rewards, which might include favored promotion opportunities and job security, are contingent on the continued survival of the firm. Therefore, all other things being equal, employees will put greater store by the promises of firms with broadly diversified assets rather than firms that rely on a few sources of differentiation.*

The connection between longevity and a broad base of assets seems to fly in the face of the current popularity of "focused" strategies. The apparent conflict derives mainly from differences in definition and perspective. The focus that many prescriptive theories recommend pertains to the assets a company directly owns and the activities its employees carry out, whereas the heterogeneity I refer to encompasses a firm's extended business system. The higher profitability found in more focused firms also usually derives from comparisons of mature companies that have already attained a high level of complexity. My argument pertains to the evolution of fledgling businesses. I am also more concerned with explaining longevity, not the maximization of financial returns; as mentioned, the investments required to build a long-lived firm may not represent the best possible economic use of resources.

My analysis departs from the popular view about focus in one important respect. As we will see next, heterogeneity does involve costs, but there is no rigid relationship between the two. Rather, the magnitude of the costs depends on how effectively firms can cope with the problems that heterogeneity creates. The inability to develop effective mechanisms to coordinate

---

* Some economic models suggest that employees will prefer to work in focused firms because this provides them with the opportunity to develop skills they can use to "hold up" their employers. In my discussions with individuals seeking employment in young firms, I can think of only one instance where the opportunity to hold up the employer was of any concern. A variation on the hold-up theme can be commonly observed, however, in the concerns of potential recruits about being able to add value in a large and diversified corporation.

Catching Up

Long-run survivors in high-technology industries seem to rely as much on their capacity to catch up and surpass others' pioneering efforts as on their own development of new markets or technologies. IBM, which has dominated the industry for over four decades, "came close to missing the computer business" writes Thomas J. Watson, Jr. (who succeeded his father as chief executive of the company). His father (and predecessor as IBM's chief executive) was "devoted" to punch cards; in the late 1940s, punch-card machines accounted for 85 percent of its revenues. IBM was also a late entrant in the minicomputer segment in the 1960s and in personal computers in the 1980s. Its marketing, sales, and service capabilities and customer relationships protected IBM, however. As Thomas J. Watson, Jr., wrote in his memoir:

> In the history of IBM, technological innovation wasn't the thing that made us successful. Unhappily there were many times when we came in second . . . [but] we consistently outsold people who had better technology, because we knew how to put the story before the customer, how to install the machines successfully, and how to hang on to the customers once we had them.[6]

HP, which has a reputation for technological leadership, derives a significant portion of its revenues from products and markets that others had developed first. An appendix in cofounder David Packard's memoir contains pages of pioneering innovations, such as the first programmable scientific desktop calculator and noninvasive fetal heart rate monitor. In its current core business, however, Packard notes, HP was a late entrant. Packard records that in 1994, HP derived 78 percent of its total sales, amounting to $20 billion, from computer products, service, and support. In 1964 HP did not have any computer sales—all of HP's revenues (amounting to $125 million) came from instruments. Writes Packard:

> This represents a remarkable transformation of our company and its business. It would be nice to claim that we foresaw the profound effect of computers on our business and that we prepared ourselves to take early advantage of the computer age. Unfortunately, the record does not justify such pride. It would be more accurate to say that we were pushed into computers.

To enter the computer business, HP first tried to acquire Digital Equipment Company and then Wang Laboratories. After these acquisitions fell through, HP introduced, in 1966, an automatic controller for measurement systems, which became its first minicomputer, the model 2116. HP found that it was selling more 2116s as stand-along computers than as controllers in measurement systems, writes Packard, but "we were slow to get the message." The cancellation of Omega, an effort to develop what would have been "the world's first 32-bit computer" provides an example of HP's "cautious approach to computers." HP did not proceed beyond the Omega prototype, because of the expense, the new technical expertise required, and the "formidable marketing challenge." Omega was scaled back to a 16-bit machine, the HP 3000, the company's first general-purpose computer, which was introduced in 1972. HP was also a laggard in the PC market—in 1992 it only had a 1 percent share of the market. Management then decided to make a determined effort in the field, and by 1998 HP had become the fourth-largest supplier of personal computers, with a 6.6 percent share of the market.[7]

Microsoft has introduced virtually all its significant revenue-generating products after rival offerings. Its first operating system, MS-DOS, came after Digital Research's CP/M was well established. The graphical user interface in Windows followed the Mac operating system. Microsoft's spreadsheet Excel and word processor Word were introduced after 1-2-3 from Lotus and Word-Perfect had achieved wide popularity. Its 32-bit operating systems Windows 95 and Windows NT followed IBM's OS/2. Microsoft initially promoted its proprietary on-line service, MSN, and allowed Netscape's Navigator to dominate the market for Internet browsers. Moreover, the first version of its products, according to W. S. Mossberg, have often had "serious design flaws, missing features, and outright defects."

But after introducing products that are late and "fall far short of promises," writes Mossberg, the company typically "mounts a massive repair effort. The fix begins with version 2.0, and usually culminates in a version 3.0 that works pretty well, or even very well." Apparently Microsoft's broad portfolio of assets—its marketing and distribution capabilities, access to capital, the capacity to incorporate customer suggestions in product revisions, a near-mythical reputation for invincibility, and an organizational norm for taking all competitors seriously—have allowed Microsoft to catch up and pass the early leaders. For instance, Microsoft did eventually embrace the Internet; and after roughly four versions, its browser, Explorer, became a serious enough threat to Netscape's Navigator to attract the interest of the antitrust lawyers in the Justice Department.

We find similar patterns in finance and professional services. Goldman Sachs in investment banking and McKinsey & Co. in management consulting, the leading and most consistently profitable firms in their respective fields, have often been late in entering new markets and offering new services and products. McKinsey, for instance, was behind other consulting firms in going overseas and developing a strategy practice. McKinsey's broad-based capabilities allowed the firm to catch up with, and eventually outdistance, the first movers in these markets and services.

heterogeneous assets and activities, not the heterogeneity itself, makes businesses "unfocused" or "overdiversified." Some cannot manage more than one location; others realize competitive advantages from worldwide operations.* The quality of a firm's coordination mechanisms has a profound influence on the long-term profitability and viability of a business with multiple assets.

3. Coordination Mechanisms

The benefits of heterogeneity have offsetting costs. Complementarities also entail potential conflicts. For example, in a business whose profits result from the joint efforts of its specialized production and marketing functions, it is difficult to evaluate their relative contributions. The two units may therefore be expected to haggle over transfer prices or attempt to ride free on each other's efforts. These problems do not arise in businesses that sell their output in an anonymous auction market. The difficulty of measuring individual contributions can also discourage talented and ambitious employees from joining the enterprise. They worry that, in a business with many interrelated parts, any out-of-the-ordinary contributions may not make much of a difference to the overall enterprise and therefore will not be rewarded.

The insurance provided by multiple assets leads to moral hazard problems that can cause firms to unravel. Most insurance schemes tempt individuals to take advantage of others in the group. Purchasers of health insurance, for instance, have an incentive to see their doctors more often than they would if they had to bear the full costs of their visits. Since all participants face the same temptation, total benefits paid increase (unless the insurance company can monitor and penalize unnecessary visits). High benefits, in turn, lead to higher premiums and induce the healthiest participants to drop out.

Similar problems may undermine the risk-pooling advantages provided by companies with multiple lines of business. Consider, for example, a company whose energy division offsets the losses of its steel-making business. As long as the corporation as a whole is in the black, members of the steel unit may be less willing to take the difficult steps needed to restore profitability than if they belonged to a stand-alone enterprise. And members of the healthy energy division will have an incentive to withhold contributions to the parent corporation—say, by slacking off or by increasing their costs. Or they may simply leave, to pursue better opportunities elsewhere. For instance, in early 1988 Bruce Wasserstein, Joseph Perella, and others in First Boston's Mergers and Acquisitions Department left the firm

---

* We see a similar pattern with national and political units. Fierce strife causes small regions such as the Balkans to disintegrate. In contrast, the right structures, rules, and traditions allow the United States to enjoy many benefits from its large size.

to start their own operation because they believed the profits generated by their department were being unfairly used to subsidize the trading operation.[8] A similar dispute has recently led to a split between the consulting and accounting units of Anderson.

As we will see below, the problems that arise due to heterogeneity defy simple "structural" remedies such as common ownership of complementary assets or the adoption of multidivisional organizational structures. Just as a nervous system that integrates specialized organs and functions pervades our bodies, so a firm's capacity to coordinate diverse assets is deeply embedded in its routines, processes, formal and tacit reporting relationships, incentive and control systems, norms, values, and other such organizational attributes that influence the behavior of the employees, customers, suppliers, and other resource providers. This capacity for coordination represents a critical meta-asset of long lived companies.* Firms cannot purchase effective mechanisms to coordinate assets off the shelf (e.g., as they might a payroll management system) or copy them from rivals; and poor coordination mechanisms cause the unraveling of the distinctive assets that comprise a firm.

Joint Ownership

Some "transaction cost" theorists relate the mitigation of the conflicts between complementary activities to their joint ownership. Below I summarize Oliver Williamson's analysis of the benefits of joint ownership and review and extend Mark Granovetter's critique.

Williamson's analysis. According to Williamson, the costs of contracting between independent firms that provide complementary functions lead to their joint ownership by a single "integrated" firm. The integration of iron- and steelmaking, he points out, cannot be explained by the thermal economies said to be available through the integration of successive stages. "Were it possible to write and enforce a complex contingent claims contract between blast furnace and rolling mill stages, the integration of these activities, for thermal economy reasons, would be unnecessary. The prohibitive cost of such contracting is what explains the decision to integrate."

In Williamson's view, two conditions make contracting between independent firms engaged in successive stages of production "prohibitively costly." One condition is the uncertainty of outcomes. The other is the small number of buyers or sellers, as may result when the minimum efficient scale is large compared to the magnitude of demand. Uncertainty makes it diffi-

---

* Henderson (1994) has discussed a different kind of "integrative competence," namely "the ability to integrate fragmented knowledge across boundaries within a firm." I am concerned here with the ongoing problems that arise in the coordination of specialized units and resources, within or across traditional firm boundaries. We arrive at the same conclusion, however, that an integrative competence represents "a potentially potent source of competitive advantage."

cult for the parties to anticipate and incorporate into their contracts all the contingencies that would be relevant to their transactions. The problem of limited contractual protection is exacerbated by the possibilities for "opportunistic" behavior (including the use of guile and deceit) that arise when the buyers or sellers have few other parties with whom they can do business. Combining successive stages into a single firm, Williamson argues, alleviates opportunism and facilitates adaptation to unforeseen events by "harmonizing interests and permitting a wider variety of sensitive incentive and control processes to be activated."[9] Instead of extended haggling between independent agents over how to deal with new circumstances, executives of a single firm, organized within a well-ordered hierarchy of authority, make the necessary decisions. The hazards of "defection and cheating" are also reduced. Claims to what might otherwise have represented two separate profit streams are permanently pooled. Members of a single firm have a common interest in preserving its infrastructure. The ability to conduct internal audits discourages misrepresentation. And the integrated firm can utilize "more refined and selective" "compliance instruments" to resolve conflicts and promote "cooperative adjustments to changing market" conditions.

Williamson acknowledges some "disabilities" of internal transactions. For instance, members of an organization may seek to promote personal goals by diverting the communication system to their own uses. Biases toward internal procurement may preserve nonviable internal capabilities. Subgroups may pursue their own objectives over those of the firm as a whole. Internal organization, Williamson claims, should therefore be regarded as a "syndrome of characteristics" with "distinctive strengths and distinctive weaknesses," which provide a clear-cut advantage only when the "defects" associated with market exchange exceed a nontrivial threshold.

Granovetter's critique. In his article "Economic Action and Social Structure," Granovetter argues that "Williamson vastly overestimates the efficacy of hierarchical power ("fiat," in his terminology) within organizations."[10] Countering Williamson's assertion about the efficiency of internal auditing and controls, Granovetter cites Dalton's research, which shows that, in practice, a variety of subterfuges can undermine internal audits and that "cost accounting of all kinds is a highly arbitrary and therefore easily politicized process rather than a technical procedure decided on grounds of efficiency." In studying a large chemical plant, Dalton found that the level of services the maintenance department provided to various production departments and how it charged for those services depended on the political standing of the department heads and their relationship to the maintenance staff. Department heads could secure favored treatment "by the use of friendships, by bullying and implied threats." Auditors, Granovetter notes, looked the other way. As one of Dalton's sources observed: "If Auditing got to snooping around, what the hell could they find out? And if they did find anything, they'd know a damn sight better than to say anything about it. . . . [The Department heads] have got lines through Cost Accounting. That's a lot of bunk about Auditing being important." [11]

Williamson's analysis relies on after-the-fact explanations. The claim that a particular business is vertically integrated because internal transaction costs are lower than those of a market exchange is a statement of "revealed superiority" akin to explanations of individual choice based on "revealed preferences." Such Darwinian arguments, Granovetter observes, can "careen toward a Panglossian view of whatever institution is analyzed." The lack of clear distinctions between the nature of some hierarchical and market "defects" cited by Williamson represents another problem. What distinguishes haggling by unit managers over internal transfer prices in order to increase salaries or bonuses, from haggling by the owners of adjacent businesses in order to increase their profits? Does lying by a manager to a downstream counterpart (or an internal auditor) have different transaction cost consequences from the misrepresentations by a vendor to a customer?

Embedded mechanisms. Granovetter's critique suggests a solution to some of the circularities of transaction cost analysis. Granovetter argues that the relative efficiency of vertical integration depends "on the concrete specific personal relations that develop within or between firms." Granovetter writes:

> Even with complex transactions a high level of order can often be found in the "market"—that is, across firm boundaries—and a correspondingly high level of disorder within the firm. Whether these occur, instead of what Williamson expects, depends on the nature of personal relations and networks of relations between and within firms. I claim that both order *and* disorder, honesty *and* malfeasance have more to do with structures of such relations than they do with organizational form. [12]

Granovetter's suggestion that some "concrete personal relations" promote order and honesty and others disorder and malfeasance corresponds to the proposition that coordination costs depend on deeply embedded mechanisms. The joint value of complementary assets depends on specific factors, such as the personality and chemistry between the players, the formal and tacit rules they follow, and the incentive and control systems rather than whether the assets have joint ownership. The degree to which internal audits become politicized or relationships with outside suppliers become acrimonious depends on many contextual factors and concrete choices. With effective coordination mechanisms the vertically integrated General Motors could become the leading U.S. automobile company, and Toyota, which relies heavily on subcontractors, could dominate the Japanese market. Similarly, Compaq and Dell have become the top leading personal computer companies in the United States with very different levels of vertical integration.

The quality of a firm's coordination mechanisms also affects its capacity to use a common asset across multiple activities. In the classical example, a business that rears sheep for mutton might also, in principle, profitably sell wool. Coordinating the wool and mutton lines—realizing horizontal complementarities—poses problems similar to those of coordinating complementary upstream and downstream activities. For instance, units sharing the same asset may conflict over cost allocations—how the wool and mutton businesses are charged for the costs of rearing the sheep. Conflicts may also arise, in spite of common ownership of the two lines, over asset use—how much attention a common sales force pays to two different lines, and over the attempts by a less profitable unit to take a free ride on the performance of a more profitable unit. And whether the benefits of sharing the common asset exceed the costs of such conflicts will depend on the concrete, deeply embedded features of the coordination mechanisms.

Organizational Structure

The adoption of multidivisional organizational structures, Williamson and other theorists suggest, also represents a powerful solution to the problem of coordinating diversified assets. As we will see below, the argument, which is based on historian Alfred Chandler's studies of the modern industrial corporation, has a reasonable empirical basis. It understates, however, the importance of all the other embedded mechanisms required for the multidivisional (or any other) organizational form to play an effective role in coordinating diverse assets.

Simply put, Chandler's analysis suggests that the transformation of American industry from small-scale manufacturing to dominance by large corporations resulted from the strategies adopted by some firms to increase the scale and scope of their businesses. Their expansion into "new areas, functions or product lines," writes Chandler, created "new administrative needs." Without changes in organizational structures, "the technological, financial and personnel economies of growth and size [could] not be realized."[13] The enterprises that came to dominate their industries developed, albeit with a lag, new organizations that met the administrative demands of their new strategies.

Chandler highlights the development of the multidivisional organizational form (later called the M-form by Williamson) as a critical innovation. Diversification into multiple businesses placed an "intolerable strain on existing administrative structures" of the traditional functional organization. "Growth through diversification into several lines increased the number and complexity of both operational and entrepreneurial activities," writes Chandler. "The problems of obtaining materials and supplies, of manufacturing and of marketing a number of product lines for different types of customers or in different parts of the world made the tasks of departmental headquarters exceedingly difficult to administer systematically and rationally. The coordination of product flow through several departments proved even more formidable."[14] The solution was a decentralized, multidivisional structure. Its adoption at General Motors "not only helped it to win the largest share of the automobile market in the United States, but also to expand and administer successfully its overseas manufacturing and marketing activities. Furthermore, because of its administrative structure, it was able to execute brilliantly a broad strategy of diversification into the making and selling of all types of engines, and products using engines. . . ."[15]

For historians, multidivisional organization represents a critical innovation: McCraw and Tedlow call it "one of the signal achievements of the twentieth-century corporation."[16] The effective administration of diversification, Chandler's data suggest, however, required a much broader effort. In Chandler's words, the "strategies of expansion, consolidation and integration" undertaken by American industrialists "demanded structural changes and innovations *at all levels of administration*" (emphasis added). Chandler defines organizational structures broadly, to include "lines of communication and authority" and "the information and data that flow through these lines of communication and authority." Chandler's descriptions show that top executives concerned themselves, administratively speaking, with much more than the principle of organizing their corporation's activities into quasi-autonomous divisions and deeply engaged themselves in numerous specific issues and decisions that determine the performance of a complex enterprise.

Between 1921 and 1925, for instance, General Motors "worked out highly rational and systematic procedures that permitted it, on the one hand, to coordinate and appraise the operating divisions and to plan a policy for the corporation as a whole, and on the other hand, to assure a smooth product flow from supplier to consumer and a fairly steady use of plants, facilities and personnel. . . ."[17] These procedures required the design and use of detailed reports and plans such as the "price study" which included each division's estimates of sales (in units and dollars), costs, and profits, as well as capital requirements and returns on investment at standard volumes and at the rate of sales forecast for the following year.[18] The leadership of General Motors was also engaged in the details of personnel decisions. For example, Pierre DuPont, whose family had a large investment in General Motors and who served as chairman of its board reviewed "in a regular and formal fashion" the performance of all its senior executives and helped decide on their salary and bonuses. [19]

The ability of General Motors to realize economies of scale and scope apparently derived from a large number of managerial decisions and activities. It developed deeply embedded and broadly based mechanisms to coordinate its diverse activities, of which its multidivisional organization was but one (albeit important and striking) element. Today the principle of decentralization through so-called strategic business units has become ubiquitous. But the complex components and architectures of effective coordination mechanisms cannot be easily replicated or purchased. Differences in coordination mechanisms therefore remain an important determinant of firm profitability and longevity. (See the sidebar "Profitable Diversification.")

To summarize: Long-lived firms resemble species that have evolved many specialized functions rather than unicellular organisms: They have many assets to sustain their profitability. Assets cannot stand alone; their value derives from association with complementary assets. A broad base of assets also contributes to firm longevity by providing insurance against the loss of value of individual components. However, heterogeneous assets also create coordination problems that defy simple solutions—conflicts between complementary functions for instance do not go away because of their joint ownership. Rather, as illustrated in Figure 9.2, the net benefits of heterogeneity depend on the quality of deeply embedded coordination mechanisms. In other words, long-lived corporations exhibit a high level of coordinated heterogeneity: Their coordination mechanisms allow them to derive more benefits than costs from complex business systems.

4. Longevity and Growth

A firm's capacity for growth has an important influence on its survival. One obvious connection between growth and longevity follows from our previous discussion of multiple assets. A small firm that relies just on the labor of its proprietors is vulnerable to the loss of their skills or motivation. To establish a more lasting source of profit than the effort of the owners can provide, the firm has to invest in assets such as proprietary technologies or brand names, increase its customer base to amortize this investment, and add employees commensurate with its expanded activities. The section

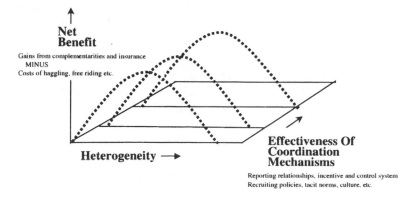

Figure 9.2. Gains from Heterogeneity

Profitable Diversification

The importance of embedded coordination mechanisms in managing multiple assets is well illustrated by the extreme case of conglomerate or unrelated diversification. Most studies suggest that the widely diversified firm produces poorer returns on capital than the single-business firm or the firm that limits its diversification to "related" businesses. Stock markets typically impose a "conglomerate discount," according companies with unrelated businesses valuations considerably lower than the estimated sum of the individual components. Apparently the cost of coordinating conglomerates usually exceeds the benefits of sharing a common managerial and fund-raising resource across several businesses. But as a 1997 *Economist* survey of the evidence on conglomeration points out, we do find exceptions.

The *Economist* noted that General Electric, a giant U.S. conglomerate, gave shareholders an annual average return of 20.8 percent, about 6 percent better than the stock market average, after Jack Welch took over as chairman in 1979. A Boston Consulting Group study of forty of the largest American, European, and Australian conglomerates showed that the top quartile of conglomerates provided annual returns that were about five points above the average returns for all stocks listed on the market. These examples suggest that whereas "on average" the costs of the conglomerate form outweigh the benefits, "unusually talented and disciplined bosses," in the words of the *Economist*, can make unrelated diversification work. There is little proprietary about GE's general approach; indeed, it is well advertised in its annual reports and presentations to Wall Street analysts. GE's reputation for motivating employees and wringing the best possible performance out of its business units indicates that its top management distinguishes itself in the details.

Even the coordination of related business activities poses difficult problems. For example, in the 1980s, several mergers in financial services attempted to create "financial supermarkets." Offering multiple products through a single distribution channel would supposedly lower sales costs and provide more convenient one-stop shopping. Under what some wags called the "socks and stocks" strategy, for instance, a Dean Witter kiosk in a Sears department store would sell insurance, brokerage services, and credit cards. These combinations failed to live up to expectations. Insurance sales staff could not, in practice, be motivated or trained to sell brokerage services, and stockbrokers would not "cross-sell" insurance. Managers of the different businesses did not cooperate. If the supermarkets had worked, their architects would likely have credited themselves with brilliant strategic foresight.

In fact, the success of strategies to realize synergies across multiple businesses lies in the details. With good procedures to select, train, control, and motivate its personnel, General Electric's value can exceed the sum of its unrelated parts. Otherwise, obvious economies from consolidating nearly identical businesses may not be realized.

below discusses a more subtle relationship between longevity and growth: A firm cannot easily stop growing after it has reached some fixed critical mass. Just as bicyclists have to keep moving to maintain their balance, so competitive forces often require firms to keep growing to survive. We will also see how the assets and coordination that influence a firm's longevity also affect its capacity to grow.

Pressures to Grow

HP cofounder David Packard writes in his memoirs that over the years, he and Bill Hewlett had "speculated many times about the optimum size of a company." They "did not believe that growth was important for its own sake" but eventually concluded that "continuous growth was essential" for the company to remain competitive."[20] When HP published a formal list of objectives in 1966, one of the seven items was: "*Growth.* To emphasize growth as a measure of strength and a requirement for survival."[21]

Penrose and subsequent theorists such as Rubin have argued that the optimal size of a firm represents a moving target because of ongoing increases in its managerial capabilities and the lumpiness of its assets. The accumulation of experience and the development of decision-making routines, they suggest, leads to a natural increase in the capacity of a firm's managerial and supervisory personnel. To quote Rubin:

> Consider a firm that has just added a new product. In planning the product, management will attempt to set up decision rules for subordinates to obey. However some problems will always arise that require consultation with top management. As the firm acquires more experience with the product, it will become possible to routinize many of these decisions. Once a decision has been made, it is no longer a problem; a precedent has been set, and a subordinate can look up the appropriate rule. Thus, if an executive was kept fully occupied when production was begun, he will find himself with more and more excess time because of this process of routinization. Further, as the executive gains experience in his job, he will find that those decisions left for him will require less time." [22]

Firms keep growing in the Penrose-Rubin model to utilize the progressive increase in their unused managerial capacity. The lumpiness of assets creates similar incentives to grow. A small, simple firm can match the capacity of its assets to its needs relatively easily, especially if the assets are versatile. In a firm with heterogeneous assets, as Penrose pointed out, lumpiness or indivisibilities will cause the underutilization of some assets. For instance, a firm may employ 2 salespersons when it really needs 1.7. The unused sales capacity provides an incentive to make more products to sell, which in turn may lead to an excess of manufacturing capacity, and so on.

External labor markets can also create incentives to grow. Hewlett and Packard believed that growth was a matter of survival because HP "depended on attracting high caliber people" who wanted to "align their careers only with a company that offered ample opportunity for personal growth and progress."[23] A stagnant firm risks losing its talented employees because it cannot easily offer them opportunities to build new skills or the financial reward of a share in the economic value they help create. Once a firm's principals commit to building something more than a small lifestyle business in which they do most of the work themselves and start recruiting ambitious talent, the process cannot be easily stopped. They have to keep growing or face the disintegration of their firms. Competitive forces have a similar effect. A firm cannot remain small if its rivals increase market share by exploiting economies of scale or if customers believe that size is a precondition for long-run survival. And, as mentioned in Part I, financial markets can tip the competitive balance in favor of rapidly growing firms by providing them with a lower cost of capital.

Growth can help reduce conflicts within the firm. Research on human behavior suggests that people weigh losses of what they already have more heavily than they do new gains of a similar magnitude. When the overall pie is fixed, increasing the rewards given to one individual requires taking something away from another individual. If the pie is growing, however, changes in relative shares do not require firm members to give up what they already have, so we should expect less rancorous disputes over the distribution of rewards. Growth also creates a sense of pride in the accomplishment of the organization and encourages individuals to internalize the interests of the overall group. (As discussed later, growth does, however, strain a firm's coordination capabilities by increasing heterogeneity.)

The incentives and the pressure to grow vary. In some organizations the key tasks of the managers may not be subject to significant learning effects and routinization—a former business school dean, for instance, says that he took just as long to perform the same functions in the fifth year of his job as he did in his first. Such organizations do not need to undertake new activities to use up their excess managerial capacity. Similarly, a high-technology company that competes in a market where there is room for only one winner, has to attract ambitious employees from a mobile pool of labor and raise capital from the public markets, faces more intense pressure to grow than a business that does not face much competition for its customers and employees and is self-financed.

Except for businesses that rely just on the labor of their principals, few firms can, however, totally avoid the pressure to grow. The owner of a building products distribution company in Massachusetts explains why he acquired a much larger company and took on debt that eventually led him to declare bankruptcy. He had built a profitable business (the "preeminent company in town"), which led him to believe he was "invincible." Labor pressures reinforced the hubris that led him to expand: "I had five guys who I had hired and trained working for me. One of them was making

$40,000 a year, which was quite a lot of money then. But he was ready to move on and I would have had to hire and train someone all over again."

The pressures to grow seem to have intensified in recent years with the increasing mobility of labor and capital and the aggressive pursuit of high returns. Anecdotal evidence suggests that business school students and seasoned executives alike are more willing to trade away some job security for the excitement and potential financial rewards of working in rapidly growing companies. The financial markets, too, as of this writing, seem to be willing to pay a high premium for the stock of such companies. But we can find evidence of such pressure from previous eras as well. The minutes of a 1956 meeting of McKinsey & Co. partners record that "the question of growth in offices and size of the staff was the most frequently raised by associates" and affirm the partners' belief that growth was "essential" (although it could "take many forms"). Apparently the pressure to grow is a pervasive feature of a market economy.

Capacity for Growth

A firm's growth potential is often related to the size of the market for its products or services. As Penrose points out, however, in the long run, firms can enter new markets, serving different customers and offering different products. This long-term growth potential depends on the productive capacity of the firm's assets and its coordination capabilities. For instance, consider a restaurant whose profits derive from difficult-to-replicate assets such as its location, ambience, and the skills of the chef. Such a business cannot profitably grow beyond a single location—the nature of its critical assets make its markets local. In contrast, a proprietary formula for operating a hamburger store allows for worldwide expansion.

A firm's coordination mechanisms affect its growth potential because growth inevitably increases the diversity of assets and activities. No two customers, locations, employees, and so on are exactly alike. As the firm expands, so do the coordination problems; in addition to having a formula for operating individual stores therefore, a company like McDonald's requires a capacity to coordinate its far-flung operations. Limits on a firm's coordination capabilities, in combination with the pressure to keep growing, can lead to its eventual demise even in the absence of significant competitive threats. This may be a reason why the natural life span of businesses is shorter than the centuries suggested by de Geus and why companies once extolled as excellent disintegrate (see Fig. 9.3).

The quality of a firm's coordination mechanisms also affects the *rate* at which it can expand—that is, add new assets. The coordination of existing assets resembles the functioning of an established marital relationship; the parties rely on prior agreements and understandings to adjust to unanticipated circumstances. Adding new assets involves problems similar to those of forming a new relationship, which requires developing agreements and

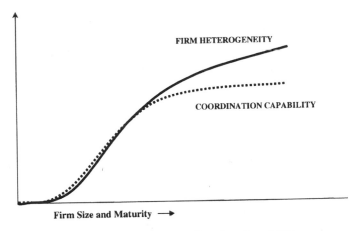

Figure 9.3. Limits to Coordination Capabilities

Note: "Coordination capabilities" refer to the maximum heterogeneity that the firm's coordination routines allow it to derive a positive net benefit from.

understandings from scratch. These problems are proportional to the firm's rate of growth; the rapid addition of new locations and employees in a restaurant chain poses greater difficulties than a slow expansion. Indeed, the demise of firms is often attributed to "excessive" growth: As HP's cofounder, David Packard, puts it, "more businesses die from indigestion than starvation."[24]

A firm's capacity to digest new assets and activities depends on embedded mechanisms such as its incentives and control systems, recruiting and training practices, and tacit norms. Effective mechanisms allow firms such as Physicians Sales and Services to add employees and customers at an extremely fast rate without impairing the quality of their output or running out of cash. (See the sidebar "Controlling Growth.")

To summarize: In the sections "Diverse Assets" and "Coordination Mechanisms" we examined the direct relationship between a firm's assets and coordination mechanisms and its capacity to generate long-lived profits. In this section we found an indirect connection: Longevity goes hand in hand with growth; and a firm's capacity for growth depends on the nature of its distinctive assets as well as its embedded coordination mechanisms.

5. Missing Requirements

Most fledgling businesses don't satisfy the requirements for long-term survival and growth. They lack a broad base of valuable assets. Rather, they resemble the undifferentiated firm found in models of perfect competition, which use similar inputs and technologies to produce similar products as their rivals. Promising start-ups, as we saw in Part I, usually imitate or

Controlling Growth

Between 1987 and 1995, Physicians Sales and Services (PSS) grew from $13 million in sales to nearly $500 million, from 5 branches in Florida to 56 branches covering every state in the continental United States, and from 120 employees to 1,800. In his book *Faster Company,* PSS cofounder and CEO Pat Kelly attributes this rapid growth to several embedded mechanisms for recruiting, training, and motivating employees. Here I will discuss just one of these mechanisms—PSS's control systems. Tight financial controls played an important role in the growth, according to venture capitalist and former board member Thomas Dickerson. Dickerson notes that the PSS organizational structure gives front-line employees considerable operating responsibility at the same time as a "nearly real-time control system" closely monitors results: "Each branch is run as a PSS in miniature and each branch manager is responsible for meeting targets for sales, profitability, inventory turns and receivables collections. The company builds these targets from the ground up—top management visits all 56 centers each year, and negotiates each of the 500 salespersons' projections individually. Each evening, headquarters captures electronically the daily sales results of each sales person and receivables and inventory information from each branch."

PSS's systems eased staffing constraints and allowed it to grow quickly without having to recruit experienced personnel. According to founder and CEO Pat Kelly, the company gave "huge amounts of responsibility to people without much experience, many of them not long out of college."[25] The control systems also allowed the company to reconcile its long-term growth objectives to the limited availability of internally and externally generated funds. The branches that PSS had to open to become a national company took about eighteen months to start making a profit. New branches consumed cash and reduced reported profits—a matter of some concern because the founder, Pat Kelly, wanted to avoid reporting losses so PSS would be able to eventually gain access to the public capital markets through a stock offering. The company's budgeting and cash management system allowed it to maximize the new center openings without violating its bank borrowing covenants or falling short of its annual targets for operating income. Many young companies that lack such systems run out of cash and "grow themselves to death."

slightly modify an existing idea. Many promising start-ups take advantage of market disequilibriums ("catch a wave") to make their initial profits. Others rely on the personal capacity of the founders to satisfy the fuzzy wants of their customers. A small number (about 10 to 15 percent of a typical *Inc.* 500 sample) do start with a unique technology or design, but don't offer a broad line of products or have deep R&D, manufacturing, distribution, and marketing capabilities. Capital constraints preclude most entrepreneurs from differentiating their business system along multiple fronts.

With few assets and a narrow range of activities, the fledgling enterprise does not require extensive coordination mechanisms. The founders perform most of the important functions and even some of the mundane tasks. In the early days of HP, the two founders, writes Packard, "had to tackle almost everything ourselves—from inventing and building products to pricing, to packaging, and shipping them; from dealing with customers and sales representatives to keeping the books; from writing the ads to sweeping up at the end of the day."[26] The young firm doesn't have formal reporting relationships, personnel policies, incentive and control systems, and so on. The founders rely on case-by-case judgment and informal systems to manage a few employees performing unstructured roles.

Such firms cannot long survive without broadening their assets. Entrepreneurs who ride the wave of a new technology, legal regime, or other such exogenous change prosper at the outset because demand exceeds the available supply. Waves crest, however; as market imbalances disappear, so do many undifferentiated suppliers. Businesses that rely on the entrepreneur's personal capacity to satisfy amorphous customer wants are vulnerable to the erosion of the principals' drive and skills and to competition from hungrier upstarts. And single-product businesses often succumb to changes in technology or customer preferences over which they have no control.

Fledgling firms also face significant growth constraints. The business that merely rides a wave has to share its market with new entrants attracted by the high profits of the incumbents. Businesses that rely on their founders' ability to serve amorphous wants are constrained by the productive capacity of their differentiating asset. And the growth of the few "better mousetrap" businesses like HP is limited by the size of their niche markets.

A fledgling business does provide a starting point for building coordinated assets. Although many of the entrepreneurs of the 1980s who assembled IBM PC "clones" from standard components folded their businesses, Michael Dell used his dormitory room operation as a platform for building a brand name and distinctive production, logistics, and marketing capabilities. Sam Walton opened his first store as a franchisee of the Ben Franklin variety store chain but soon developed the know-how to run standardized franchised stores in different and more profitable ways and then discovered opportunities in discounting. Hewlett and Packard reinvested the profits from their audio-oscillators to develop a broad line of electronic test equipment.

Entrepreneurs who operate even precarious businesses have a chance to discover opportunities that outsiders cannot see. A going business also enjoys advantages in securing the capital, customers, employees, and other resources required to build the firm's assets. Vinod Khosla, cofounder of Sun Microsystems, recalls how he made over a hundred phone calls trying to recruit an experienced marketing manager to help launch the company:

"Most of them just hung up on me. When you are twenty-six years old, look like a little kid, talk with a funny accent, and have two people in your company, and you're calling the vice president at DEC and HP, you don't get very far. . . . Besides, nobody wants to leave established companies to join someplace where they can't even see six months of salary." One year later, when Sun booked a profit and reached $1 million dollars in monthly revenues, it was able to hire a senior executive, Owen Brown, away from Digital Equipment. Khosla observes: "People feel a lot more comfortable with something there and running and profitable and operating, even if it is small, relative to nothing there. There's a radical nonlinear function between those two."

Although having "something there" provides a valuable platform for building something on, the progression to well-established business is unusual. As we will see in subsequent chapters, it takes decades of sustained effort by exceptional entrepreneurs to bridge the wide gap that separates the "promising" Wal-Mart, Sun, or HP from the well-established *Fortune* 500 enterprise.

6. Summary and Conclusions

The material above provides some basic building blocks for analyzing the growth and longevity of firms. We adopted the resource-based view of a firm as comprising a distinctive bundle of tangible and intangible assets. We associated its life span with the continuity of its assets and its size with its area of economic influence. Long-lived firms, we found, have a broad portfolio of assets, and effective mechanisms for coordinating these assets. We also discussed the close connection between longevity and growth. These determinants of longevity suggested a wide gap between fledgling and well-established firms.

Going forward, we can think of the building of long-lived firms as the process of closing that gap—that is, of investing in a broad base of assets, developing mechanisms to coordinate these assets, and overcoming growth constraints. We may also contrast the challenges of firm building with those of managing a well-established business. Building a firm requires the entrepreneur to develop assets and coordination mechanisms more or less from scratch. The concerns of the top managers of established businesses revolve around existing assets and mechanisms. Given the current set of market opportunities, are the firm's assets being put to their best possible use? Would investing in new, complementary assets increase the value of the firm's portfolio? Should some components be divested because they would be more valuable to another firm? Similarly, where the entrepreneur has to build coordination mechanisms, the executive has to resist being overwhelmed by them. The "way things are done around here," formal and informal organizational rules, and multiple levels of decision-making can all marginalize the efforts of top management and eventually lead to the demise of venerable business institutions.

The coordinated heterogeneity of large corporations influences the economic role they play. In Part I, I suggested that the control systems and decision-making processes of large corporations allow and encourage them to undertake initiatives that require significant up-front investment. The analysis of this chapter suggests that the systems also facilitate the coordination of heterogeneous assets and activities. The comparative advantage of large corporations thus encompasses high capital requirements as well as complexity. In contrast to hedge-fund manager George Soros's billion-dollar currency speculations, the projects undertaken by companies such as IBM and Intel have many moving parts.

This perspective bears a close relationship to the theories of Chester Barnard, Herbert Simon and Alfred Chandler that connect the multifaceted administrative and social structures of firms to their economic role. Its correspondence is not as close, however, with the "transaction costs" theories pioneered by R. H. Coase and extended by scholars such as Williamson. Transaction costs theories focus on bilateral exchanges that can either take place between two autonomous agents through market transactions or within a firm whose owners have a claim on the cash flows of both the parties. While transaction cost analyses provide many useful insights, I believe they miss important aspects of the coordination mechanisms found in real-life business organizations.

Large corporations—from the early railroads to the modern Microsoft or Intel—do not just coordinate transactions between two parties. They undertake and manage initiatives that involve the joint effort of a heterogeneous group of agents. Joint ownership (or employment) represents but one tool for such multilateral coordination; the effectiveness of the joint effort of many agents depends on a multifaceted, deeply embedded organizational nervous system. And the dichotomy between "firms" and "markets" overlooks important differences in the coordination capacities of firms and therefore the kinds of activities they tend to specialize in. Small firms whose owners personally do most of the coordinating have an advantage in undertaking activities that do not involve many specialized assets. As firms develop more extensive coordination capabilities they tend to undertake activities where the returns from managing complexity can justify the increased administrative costs. The evolution of a firm thus involves basic changes in its economic role.

10

Existing Theories and Models

This chapter examines existing theories and models that might help explain why some promising new ventures undergo the transformation into large and long-lived businesses. Section 1 suggests that although the transformation is radical, it takes place gradually. Sections 2 through 5 examine possible explanations from mainstream economic theory, life-cycle models, evolutionary theory, and the business strategy literature.

Most businesses mature gradually. Only exceptional businesses start with the talent, capital and strategies that rapidly propel them into the ranks of large, well-established companies. Compaq, as we saw in the Introduction, had an experienced team, $20 million in venture capital, and a plan that allowed it to behave like a large sophisticated company from the start, selling $100 million of its computers in its very first year. To use a biological analogy, ventures such as Compaq are like the "precocial" offspring of horses, which are relatively mature at birth and can see and walk in hours. Most start-ups, however, resemble the "altricial" young of creatures such as birds, red foxes, and humans, who are born in an immature and precarious state. Altricial start-ups take many years, often decades, to build the assets and coordination mechanisms that characterize well-established firms. Moreover, most don't: In contrast to human offspring, an early demise or arrested development is the rule with start-ups, survival and growth the exception. In this chapter we will examine a variety of theories and models that might explain why only a few start-ups go on to become large and long-lived firms.

1. A Gradual Process

Fledgling businesses turn into long-lived companies through a protracted, multistage process rather than through a one-shot transformation. It often requires decades of sustained investment to develop the necessary systems of coordinated assets, for several reasons:

Capital constraints. Developing the assets that sustain a long-lived firm requires much more investment than does starting a promising business. Entrepreneurs have to undertake initiatives that require considerable out-of-pocket outlays or opportunity costs to develop brand names, technologies, broad product lines, distribution channels, and so on. As we have seen, few entrepreneurs can undertake such initiatives at the outset because they lack credibility with the providers of capital and their businesses have highly uncertain prospects. As entrepreneurs build a track record, uncertainties about their ability and business propositions diminish. They gain access to more capital and can move their initiatives from the upper-left-hand corner to the middle of the investment-uncertainty-profit diagram. But because it takes time for capital constraints to ease, entrepreneurs cannot make a one-shot investment in a system of complementary assets. Rather, they tend to invest in a few assets that have the highest likely pay-off and to use standard, readily available elements in the rest of their business system. Subsequently, as they gain access to more capital, they can invest in a broader portfolio of assets. Michael Dell, the founder of Dell Computer, for example, made low price an option for sophisticated personal computer buyers by assembling standard components and selling by mail order without frills or much sales support. As internally generated profits grew and as Dell gained access to public equity markets, the company was able to build a brand name, an extensive logistics system, sales and support functions, and close relationships with its suppliers.

Foreknowledge. Entrepreneurs cannot easily envision the design of an effective system of complementary assets in advance. For instance, the distinctive features of the Wal-Mart discount chain—its focus on underserved rural areas, low prices, purchasing skills, investments in information technology, employee culture, and even the greeters at store entrances—have an impressive logic and coherence. But while we might admire the system now, Wal-Mart's history suggests that its founder, Sam Walton, did not envision its components beforehand. Walton started by buying what he called a "real dog" of a franchised store in a small town in Arkansas. He added more franchised stores through the 1950s and did not open his first "Wal-Mart" until 1962. The Wal-Mart system then evolved, over more than a decade, after much trial and error and some failed initiatives, rather than through the execution of a master plan.

Learning by doing. Some critical assets, such as know-how and reputations, can only be developed through repeated action. A pharmaceutical company develops an effective capability to discover new drugs by undertaking many research projects and by distilling effective management routines and practices from them.[1] Experience leads firms that have produced more output over time to enjoy lower costs.* In some cases the ability to

* Per the well-known learning curve effects popularized by the Boston Consulting Group, manufacturing costs in many industries are a function of cumulative output.

get any output at all from a technology requires, according to Polyani, an "indefinable knowledge" built through experience. Polyani recalls observing "in Hungary a new, imported machine for blowing electric lamp bulbs, the exact counterpart of which was operating successfully in Germany, failing for a whole year to produce a single flawless bulb"[2]

Firms build relationships with customers by consistently providing high-quality service and products. They develop valuable brand names and distribution capabilities after decades of effort and investment. For example, according to Ip, Coca-Cola owes its 50 percent share of the world soft drink market to its "painstakingly developed brand" on which it spent, between 1919 and 1998, $78 billion (inflation-adjusted 1998 dollars).[3] We can in fact reasonably argue that the time and experience required to develop such intangible assets make them valuable and difficult to replicate.

The evolution of coordination mechanisms follows the gradual development of assets. In exceptional ventures such as Compaq, experienced founders quickly delegate many of their responsibilities to employees who are recruited for well-defined positions. Administrative structures and systems are established well before they are necessary. This is unusual: In *Inc.*'s survey of the founders of companies who made the 500 lists from 1982 to 1989, only 2 percent reported that they had the systems in place for fast growth when they first began operations.[4] The typical fledgling company cannot afford the fixed costs of maintaining an extensive administrative infrastructure, and its simple, small scale of operation does not require formal systems and structures. It confronts the issue of developing coordination mechanisms after its assets and activities exceed the entrepreneur's personal limits and it has the financial capacity to support organizational overhead. (See the sidebar "The Lagged Development of Organizational Structures and Systems.")

Although the process of building coordinated assets is gradual, it ultimately results in a radical transformation. Microsoft of the 1990s bears little resemblance to the Microsoft of the 1970s. Moreover, as we will see, turning a fledgling business into a well-established one requires entrepreneurs to effect a U-turn and abandon, albeit gradually, the very policies that allowed them to get up and running with limited capital. They often have to emerge from their hospitable niches and compete with large companies. When John Katzman launched the *Princeton Review* he competed against private tutors of uneven quality in Manhattan. To become a nationally franchised operation his company had to confront the established Stanley Kaplan chain. To realize economies of scale, entrepreneurs have to make more standardized products and stop offering extensive modifications and customization to their customers. Nor can they rely on employees with low opportunity costs. The growth of a business often requires replacing cheap but inexperienced staff with well-paid professional managers. They must become more selective about the opportunities they pursue. Building

The Lagged Development of Organizational Structures and Systems

Few long-lived companies devote much effort at the outset to building their organizational capabilities, and they continue to operate without formal organizational systems and structures for quite a long time. "For several years," Wal-Mart founder Sam Walton writes, "the company was just me and the managers in the stores."[5] There was no time for "building the company up" because "we were too busy concentrating on day to day operations."[6] Coordination was accomplished by "a bunch of store managers getting together early Saturday morning" when "we would review what we had bought and see how many dollars we had committed to it." The company made up for a "a lot of shortcomings—an unsophisticated buying program, a less than ideal merchandise assortment, and practically no back office support" by emphasizing item promotion—by "being merchants."[7] Similarly, for the first decade or so, the emphasis at McKinsey & Co. was on building a reputation and a top-quality clientele. The firm had few written policies or committees; its ten or so partners would meet as a group and agree on all major decisions.

Eventually the lack of formal structures and systems limits the evolution of the enterprise. Entrepreneurs cannot personally direct the activities of a large firm with heterogeneous assets. They need to develop mechanisms such as compensation systems, financial controls, and organizational cultures to coordinate specialized activities and units. The growing firm also has to cope with capital constraints; it therefore needs systems to forecast and monitor the availability of cash and to satisfy banks and other capital providers, who will often refuse to advance funds to companies with weak controls and weak organizational infrastructures.

By the mid-sixties, Marks writes, Walton was deeply in the "absentee ownership situation" of "putting your stores out where you, as management, aren't" and realized the need to develop systems to "control his operations, no matter where they might be." Walton became "the best utilizer of information to control absentee ownership that there's ever been," which allowed him to open a large number of far-flung stores and operate them at exceptional levels of profitability. Similarly, after McKinsey had established its client base, Marvin Bower initiated several measures in the 1950s to formalize and revamp its governance structures and recruitment and promotion policies. For instance, the firm adopted written guidelines for sharing profits and electing new partners and formed profit-sharing, executive, and planning committees. These initiatives allowed McKinsey to transform itself from a five-office U.S. firm to an international enterprise: Between 1959 and 1966 the firm opened overseas offices in London, Geneva, Melbourne, Paris, Amsterdam, and Dusseldorf. The expansion would likely not have been possible if the informal style of decision-making by all the partners had been retained.

know-how and reputations in a certain field often requires entrepreneurs to forgo diversionary profit opportunities.

These changes imply a basic shift in objectives. As Phil Bookman of the software company Silton-Bookman put it:

> In the early days, managing cash is the most important thing. It is cash that matters and cash alone. Early on, I was a cash management fanatic. I made everyone crazy. I scrutinized every expenditure. If people overspent their cash budget they had to explain that. In the early days, $100 meant a lot. Today, I have to tell people that they should not worry so much about the little expenditures and think about the big picture.[8]

Few entrepreneurs successfully undertake the changes necessary to transform fledgling firms, however. The remaining sections of this chapter review the existing research that might explain why the evolution of large and long-lived firms is so unusual. We will examine the following models: mainstream economic theories; "biologically" inspired life-cycle models; and Nelson and Winter's evolutionary theory; and business strategy models. The exercise will suggest some ideas and concepts for use in the next chapter, but we will find that the ability of the theories to explain differences in the evolution of new firms is limited. Readers who are already familiar with the ideas (summarized in Table 10.1) may choose to skim the rest of the chapter.

2. Mainstream Economic Theories

Mainstream economics has little to tell us about how and why some firms survive and grow and others do not. In the standard microeconomic theory

Table 10.1. Existing Theories and Models

Mainstream economic theories	• Do not attempt to explain why certain firms attain noteworthy size and longevity.
Life-cycle models	• Directly address the issue of new venture growth. • Accurately reflect the gradual nature of firm evolution. • Inappropriately assume the firms conform to a uniform path of growth. • Oversimplify the nature of the entrepreneur's role.
Evolutionary theories (Nelson and Winter)	• Address issues such as innovation and economic change. • Assume that firms grow through a combination of luck and routines rather than through the purposive choices of a decision-maker. • May reflect realities of large corporations but underplay the role of entrepreneurs in fledgling firms.
Business strategy models	• Emphasize role of top decision-maker. • Provide framework to analyze multiperiod, multidimensional initiatives. • Implicit perspective of large company CEOs; need adaptation for analysis of transitional firms.

that focuses on perfect competition among many identical competitors, the question never arises. Variations in the size and longevity of firms have no influence on outcomes, and the evolution of a specific firm is irrelevant—it makes little difference in this theory whether changes in characteristics are treated as altering the existing firm or creating a new firm. Some theorists, in fact, prefer the latter approach—Penrose cites Robert Triffin, who stated that it was better to say that a new firm was created when the producer's appraisal of cost and revenue conditions changed.[9]

The industrial organization (IO) subfield of economics, which studies oliogopolistic rather than perfect competition, does take notice of differences in firm size and growth. IO research suggests that the structural characteristics of an industry, including the number of competitors and their relative market shares, have a significant impact on economic outcomes. For instance, a seminal paper by Joe Bain in 1951 showed that the profitability of manufacturing industries where the eight largest firms accounted for 70 percent of sales was nearly twice as great as more fragmented industries where the top eight firms had a lower than 70 percent share of the overall market. Much of the IO research that extended Bain's paper was cross-sectional—it studied how differences in structures (and the conduct of the competitors) across industries led to different levels of profitability, efficiency, innovation, and so on.

Some researchers have also studied how the structures of industries evolve over time. In keeping with the finding of low overall survival rates of start-ups, studies of industry evolution also point to the failure of a considerable proportion of the early entrants. According to Jovanovic and Mac-Donald, for instance, the growth of the automobile tire industry in the United States attracted 275 firms in 1922. Six years later, in 1928, the number of tire producers had more than halved to 132, and then halved again, to about 60 in 1932. Gort and Klepper found the same patterns of widespread exit in the 46 industries they analyzed.

IO researchers did not probe deeply into why particular firms survive. Thus a structural analysis might rely on factors such as economies of scale to explain why the number of viable long-run competitors in the automobile industry would be smaller than the number of management consulting firms. But structural variables cannot explain why GM and Ford in particular came to dominate the U.S. automobile market when scores of other start-ups folded, or why McKinsey & Co. has flourished through several generations of partners whereas most consulting firms fail to outlive their partners. Detailed answers to such questions seem unnecessary for economists who are more interested in the degree of concentration in an industry and its consequences for economic efficiency.

Consider Jovanovic and MacDonald's work on the tire industry. "In the U.S. tire industry," they write, "several key inventions appeared in the 1910–20 period. Once put to work, they allowed a dramatic increase in scale. Firms that were able to implement early were rewarded with growth in output and value; the others joined a mass exodus."[10] But why did only some firms implement the "key inventions," (such as the 1916 Banbury mixer that greatly accelerated the process of mixing rubber with other compounds), that were, in principle, available to all? Was it, for instance, because some decision-makers had more foresight, willingness to bet on new technology, access to capital, or the ability to build organizations needed to effectively implement the new inventions? For Jovanovic and MacDonald's purpose, which is to explain why "firm numbers first rise, then later fall, as an industry evolves,"[11] it is sufficient to assume a model in which "innovative success is stochastic, so that some firms succeed before others."[12]*

3. Life-Cycle Models

"Stages of growth" or life-cycle models offer predictions on how firms develop as well as advice to entrepreneurs on nurturing their new ventures. The models recognize that businesses evolve in a gradual way; but as we will see, they assume an excessive preordination of development and they understate the entrepreneur's role.**

The life-cycle approach posits that just as humans pass through similar stages of physiological and psychological development from infancy to adulthood, so businesses evolve in predictable ways and encounter similar problems in their growth. Managers of firms at different "stages of growth" have different tasks and priorities, just as parents of children of different ages face different challenges. "A company's development stage," write Churchill and Lewis, "determines the managerial factors that must be dealt with."[13]

Their resonance with the biological world gives these models intuitive appeal. They give entrepreneurs the comfort that an authoritative child-rearing book can provide parents by, for example, telling them what to do and expect during their child's "terrible twos." They suggest that as the business matures, the entrepreneur's job is to progressively "let go." Founders who do not delegate stunt the growth of their firms, just as over-controlling parents can retard the development of their offspring. "As the company grows," write Churchill and Lewis, "the owner must spend less time doing and more time managing. He or she must increase the amount

---

* Some IO-based researchers, such as Michael Porter, relate the survival and growth of a business to the strategy its managers choose; and I will discuss some of their contributions in the section "Business Strategy Models" in this chapter.

** In the discussion of life-cycle models below I will focus on Neil Churchill and Virginia Lewis's article "The Five Stages of Small Business Growth" (Churchill and Lewis [1983]), which built on prior work by McGuire, Steinmetz, and Griener and is considered a seminal piece in the genre.

of work done through other people, which means delegating. The inability of many founders to let go of doing and to begin managing and delegating explains the demise of many businesses in substage III-G [the 'success-growth' stage] and stage IV [the 'Take-off' stage]."[14]

As discussed in Section 1, the data seem consistent with a characterization of firm development as gradual and "altricial" rather than one-shot or "precocial." Life-cycle models overextend the biological metaphor, however, by asserting that businesses progress through predictable phases. We see little evidence to support the details in the Churchill-Lewis model, which suggest, for instance, that operational planning is introduced in stage III-D (the "success-disengagement" stage) and extensive strategic planning in stage III-G (the "success-growth" stage). My observations suggest that ventures evolve in unpredictable, idiosyncratic ways that do not conform to one-size-fits-all models of development. Life-cycle models fail to adequately account for the great variety in the manner in which firms grow.

We cannot easily map, for example, the histories of Ford and General Motors into a common evolutionary story. Rather, as described in the sidebar "Ford vs. General Motors," we find great differences in how the two competitors developed their assets and routines, and in the role of their founders. If we look at firms across a range of industries, the case for a one-size-fits-all model becomes even weaker. A well-run professional firm is bound to develop along very different lines from a discount retailer. While Wal-Mart and McKinsey both built organizational capabilities gradually, the development of their control, budgeting, incentive, governance, and other such routines had very little in common. Wal-Mart invested heavily in automated inventory and logistics systems. McKinsey focused on establishing committees and devoted considerable time to develop and implement criteria for evaluating and compensating its staff. Wal-Mart stuck to out-of-the-way locations in the United States; it did not have any overseas locations until 1992, the year in which it recorded $55 billion in domestic sales. McKinsey opened its first international office in 1959, when the firm's total billings were just $5.7 million. In 1992, the year of Wal-Mart's first overseas initiative, McKinsey operated in thirty-one countries.

I do not mean to suggest that the absence of preordained development paths precludes some common features in the growth of companies and industries. We have to distinguish, however, between the identification and explanation of historical patterns and propositions with predictive value. For instance, Alfred Chandler's work on the evolution of large industrial companies suggests that the adoption of a multidivisional organizational structure followed strategies of diversification into multiple lines of business, after a significant period of experimentation. Today, as the benefits of decentralized business units have been widely accepted, we should not expect to find a similar lag—the durable hypothesis one can draw from Chandler's work is that the effective implementation of strategy requires

Ford vs. General Motors

The Ford Motor Company and General Motors, which came to dominate the U.S. automobile industry, evolved in markedly different ways. Ford's evolution reflects founder Henry Ford's engineering and manufacturing interests. Henry Ford, who was born on a Michigan farm in 1863, pursued mechanical hobbies from his boyhood. He joined the Detroit Edison Company as an engineer, built internal-combustion engines in his spare time, and sold his first "gasoline buggy" in 1892. In 1899 Ford was dismissed as chief engineer of Detroit Edison because his superiors believed he had become excessively preoccupied with his side interests. He then started the Detroit Automobile Company, but soon withdrew after a dispute with his financial backers. After a stint as a developer of racing cars, he started the Ford Motor Company (FMC) in 1903, using capital that he raised from friends. FMC produced more than seventeen hundred cars in its first year, in a converted wagon factory. The company soon relocated to a larger facility in Detroit and opened a plant in Canada.

Ford wanted FMC to use large-scale production to manufacture cars that everyone could afford, but some of the company's investors did not share his vision. Ford thereupon bought them out, secured majority control, and assumed the presidency of FMC in 1906. In 1908 the company introduced the Model T. It was produced on a moving assembly line, with machines specialized for minute tasks and extreme division of labor. The system of mass production of a single, standardized product yielded cost savings, which allowed for low prices, which in turn helped expand consumer demand.

FMC grew by replicating this system in ever larger and more vertically integrated facilities. In 1919, after minority investors objected to Ford's plan to build a gigantic manufacturing complex, complete with its own steel mill, he bought them out and reregistered the company as a Delaware corporation. Ford proceeded to build the complex at River Rouge, near Detroit, and continued to manufacture the Model T until 1927.

General Motors (GM), which caught up with and then surpassed FMC in the late 1920s, followed a different trajectory. In its early years it grew through acquisitions rather than by building its own plants. Founder William Durant, the son of a Michigan governor, had been in the carriage-making business in the 1890s. In 1904 he bought the failing Buick Motor Company, one of many small companies then in automobile production. Using Buick as his base, he persuaded the suppliers who had previously made him carriages to make automobiles, and bought more companies in the automobile business. In 1908 he formed GM as a holding company for further acquisitions. Starting with Buick, Oldsmobile, and a bodymaker in Flint, GM acquired, within eighteen months, large blocks of stock in Cadillac and Oakland (renamed Pontiac), six other automobile companies, three truck firms, and ten parts and accessories companies.

These rapid acquistions caused a financial crisis. In 1910 GM's lenders forced Durant to relinquish control. Five years later, with the financial support of the du Pont family, Durant managed to regain control and resumed his acquisition spree. By 1920 GM had acquired more than thirty companies. A business downturn that year, however, precipitated another debt crisis. Durant relinquished the presidency of GM to Pierre du Pont, who had the confidence of the company's creditors. Du Pont turned to Alfred Sloan, Jr., to run the company. According to McCraw and Tedlow, Sloan reveled in the subtleties and nuances of organizational issues and helped create "a system for managing human relations that was just as rationally planned and efficient for business organization as Henry Ford's assembly line had been for production."

Under Sloan, GM adopted a multidivisional structure that "combined the virtues of centralized control with those of decentralized decision-making."[15] GM was organized into several divisions (such as Buick, Olds, and Pontiac), each of which was responsible for a distinct price segment of the market. Where Ford offered a single Model T, GM's divisions catered to the increasingly differentiated tastes of different customer segments. At the same time GM did not lose the cost advantages of high-volume production, because it used common components that went into several makes and models.

the adoption of appropriate organizational structures and routines.[16] Therefore, the model of firm evolution that I will propose does not try to force empirical regularities into a recurring temporal sequence. Rather, I will use these regularities to identify the critical tasks that entrepreneurs have to perform to build a large and long-lived firm and the skills and traits they need to perform these tasks.

Another noteworthy limitation of life-cycle models lies in their oversimplification of the entrepreneur's role. One cannot dispute the proposition that as their businesses grow, entrepreneurs "do less and delegate more," making a smaller proportion of the decisions. The simple injunction to "let go" does not however reflect the complex nature of the tasks that entrepreneurs such as Henry Ford, Alfred Sloan, Sam Walton, and Marvin Bower performed over several decades. For reasons that we will analyze in the next chapter, these entrepreneurs combined the visionary tasks formulating long-term strategies with a "hands-on" role in their implementation. Walton not only formulated his company's strategy of putting "good-sized discount stores into little one horse towns which everybody else was ignoring,"[17] he also scouted for locations from a plane he personally flew. Walton writes:

> From up in the air we could check out traffic flows, see which way cities and towns were growing, and evaluate the location of the competition. . . . I loved doing it myself. I'd get down low, turn my plane up on its side, and fly right over a town. Once we had a spot picked out, we'd land, go find out who owned the property, and try to negotiate the deal right then. . . . I guarantee you not many principals of retailing companies were flying around sideways studying development patterns. . . .[18]

Walton picked the first 120 or 130 stores in this fashion, and until Wal-Mart grew to about 500 stores continued to "keep up with every real estate deal we made and got to view most locations before we signed any kind of commitment" because "a good location and what we have to pay for it, is so important to the success of a store." Similarly, in his long stint at the helm of McKinsey & Co., Marvin Bower played an important role in securing and directing several pivotal studies. He directed a study for Shell Oil's operating company in Venezuela in 1956 that was a "tryout" for an overall study of Shell's organization structure, "spending several weeks at a time on location."[19] In 1957 he negotiated the follow-on organizational study that provided the basis for opening an office in London. On learning in 1962 that the chairman of Imperial Chemical Industries (ICI) had expressed an interest in meeting Bower when he was "next in London," Bower flew over immediately. The study he negotiated with ICI, the largest industrial enterprise in the United Kingdom, provided the "client breakthrough" after which the London office was "swamped with major new British clients."

Few entrepreneurs who build durable companies, in fact, *ever* adopt a purely visionary or statesmanlike role within their organizations. Marvin Bower did not stop working on client studies until he was about ninety. Sam Walton writes that until he got "really sick" in 1991 (he died of cancer in 1992) he remained fully engaged in the operational details: "If I wasn't in the stores trying to pump up our associates to do an even better job, or in the office looking over the numbers to see where the next trouble spot was going to pop up, or leading cheers at a Saturday morning meeting, I was probably at the stick of my airplane . . . checking out the number of cars in those Kmart parking lots."[20] Bill Gates, cofounder and CEO of the multibillion-dollar software powerhouse Microsoft, still reportedly reviews the code programmers write. Psychoanalyst and emeritus HBS professor Abraham Zaleznik argues that the effective leadership of an enterprise requires top executives to engage in the "real work" of "thinking about and acting on products, markets and customers." When top executives "put interpersonal matters, power relations and pouring oil on troubled waters ahead of real work" subordinates follow their lead. Group norms appear to "foster the appearances of getting along. . . . Process takes precedence over substance. Attention turns inward to the organization's politics rather than outward to the real work of making and marketing goods and services."[21]

This is not to suggest that Walton's or Bower's role remained the same as their companies grew. In fact, the next two chapters suggest that building a long-lived firm entails radical changes in the entrepreneur's role. But these changes, I will argue, involve a broadening and expansion of responsibilities rather than the narrowing implied in "letting go."

4. Evolutionary Theories

The evolutionary approach (in contrast to life-cycle models) has attracted considerable interest in recent years. Some scholars believe that models based on natural selection can better explain "real world" phenomena than standard economic theory. Rather than review this growing literature, however, I will concentrate below on Nelson and Winter's pioneering work, which has almost become synonymous with evolutionary theory. After summarizing the features of the Nelson and Winter models, which distinguish them from mainstream economic theory, I will examine the degree to which they explain observed patterns of the evolution of fledgling businesses.

Evolutionary theories, like life-cycle models, are based on a biological analogy but with an important difference. Life-cycle models implicitly compare the development of firms to the predetermined aspects of biological maturation that are programmed into the genetic code of a species. Evolutionary theories are inspired by models of how the inherited traits of a species change through chance variation and natural selection. There is accordingly nothing predestined about firm development in evolutionary models. Different firms grow at different rates. History matters—firm development is "path-dependent."

Distinguishing Features

Unlike the formal mathematical analysis found in standard economic models, Nelson and Winter use multiperiod computer simulations to address problems such as explaining rates of technical change, how industry structures influence and are influenced by the R&D activities of firms and the interaction of innovation and imitation. They typically start with a population of firms (or an "industry") that follow specified rules to search for new techniques or investments in research and development. A stochastic process follows—the model assigns random probabilities to the success of the efforts of each firm. The cumulative or accretive effects of these random draws over many rounds lead some firms to grow faster than others and help determine the structure of the industry.

Besides using different modeling techniques, Nelson and Winter also depart from some basic assumptions of standard economics in the decision-making processes they assume their firms follow. In the conventional microeconomic theory, the perfectly informed, perfectly rational decision-maker finds optimal solutions to problems. In the Nelson and Winter models the search by firms for new techniques—assumed to be an important precursor for their growth—is based on "satisficing" rather than "optimizing" behavior. In their early models of growth, firms retain their existing techniques if their profitability exceeds a certain threshold; otherwise they search for new techniques or imitate those of other firms. Later models assume that firms satisfice on the levels of their R&D spending, routinely investing fixed proportions of their available funds in the search for new techniques.

Another feature that distinguishes the Nelson and Winter models from the usual assumptions of microeconomics is their emphasis on "routinized" decision-making. Traditional microeconomic theory assumes that decision-makers respond optimally to changes in exogenous market conditions. In the Nelson and Winter models the internal routines of a firm drive their behavior.[22] Summarizing their view on "the realities of organizational functioning," Nelson and Winter write:

> As a first approximation, therefore, firms may be expected to behave in the future according to the routines they have employed in the past. This does not imply a literal identity of behavior over time, since routines may be keyed in complex ways to signals from the environment. It does imply that it is quite inappropriate to conceive of firm behavior in terms of deliberate choice from a broad menu of alternatives that some external observer considers to be "available" opportunities for the organization. The menu is not broad, but narrow and idiosyncratic; it is built into the firm's routines, and most of the "choosing" is also accomplished automatically by those routines.[23]

Explaining Firm Evolution

Some features of the Nelson and Winter models suggest useful ideas for analyzing the evolution of fledgling businesses. The concept of "satisficing" search is crucial. An entrepreneur's thresholds of satisfaction make a significant difference to the growth of the firm: Ambitious entrepreneurs are much more likely to search for ways to broaden their firm's assets than individuals who are satisfied with the status quo. Similarly, Nelson and Winter's emphasis on organizational routines as an important determinant of firm behavior corresponds closely to our previous discussion of embedded coordination mechanisms as a necessary condition for firm longevity: one could easily substitute the term "embedded coordination mechanisms" with "organizational routines."

The complete exclusion of differences in the skills and efforts of individual decision-makers from the models limits their utility, however, in explaining the evolution of firms. Nelson and Winter repeatedly insist that their theories are "Schumpeterian." They are, to the degree that the models involve continuous change through an infinite number of periods rather than the instantaneous attainment of equilibrium. But the theories do not, Jon Elster observes in his insightful review of Nelson and Winter's work, incorporate Schumpeter's "emphasis on supernormal ability and energy."[24] They implicitly assume that all decision-makers are endowed with identical drive, foresight, and ingenuity. Judgment plays no more a role in their view of decision-making than it does in standard microeconomics. Instead of an omniscient decision-maker who always finds the unique optimizing solution, we have equally mechanistic organizational routines.

The assumption of purely routinized decision-making leads Nelson and Winter to throw the responsibility for outcomes into the hands of chance, on the grounds that the results of decisions based on organizational routines are hard to predict. They write that

> even the sophisticated problem-solving efforts of an organization fall into quasi-routine patterns, whose general outlines can be anticipated on the basis of experience with previous problem-solving efforts of that organization. But the patterning of the problem-solving activity is reflected only vaguely in the immediate outcomes of that activity and even less clearly in the gross changes in firm behavior that these problem solutions may trigger. From the viewpoint of an external observer who has no access to the sophisticated workings within the organization, the results are hard to predict and on that ground are best regarded as stochastic. [25]

Elsewhere, Nelson and Winter argue that in a typical competitive situation, "luck is the principal factor that finally distinguishes winners from near-winners—although vast differentials of skill and competence may separate contenders from non-contenders."[26]

The Nelson and Winter assumptions may fit mature firms. In *An Evolutionary Theory of Economic Change* they write that their

> framework applies most naturally to organizations that are engaged in the provision of goods and services that are visibly "the same" over extended periods—manufacturing hand tools, teaching second graders, and so forth—and for which well-defined routines structure a large part of organizational functioning at any particular time.

They also focus on organizations that are already large and complex:

> The organizations we envisage are ones that face a substantial coordination problem, typically because they have many members, performing many distinct roles, who make complementary contributions to the production of a relatively small range of goods and services. In such organizations, most of the working interactions of a large number of the members are primarily with other members rather than with the organization's environment. Also, while the organizations we describe are of the sort that have a top management that is concerned with the general direction of the organization, the scale and complexity of the organization are presumed to make it impossible for that top management to direct or observe many of the details of the organization's functioning.[27]

This inquiry has a different focus. We want to explain how small firms become large and complex. Firms that have not yet established well-defined organizational routines or settled on providing "goods and services that are visibly 'the same' over extended periods" are of crucial concern. We are interested in stages of competition where "differentials in skill and competence" matter at least as much as luck. As Edith Penrose argues in her classic *The Theory of the Growth of the Firm*, "enterprising management is the one identifiable condition without which continued growth is precluded."[28] To assume that all firms are equally endowed with enterprising management seriously misrepresents the realities of growing businesses.

In our universe of interest, conscious choices matter. In a large, complex firm, organizational constraints may limit the influence of top managers to shape broad policies (or "meta-routines"). More specific decisions may, as Nelson and Winter propose, represent reflexive or automated responses of organizational routines to the stimuli they are exposed to. In a small, fledgling business, the principals make conscious choices—albeit within their informational and cognitive limits—about products, technologies, personnel, and so on. Without stretching the meaning of randomness and routine to a point where they explain "everything and nothing" we cannot avoid relating these conscious, concrete decisions to the fledgling firm's maturation.

Entrepreneurs who start promising niche businesses usually do not face obvious growth opportunities. It takes an act of will—and dissatisfaction with the status quo—to search for larger opportunities and invest in a portfolio of assets. As Penrose put it:

> The decision on the part of the firm to investigate the prospective profitability of expansion is an enterprising decision, in the sense that whenever expansion is neither pressing nor particularly obvious, a firm has the choice of continuing in its existing course or of expending effort and committing resources to the investigation of whether there are further opportunities of which it is not yet aware. This is a decision which depends on the "enterprise" of the firm and not on sober calculations as to whether the investigation is likely to turn up enticing opportunities, for it is, in effect, the decision to make some calculations. This is truly the "first" decision, and it is here that the "spirit of enterprise," or a general entrepreneurial bias in favor of "growth" has perhaps its greatest significance.[29]

Today, companies such as HP may, per the Nelson and Winter models, "routinely" invest a certain percentage of profits in developing new products or technologies. But such routines do not create themselves or emerge by chance. HP grew from a company making one product in 1938, the Model 200B audio oscillator, to more than one hundred items in 1952 to more than three hundred in 1957. The founders consciously chose to reinvest all profits (and pay themselves low salaries) to broaden the product line. In early 1939, David Packard recalls, their sales representative, Norman Neely, impressed on them the importance of offering more than one product, so they decided to develop a full line of audio-frequency measuring instruments.[30] The software firm Intuit's first product, Quicken, had more attractive features and was easier to use than other personal-finance software programs. Intuit's founders believed that competitors could also make their products easy to use, so to enhance its position with distributors, the company developed a family of products for small businesses and invested heavily in marketing and sales support.

All entrepreneurs do not reflexively invest in broadening their product line and marketing capabilities. As I will argue in Chapter 12, developing the broad base of assets that sustain long-lived firms exposes entrepreneurs to considerably greater personal risk than does starting a new business or expanding one after it has become well established. As we have seen, founders of the typical bootstrapped start-up do not face much financial risk. The CEOs of large, well-diversified corporations do not face much personal financial loss from unsuccessful initiatives. Entrepreneurs who reinvest profits or secure loans against personal guarantees to invest in new assets (after the venture has passed the start-up stage) risk losing most or all of the wealth they have accumulated. If, as is sometime the case, entrepreneurs borrow against personal guarantees to finance their firms' investments, they can face personal bankruptcy. Therefore, only individuals with unusual ambition and tolerance for risk make the sustained investments needed to build long-lived companies.

Bold, purposive changes are especially important for young businesses that are caught in a rut. As discussed in Chapter 2, myopic choices made by cash-constrained entrepreneurs can lead a business into undesirable "local maxima" from which it cannot escape by undertaking small "evolutionary changes." But as the examples of several of today's well-established companies show, a determined entrepreneur can transform a dead-end business through radical changes. IBM, for example, started as the Computing-Tabulating-Recording (C-T-R) Company in 1911 through the merger of several small firms. Its product lines included scales, coffee grinders, meat slicers, time clocks, and a line of punch-card tabulating machines. In 1914 Charles Flint, the financier who had put together C-T-R, hired Thomas J. Watson to run the company. According to the historian Rowena Olegario, Watson had "grandiose visions" for C-T-R. He eliminated the coffee grinders and meat slicers and renamed C-T-R as the International Business Machines Company, "even though at the time the firm was not actually very international." Watson introduced several innovations that he had observed in his previous employment at the National Cash Register Company that transformed the motley conglomerate into an organization with exceptional sales and marketing capabilities.[31]

IBM is by no means an isolated illustration of the consequences of deliberate choice. In historian Alfred Chandler's *Scale and Scope*, which analyzes the histories of the two hundred largest manufacturing companies in the

United States, Great Britain, and Germany, we find a recurring pattern. "The institutional history told here," Chandler writes,

> is the outcome of innumerable decisions made by individual entrepreneurs, owners, and managers. For these decision-makers the choices among alternatives were limited and the outcomes uncertain, but almost always there *were* choices. Indeed, where they made decisions collectively, the decision-makers disagreed as often as they agreed.[32]

These "decisions and actions," Chandler continues, "did much to determine the performance of individual firms, industries and even nations."[33]

To conclude: Natural selection offers an attractive metaphor for describing the dynamic world of business. We can speak of Darwinian struggles for survival and—as in the very title of this book—of the evolution of businesses. In using these terms, however, we should bear in mind Elster's analysis of the differences between purposive human action and natural selection. As mentioned in Chapter 2, natural selection is mechanistic and myopic. The "evolutionary machine" accepts any randomly generated mutation if it endows an organism with a superior reproductive capacity without regard to its long-term consequences. It has no capacity to wait or to invest in the future. Human action involves judgment. We do not automatically accept good variations and reject bad ones. We can imagine variations that have not actually occurred. We can defer gratification and invest in the future. We can attempt radical changes to escape undesirable local maxima. And we can drastically alter our environment instead of just adapting to it.

These distinctive human qualities have a profound influence on the "evolution" of businesses. Differences among entrepreneurs' capacity for good judgment, imagination, willingness to make long-term investments, and not just chance, affect the longevity and size of firms and the structure of their markets. The path dependency of natural selection may preclude wooly mammoths from evolving into giraffes, but a determined and capable Thomas Watson can turn a C-T-R into an IBM and in so doing shape the worldwide structure of the computer industry. To incorporate these purposive factors into an explanation of business evolution requires constructs beyond those of natural selection or the life-cycle concept of "letting go." The following section shows how we can derive appropriate constructs and terms from the field of business strategy that will help us identify entrepreneurs' contributions to the apparently idiosyncratic evolution of their businesses.

5. Business Strategy Models

Business strategy research highlights the importance of broad rules or policies. Strategy models assume that the chief executive or top manager of a large and diversified corporation cannot effectively attend to every detail. They can, however, make a significant contribution to their firms' long-run profitability by formulating and implementing a strategy for the enterprise. This proposition, which stands in clear contrast to the focus on randomness and routine in Nelson and Winter's models, helps us relate the multifaceted, multiperiod initiatives required to build a long-lived firm to the entrepreneur's willingness and ability to adopt a strategic approach. So although strategy research implicitly takes the perspective of executives of corporations that are already large and well established, we can adapt the framework to analyze the evolution of young firms as well.

In the section below I briefly sketch the development of some key ideas in the field of business strategy, review criticisms of the approach, and discuss the adaptations that will help us analyze the entrepreneurs' role in a transitional firm.

A Brief Sketch

The concept of strategy, Nelson and Winter write, has been "developed by a number of investigators associated with the Harvard Business School."[34] As the following abbreviated sketch will show, the field of strategy has a broad ancestry.* It likely emerged from the increasing number of large and complex organizations whose top executives could not micromanage their businesses and did not wish to abdicate control to invisible and unplanned "routines." For instance, James O. McKinsey ("Mac"), a professor at the University of Chicago, articulated an "integrated" or "top-management approach" in *Business Administration*, published in 1924. Mac expanded on this approach in the General Survey Outline after he launched a consulting partnership in 1929. The outline, Marvin Bower noted, was "a checklist for making a strategic general survey of a business."[35] It required consultants to analyze the industry and the client's competitive position before considering anything specific to the organization. It also forced

> ... an orderly approach by requiring examination of the elements of managing in an undeviating sequence: goals, strategy, policies, organization structure, facilities, procedures, and personnel—*in that order*. To emphasize the sequential approach, Mac would ask: "Would you polish the brass on a sinking ship?"[36]

Mac's firm was subsequently dissolved, but his approach was adopted and extensively applied in the corporate world by the successor firm, McKinsey Co., launched by Marvin Bower and two partners in 1939.

In 1962 Alfred Chandler, then a business historian at MIT, published

---

* See P. Ghemawat's *Competition and Business Strategy in Historical Perspective* for a more comprehensive overview.

the influential *Strategy and Structure*. The book studied the evolution of DuPont, General Motors, and Sears, primarily through the eyes of the top executives of these companies. To classify their decisions and actions, Chandler used strategic decision-making as a critical component of top-executive work. Chandler distinguished between strategic decisions that "clearly deal very largely with defining basic goals and the course of action and procedures necessary to achieve these goals" from decisions about "day-to-day operations carried out within the broader framework of goals, policies and procedures." Chandler's classification and descriptions of executive tasks helped frame the language of business strategy.

Kenneth Andrews published a comprehensive synthesis, *The Concept of Corporate Strategy*, in 1980. A firm's strategy was "the pattern of purposes and policies defining the company and its business" that the chief executive or president had to formulate and then implement.[37] Formulating strategy ("deciding what to do") required the consideration of factors such as the goals and values of the decision-makers, the company's resources and competencies, and the external or market opportunities and threats. An optimal strategy involved good "matches" among goals, resources, and opportunities. The implementation ("achieving results") of strategy comprised "primarily administrative" activities such as establishing or modifying the organizational structures, incentive and control systems, and the recruitment of personnel.

Michael Porter, who started out as an IO economist, revolutionized the field of strategy, in part by recognizing that variables IO research had shown to affect the profitability of an industry could be used by strategists to identify the attractiveness of a business. As Ghemawat has put it: "IO economists focused on issues of public policy rather than business policy: they concerned themselves with the minimization rather than the maximization of "excess" profits. Porter instead tried to "turn IO on its head by focusing on the business policy objective of profit maximization rather than the public policy objective of minimizing 'excess" profits.'"[38] Porter's 1980 book *Competitive Strategy*, Ghemawat writes, "owed much of its success to Porter's elaborate framework for the structural analysis of industry attractiveness."

Porter's "five forces" framework also incorporated practical rules of thumb that did not come out of the IO research.* The incorporation of experiential rules into a framework with *prima facie* plausibility and con-

---

* According to Ghemawat, "[M]anagers routinely have to consider much longer lists of variables than are embedded in the simple models used by economists. In the case of the five forces, [Richard Schmalensee's] survey of empirical literature in the late 1980s—more than a decade after Porter first developed his framework—revealed that only a few points were strongly supported by the empirical literature generated by the IO field" (Ghemawat [1997], p. 13). Ghemawat's accompanying diagram indicates that only 6 of 47 points have strong empirical support, but he points out: "This does not mean that the other points are in conflict with IO research; rather, they reflect the experience of strategy practitioners, including Porter himself."

sistency had a profound influence on the process strategy formulation. Porter's framework made the ad hoc process of matching a company's goals, opportunities, and assets much more systematic and standardized. He also gave business strategists a common vocabulary that helped establish strategy formulation as a specialized business function.

Criticisms

Quinn has criticized the "top-down" approach to strategy on the grounds that companies rarely use "grand design" strategic plans in practice. After studying companies such as General Mills, Pilkington, IT&T, and Exxon he concluded that when successful, well-managed companies make strategic changes, "the approaches they use frequently bear little resemblance to the rational, analytic systems so often described in the planning literature."[39] Strategies, Quinn found, were typically formulated at a subsystem level, in response to precipitating events over which top managers did not have much control—a finding consistent with Nelson and Winter's claim about routines. Given these organizational realities, Quinn recommended that managers adopt a process of "logical incrementalism." In contrast to the traditional, top-down, anticipatory approach to strategy formulation Quinn suggested that "the prudent and rational executive make final commitments *as late as possible* consistent with the information available."[40]

Arguably, the incrementalism discovered by Quinn might have been even more disruptive and chaotic in the absence of a top-down strategy. Selznick's studies of large organizations suggest an interactive relationship between routines and policies formulated by the organizations' leaders. Selznick wrote that "organizational processes profoundly influence the kinds of policy that can be made, and policy in turn shapes the machinery of organizations. . . ."[41] Abdication of the policymaking role by top executives could lead to the disintegration of the enterprise or at least to an inability to perform what Selznick calls its "mission." Furthermore, the resistance of subunits and entrenched routines is less likely to limit the influence of top management in a small, young organization[42] thus making the strategic model an especially appealing one for analyzing the actions and choices of entrepreneurs. For our purposes, the proposition that the growth and longevity of a firm are functions of the entrepreneur's ability to formulate and effectively implement an appropriate long-term strategy seems a reasonable one.

Modifications

I will make two modifications, however, to adapt the strategy models, which are implicitly based on the perspective of the CEO of a large corporation, to the domain of fledgling enterprises. First I will emphasize the goals of a firm's top decision-makers, which are often glossed over in the strategy literature. For instance, Andrews does suggest that the personal values and aspirations of senior management be considered in the formulation of strategy. But he lists this third in the list of factors to be considered, after "market opportunities" and "corporate competence and resources."[43] In the subsequent work of Porter we find little mention of the decision-maker's personal goals.

We cannot evaluate the effectiveness of a strategy without reference to the goals it is supposed to achieve. Similarly, if we expect a causal link between consciously formulated strategies and outcomes we should also expect a prior link between goals and the strategy. With a CEO of a public corporation with diffused stockholding, it may be reasonable to suggest, at least in a prescriptive way, that the decision-maker should seek to maximize shareholder wealth without consideration of personal preferences. With entrepreneurs who own their businesses outright or who can choose to raise money from like-minded investors, personal goals must come before—in a prescriptive or predictive analysis—the formulation or implementation of strategy. In explaining differences between the growth and the longevity of different firms, therefore, I will treat the goals and preferences of the entrepreneur as a distinct variable that precedes the formulation and implementation of strategy.

Second, I will modify the strategy model to suit firms that have not yet developed their portfolio of assets and coordination mechanisms. The orientation of strategy theorists toward established companies leads them to assume a more or less stable preexisting base of business activity. For instance, in choosing between or among strategic alternatives, Andrews suggests that "the company's strengths and weaknesses should be appraised together with the resources on hand and available" to match "opportunity and corporate capability at an acceptable level of risk."[44] An existing, going business is also assumed in Andrews' classification of strategies as low-growth or forced growth (through the acquisition of competitors, vertical integration, geographic expansion, and diversification). Such assumptions, we will see in the next chapter, lead to a more analytical or deductive process of strategy formulation than is practical for the CEO of a fledgling business, who starts with a more or less clean slate.

The assumption of an established business also affects the variables that decision-makers can manipulate. For instance, organizational policies and norms help determine the effectiveness of a firm's coordination mechanisms, and by extension, its longevity and growth. Once policies are in place, however, changing them entails great disruption; and because CEOs of established companies cannot easily change organizational policies and norms, they are therefore often glossed over in the strategy literature. In the management literature, the reformulation of organizational policy typically falls under the specialized rubric of "change" or "crisis management."

In a fledgling business, which has yet to establish its coordination mechanisms, organizational choices represent important variables in the formulation of a strategy.

6. Summary and Conclusions

The previous chapter identified a wide gap between fledgling and well-established firms in terms of their assets, coordination mechanisms, and capacity for growth. In this chapter I suggested that filling this gap requires entrepreneurs to undertake many complementary initiatives that occupy the middle of the investment-uncertainty-profit diagram. Existing models of firm growth do not adequately explain why only some entrepreneurs effectively undertake a program of such initiatives. Nelson and Winter's evolutionary theory (and some industrial organization models) attribute differences in firm growth to chance. Life-cycle models assume that firms will progress through preordained stages as long as the entrepreneur is willing to "let go." Business strategy models emphasize the role of the top decision-maker in shaping the development of a firm through the formulation and implementation of a long-term strategy. The concepts of strategy formulation and implementation offer a useful framework for analyzing the purposive, multidimensional, multiperiod entrepreneurial efforts required to transform fledgling ventures into a well-established corporation. The framework, which implicitly addresses the concerns of the executives of mature firms, needs to be modified, however, to fit the distinctive problems of the fledgling enterprises.

11

Critical Tasks

This chapter analyzes the critical tasks that entrepreneurs face in turning fledgling businesses into long-lived corporations. The sections cover, in sequence, the three tasks of goal-setting, strategy formulation, and implementation. Each section discusses the nature and importance of the tasks and their distinctive aspects in the transitional phase of a firm. Examining these tasks will help us, in the next chapter, to infer the personal qualities and skills that affect an entrepreneur's propensity and capacity.

Transforming a fledgling enterprise into a large and long-lived corporation requires entrepreneurs to adopt a strategic rather than an opportunistic approach. Drawing on the business strategy framework outlined in the previous chapter, I will discuss three tasks entrepreneurs must perform:

1. Articulation of audacious goals and "purpose" for the enterprise;
2. Formulation of a "strategy"—a set of general rules or boundary conditions—for realizing their goals; and,
3. Effective implementation of the strategy—that is, translating the general rules into specific actions and decisions.

To clarify the nature of the tasks required to transform a fledgling business, I will distinguish them from the challenges involved in starting a new venture and managing a large corporation. Audacious goals do not play an important role in starting a promising business. And, as we saw in Part I, the survival of such businesses depends more on effective adaptation to unexpected problems and opportunities than on the entrepreneur's ability to formulate and implement a strategy. Long-term strategies do play an important role in the management of large corporations. But we will see that the process of formulating a strategy and its content is different in the transitional phase than it is after a firm becomes well established.

1. Goals

Entrepreneurs who build long-lived firms establish audacious goals for their companies. The goals are audacious in that they envision a sharply different and difficult-to-realize future state, in terms of revenues, competitive rank, geographic scope, and so on. Entrepreneurs also articulate a long-run purpose for the organization that helps define the broad class of products or services it will offer and the types of wants it seeks to satisfy.

Founders of promising businesses may have a far-reaching vision, but it is not necessary for starting their ventures. Len Bosack and Sandy Lerner did not articulate audacious goals when they started Cisco Systems in their home in 1984. Five years later Cisco's VCs recruited John Morgridge as CEO, and he established a revenue goal of $100 million—a twentyfold increase from 1989 revenues of $5 million. The top executives of large corporations do not have to establish visionary goals for the enterprise either, unless it is stagnating or failing.

The following section below discusses how the adoption of audacious goals plays an important role in building a long-lived firm and, by contrast, why it is not as crucial in the start-up or mature stages.

Importance of Goals

Audacious goals help entrepreneurs build large, long-lived firms in several ways.

Impetus. Fledgling businesses do not automatically undertake the initiatives and investments needed to build a system of coordinated assets; according to the satisficing principle, audacious goals stimulate the search for these initiatives and investments. In 1989, for instance, Pat Kelly declared that PSS would become the first national distributor of medical products to physicians' offices in the United States. At the time it was an "itty-bitty company in Florida" with seven branches. PSS had made *Inc.*'s 1988 list of the 500 fastest-growing companies in the United States, but with just $20 million in revenues it had no significant economies of scale that would justify nationwide operation. Like a lot of young companies, Kelly recalls, PSS relied on "hard work," "good people," "seat-of-the-pants navigation," and "a lot of luck."

The goal of becoming a national company was displayed in big banners in every branch, mentioned in every company document, and repeated by Kelly and his top managers.[1] It provided the impetus to search for initiatives that created economies of scale. In 1991 PSS started rationalizing its product lines—the company standardized on one or two suppliers in several lines so it could negotiate price breaks for bulk purchases. In that same year it opened "PSS University," which provided economies in training recruits. In 1994 PSS developed ICON, an order entry system based on handheld computers that increased the speed of deliveries and enabled PSS to reduce the inventories it had to carry.

Justification. As discussed in Chapter 3, providing even illogical "reasons" ("May I use the Xerox machine, because I have to make some copies?") can provide a psychological inducement to make a certain choice. Entrepreneurs cannot easily justify the initiatives required to build a large corporation just on the basis of financial projections. Although the uncertainty of firm-building initiatives is usually lower than the uncertainty of start-up opportunities, the irreversible investment and the personal financial exposure of the entrepreneur are substantially greater. The initiatives required to build a large corporation, as I will argue in the next chapter, may not represent a wealth-maximizing investment of resources. But when entrepreneurs convince themselves and other resource providers that their long-term goal or vision is, in and of itself, worthwhile, that goal becomes a cognitive anchor or objective function that justifies a variety of investments whose financial merits cannot be easily demonstrated.

To illustrate: In 1959 McKinsey & Co. opened its first overseas office (in London), and in the eight years following added offices in Switzerland, Holland, France, Germany, and Australia. The expansion involved significant out-of-pocket and opportunity costs. The firm did not have the manpower to satisfy the demand for its services from its United States clients, and the consultants who transferred overseas lost the client relationships in the cities they left behind. Moreover, the senior partners of the firm could not hope to recoup their share of forgone firm income through a long-term capital gain: Under the terms of McKinsey's ownership plan, retiring partners had to sell their shares at their "book" rather than their true economic value. Nevertheless, the McKinsey partners unanimously supported Managing Director Bower's drive to expand overseas. Apparently the firm members had bought into the goal of building the world's leading consulting company. This goal justified investments that might fail the test of personal wealth maximization.

Securing resources. Ambitious goals help businesses secure commitments from resource providers. The publicity generated by the promise of a grand adventure and the psychic benefits it can afford can help persuade employees and customers to take a chance on a fledgling business. For instance, the founders of Sun adopted the goal of competing with IBM and Digital in their mainstream businesses.[2] Sun's ambitious goals helped it attract top-quality talent and gain exposure with potential customers. Sun's concept, of building workstations with a Motorola 68000 microprocessor, a bit-mapped display, and the UNIX operating system connected to an Ethernet network, was hardly unique in 1982. These were, according to Sun's cofounder and former CEO Vinod Khosla, "the only reasonable specs," and by 1983 "there were maybe thirty companies implementing exactly the same spec." As Datamation noted in March 1983: "The new venture uniform of UNIX and the Motorola 68000 is getting as fashionable as IBM's blue and white stripes."[3] But only Sun's founders claimed they would build a company on the scale of an IBM or a Digital. This audacity helped Sun attract top-quality talent and gave Sun high visibility in the industry: At the UNIX trade show in 1983, Khosla reports, "one of the most important sessions was 'News from AT&T, DEC and Sun.'"[4]

Management scholars Bartlett and Ghoshal emphasize the value of goals that embody a higher "purpose" with which employees can identify and find satisfying. "Companies that assert more boldly what they stand for," they write, "typically attract and retain employees who identify with their values and become more deeply committed to the organization that embodies them."[5] Similarly, customers also can develop attachments to firms that they believe have a worthwhile mission. The loyalty of Apple's customers, for example, seems to go beyond a rational financial interest in having their vendor survive. Conversely, customers who disdain their vendor's goals and values will more eagerly search for alternative sources of supply.

Cooperation. Articulating an audacious goal and "purpose" for the firm can help reduce conflicts and among member firm members within and across specialized functions and subunits. As discussed, long-lived firms have to coordinate complementary assets. These coordination problems cannot be easily solved because it is difficult to foresee and contract for all contingencies and because the relative contributions of the complementary assets to what they jointly produce cannot be accurately assessed. For instance, the satisfaction of PSS's customers with the quality of service it provides depends on the efforts of its sales people as well as its logistics and delivery staff, but it is difficult to assess and provide appropriate compensation for the contribution of the two groups. Interests may be aligned to some degree by providing all contributors with a stake in the long-term financial success of the enterprise. But even with rewards tied to the overall success of the business (e.g., through stock options) there is still room for conflict. For instance, disagreements may arise over how many options the delivery staff get as compared to the sales personnel.

Internalization of the firm's long-term goals by its members reduces such conflicts. In contrast to bonuses or options allocated from a finite pool, the satisfaction an individual derives from contributing to a common goal does not curtail anyone else's satisfaction. The intrinsic and intangible nature of the satisfaction also eliminates the envious comparisons that can follow from the tangible rewards and recognition awarded by superiors. Employees whose individual contributions cannot be accurately measured are therefore more likely to tolerate perceived errors in the distribution of financial rewards if they are joined by a common interest in the firm's goals and purpose. The shared excitement of rapid national expansion at PSS or the challenge of taking on IBM at Sun Microsystems can play an important role in facilitating the coordination of individuals and functions.

Distinctive Features and Contrasts

Audacious goals do not play as significant a role at the start-up stage of a promising business as they do in the transitional phase of a business. Some founders may have one—Allen and Gates reportedly had the vision of having a computer on every desk and in every home, all running Microsoft software—but audacious goals do not represent an important precondition for starting a promising business. As we saw in Part I, promising businesses start out on a small scale. Their founders do not have to coordinate many employees and (unlike Bower and his partners) do not face much financial risk. They generally do not have in mind the idea of building a firm that will last in perpetuity. Entrepreneurs often start their businesses with the modest objective of becoming their own boss, to earn a little money, or just as a lark. Bill Hewlett and David Packard started with "tentative plans to try to do something on our own."[6] As they built various devices "to make a little money," Packard writes, the notion grew "in the back of our minds" that "maybe one of these devices could be developed into a viable product."[7] In 1995 The Princeton Review had attained the leading position in the SAT preparation market, claiming a 40 percent share, compared to Stanley Kaplan's reported 20 percent.[8] When John Katzman launched the business in 1981, he "never intended to make Princeton Review into a national company; all I wanted to do was to make some profits to start a software company." *Inc.* asked the founders of companies that made its "500" lists from 1982 to 1989 about their original intentions for their firms. Only a third had planned to grow as fast as possible, 12 percent had planned to stay small, 27 percent had planned to grow slowly, and the rest didn't plan at all—they "just wanted to get started."[9]

Articulating audacious goals and a well-defined "purpose" at the outset seems to be more important however for the unusual entrepreneurs who put themselves at considerable risk from the start or who have to raise significant outside funding. For instance, Marvin Bower and two partners took on the unprofitable East Coast practice and lease obligations (for which they assumed unlimited personal liability) of a struggling consulting firm to launch McKinsey & Co. Bower recalls that in the midst of the Great Depression, the partners "established, in our minds, the goal of becoming the leading management consulting firm in the United States," which would "continue into perpetuity." Although they did not make a formal declaration of their goal, the three discussed their "lofty ambitions almost constantly among ourselves. If we had not been ambitious, optimistic and visionary, we would never have had the courage to go ahead at all."[10]

Adopting audacious goals or defining an uplifting "purpose" for the enterprise does not represent an important task for the top executives of an established enterprise either. Having audacious goals is a necessary condition for building a long-lived firm, but once an enterprise has matured, its basic goals and values cannot be easily changed. Top managers' role can modify or reaffirm existing goals, but they don't have a clean sheet on which they can sketch new ones. As Bartlett and Ghoshal advise executives: "New values cannot be instilled through a crash program. . . . In fact, the goal for most companies should be to build on the strengths and modify the limitations of the existing set of values, not to make radical changes in values"[11] Moreover, past accomplishments limit the audacity of an established company's aspirations. The founders of a fledgling Sun Microsystems can make bold declarations about taking on IBM—a goal that involves exponential growth. The CEO of IBM, whose current market value of $154 billion[12] exceeds the GNP of nations such as Chile, Israel, Nigeria, and Singapore, cannot hope to attain similar rates of growth. Audacious goals in large companies typically are set at the level of specific initiatives ("become the number one company in PCs") and business unit level (see Fig. 11.1).

2. Strategy

Building a durable corporation requires long-term goals as well as rules to channel investments and initiatives toward the achievement of these goals. These rules—which I will call a "strategy"*—have several dimensions. A strategy defines in broad terms where and how the firm will seek to add value, the opportunities it will pursue, the breadth and attributes of the firm's product lines, its pricing policies, distribution channels, technologies, R & D efforts, and so on. As I use the term, a strategy includes organizational rules pertaining to matters such as the firm's hierarchical structure, the personalities and qualifications of its staff, and informal norms or culture. PSS, for example, adopted a policy of carrying a broad

Figure 11.1. Importance of Articulating Audacious Goals

---

* The strategy literature contains many definitions; I have chosen a relatively simple and broad definition that I believe best reflects the role of strategy in a transitional firm.

line of products and charging higher prices than its competitors while offering prompter deliveries and higher-quality service. Its target customers were physicians working solo or in small practices. Organizationally the PSS policy was to hire young, good-looking college graduates (rather than experienced personnel) for its sales staff, train them intensively, set challenging sales quotas, pay handsome commissions, keep a flat structure, and foster a gung-ho, "work hard, play hard" culture.

The following section discusses the importance of such strategies, how they develop, and their distinctive features in the transitional period of a firm.

Importance of Strategy

Many entrepreneurs start their businesses in an improvised way and rely on imitation or small modification of existing ideas to serve niche markets. Their subsequent search for a more differentiated and larger business also tends to be ad hoc rather than systematic. The entrepreneur may find a new combination that is closely related to the initial business or only very tangentially so. The discovery may be immediate, take several years and false starts, or the entrepreneur may never find a better business model. Factors such as luck, the intensity of dissatisfaction with the current situation, and the willingness to take a chance on an unconventional perspective rather than a strategy play a determining role. In Karl Popper's terms, finding a source of differentiation tends to be an inductive rather than a deductive process.

Whenever or however the entrepreneur establishes a venture's first differentiation, it will usually be of limited scope.* The subsequent broadening of the firm's assets and the development of routines require a more systematic effort than the typically opportunistic search for the initial source of differentiation. Investing in opportunities with positive expected returns without regard to their interactive effects may make an entrepreneur rich. Many individuals have prospered through a sequence of unrelated transactions in real estate and other such deals. But barring an extraordinary coincidence, one-off investments will not create a firm with a system of complementary assets. To build such a system, entrepreneurs have to formulate a strategy. As we will see next, strategies complement the role that an entrepreneur's goals play in building complementary assets. They promote consistency and coherence across multiple initiatives, help develop intangible assets such as expertise and reputation, and help solve coordination problems by fostering cooperation and teamwork.

Coherence of initiatives. Firms develop new assets through an ongoing process of searching for and experimenting with new initiatives. A strategy

---

* As we saw in the previous chapter, entrepreneurs lack the capital to acquire a portfolio of complementary resources in one shot as well as the foreknowledge of the components and their linkages.

defines the boundary conditions or envelope within which new initiatives are more likely to result in complementarities or synergies than if they were randomly selected. For instance, the Wal-Mart system is the result of many years of continuous change. Sam Walton was an avid innovator and imitator who quickly tried out many new ideas. But his experiments all fit a long-term strategy of low-cost, mass-market, discount distribution and thus cumulatively provided Wal-Mart with significant competitive advantages. The evolution of McKinsey's system is similarly characterized by considerable experimentation within the framework of a long-term strategy of providing independent, high-quality advice to the top managers of prestigious companies. The partners discarded or modified initiatives and activities that fell outside the framework and kept those that fit. For example, in 1951 McKinsey abandoned a profitable executive recruiting practice after twelve years when the partners concluded it might compromise the objectivity of their consulting services.

Thomas J. Watson, Sr. (who came to be known as "T. J.") introduced a variety of innovations at IBM. These included, according to Olegario, "providing professional training for all new sales recruits, giving sales people exclusive rights to their territories, and implementing sales quotas."[13] Although he was not an engineer, "T. J. played the key role in developing new products" and through the 1920s and 1930s "moved IBM's focus away from low-tech machines and into that period's state-of-the-art tabulating instrument, the punch-card machine."[14] He added printers to IBM's line so that the tabulating instruments "could be adapted for use in every large office in America."[15] He implemented a policy of leasing rather than selling products to customers. Under T. J., IBM expanded overseas, opening offices in 78 countries by the end of World War II. T. J. adopted a "decentralized approach by establishing wholly owned national companies that were managed and staffed primarily by local citizens."[16]

These varied initiatives did have a common theme, however. Through the 1940s T. J. focused on punch-card machines. A memorable consequence of what Olegario calls a "stubborn adherence"[17] to punch-card technology was that T. J. turned down the chance to buy the patents for xerography. T.J's son, Thomas J., Jr., recalls in his memoirs that "the inventor Chester Carlson came over from Queens and offered [the patents] to Dad. That was the biggest opportunity my old man ever missed." Thomas, Jr., also notes that although "sometimes Dad stuck to his last a little too closely," without his "devotion to punch cards, IBM would have lost its focus; it might have become a hodgepodge conglomerate like Remington Rand."*[18] (And as we previously discussed, the cash flow and complementary assets from punch-cards allowed IBM to make a late but successful entry into computers in the 1950s.)

---

* In the 1920s Remington Rand and IBM had shared leadership of the U.S. tabulating equipment market.

Reputations and expertise. Besides promoting synergies across different initiatives and investments, rules and boundary conditions also help firms develop assets such as know-how and reputations that, as discussed in the previous chapter, require repetition and constancy of effort. McKinsey's policy of serving top managers of prestigious companies entailed turning down profitable assignments that fell outside this definition. Over time this focus enabled McKinsey to build a reputation and ability in the field of top-management consulting that rivals who were more opportunistic in the assignments they chose to pursue have found hard to match. Similarly, HP developed technological expertise by focusing its product development efforts. David Packard writes that as the company expanded its product line during World War II, it stuck with instruments "designed to test electronic equipment. They reflected our strategy to concentrate on building a group of complementary products rather than becoming involved in a lot of unrelated things." Accordingly, HP turned down some big production contracts during the war; Packard felt the company should build a "solid base [in] designing and manufacturing high-quality instruments."[19]

Cooperation. Organizational policies can promote cooperation and mitigate a firm's coordination problems in both direct and indirect ways. Many long-lived companies, such as HP, adopt policies directly intended to promote what David Packard calls "commonness of purpose and teamwork." In the early years, according to Packard, the company did not need explicit policies because "we were all working on the same problems" and "each employee felt that he or she was a member of the team." But as the company grew "we could no longer take teamwork for granted. We had to emphasize and strengthen it."[20] HP developed personnel policies whose "underlying principle," writes Packard, "became the concept of sharing— sharing the responsibilities for defining and meeting goals, sharing in company ownership through stock purchase plans, sharing in profits, sharing the opportunities for personal and professional development, and even sharing the burdens created by occasional downturns in the business."[21]

Similarly, McKinsey's founders adopted a management philosophy that gave "broad participation in the affairs of the firm to as many partners as possible." All the partners had to agree to all major decisions even if this practice resulted in considerable delays. Unlike some other professional firms, McKinsey did not concentrate decision-making power with the managing partner or a small executive committee. To mitigate conflicts between offices, the firm formulated a "one firm" policy. Under the policy, all consultants would be recruited and promoted by the firm rather than by an office; partners' profit shares would derive from a firm pool, not an office pool; and each client was to be treated as a client of the firm, not of an office or even a particular partner.

Organizational rules also facilitate teamwork and mitigate conflict in indirect ways. Microsoft's policy of hiring the brightest individuals it can find or PSS's policy of recruiting young, personable college graduates and putting them through a boot-camp-style training program (with a dropout rate of about 30 percent) helps create a cadre of like-minded individuals who understand and can work with each other. Policies that shape the firm's culture reinforce the selection criteria by encouraging the individuals who don't fit to leave the firm. Long-term rules and norms also provide a "constitutional framework" for adjusting to unexpected circumstances and increase the mutual predictability of firm members' behavior. When faced with unexpected contingencies and conflicts, the concerned parties can rely on shared principles for problem-solving and renegotiations of past agreements. So even consistent norms of aggressive individualism can promote coordination.

As the above discussion suggests, effective strategies have an optimal level of precision. Broad strategies provide the latitude to adapt to unexpected setbacks and opportunities and guide the search for complementary assets. For instance, the decision by a tent manufacturing company to define itself as a provider of "high-performance outdoor equipment" can stimulate the development of a line of products sold through the same channel and a versatile brand name. At the same time, defining goals and rules too broadly limits their utility in coordinating the firm's efforts. A useful strategy precludes not just palpably unprofitable activities but also ones that could be reasonably undertaken by a firm following a different strategy. A strategy that is so broadly defined that it encompasses anything a company does is tantamount to not having a strategy. For instance, claiming to be in the leisure and entertainment business does not preclude a tent manufacturer from operating casinos or making films and therefore does not provide much focus to the company's efforts.

The difficulty of communicating an imprecise strategy also limits its utility. The value of long-term rules partly depends on the degree to which they are understood by the firm's key constituents, such as employees, customers, and investors. Clearly understood do's and don'ts, for example, help direct the search by employees for new innovations and investments. Similarly, acquiring useful external reputations also requires outside constituents to know what the firm stands for and what it can or cannot be counted on to do. Such understandings are obviously difficult to establish if the firm's leaders cannot clearly and concisely communicate their strategy.

To summarize: The previous chapter suggested that long-lived firms do not acquire coordinated assets through one-shot or even a preplanned sequence of investments. The process is evolutionary but not random, as with the proverbial monkeys who type out *The Origin of Species* by chance. Rather, building a long-lived firm requires entrepreneurs to formulate a strategy to achieve their firm's long-term goals that guides their initiatives and investments.

Distinctive Features and Contrasts

Long-term strategies, we saw in Part I, play a limited role in the launch of promising businesses. The formulation of an overall strategy does represent an important concern for the top managers of large, diversified companies such as IBM, who have to delegate considerable responsibility to more knowledgeable subordinates and who face the risk of being overwhelmed by diffused firm routines. As discussed next, however, we find important differences between transitional firms and large corporations in the content and process of the formulation of their strategies.

The strategies that bring order and focus to a fledgling company's efforts are not themselves the result of a systematic research and careful analysis of alternatives. Rather, strategies emerge from the entrepreneurs' goals and past experiences and adaptation to unforeseen circumstances rather than through a structured approach to maximizing returns.

Goals and prior experiences. The entrepreneur's overall goals can lead to rules about specific policies. Vinod Khosla recalls how Sun's goal of building a general-purpose workstation to take on IBM and DEC in their mainstream business shaped the company's product development choices:

> We wouldn't develop any applications software [and] whenever we had a trade-off we'd go after the general computing environment. For example, should we use our resources to build better compilers in the UNIX development environment, or should we build a fast graphics thing like Silicon Graphics was doing? We'd pick the general one [i.e., the compilers], which we'd need to compete against DEC.

The goal of building a large computer company led Sun to build a direct sales force, because, says Khosla:

> . . . that was what all the successful computer companies had. I did not know anybody who had been successful through third-party distribution and third-party support. It was very hard, because you didn't know how you were going to get revenue with a direct sales force, and you knew on the distribution side you could probably pick up revenue fairly quickly. . . . Our calculations showed we would not have money for anything besides a direct sales force and direct support. So marketing went out of the window at Sun. We couldn't afford a PR firm and all those things, so we did without those. If we did not get money to put a color brochure together, that was OK.

Formative experiences that shape the worldview of the entrepreneur play an important role in determining firm strategies. The origins of Wal-Mart's strategy of serving out-of-the-way markets can be traced back to chance events that lead the founder, Sam Walton, into discount retailing in rural Arkansas. Walton worked briefly in the department store business, for JC Penney, before joining the United States Army. When he returned to civilian life in 1945, he and a friend decided to become partners in a franchised store in St. Louis. But because Walton's wife insisted they live in a town with fewer than ten thousand inhabitants, he bought a franchised store in Newport, Arkansas, instead. When the landlord declined to renew the lease three years later, Walton decided to move to Bentonville, another small town, in northwestern Arkansas. Bentonville was closer to his wife's family, and its location allowed Walton to more fully satisfy a passion, acquired from his father-in-law, for quail hunting. By 1960 Walton had fifteen stores with total sales of $1.4 million in and around Arkansas. If circumstances had let Walton start in St. Louis or if he had developed different recreational tastes, he might have adopted a different strategy for Wal-Mart; perhaps he might have developed a chain of upscale specialty stores in large cities like the Nordstrom chain.*

John Chambers's prior experiences influenced Cisco Systems' technology strategy. In 1991 Cisco's then CEO, John Morgridge, recruited Chambers to succeed him. Chambers had worked at Wang Laboratories, where he witnessed "a painful downsizing." One lesson he drew from the experience was to avoid relying on a single technology—Wang was a company built around minicomputers. When Chambers assumed the leadership of Cisco, he sought to diversify its portfolio of technologies through acquisitions of or minority investments in small firms. Between 1993 and 1996 Cisco made seventeen such acquisitions or investments. In 1996, according to its chief technical officer, Cisco's technological base comprised about a dozen technologies.[22]

Many of the policies Marvin Bower adopted at McKinsey & Co. derived from a previous stint at Jones, Day & Co., a leading law firm in Cleveland. When he joined Jones, Day in 1930, Bower recalls, he got "a chance to work for Mr. Ginn, the senior partner. Because I had heard so much about him and the firm he had shaped, I made it an immediate objective to learn why it had been so successful. From observation and analysis during my Jones, Day years began the formulation of the program that I later brought with me to McKinsey." Bower made note of Jones, Day's professional approach, recruiting standards, and the prominence of its partners in Cleveland's charitable, social, and cultural organizations. If Bower had worked at an advertising or accounting firm instead of Jones, Day, he might not have emphasized the prestige and standing of McKinsey and its partners as much.

McKinsey's organizational principles likewise reflect Bower's dissatisfaction with the discord and authoritarian leadership he had witnessed at

---

* Nordstrom's history also illustrates the influence of formative experiences on long-term strategies. Nordstrom began as a shoe store in Seattle in 1901. The founder, John W. Nordstrom, had three sons who built a national shoe chain before branching out into fashion retailing. According to the company, Nordstrom's strategy of emphasizing customer service derives from its origins in the shoe business: "Selling shoes is the epitome of one-to-one service—nowhere else in the fashion business will you find a sales person on his or her knees in an effort to please the customer" (Moskowitz, Levering, and Katz [1990], 223).

the antecedent firms, James O. McKinsey & Co. and McKinsey Wellington. Bower's distaste for the "controlling type of leadership" practiced by
McKinsey Wellington's managing partner (and to a certain extent by James
O. McKinsey) led to the adoption of a consensual form of governance. Similarly, his unhappiness with interoffice rivalries at McKinsey Wellington
led to McKinsey's one-firm policy.

Adaptation. Entrepreneurs do not formulate their strategies all at once—
they adapt and expand the scope of their policies in response to unforeseen
problems and opportunities. HP's founders, for instance, did not formulate explicit organizational policies for nearly twenty years. Writes Packard:
"We did not much concern ourselves with organizational matters until well
into the 1950s. There was no need to. We had a well-defined line of related
products, designed and manufactured in one location, sold through an
established network of sales representatives, and had a highly centralized
company in which management was organized on a fundamental basis with
vice presidents for marketing, manufacturing, R&D and finance."[23] Continued growth and diversification of product lines "brought to light some
organizational weaknesses"[24] and led the founders to "consider some sort of
decentralized strategy."[25] In 1957, they divided the ninety engineers
engaged in product development into four groups, each of which concentrated on a family of related products.[26] The formation of product development groups was followed by further "divisionalization steps" spurred by
geographic expansion of manufacturing operations in Colorado and Germany and by the acquisition of new businesses. By the mid-1960s HP had
more than a dozen "integrated, self-sustaining" operating divisions responsible for developing, manufacturing, and marketing their own products.[27]

Hewlett and Packard also codified organizational norms in response to
the company's growth and diversification. In 1957 the company held its
first off-site meeting of senior managers. A group comprising about twenty
people reviewed and studied a set of corporate objectives that Packard had
previously drafted and discussed with Hewlett. As Packard describes it:
"Bill and I often thought about how a company like ours should be organized and managed. We thought that if we could get everybody to agree on
what our objectives were and to understand what we were trying to do,
then we could turn them loose and they would move in a common direction." The principles discussed in 1957 were subsequently refined based
on experience and on changes in the business environment."[28]

Limited growth opportunities in the businesses it had initially concentrated on lead HP to change its product-market focus. "By the late 1950s,"
Packard writes, "the need for diversification was clear. We were becoming
the largest supplier in most of the major segments of the electronic-instru-
mentation business. But these segments, in total, were growing at only 6
percent per year, whereas we were growing out of profits, at 22 percent.
Obviously, that kind of growth could not continue without diversifica-

tion."[29] HP subsequently established an operation to engage in solid-state research and development. As previously mentioned, it entered the medical field by acquiring the Sanborn Company, and the field of instrumentation for chemical analysis by acquiring F&M Scientific[30]. These strategy-defining acquisitions provided a base for entering new markets where HP could exploit and extend its capacity for developing technology-based products.

Similarly, important elements of Wal-Mart's strategy evolved over several decades, in response to unanticipated problems and opportunities. Distribution centers or warehouses have been a cornerstone of the company's expansion: Wal-Mart grew from state to state, methodically saturating markets surrounding distribution centers with its stores. With each store located within a day's drive of a distribution center, Wal-Mart could replenish store inventories, Walton estimated in 1992, more than twice as fast and at about a 35–40 percent lower cost than its competitors.[31] The strategy was born out of necessity. The company started building its first center in 1968, according to Walton, because "we didn't have distributors falling over themselves to serve us like our competitors did in larger towns. Our only alternative was to build our own warehouses so we could buy in volume at attractive prices."[32]

Investments in computer and communications systems have been another important critical element of the retailer's strategy. Abe Marks, the first president of the National Mass Retailers Institute, writes that without computerization, it would have been impossible for Walton to "have built a retailing empire the size of what he's built, the way he built it. He's done a lot of other things right, too, but he could not have done it without the computer."[33] For many years, however, Walton relied on rudimentary, labor-intensive systems. Writes Walton:

> By the early sixties, we had eighteen variety stores and a handful of Wal-Marts. . . . We kept a little pigeonhole on the wall for the cash receipts and paperwork of each store. I had a blue binder ledger book for each store. When we added a store, we added a pigeonhole. I know we did that at least up to twenty stores. Then once a month, Wanda Wiseman and I would close those books—enter the merchandise, enter the sales, enter the cash, balance it, and close them.[34]

In 1966, Walton enrolled in an IBM course for retailers. He recognized that Wal-Mart "had to get better organized" and that "quite a few people were beginning to go into computerization."[35] After this course, Walton began to recruit the personnel who would develop Wal-Mart's systems. In 1968 Wal-Mart hired Ron Mayer, and from that point on, Walton writes, "we as a company have been ahead of most other retailers in investing in sophisticated equipment and technology."[36] So it was more than two decades after Walton had opened his first store that a critical element of Wal-Mart's strategy was put in place. The principle of "treating employees as partners" through profit sharing and other benefit programs was adopted even later. Initially, Walton writes, "I was so obsessed with turning in a profit margin of 6 percent or higher that I ignored some of the basic needs of our people."[37] Subsequently, after skirmishes with unions led Walton to start "experimenting with this idea of treating our associates [employees] as partners, it didn't take long to realize the enormous potential it had for improving our business."[38]

Although policies often result from adaptation, this does not mean that effective strategies are in a state of constant flux: Rules need some stability to guide a firm's activities. At the same time, effective strategies for building a long-lived firm are not static either. Goals and prior experiences shape the initial policies. External developments such as a union organization drive or the availability of cheap computing power cause entrepreneurs like Sam Walton to reformulate their initial strategies. As the example of HP shows, firms may also develop new policies because they outgrow their target markets and their organizational structures and routines. Thus we find fledgling firms undertaking two kinds of initiatives. Some initiatives, such as HP's efforts to develop new electronic instruments, fall within the framework of the existing strategy. Other initiatives, such as HP's search for new markets, attempt to modify the framework. Successful frame-modifying initiatives lead to new policies—for instance, HP's acquisition of the Sanborn Company lead to a long-term commitment to the medical products market. Like a system of common law, effective strategies are both consistent and responsive to changing circumstances.

Analysis and research. Although entrepreneurs formulate their strategies in a purposeful and goal-oriented way, little formal analysis or research informs their choices: They pick long-term rules without much study of whether an alternative set would lead to superior results. For instance, McKinsey's "top management approach" of working only "with the approval and liaison of its client's chief executive officer" and "probing deeply the overall aims and abilities of its client" was a matter of faith.[39] A cover story in the September 24, 1955, issue of *Business Week* noted:

> Some of McKinsey's competitors laugh at the "top management approach." One of them says, "While they're talking to the president, we've moved into the sales promotion manager's office and gotten the order for a new marketing survey." To this, a McKinsey partner says, "That doesn't bother us one bit. We decided long ago that in our consulting we would take into account more than just one piece of the picture. And we haven't suffered for it."

As the phrase "haven't suffered for it" suggests, entrepreneurs make satisficing rather than "maximizing" strategic choices. Indeed, entrepreneurs cannot determine whether they made the best possible choice even after the fact. In their formative years, firms confront a vast number of options that are difficult to enumerate, let alone subject to a rigorous comparative analysis. Consider, by way of illustration, the case of Steve Belkin, the founder of TransNational Travel (TNT). In 1972 Belkin began working at Group Touring Associates (GTA). GTA developed and sold charter travel tours to various affinity groups by mail, using the membership lists of these groups. About a year later, Belkin left to start a company, TNT, which replicated GTA's business. As the charter travel industry was in its infancy and profit margins were high, TNT generated significant cash flows right from the outset. Belkin then built on TNT's direct-mail capabilities to sell products such as affinity credit cards by mail order. TNT's direct-mail strategy proved rewarding; in the early 1990s, Belkin sold off the credit card businesses for $200 million. But the redefinition reflected Belkin's dislike for investing in fixed assets rather than a careful financial comparison of all possible alternatives. Otherwise Belkin could have decided to build a vertically integrated travel service company and perhaps made a fortune developing hotels and resorts instead.

The risks of seemingly arbitrary choices are, to a degree, mitigated by the gradual evolution of a firm's strategy. Although entrepreneurs like Sam Walton, Bill Hewlett, and David Packard have limited experience when they start, over time they gain a deep, almost intuitive understanding of the businesses and markets, which can compensate for the sketchiness of their formal research and analysis. The twenty-seven-year-old Sam Walton had limited business knowledge when he opened his first store in 1945. He got "suckered into . . . an awful lease"[40] that didn't have a renewal option. By the time Walton refined the Wal-Mart formula in the late 1960s and 1970s, he had accumulated a deep knowledge of retailing through firsthand experience and by studying others' operations. "I probably visited," Walton writes, "more headquarters offices of more discounters than anyone else—ever."

And although the breadth of possible options makes it impossible to identify the best possible choice, entrepreneurs can analyze the merits of their intuitive leanings. We have previously noted that as firms evolve, they pursue opportunities that require more initial investment and involve less uncertainty. Accordingly, entrepreneurs have both the option and the incentive to make a serious effort to investigate the risks and the returns of their strategy-defining initiatives. Walton's 1945 store was a leap into the dark. The returns were highly uncertain because they depended on Walton's unproven capacity to manage a small franchised store. The economic contribution of Wal-Mart's first distribution center was less uncertain and could be more easily analyzed. The much larger capital required for the seventy-two thousand-square foot facility also gave Walton an incentive to do more research and planning. Similarly, in the early 1960s, when HP could have diversified into many fields, the founders could not determine whether medical products and instruments for chemical analysis represented the optimal choice. But they had the incentive and the means to analyze their acquisition of the Sanborn Company and F&M Scientific more thoroughly than they had the development of their Model 200A audio oscillator in 1939.

Corporate strategies. Strategy formulation in a mature business involves the consideration of a limited number of options because of a large preexisting stock of assets and embedded coordination mechanisms. Companies such as IBM today already have a base of customers, a broad line of products, reputations, know-how, personnel policies, transfer pricing mechanisms, norms, and so on. These assets and mechanisms cannot be easily altered, and the costs for their acquisition are already sunk. Strategy formulation in such companies, according to business school theorist Andrews, involves "matching" the firm's assets with its market opportunities. Similarly, IO economist Richard Caves represents "strategic choice" in a large firm as a "constrained optimization problem"; the "best strategy" maximizes some objective function, subject to constraints set by the firm's assets and market environment. [41]

In this process of matching (or constrained optimization), decision-makers face limited choices. When Hewlett and Packard sought to enter new markets in the late 1950s, they could have considered opportunities in telecommunications or process control instead of medical products. In the early years, Michael Dell could have decided to enter computer retailing or the manufacture of peripherals instead of desktop computers. Today the existing assets of HP and Dell limit the range of complementary new markets and businesses they can enter. Prior commitments and assets similarly limit the number of options that mature companies have in the choice of their technologies, manufacturing capacity, product features, pricing, joint venture partners, policies, distribution channels, and other such strategic variables.

History (or "path dependencies") not only limits the feasible range of values or states that a strategic variable can take, it also limits the number of variables that decision-makers can consider manipulating. As one important example, top managers of mature firms cannot easily alter basic organizational policies and rules. Entrepreneurs like Bower, Hewlett, and Packard pay considerable attention to policies regarding compensation, promotion, recruiting, and firm governance and to establishing the basic norms or values of their organizations. The choices they make in the formative period of their organizations have a profound impact on their firm's coordinative capacities and longevity. McKinsey's managing director or HP's CEO cannot easily change core organizational policies. They also have little reason to try to do so: Firms don't enjoy the long-term success of an HP or a McKinsey with obviously flawed organizational policies. Therefore, unless a mature firm faces a crisis, its organizational rules represent more of a constraint than a variable; and indeed, strategy models that take the perspective of the CEOs of large companies often exclude the organizational dimension. (See the sidebar "Organizational Variables in Strategy Models.")

Organizational Variables in Strategy Models

Organizational variables have long occupied an ambiguous place in the business strategy literature. The definitions of strategy used by Chandler in 1962 ("defining basic goals and the course of action and procedures necessary to achieve these goals") and then by Andrews in 1980 ("pattern of purposes and policies defining the company") should include the organizational policies that help firms achieve their goals and "define the company." Chandler's central thesis, that organizational structure follows strategy, however, implies a distinction between the organizational and the strategic. A similar ambivalence is reflected in Andrews' discussion of "economic strategy," and classification of some organizational policy issues under the rubric of strategy "implementation." Porter's framework, which so profoundly influenced the field of strategy, excluded organizational variables altogether. Porter dealt almost exclusively with the formulation of what Andrews would call "economic" strategy and unlike Chandler and Andrews, did not discuss organizational issues much, either as separate variables or under the rubric of implementation. There was similarly little analysis of what Philip Selznick had called the firm's "mission" or "purpose"—an organizational concern that pervades Andrews' view of strategy.

Stanford economist David Kreps offers the following description of how Porter and other scholars who have been "weaned on the economic paradigm" ignore variables such as firm culture in their approach to business strategy. In the Porter approach, Kreps writes:

> The firm and its capabilities are more or less taken as givens, and one looks at the tangible characteristics of an industry to explain profitability. It sometimes seems, in this approach, that there are good industries (or segments of industries) and bad: Find yourself in a bad industry (low entry barriers, many substitutes, powerful customers and suppliers, many and surly competitors), and you can do nothing except get out at the first opportunity. Now, this is assuredly a caricature of the Porter approach. The size of entry barriers, relations with suppliers/customers, and, especially, competitive discipline within an industry are all at least partially endogenous. Bad industries can sometimes be made good, and (perhaps a more accurate rendering of Porter) good niches can be found or formed even in bad industries.
>
> This approach carries with it a powerful legacy from textbook microeconomics: The firm is an exogenously specified cost function or production possibilities set, and market structures (also exogenous) determine how it will fare. The actual purpose of the firm qua organization is not considered. This is rather strange, for if one has an economic mind-set, one must believe that the firm itself performs some economic (efficiency-promoting) function. From there it is a short step to consider as part, perhaps the largest part, of successful strategy those actions designed to increase the firm's organizational efficiency. But since textbook economics doesn't explain firms qua organizations, it comes up empty as a discipline for analyzing this part of strategy.[42]

Recent work in the strategy field has begun to emphasize the organizational dimension. According to Henderson (1994) the growing popularity of the resource base view (RBV) has led to "a renewed interest in heterogeneous organizational capability," with several scholars suggesting that "organizational knowledge, structure, culture, or 'capabilities'" represent an important source of competitive advantage.[43] How firms developed their organizationally embedded advantages is often, however, not well specified. Some RBV theorists who have followed in the intellectual traditions of Nelson and Winter do not include a purposive top manager. Valuable organizational capabilities in their models develop by chance rather than by choice. This assumption seems inconsistent with the great effort that entrepreneurs who build long-lived firms put into organizational development. There may not be a simple relationship between intentions and outcomes, but it is implausible that conscious choices don't matter.

The exclusion of organizational variables, especially in "prescriptive" strategy models, derives, perhaps, from their established company orientation. From the point of view of the executive of an established company, organizational policies are much more difficult to change than the traditional strategic variables of product line, markets, capacity expansion, and so on. In empirical studies, measurement problems likely lead to the exclusion of organizational variables. Researchers cannot readily quantify the efforts and investment that go into building an organization, as they can the expenditures on R & D, advertising, or physical plant. In a young enterprise, however, whose routines have not yet been established, consciously formulated organizational policies have a significant influence over the firm's ability to develop a portfolio of assets and to overcome growth constraints. And our inability to quantify the efforts of an Andy Grove at Intel or a Bill Gates at Microsoft to root out complacency and build an intensely competitive organizational culture should not lead us to discount its importance.

Internal control systems also limit a mature corporation's options. As discussed in Part I, the fixed costs of evaluating and monitoring new initiatives lead to a high threshold of expected profit. Instead of considering many niche opportunities, top decision-makers restrict their attention to a few large investments. A critical strategic issue for HP in the early 1990s, for instance, was whether to withdraw from or increase its commitment to the multibillion-dollar personal computer market. For Wal-Mart it was whether or not to expand overseas.

Fewer options permit a more detailed evaluation of strategic alternatives. In fledgling companies, where entrepreneurs have to decide what assets they want to develop rather than match opportunities to existing assets, the overwhelming number of possibilities leads to intuitive, satisficing judgments. The constrained optimization of strategy formulation in large corporations facilitates research and analysis to pick the best option.

Decision-makers in HP could systematically investigate the pros and the cons of a commitment to PCs in the 1990s.

The control systems of mature corporations also provide the capacity to evaluate strategies in a systematic way. Fledgling companies usually lack the personnel to conduct detailed analysis of strategies. The system of checks and balances of mature corporations includes a staff specialized in evaluating strategies. Although the size of their staffs vary, practically every *Fortune* 500 company has senior executives and analysts dedicated to strategic planning and established routines for formulating and evaluating strategies. They also make extensive use of management consultants. Strategy assignments for large corporations generated, according to one estimate, worldwide revenues of about $6.3 billion for the top twenty consulting firms in the field in 1997.[44] In the 1960s, by contrast, Sam Walton personally did much of the analysis and research that went into formulating Wal-Mart's strategy.

Business school faculty and management consultants have developed many analytical tools and processes for the systematic formulation of corporate strategy. In Porter's "five force" framework, the analyst evaluates strategic options in terms of their effect on five categories of factors that affect the profitability of the firm's industry—the degree of rivalry between direct competitors, the likelihood of new entry, the threat from substitutes, buyer power, and supplier power. Porter provides numerous heuristics or checklists for analyzing these factors and for evaluating the effects of different types of strategic moves. The exercise involves extensive collection of data on customers, internal cost structures, competitors, potential entrants, and so on. In his book *Competitive Strategy*, Porter observes that "a full blown analysis is a massive task."[45] In the appendix "How to Conduct an Industry Analysis" Porter defines thirteen principal categories on which data should be compiled by company, by year, and by functional area.* Corporate analysts may not, in fact, develop this "comprehensive picture of industry structure and competitors' profiles"[46] that Porter recommends; but compared to decision-makers in fledgling companies, they at least have the resources to aspire to do so.

To conclude this section, we may thus sketch the following progression in the evolution of the strategies of promising ventures. Entrepreneurs start their business in an ad hoc way, without any systematic effort to find the best possible opportunity. They serve small markets and often rely on their

---

* These categories, with subcategories in parentheses, comprise: product lines; buyers and their behavior; complementary products; substitute products' growth (rate, pattern, and determinants); the technology of production and distribution (cost structure, economies of scale, value added, logistics, and labor); marketing and selling (market segmentation and marketing practices); suppliers; distribution channels; innovation (types, sources, rate and economies of scale); competitors (strategy, goals, strengths and weaknesses, and assumptions); social, political, and legal environment; and macroeconomic environment.

personal efforts and market disequilibriums to turn a profit. Through a determined, but usually not systematic, search, some entrepreneurs find larger opportunities that provide a platform for building a coordinated system of assets that can sustain a long-lived firm. The development of the system is neither random nor fully planned; rather, it evolves through experiments conducted within the framework of the firm's strategy. Although the long-term rules, which comprise the strategy, provide a consistent, systematic structure for the firm's initiatives and investments, the formulation of the strategy itself is arbitrary and evolutionary. Entrepreneurs make a priori choices about the type of firm they would like to build and rules they will adopt to do so. The entrepreneur conducts many experiments within the guidelines of long-term rules and also experiments to refine and expand the rules.

Over time the firm accumulates a distinctive bundle of assets that are best deployed against a limited number of market opportunities. These accumulated assets rather than the entrepreneur's intuitive choices set the boundary for subsequent initiatives and make the formulation of strategy more deductive and analytic than is possible in the transitional phase (see Table 11.1). Arguably, overconstrained strategies deduced from the existing asset base can prove ossifying and may lead to the slow demise of the corporation. Management gurus like Hamel and Prahalad suggest that senior managers "unlearn" the successful strategies the corporation has used in the past and "write off its depreciating intellectual capital" quickly.[47] The analysis of such advice is beyond the scope of this work; for our purposes it is sufficient to note that as an empirical matter, mature companies rarely offload their core assets and successfully make significant changes in direction.

Table 11.1. Strategy Formulation: Transitional Firms vs. Large Corporations

	Transitional Firms	Large Corporations
Role	Helps create a coordinated system of assets	Helps maintain and expand system
Content	Many variables and options	Variables and options limited by existing assets and past choices
Process	Based on entrepreneur's goals and past experiences and adaptation to unexpected circumstances	Limited options and availability of staff permit extensive comparative analysis

3. Implementation

In addition to the formulation of a strategy, building a durable firm requires its consummate implementation. By implementation I refer to concrete decisions and actions, in contrast to the choice of general rules or principles involved in strategy formulation. For example, Wal-Mart's adoption of a rule to locate stores in small towns, and Microsoft's policy of recruiting and training programmers straight out of college (rather than hiring experienced personnel) represent, in the terminology I use, strategy formulation choices. Finding specific store locations (or candidates) and negotiating leases (or compensation arrangements) represent, in my usage, the implementation of the strategy. Similarly, adopting the principle of having a decentralized organization represents a formulation choice. Determining the specific division of functions between headquarters and the decentralized units; designing, negotiating, and reviewing budgets; selecting managers for the units and setting their pay and bonuses, and so on, all represent implementation choices.

The difference between formulation and implementation does not, in my usage, correspond to the distinction between short-term or "tactical" decisions and long-term or "strategic" decisions. As discussed below, choices about specific store locations and personnel can have a significant long-term impact on firm evolution.

Importance of Implementation

The quality of implementation matters at least as much as, and sometimes more than, the formulation of rules and policies. A typical business strategy resembles a map of Everest rather than directions for making withdrawals from a numbered Swiss bank account. In the latter case, the directions are of value, while the execution is routine. In contrast, getting to the top of Everest is challenging, not because of the scarcity of reliable maps but because of the difficulty of the climb. Reaching the summit of Everest requires, in addition to a reliable map, exceptional determination, technique, endurance, and the ability to make judgments under difficult conditions. Similarly, while goals and rules help direct and coordinate effort, building a durable firm also requires an exceptional capacity to execute or implement strategy. Implementation is especially important when competitors monitor each other's strategies. A firm's general rules and objectives are typically intended for wide communication and thus may be easily observed by rivals. If rivals choose to adopt the same broad approach, success will be largely determined by differences in the quality of implementation.

Implementation has obvious importance at the level of the individual functions of a business. Wal-Mart would not have become a multibillion-dollar enterprise without excellence in buying and merchandising goods and Sam Walton's talent for picking good locations from his airplane. If Sun Microsystems had been weak in its software or hardware engineering efforts, it would not have captured a significant share of the workstation market—according to Vinod Khosla, several other companies that started with the same product specifications and technology as Sun were simply unable to do the follow-on engineering required to make a good product. The inability to get products to work is a common reason for the failure of high-technology ventures. Apple Computers, for example, launched the handheld Newton in 1993 with great fanfare. It became an object of derision, not because of a strategic or marketing mistake; the Newton's handwriting recognition capability—a crucial feature of the product—just did not work satisfactorily.

Implementation also affects a firm's capacity to coordinate multiple assets and activities. The effectiveness of deeply embedded coordination mechanisms depends on many specific choices, not just a few overall principles. For instance, whether a policy of hiring team players instead of brilliant but difficult stars has the desired consequences will depend on the traits of the individuals actually recruited. We might further expect that the effectiveness of specific choices depends on changing contextual factors. The marketing and production heads may, for instance, develop a mutual dislike; effective coordination of the two units may therefore require replacing one or both heads.

Distinctive Features and Contrasts

Although the success of a strategy depends on its effective implementation regardless of a firm's age or size, we can find differences between mature and fledgling firms in the role played by the top decision-makers and in the nature of the implementation tasks.

Role. The top managers of large, well-established firms often focus on broad policies and delegate the responsibility for specific choices to subordinates. (As the sidebar "Implementation in Strategy Models" suggests, many prescriptive strategy models reflect the interest of large-company executives in strategy formulation.) In contrast, for reasons we will explore in the next chapter, the principals of a fledgling enterprise cannot delegate the responsibility for implementation as easily. They have to play an active role in the formulation of general policies as well as in their translation into concrete initiatives and investments.

Consider, for instance, Sam Walton's role at Wal-Mart. Wal-Mart took a large number of ideas from other retailers to implement its overall strategy of providing exceptional value to discount shoppers. Walton told employees, a former store manager recalls, to "check everyone who is our competition. And don't look for the bad. Look for the good. If you get one good idea, that's one more than you went into the store with and we must try to incorporate it into our company."[48] Moreover, Walton did not rely just on store managers to find these ideas. Don Soderquist, who used to run the data processing operations for a chain of variety stores, describes how Walton met with him to talk about computers:

He wanted to know all about how we were using them, and how we were planning to use them. And he took everything I said down on this yellow legal pad.

The next day was Saturday, and I went shopping . . . at the Kmart near my house. I walked over into the apparel section and saw this guy talking to one of the clerks. I thought "Jeez, that looks like that guy I met yesterday. . . . He's writing everything [the clerk] says in a little spiral notebook." Then Sam gets down on his hands and knees and he's looking under this stack table, and he opens the sliding doors and says, "How do you know how much you've got under here when you're placing that order?"[49]

Tasks. Strategy implementation in a transitional firm also involves some distinctive tasks. Below, I discuss two special challenges that entrepreneurs face in implementing strategies: upgrading the firm's resource providers and building the organizational infrastructure.

Upgrading resources. The existing base of resource providers in a mature company represents a constraint or a "given" in the formulation of its strategy. In young firms, where strategies derive more from the entrepreneur's hopes than from the existing stock of resources, entrepreneurs often have to "reconstitute" their resource providers to close the significant gap between their aspirations and their current position. They have to find new employees, customers, and sources of capital.

As we saw in Part I, many new ventures cannot initially attract top-notch employees. Moreover, while the basic strategy is still in flux and it is not clear what kind of workforce will be needed in the long-term, it may be imprudent to hire expensive, high-quality talent. If the initial business concept proves to be unviable, the entrepreneur has to change course while paying high salaries of underutilized employees. In the early stages, therefore, expediency rules: The founders provide most of the crucial skills and recruit whomever they can for tasks they are too stretched to perform themselves.

After they have formulated long-term goals and policies, however, entrepreneurs require more qualified personnel. The urgency of rapid expansion may preclude training underqualified or inexperienced initial employees for critical positions. Some individuals may also lack the innate ability or motivation to take on increased responsibility. And recruiting experienced staff provides evidence of the firm's long-term prospects and a signal of the entrepreneur's commitment to building a long-lived firm.

Recruiting Steve Ballmer, for instance, helped Microsoft secure the crucial contract to provide an operating system for IBM's PCs. Ballmer joined Microsoft in June 1980. Steve Wood, the general manager, and his wife, Marla, who kept the books, had just left. Marla had been overwhelmed by the workload; her husband was drawn by the greater opportunity he saw at Datapoint: At the time, Microsoft owners Bill Gates and Paul Allen did not

Implementation in Strategy Models

Many models underplay the role of the implementation of strategies. They suggest that choices along a few policy dimensions are the main determinants of long-run profitability; implicitly or explicitly, they assume a firm can readily acquire the capacity to implement the right policy choice effectively. For instance, in his 1980 book *Competitive Strategy*, Porter emphasized the importance of picking inherently profitable industries and subgroups of industries. His formulation of strategy has evolved since then, but the emphasis on policy choices remains. In an award-winning 1996 article, "What Is Strategy?," in the *Harvard Business Review*, Porter argues that operational effectiveness ("performing similar activities better than rivals perform them") has limited value. "Few companies have competed successfully on the basis of operational effectiveness over an extended period," Porter writes, because of "the rapid diffusion of best practices. Competitors can quickly imitate management techniques, new technologies, input improvements, and superior ways of meeting customers' needs." Rather, long-run profits derive from differences in strategic positioning: "performing different activities from rivals" or "performing similar activities in different ways."

The new formulation of strategy contains ambiguities. How can a firm achieve operational effectiveness—"perform similar activities better than rivals"—without performing them in at least slightly different ways? And how could we expect any differences in the profitability of firms performing the same activities in the same way? More important, the spirit of the claim seems to lack empirical support. We can find several examples of companies making similar policy choices but enjoying quite different levels of long-term profitability because of differences in the implementation of strategies. When it gets down to the details, competitors cannot "quickly imitate management techniques," and "best practices" do not diffuse as readily as Porter suggests. Goldman Sachs and Morgan Guaranty, for instance, have enjoyed exceptional returns over several decades, providing the same services, drawing professionals from the same labor pool, and using the same technologies as their rivals, primarily because their capacity to provide higher-quality service or control risk has proved difficult to replicate. And, the sociologist Paul Adler's work on the General Motors-Toyota joint venture NUMMI describes the practical difficulties of transplanting manufacturing and human relation practices even when managers can observe them at close range.[50]

The focus of the Porter and similar models on strategy formulation likely reflects their interest in the top managers of large, established firms who delegate many implementation decisions to subordinates. Moreover, a mature firm's effectiveness in implementing strategies often derives from difficult-to-change routines and procedures. Like established organizational policies, therefore, the firm's "capacity to implement" represents more of a constraint than a decision variable. In fledgling firms, however, specific implementation choices made by the top decision-makers have a considerable impact on long-run profitability.

offer employees equity. Ballmer, a former college roommate of Gates, had previously worked at Procter & Gamble and attended Stanford's business school. Gates recalled later:

> When we got up to 30 (employees), it was still just me, a secretary, and 28 programmers. I wrote all the checks, answered the mail, took the phone calls—it was a great research and development group, nothing more. Then I brought in Steve Ballmer, who knew a lot about business and not much about computers.[51]

One month after Ballmer joined, IBM approached Microsoft to secure software for its planned introduction of a PC. Ballmer's corporate experience (and, jokes Gates, possession of a business suit) helped Microsoft allay IBM's concerns about entrusting the development of the PC's operating system to a small company that might not be able to provide ongoing service and support.

The growth of Cisco Systems required substantial changes in the composition of its workforce. Len Bosack and Sandy Lerner persuaded friends and relatives to work for deferred pay when they started the company in 1984. The founders continued to rely on improvised staffing for five years: a seventy-year-old retired physicist served as a plant manager for instance.[52] John Morgridge "built the management structure" after he was recruited to run the company in 1989. According to Morgridge, the company hired "professional and experienced people in all the main functional areas—a chief financial officer, a vice president of engineering, a vice president of manufacturing, and a marketing person" and recruited a professional sales staff.[53]

In 1996 Cisco had more than seven thousand employees, making it one of the largest employers in California's Silicon Valley. The company, which took on a thousand employees in each quarter of that year, had completely changed its initial recruitment policy. Instead of relying on individuals with low opportunity costs, it sought out "passive job seekers," who were happy and successful in their jobs. According to Cisco's vice president for human resources, the "top 10-percent" type staff that the company tried to recruit were not "typically found in the first round of layoffs from other companies" and weren't "cruising through the want ads."[54]

Customers represent another important area for upgrading. The customers who are most willing to buy from a new venture may not fit the firm's long-term strategy. As the example of Sun Microsystems illustrates, survival of the enterprise may hinge on making a sale to a new type of customer. In its first year, Sun sold what Vinod Khosla calls its "half-baked" workstations to a relatively small academic market. Universities could use "a not-fully developed machine," Khosla recalls, "because they did all kinds of kludgy stuff themselves and they did not mind putting in the resources. Typically, they were trying something new so they did not have to rely on the whole hardware as much."[55] Sun could not initially sell to commercial "system integrators" or OEMs, who might also have been able to use its unfinished workstations, Khosla found, because Sun lacked credibility. The OEMs instead turned to Apollo which was nearly ten times better capitalized than Sun. Apollo also had "well-connected senior management," an area in which Sun had "diddly-squat."

Sun had managed to sell its workstations to forty-two of its target list of the top fifty computer science departments in the United States in its first year. In the meantime, Apollo had secured Calma, Autotrol and Mentor Graphics, the three largest commercial customers for workstations, and was rapidly on the way to establishing its platform as the industry standard. In the following year Sun managed to secure an order from Computervision, which had decided to buy rather than make its own workstations. According to Khosla, if Apollo had gotten the Computervision order it would have been "all over" for Sun.[56]

Cisco founders Bosack and Lerner initially secured orders from fellow engineers in universities. According to Morgridge: "They were basically selling to their peer group, through word of mouth. The initial customer set started with the lunatic fringe—the kind of people who are way out on the leading edge. The early people were very technical and tolerant."[57] Morgridge established a systematic marketing program, hired professional sales staff, and targeted business customers. The company's sales grew from $5 million in 1989 to $183 million for the 1991 fiscal year as it secured more than a 75 percent share of the market for routers.

Finally, ventures may need to change their sources of capital. We have seen that start-ups are usually bootstrapped, using personal funds or money provided by friends and family. Bank loans are provided, if at all, by small local banks that cannot find larger, more creditworthy borrowers. Such sources often cannot provide much additional capital, however. The subsequent growth of the firm therefore often requires upgrading to professional venture capital, credit from larger banks, or the public markets to fund faster growth and for the credibility that the more well-known sources provide.

To illustrate: Sam Walton opened his first store, a Ben Franklin franchise, in 1945 with $5,000 of personal funds and $20,000 borrowed from his father-in-law. He financed more franchised stores through limited partnerships, in which the managers had a roughly 2 percent share, with Walton and his relatives holding the rest. Walton financed 95 percent of the first Wal-Mart in 1962 by taking out a personal loan against his assets; his brother and the store manager provided the other 5 percent of capital. Internally generated funds and a bank line of credit financed Wal-Mart's growth until 1969. In May 1969 Wal-Mart narrowly averted a liquidity crisis when a new banker became nervous about expansion plans and refused to allow the company to draw on its line of credit. Walton, who planned to open at least a dozen stores a year, then secured a term loan of $2.5 million from the Prudential and Mass Mutual insurance companies, and in October 1970 completed a public offering that raised $4.6 million.

Bosack and Lerner financed Cisco Systems with their personal savings and borrowings. In 1987 they raised funds from Sequoia Capital, a venture capital firm. In February 1990 the company went public, and the value of its stock rose about seventy times over the following seven years. The rapidly appreciating stock provided the currency to acquire other companies and broaden its portfolio of its products, technologies, and customers.

Building the organizational infrastructure. Just as the employees of a large firm are relatively fixed, so are the organizational structures and routines through which they work and interact. The formulation and implementation of new organizational policies become issues mainly in times of crises. Most start-ups have no organization to speak of; entrepreneurs who want to build long-lived firms face the task of formulating and implementing policies to build the firm's organizational infrastructure from scratch.

In building the hard elements of the infrastructure such as the formal reporting relationships, incentive plans, and control systems, entrepreneurs often seek to capture the knowledge and experience of mature firms by recruiting experienced managers from them. For instance, although Sam Walton had a keen intuitive sense for financial controls and had developed reasonably effective paper-based systems, he relied heavily on recruits, such as Ron Mayer from Duckwell Stores, to install the computerized systems that allowed Wal-Mart to grow rapidly. Consultants represent another means for acquiring expertise on the design of formal structures and systems. In the first half of the twentieth century, firms such as DuPont and General Motors had to invent their organizations without the benefit of existing models. Knowledge of the formal components of organization can now be directly or indirectly purchased.

The "soft" elements of organizations such as appropriate norms and culture cannot be acquired in the same fashion, however. Edgar Schein's study of how organizations "create cultures through the actions of founders" identified five "primary mechanisms for culture embedding and reinforcement." These were:

1. what leaders pay attention to, measure, and control;
2. leader reactions to critical incidents and organizational crises;
3. deliberate role modeling, teaching, and coaching by leaders;
4. criteria for allocation of rewards and status;
5. criteria for recruitment, selection, promotion, retirement, and excommunication.[58]

Schein's analysis and other studies of company cultures show that effective norms cannot be built simply by hiring experienced managers or consultants. Nor can entrepreneurs easily copy the cultures of the firms they admire; they have to customize the specific mechanisms for "embedding" culture to their specific circumstances. We thus see great variety across long-lived firms: The culture at Wal-Mart, according to Walton, reflects the traditions of small-town America, whereas the McKinsey culture is that of an elite, prestigious professional firm. The mechanisms used by the founders to implement the culture were also different. At Wal-Mart, Walton used to start executive meetings by doing the University of Arkansas' Razorback cheer and once wore a grass skirt to do a hula on Wall Street. Walton describes several other "corny" activities undertaken by executives to "make our people part of a family"[59]: a persimmon seed-spitting contest with the general counsel as target; wrestling a bear; and dressing up a male in pink tights and a long blond wig for a horse ride around the town square in Bentonville.

Bower, in contrast, insisted on a conservative dress code; until the 1960s, consultants were expected to wear hats and calf-length socks. He concerned himself with the look of reports to clients and wrote cautionary memos to firm members on the excessive use of ellipses. Bower describes his efforts to build "professionalism," a key element of McKinsey's culture, thus:

> The history of our program to establish professionalism in the firm reflects few dramatic highlights. It has been slogging work. The hours devoted to it cannot be numbered. I put out what I am sure was for many a monotonous series of memorandums and made an equally monotonous series of speeches at firm and office training meetings. Untold hours were also devoted to applying the professional approach to all aspects of our thinking, client work, prospective client relationships, and relationships among ourselves.

Although Bower's efforts to mold the McKinsey culture seem very different from Walton's, they did have in common a concern with detail: Establishing the high principle of professionalism in the McKinsey culture involved attention to consultants' purchases from the haberdashery.

4. Summary and Conclusions

In the previous chapter we saw that the transformation of a fledgling enterprise into a well-established corporation involves a gradual accretive process that requires a purposive coordination of effort across functions and across time. In other words, entrepreneurs have to adopt a "strategic" approach. In this chapter we examined the importance and nature of three elements of the strategic approach: the adoption of audacious long-term goals for the firm; the formulation of general rules and policies to achieve the goals; and the translation (or "implementation") of the general rules into concrete decisions.

The strategic approach to building a firm stands in obvious contrast to the opportunistic or improvised approach adopted by the founders of promising new ventures. The strategic approach also has some noteworthy differences, we saw, from the strategic tasks of the top executives of mature firms. The existing assets and norms limit the variables that the top managers of mature firms can manipulate; for instance, they cannot easily change the firm's basic purpose or its organizational climate. The need to match new initiatives with existing assets similarly limits technology and product market choices. And with fewer choices (and greater resources) they can derive strategies in a more deductive, analytical way. In a fledgling venture, by contrast, entrepreneurs can choose the long-term goal for their firm, the norms it will seek to develop, the customers it will target, and the assets it will invest in. These choices are made in an intuitive and adaptive fashion. In a young firm, policies reflect the entrepreneurs' beliefs and adaptive responses to unexpected events rather than a formal process to deduce a strategy.

12

Exceptional Qualities

This chapter examines the traits that entrepreneurs must have in order to build a large and long-lived firm. The first three sections discuss the traits that determine an entrepreneur's willingness and capacity to undertake the tasks involved in building a long-lived firm. They conform to the taxonomy used in the previous chapter: Section 1 discusses the traits that predispose individuals to adopt audacious goals. Sections 2 and 3 discuss the traits that affect an entrepreneur's ability to formulate and implement long-term strategies. Section 4 examines why entrepreneurs who lack the qualities needed to build long-lived firms cannot delegate or transfer responsibility to others. Section 5 contrasts entrepreneurial qualities with innate economies of scale and scope as an explanation for firm longevity and size.

Building a firm requires different qualities from starting a new business because it involves different tasks. In Chapter 4 we discussed how starting a business in an uncertain niche through a process of opportunistic adaptation requires qualities and skills such as a tolerance for ambiguity, open-mindedness, perceptiveness, tactical ingenuity, and a capacity for face-to-face selling. Adopting a strategic rather than an opportunistic approach to building a large, long-lived firm, we should expect, involves a different set of qualities. For instance, pursuing ambitious long-term strategies, we will see, requires considerably greater tolerance for risk than does starting a niche business.

Many entrepreneurs who start promising businesses don't have the traits necessary to build long-lived corporations. Nor can they easily delegate or transfer the responsibility for critical firm-building tasks to other individuals who may be better equipped to handle them. The very small number of individuals who have the willingness and the capacity to both start *and* build a business helps explain why few new ventures attain the longevity and size of an HP, a Wal-Mart, or a Microsoft. This explanation stands in contrast to the idea that natural economies of scale and "barriers to entry" determine the size and longevity of firms. Unusually driven and capable entrepreneurs like Sam Walton and Bill Gates, I will argue, help create the economies of scale and the barriers to entry that allow their companies to dominate their markets.

1. Predisposition

Audacious goals, we saw in the previous chapter, provide impetus and
direction to an entrepreneur's efforts to build a long-lived firm. The sections below relate the audacity of goals to the nature of an entrepreneur's
ambitions and willingness to take risks.

Nature of Ambitions

Starting a promising niche business does not require exceptional ambition.
The goal of building a long-lived enterprise derives from what Schumpeter
described as "the dream and will to found a private kingdom; the will to
conquer, to succeed for the sake not of the fruits of success, but of success
itself; and finally the joy of creating, of getting things done."[1]
  Entrepreneurs vary in the degree of their ambitions. Some "very good
businessmen," Penrose writes:

> . . . may have a high degree of managerial skill and imagination; they may
> be hard and efficient workers, but the ambition that would drive other men
> in the same circumstances to expand their operations in an unending search
> for more profit, and perhaps greater prestige, may be lacking. There is no
> inconsistency here: a good businessman need not be a particularly ambi-
> tious one, and so long as a firm is dominated by men who are not ambitious
> always to make profits it is unlikely that the firm will grow very large.[2]

  The nature of an entrepreneur's ambitions also matters. The "dream and
will to found a private kingdom" has different consequences from "an
unending search for more profit." The desire for profit does not require the
entrepreneurs to adopt the goal of building a long-lived firm. The profit-
maximizing individual can take advantage of transient opportunities and
move on without making an effort to leave a permanent mark. To illustrate, consider Sam Walton's contrast of his motives with those of the other
entrepreneurs who also started discount stores at about the time he did.

> . . . discounting attracted mostly promoters in the beginning—people who
> had been in the distribution center business or who were real estate pro-
> moters, guys who weren't really even aspiring merchants but who saw a
> huge opportunity. You didn't have to be a genius to see discounting as a
> new trend that was going to sweep the country, and all kinds of folks came
> jumping into it. . . . They would take a carbon copy of somebody's store in
> Connecticut or Boston, hire some buyers and some supervisors who were
> supposed to know the business, and start opening up stores. From about
> 1958 until around 1970, it was phenomenally successful.[3]

  Many promoters eventually "fell apart" after established mass merchandisers such as Kmart "got their machine in gear and began to do it

better and better."[4] Others "built their companies to a point, and then said, 'I've had enough!' and sold out and bought an island."[5] Walton had the personality of a showman and promoter, he writes, but underneath he had the soul of "somebody who wants to make things work well, then better, then the best they possibly can be." He was mistaken for a "fly by night" operator—in the discount business one day, and "selling cars or swamp-land the next." In fact, he was "never in anything for the short haul; I always wanted to build as fine a retailing organization as I could."[6] Wal-Mart didn't remain a regional operator or sell out to a national chain[7] because Walton wanted to "leave a legacy."

The distinction between accumulating wealth and leaving a legacy seems especially important today because of an active mergers and acquisitions market. Many ambitious individuals today start ventures that they expect to sell to a larger company; their goal is to develop products or technologies that complement another firm's assets rather than to build their own long-lived firms. And several entrepreneurs have indeed become wealthy in recent years by selling their businesses at the peak of what has later turned out to be a transitory success.

In some cases entrepreneurs who start their businesses for purely pecuniary reasons later develop different ambitions. Patrick Kelly recalls that when he and his cofounders started PSS in 1983, they "wanted to make money. We figured that's what it was all about: making money. If you could make money you could have all the stuff you wanted." In five years, they were "making plenty of money." They had "nice homes, boats, a couple of cars apiece." If they sold PSS, then a $20 million revenue company, the founders would have realized a few million dollars. Kelly felt he had earned enough to satisfy his personal consumption needs when a chance encounter with a speaker at a conference convinced him of the need for "a new challenge. Something big. Something no one had done before." Kelly then adopted the goal of making PSS the first national distributor of supplies to physicians.[8]

Willingness to Take Risks

The pursuit of audacious goals requires entrepreneurs to assume more risks than they usually do in starting their businesses. As we saw in Part I, start-ups usually exploit opportunities that do not require much up-front investment. Entrepreneurs perform an arbitrage function in turbulent markets or provide customized services to satisfy the amorphous wants of their customers. They do not sink much money or time to develop specialized assets; and they persuade customers and resource providers to bear much of the risk. Building a large corporation, however, requires initiatives with greater up-front investment. Wal-Mart constructed dedicated warehouses instead of relying on distributors. Microsoft invested in an advertising campaign to build durable brand names after initially relying on word of mouth and contracts with hardware manufacturers to sell its software. Dell developed its own design and engineering capabilities after selling computers assembled from off-the-shelf components. These initiatives happened to pay off, but ex ante they represented risky irreversible commitments. Moreover, because it takes many initiatives to develop the system of coordinated assets that sustains a large corporation, the aggregate investment is substantial.

Although entrepreneurs who start by bootstrapping their ventures often bring in outside investors to help finance these investments, they still face considerable personal financial risk. Usually they cannot withdraw their share of their capital and must keep reinvesting their share of the profits. If the firm fails, they stand to lose much of their wealth. They face the risk that the new investors they take on will force them to relinquish control. They may also have to sign personal guarantees for bank loans that put their personal assets at risk. Until 1970, when Wal-Mart went public and could retire its bank debt, Sam Walton and his wife, Helen, were "always borrowed to the hilt." Helen cosigned notes with Sam, pledging "houses and property, everything we had."[9]

Overcoming growth constraints also involves risk. Promising firms have to emerge from their niche and compete with large companies in mainstream markets. For instance, Wal-Mart initially served rural markets, where, according to one analyst, its pricing did not have to be "so sharp" and having the right merchandise wasn't critical "because customers had no alternatives."[10] To expand to a national scale, Wal-Mart subsequently "butted heads with other regional discounters like Gibson's and the Magic Mart" and in 1972 started competing against the multibillion-dollar industry leader, Kmart.[11] Growth may require entrusting inexperienced employees with decisions that could potentially sink the company. As mentioned, PSS had to give "huge amounts of responsibility to people without much experience."[12] Growth involves developing formal structures and systems that increase the firm's fixed costs and hence the risk of bankruptcy. And growth involves some irreversible investment in working capital—the cost of a firm's inventory and accounts receivable usually exceeds its liquidation value.

Many entrepreneurs who readily start with a small, "nothing to lose" business find it psychologically difficult to make the investment required to build a large, long-lived firm. As the founder of a chain of outpatient diagnostic clinics noted: "When you start, you 'Just do it,' like Nike says. You are naive because you haven't made your mistakes yet. Then you learn about all the things that can go wrong; and, because your equity now has value, you feel you have a lot more to lose. We have a hard time taking risks today that we once took almost without thinking." From an objective point of view, the failure of the twenty-first clinic did not pose as great a threat to the survival of the enterprise as would have the failure of the second or the third clinic. But the equity the entrepreneur had built in the business brought out an innate tendency toward "loss aversion" and (together with the greater knowledge of what could go wrong) made investments in additional clinics seem more, rather than less, risky.

The fear of losing the wealth they have accumulated leads some entrepreneurs to sell their businesses. In Chapter 1 we encountered Bob Reiss, whose company, Valdawn, capitalized on the trend toward fashion watches. Starting with $1,000 of initial capital, by 1994 Reiss had turned Valdawn into an *Inc.* 500 company with more than $7 million in revenues and pre-tax profit margins exceeding 15 percent. To finance Valdawn's growing inventories and receivables, however, Reiss had to reinvest most of the profits, and by 1994 he had more than $1.4 million tied up in the business. In November of that year Reiss sold Valdawn to a group of investors. "I am pretty confident that I could have continued to grow the business and achieved a greater payoff from selling later," says Reiss. "But I would have had to put in more capital and if there was a downturn in sales I would have to forfeit the payoff that was available."

The unwillingness of many entrepreneurs to take the risks needed to build long-lived businesses is consistent with the claim made in Chapter 4 that the predisposition to start a promising business depends on an individual's tolerance for ambiguity rather than for risk. And, as mentioned in that chapter, the experimental evidence suggests that ambiguity aversion is uncorrelated with risk aversion. The typical entrepreneur who has a high tolerance for ambiguity will likely have only an average tolerance for risk. Only very unusual individuals like Sam Walton will have the ambiguity tolerance needed to start an uncertain business and the risk tolerance needed to build it.

Relationship to Financial Returns

Although the analysis above suggests that in the long run, ambitious entrepreneurs with a high tolerance for risk are more likely to dominate their markets, this does not mean that they earn superior financial returns. Starting a business without putting up much capital and subsequently developing the assets that facilitate its acquisition by other companies or by investment groups offers attractive rewards compared to the risks. The likely cash flows do not easily justify the protracted investment and effort required to build a large corporation, however. The most aggressive entrepreneurs may be victims of a winner's curse who overpay for the market share they secure.

In fact, the best financial course for an entrepreneur may be to sell out to a more optimistic or ambitious competitor. Acquisition by a large corporation seeking to enter a new market represents another attractive exit option. Corporate executives often believe that they can exploit the assets of smaller firms more effectively, and are willing to offer entrepreneurs a price that reflects the value they think they can add. The pressure to grow also makes large corporations eager acquirers of up-and-coming businesses.

At the same time, the decision to avoid growth or exit can be myopic and riskier in the long run than taking a bet on expansion if rivals have aggressive growth plans. For example, as long as the hardware distribution industry was fragmented, the size of a business was a matter of the owner's choice—some were content with a single store, whereas others built, small regional chains. However, once companies such as Home Depot started investing in megastores and committed resources to finding national economies of scale through bulk purchasing and so on, small operators could not, in the long run, afford to stand still. Labor and capital markets may also preclude niche strategies. In Silicon Valley, for instance, a high-technology company that does not espouse a strategy of high growth will likely face difficulty today in recruiting engineers or raising venture capital.

Moreover, even entrepreneurs who run small, profitable ventures cannot count on enjoying the quiet life. An entrepreneur's long hours often never come to an end because of the inability to attract talented employees; besides, without sharp colleagues, they find their existence lonely and boring. Founders may also get locked into their business because personal franchises are difficult to sell, and face financial distress if they fall sick or get burned out. "I'm always running, running, running," one entrepreneur told my class. Although his business made the entrepreneur $500,000 per year, he complained: "I work fourteen-hour days and I can't remember the last time I took a vacation. My wife spends everything I make so I can't let up. I would like to sell the business, but who wants to buy a company with no infrastructure or employees?"

To summarize: Entrepreneurial ambitions matter a great deal in determining which firms will grow. In a world populated with perfectly rational and prescient decision-makers, if one entrepreneur decided to grow aggressively, competitors (for customers or resources) would either follow suit or exit if they had that choice. But "loss aversion" and the fear of change can lead to a myopic disregard for the loss of competitive position over the long term. Many individuals will stand pat, especially if they are satisfied with the status quo. Entrepreneurial ambition, even if it does not have pecuniary roots, can therefore lead to superior financial outcomes. Entrepreneurs with the will to grow a large firm can even enjoy more leisure in the long run than those who restrict their ambitions, supposedly to enjoy a better lifestyle.

Ambition and risk-taking do not play as important a role in starting a promising business or after it becomes large and well established. The question of risk-taking is moot in start-ups where an entrepreneur does not have much capital to lose and does not face high opportunity costs (see Fig. 12.1). Similarly, ambition and risk-taking are not critical in managing a

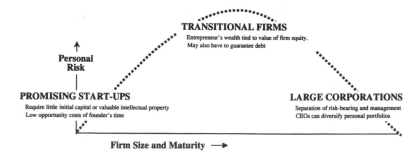

Figure 12.1. Risks Faced by Top Decision-Makers

large corporation. Executives of firms whose distinguishing characteristic is the separation of risk-bearing and management do not have to put their personal wealth on the line. And, as mentioned in the previous chapter, the existing assets and activities of their firms limit their capacity to act boldly.

2. Formulating Strategies

The task of formulating a long-term strategy for a fledgling business involves mental faculties that do not play a significant role in starting a venture. These faculties include the imagination to envision a different kind of future, a capacity for creative synthesis, and a capacity for abstraction.

Imagination

As we saw in the previous chapter, entrepreneurs cannot deduce the long-term strategy for a fledgling business by matching existing resources with market opportunities. Starting with a relatively clean slate, they have to use their imaginations to envision what their firms could become along several dimensions, such as the markets they will serve, the tangible and intangible assets they will acquire, and their organization's climate and norms. The capacity for seeing the possibilities does not correspond to a gift of prophesy; the process of building a long-lived firm represents an effort to make the future conform to one's vision rather than to make accurate long-term forecasts.

Creative Synthesis

Entrepreneurs often copy many elements of their strategy from other firms. Patrick Kelly of PSS writes: "I don't think I've ever had an original idea in my life. At PSS all the great ones were borrowed from somebody else. . . ."[13] But unlike the nearly complete replication of someone else's model that we often find at the start-up stage, entrepreneurs creatively select and integrate ideas from several sources. Kelly credits a variety of sources for providing the building blocks of PSS's strategy, ranging from an airline (SAS),

Federal Express, an automotive component manufacturer (Dana Corporation), motivational speakers, and popular business books. Marvin Bower derived several elements of McKinsey & Co.'s strategy from his experiences as a lawyer at Jones, Day, a leading law firm in Cleveland. He borrowed the principle of providing objective, independent counsel and cultivating a prestigious clientele; he implicitly rejected, however, the Jones, Day, strategy of having a single office in Cleveland. Similarly, McKinsey & Co. retained the "top management approach" and emphasis on training from its predecessor firm James O. McKinsey & Co., but Bower consciously rejected its strategy of offering both accounting and consulting services and its centralized management style.

Abstraction

The strategies of fledgling firms, we have seen, evolve as entrepreneurs adapt to unforeseen opportunities and problems. The choice of new policies involves a conscious, "artificial" selection of the sort employed by livestock breeders rather than a mechanical process of natural selection. The entrepreneur has to go beyond solving a concrete problem, and distill (from often quite sketchy data) a general rule that guides subsequent investments and initiatives. As mentioned, Wal-Mart started building its own warehouses because it couldn't get distributors to serve its rural stores. It expanded around the warehouses, so that each store would be within a day's drive from a warehouse. "We would go as far as we could from a warehouse and put in a store," writes Walton, and then "fill in a map of that territory . . . until we had saturated that market area."[14] Deriving this rule took more than just problem-solving. "Our growth strategy was born out of necessity, but at least we recognized it as a strategy early on,"[15] writes Sam Walton. "We just started repeating what worked, stamping out stores cookie-cutter-style."[16]

Many entrepreneurs who start businesses to seize short-term opportunities cannot make the transition from a purely tactical to a strategic orientation because they don't have the necessary imagination and capacity for synthesis and abstraction. Some individuals are "doers" with a great faculty for operating detail but lack the imagination needed to envision a large enterprise. Others have imaginations that seem optimized for short-term projects or deals. As discussed in Chapter 4, they may show great "tactical" creativity in making a sale, securing extended payment terms, or finding underutilized production capacity that they can rent for a low price. But they may be uncomfortable going beyond the here and now to imagine what their firms might become after a decade. We often find such deal-oriented imaginations in the fields of finance and real estate. For example, the "raiders" in the "eighties," such as Sir James Goldsmith, Irwin Jacobs, and Ronald Perelman, showed noteworthy creativity in acquiring diversified companies such as Crown Zellerbach, AMF, and Revlon and selling off several of their business units for a considerable profit. The same individuals have not enjoyed similar success in building and growing businesses.

An entrepreneur's imagination and creativity may also be limited in scope. For instance, in the high technology field we often find entrepreneurs with technical foresight but limited interest in formulating marketing or organizational policies. As a result, the marketing function may consist of little more than order-taking personnel. The firm may develop dysfunctional norms because its culture is shaped, by default, by employees recruited mainly for their technical skills and credentials. Without the active efforts of entrepreneurs like Bill Gates at Microsoft or Andrew Grove at Intel to proactively develop a culture of insecurity and paranoia, success may engender hubris and slack. Unlike Intel, Microsoft, or HP, such a firm will tend to disintegrate when a rival develops a superior technology, because it lacks the buffer of good marketing, high employee morale, and the capacity to respond quickly to setbacks.

3. Implementation

In the previous chapter we found that implementing strategies to build long-lived firms required the upgrading of resources and the building of an organizational infrastructure. Now we turn to looking at the qualities that determine an entrepreneur's capacity to perform these tasks. These are: constancy, the capacity to inspire and intimidate, and the ability to learn new skills.

Constancy

The congruence of broad strategic rules and concrete actions depends on the entrepreneur's constancy—"the steadfastness of attachment to a cause," according to one definition in the dictionary. This is not an important trait in the "opportunistic" start-up phase of a promising business; a strong commitment to an idea may in fact conflict with the "open-mindedness" required to adapt to fluid markets and customer needs. Constancy is critical, however, in implementing strategies to build customer relationships, reputations, and organizational infrastructure.

Focusing on a particular set of customers or needs usually involves the willingness to incur opportunity costs. As previously mentioned, the McKinsey partners turned away market survey work and studies for sales managers to build a "top management clientele." Hewlett and Packard turned down large production contracts during the World War II to focus on developing high-quality instruments.[17] The implementation of organizational principles can require terminating productive employees. Patrick Kelly describes letting go one of his early partners because his managerial style conflicted with the values Kelly wanted to instill at PSS.[18] McKinsey started implementing an "up or out" policy for associates in 1952 to build an "elite" organization, even though the policy reduced the firm's productive capacity (and the incomes of the partners). The willingness to incur such opportunity costs likely derives from a strong conviction about the merits of the underlying principle, as well as considerable self-control and capacity to delay gratification.

In extreme cases, constancy may entail betting the company, not just forgoing incremental profit opportunities. A strategy of replacing second-tier customers or employees may be crucial for long-run survival. But the rate at which the new resources become available is unpredictable; giving up the cash flow generated by the current customers and employees can sink the company. To proceed with the upgrade, therefore, entrepreneurs require an unusual tolerance for risk as well as self-control and conviction in the strategy. (See the sidebar "Upgrading the Telluride Company's Client Base" for an example.) For individuals with "bounded will power" the incentive to procrastinate can be strong.

Entrepreneurs' "steadfastness of attachment" to a strategy for upgrading resources may conflict with their personal attachments. Many cannot easily reconcile their desire to build the firm with a sense of loyalty or obligation to their initial employees. Bill Nussey, who cofounded the software company Da Vinci Systems, recalls that as the company grew, "it became increasingly obvious that the demands of the company had outgrown the people." Terminating these employees who had "struggled and cried and sacrificed with the company" was "the hardest thing he ever had to do." Loyalty to individuals can also reinforce, and provide a rationalization for the fear that changing even a suboptimal organization may make things worse.

Inspiration and Intimidation

Building a firm requires a different kind of persuasiveness than does starting a new business. In the start-up phase, we saw in Part I that perceptive entrepreneurs get others to take a relatively modest chance on the venture by understanding and adapting to their needs. For instance, they provide customized products and services to customers and jobs for individuals with limited employment prospects. The entrepreneur's challenge subsequently shifts from adaptation to others' wants and beliefs to bending others to the entrepreneur's will.

At this stage an entrepreneur's capacity to inspire others assumes a more significant role. As charismatic leaders, entrepreneurs have to shape the preferences and wants of others: Patrick Kelly, for instance, had to persuade his staff to adopt and internalize his goal of building a national distribution company, and Bower had to convince his partners that creating a professional firm that would "last in perpetuity" was a worthwhile enough cause for them to sacrifice some income. Entrepreneurs also have to get others to share their convictions about means as well as ends—that the steadfast adherence to the firm's strategy will lead to the attainment of

Upgrading the Telluride Company's Client Base

Jeff Behrens, founder of the Telluride Company, a provider of computer-related services, recalls:

> I started Telluride from my bedroom. I worked alone and did whatever clients wanted for $50 an hour: I installed computers and software, fixed bugs, researched software, did some database programming and some network and systems administration. It amazed me then that people would pay an untrained kid $50 an hour. I didn't know how to do things very well and had to figure them out with some trial and error.
>
> Within three years I had hired an associate and rented office space. I was still doing anything and everything on an hourly basis. It became a real drag. Cash flow was hard to predict and perhaps most infuriating were clients who I had worked for one to two years and who I billed regularly—perhaps $500 to $1000 per month: They would pick apart my bills, demanding to know why X had taken 1.5 hours and not 1.2. In order to grow and build a sustainable business we needed more predictable cash flow and less painful client relationships. We devised the "SMP"—System Management Plan—where clients would pay a fixed fee each month depending upon their size and complexity and get all services they needed.
>
> The transformation was difficult and painful. No one wanted the SMP: Clients liked the feeling that if they didn't call me, they didn't incur any charges. Finally I made the scary and risky decision to tell clients that they would have to do the SMP or find someone else to work with. Over the course of twelve months we lost 75 percent of our clients and over eighteen months we lost all but one client. But we were able to find much better clients during this process, in essence replacing bad revenue with good. We became much more profitable and average revenue per client went way up. But if I had known that I would lose all but one client I am not sure I would have had the resolve to do it.
>
> Today, two years later, we are facing another transition point. The company has grown to eleven people and our SMP and associated services bring in good cash flow. We can find business easily and convert leads to clients well. However, hiring technical managers has become the most difficult aspect of the business. Good technical managers are expensive and are paid 50 to 75 percent more than we pay our current personnel. I have to create a compensation plan that will allow us to bring in more management talent. This may force us to revisit our rates, evaluate or even fire existing managers, and will potentially be equally transformative and devastating as the SMP introduction. I guess I don't have much choice if I want to keep growing Telluride. What makes it hard is now I am making a good living and have a viable if small business—I have far more to lose!

long-term goals. (I do not mean to suggest that individuals like Kelly and Bower ignore the innate wants and beliefs of others; their perceptiveness about how others see the world can be of considerable use in getting others to see the world their way.)

A capacity for intimidation, or what Herbert Simon might call the provision of "inducements" that cause others to suspend their "critical faculties for choosing between alternatives,"[19] reinforces the entrepreneur's ability to inspire. The capacity matters little in the early stages of a business, when the entrepreneurs have little bargaining power and must often adopt the role of a supplicant. In fact, as mentioned in Chapter 4, to make a sale they have to be disarming and nonthreatening. Intimidation plays a role after a business has acquired the capacity to offer positive and negative inducements. For instance, Microsoft's principals had to be very responsive to the demands of IBM executives to secure the crucial order for MS-DOS from IBM in 1980. After the success of the IBM PC, Microsoft could drive hard bargains with PC manufacturers to consolidate its position in the operating system market.

Although intimidation requires an objective basis, its effective use depends on the entrepreneur's skill in shaping the perceptions of others. Entrepreneurs have to understand and exploit others' loss and ambiguity aversion—the fear of losing what they have, and uncertainty about their alternatives. Entrepreneurs also have to have or project an unusual willingness to take risks to achieve their goals. By managing perceptions effectively, entrepreneurs can secure much greater compliance than their actual bargaining position merits. It is not coincidence that entrepreneurs like Bill Gates who build long-lived businesses are frequently described as "tough" or "ruthless" and seem to follow Machiavelli's advice to be more "feared than loved."

Learning New Skills

Implementing a strategy to build a firm involves different concrete tasks from those required to start a new venture. For instance, the entrepreneur has to negotiate with bankers instead of extending payment terms to suppliers; focus more effort on developing marketing programs and less on personal selling; determine reporting relationships and shape norms rather than using under-qualified staff to somehow get the product out the door. These tasks require skills, which we might broadly call business or administrative skills, that few founders have at the outset. As we saw in Part I, entrepreneurs like Rod Canion who had extensive business and managerial experience are unusual. More commonly, long-lived firms are started by young individuals like Bill Gates, Michael Dell, Sam Walton, William Hewlett, and David Packard, who do not have much experience or formal training in business.

The capacity of such individuals to broaden their skills, to transform themselves from scrappy bootstrappers to managers of a complex business, helps determine whether they can effectuate a corresponding transforma-

Microsoft, and Michael Dell has long given up assembling computers. It is also obvious that entrepreneurs have to make a transition from spending virtually no time on formulating long-term policies to devoting a considerable effort in this area. This does *not* mean, however, that they can concentrate just on strategy formulation and leave its implementation to others. Although the nature of concrete tasks entrepreneurs have to perform changes, their capacity as "doer" remains crucial for a long time.

The delegation of implementation tasks is limited by the degree to which customers, employees, investors, lenders, and other resource providers trust the entrepreneur rather than the firm. The credibility and reputation of a young firm is closely linked to that of the entrepreneur. In placing an order or extending a line of credit, customers and bankers will, therefore, typically require the entrepreneur's close involvement with the transaction. Sun Microsystems secured its all-important commercial order from CVD only after the all-out effort of Sun's cofounder and chief executive Vinod Khosla. Similarly, Marvin Bower personally negotiated studies with McKinsey's breakthrough overseas clients Shell and ICI.

The derivation of policies from concrete choices makes it difficult to separate the formulation and the implementation of strategies. Entrepreneurs like Sam Walton can distill policies from specific problems and opportunities because of their close involvement with the day-to-day activities of the enterprise. Such involvement also helps them control the inadvertent adoption of inappropriate policies, as may occur when a special favor done for a customer or employee sets the precedent for poor marketing or compensation practices.

Entrepreneurs have to apply case-by-case judgments to reconcile long-term strategies and immediate financial constraints. Although transitional firms have access to more funds than start-ups do, their opportunities for strategic investment usually outstrip their available capital. While enunciating visionary strategies, therefore, entrepreneurs have to maintain tight controls over specific expenditures. Walton, for instance, balanced a long-term commitment to computerization at Wal-Mart, with a close scrutiny of individual projects. Writes Walton:

> Everybody at Wal-Mart knows that I've fought all these technology expenditures as hard as I could. All these guys love to talk about how I never wanted any of this technology, and how they had to lay down their life to get it. The truth is, I did want it, I knew we needed it, but I just couldn't bring myself to say, "Okay, sure, spend what you need." I always questioned everything. It was important to me to make them think that maybe the technology wasn't as good as they thought it was, or that maybe it really wasn't the end-all they promised it would be. It seems to me that they try just a little harder and check into things a little bit closer if they think they might have a chance to prove me wrong. If I really hadn't wanted the technology, I wouldn't have sprung the money loose to pay for it.[21]

Concrete choices made by a firm's top leaders help determine its culture. The founders of HP, McKinsey, or Wal-Mart articulated broad principles and brought them to life by taking advantage of specific opportunities to celebrate their application and to punish transgressions. Unless entrepreneurs "lead by example" and closely monitor the behavior of subordinates, opportunistic deviations lead to sharp differences between the espoused and the actual norms of the organization.

The Value of Continuity

It might seem optimal for the many individuals who only have the skills needed to start a business to transfer control to individuals who have the capacity to build a firm but not the capacity to start one. This does not seem to commonly occur, however: In the case of all but one of the companies from the *Inc.* class of 1985 that had crossed $500 million in revenue in 1995 (including Microsoft and Oracle), the same CEO was still involved in management.[22] The evidence suggests that long-lived firms such as HP, Wal-Mart, Microsoft, and McKinsey are built, over several decades, by the individuals who started them. In some cases, such as IBM, 3M, and McDonald's, where the founders bowed out early, we find a similar continuity of leadership provided by individuals who took control when the firm was still in an unformed state. As mentioned, Thomas J. Watson, Sr., joined C-T-R in 1914, three years after its formation. He ran the company (which he later renamed IBM) for forty years thereafter. William McKnight, who turned a failing sandpaper manufacturer into 3M, served as its president and then chairman between from 1929 to 1969.

Of course, exceptions can be found. For instance, Sandy Lerner and Len Bosack started Cisco Systems in 1984. Venture capitalists recruited John Morgridge to run the company in 1989, when it was a $5 million concern with thirty-five employees. Morgridge hired Chambers from Wang in 1991; Chambers was appointed CEO when Morgridge became the chairman of the company's board. According to Morgridge, he had reached his goal of building a $1 billion in sales company; he believed that Cisco had the potential to reach $10 billion, but at age sixty-one, didn't want to make the five-year commitment it would take.[23]

The goals and incentives of a company's founders limit the frequency of top management changes. The individuals who start businesses are often unwilling to relinquish control: Venture capitalists more or less forced out Lerner and Bosack from Cisco's management team. Some founders do not realize they lack the ability to build a large corporation. Others consciously choose to operate a small business that provides a comfortable income and a congenial lifestyle. Limited alternatives may encourage entrepreneurs to stay with their firms: It is not obvious, for instance, that Hewlett and Packard or Bill Gates would have found a more rewarding use for their time if they had departed from their companies in the transitional phase.

The entrepreneurs who do choose to move on, often find it financially more rewarding to sell their businesses to another firm than to hand over control to another individual. As mentioned, up-and-coming businesses can have a higher value as acquisition candidates than as stand-alone firms. Such acquisitions, which extinguish the independent existence of the selling firm, contribute to infrequency of top management changes in long-lived firms; they lead to a transfer of assets from one firm to another rather than a passing of the CEO's baton from one individual to another.

On the positive side, when entrepreneurs have (or can develop) the requisite skills, their ongoing leadership can also help their firms attain noteworthy size and longevity. As mentioned, the value of a firm in its very early stages is closely tied to the entrepreneur's personal knowledge, skills, reputation, and legitimacy; ownership of the firm cannot be transferred to others. The examples of firms such as HP and Microsoft suggest that even after firms acquire an independent portfolio of assets, continuity of leadership remains valuable. Temporal specialization—passing on control of the firm to new individuals as the set of desirable skills changes—apparently has drawbacks similar to those of dividing up entrepreneurial responsibilities. Instead of a relay race or a frequent changing of the guard, we usually find in long-lived firms an evolution in the roles and skills of the entrepreneur.

To summarize: Transforming a fledgling enterprise into a large, long-lived corporation requires entrepreneurs to perform many interrelated tasks. They have to exercise their imagination to formulate long-term strategies, design their organization's structure and systems, and mold its culture and character. Besides performing these creative and visionary roles, entrepreneurs have to remain engaged in the day-to-day activities and make difficult, specific trade-offs. While they sketch out an expansive view of the possibilities to inspire and attract constituents, entrepreneurs have to keep firm control over expenses and cash, and closely monitor operating performance. The interrelationships among these tasks make it difficult to delegate them. Nor can entrepreneurs easily transfer their knowledge, contacts, and legitimacy to another person. Companies typically attain noteworthy size and longevity under the leadership of individuals who have an exceptional capacity and willingness to broaden their skills and roles.

5. Relationship to Industry Structure

In Chapter 10 I briefly alluded to the view of industrial organization researchers who provide an alternative to the proposition that it takes entrepreneurs with unusual will and capacities to build large and long-lived companies. The IO research holds that factors such as technology and consumer tastes determine the economies of scale and scope in an industry and thus the optimal number of competitors. If economies of scale are high, competitive forces eliminate all but a few firms, whereas in their absence we find fragmented industries with many small firms. Exogenous innovations that increase the economies of scale reduce the number of viable firms and increase their average size: recall Jovanovic and MacDonald's example of the appearance of the Banbury mixer in 1916 that led to a shakeout in the tire industry. Surviving such shakeouts does not require exceptional ambition or multifaceted capabilities, merely the luck or the foresight to adopt the innovation quickly.

To evaluate the claim that economies of scale and scope predetermine the number of survivors in a market, we will first review the evidence. Then we will look at the direction of the causality. I argue that the efforts of entrepreneurs to build large and long-lived firms, not just exogenous factors, are important determinants of the economies of scale and scope found in an industry.

Evidence

According to Scherer's 1980 text, standard IO theory posits that "market structures [i.e., the number and size of competitors in an industry] are the more or less determinate result of variables such as technology [and] the receptiveness of consumers to advertising."[24] Cross-country comparisons of concentration ratios (usually measured as the market shares of the top four firms) in different industries seem to support this assumption. "Sufficient similarity in concentration patterns exists among nations to suspect that some common cluster of concentration determining forces is at work,"[25] writes Scherer. Sutton's 1996 review also notes that "the ranking of industries by concentration level tends to be closely similar from one country to another: An industry that is dominated by a handful of firms in one country is likely to be dominated by a handful of firms elsewhere, too. The large majority of studies argue in favor of such regularity and interpret it as a reflection of the fact that the pattern of technology and tastes that characterize a given market may be expected to be similar across different countries."[26]

Exogenous variables that limit the number of competitors in a market, according to IO models, also contribute to the longevity of the incumbents. High irreversible investments required to reach the minimum efficient scale, the argument goes, protect the "first movers" against new entrants. So if the "minimum efficient scale" of production is one-tenth the total demand, we will find no more than ten firms serving the market at any time, *and* over time, we would find the same ten firms.

Business historians echo the claim of IO research that exogenous factors such as technology determine the size and longevity of firms. Consider, for instance, Alfred Chandler's observations about the "clustering" of the large modern industrial enterprise in "industries having similar characteristics."[27] In his 1990 book *Scale and Scope*, Chandler analyzed the distribution of all the industrial corporations in the world that employed more than 20,000 workers in 1973. Of 401 such companies, 289 (72 percent) were clustered in the food, chemicals, petroleum, primary metals, machinery, and transportation equipment industries. Just under 23 percent were in cigarettes, tires, newsprint, plate and flat glass, cans, razor blades, and cameras. Only 5.2 percent were drawn from the textiles, apparel, lumber, furniture, leather, printing, and publishing industries.[28] The clustering of large companies in certain industries, according to Chandler, reflects the invention or vast improvement in "processes of production" that led to "unprecedented" opportunities to realize "cost advantages of the economies of scale and scope."[29] In apparel, lumber, furniture, printing, and other such industries in which "the large modern firm remained relatively rare," improvements in equipment and plant design did not bring "extensive" economies of scale. Large companies could not enjoy "striking" cost advantages over smaller competitors in these industries.[30]

Another historian, McCraw, writes:

> Only certain kinds of industries lend themselves to large operations. Such industries either have major economies of scale (electric utilities, steel, oil refining, chemicals, automobile manufacturing) or economies of scope (pharmaceuticals, discount retailers, branded snack foods). Throughout American history, entrepreneurs have tried, sometimes desperately, to create big businesses out of naturally small-scale operations. It has not worked. Everyone knows about National Biscuit (RJR Nabisco) but few people have ever heard of National Novelty, National Salt, National Starch, National Wallpaper, and National Cordage, all of which perished soon after they were incorporated. Standard Oil became one of the world's largest companies, but Standard Rope and Twine quickly dropped from sight. United States Steel prospered, but United States Button came and went in a flash.[31]

The Entrepreneur's Role

A simple reconciliation of predetermined industry structures and entrepreneurial talent would be as follows: Exogenous economies of scale determine the number of competitors in a market, whereas the capacities of the individual entrepreneurs determine their identities. Many qualities, not just chance, determine which entrepreneurs can successfully adapt to the appearance of innovations like the Banbury mixer that increase the efficient scale of operation. The survivors are hungrier for market share. They are more willing to take the risks of investing in a new technology and have the capacity to raise the necessary finances. They can market and sell a high volume of output. And they can establish effective mechanisms to solve the coordination problems involved in realizing economies of scale (such as the conflicts between the production and the marketing functions).

Similar logic can be used to explain why many firms have market shares greater than what we would expect from scale effects alone. Scale effects establish a lower bound to the level of concentration—the minimum efficient scale determines the maximum number of viable firms in a market. In fact, we usually find fewer competitors. Several observers have noted that "actual concentration levels seem to lie far above the levels warranted by [minimum efficient scale] arguments."[32] We might attribute the difference to exceptionally capable entrepreneurs who can extract greater economies than are "predetermined" by factors such as technology or taste.

We can, however, go beyond this simple reconciliation. In *Business Cycles* (1939) Schumpeter argued that innovations "are neither transcendental and unknowable, nor mechanical and foreordained," and that only an exceptional entrepreneur could take advantage of the latent opportunities to innovate.[33] Both the cotton and the wool industries provided opportunities to innovate in late eighteenth-century England, Schumpeter pointed out, but only the cotton industry had the entrepreneurs who could take advantage of the possibilities. We can extend the relationship between entrepreneurial ability and innovation to industry stucture: Below I argue that the apparently exogenous determinants of industry structure often result from the efforts of entrepreneurs. Differences in the technology and tastes that lead to differences in production, marketing, or other such economies across industries reflect the ambition and talent of the entrepreneurs who sought to build their business in their industries.

Production economies. As mentioned, Chandler contrasts industries where new processes of production led to the realization of significant economies through large-scale production with industries where the processes of production did not allow steep reductions in costs with increasing scale. But where did the new processes of production in the former category come from? The research of Chandler and other historians points to the efforts of ambitious entrepreneurs with multifaceted talents.

Henry Ford, for instance, transformed the manufacturing of automobiles from a batch process to mass production on an assembly line. Ford was more than a "mechanical genius." Historians McCraw and Tedlow note a variety of his innovations and talents that made mass production a success. Ford introduced the $5 day for his workers—more than twice the prevailing wage—to reduce worker turnover, which sometimes reached 300 to 400 percent per year because of "the strength-sapping and mind-numbing character" of assembly line work.[34] Ford had a "brilliant" intuition about "the nature of a car for the masses," and saw that "the proper *design* of the car must precede all other considerations."[35]

For his time, we may also credit Ford with an unusual capacity for organization. McCraw and Tedlow write that Ford "had great difficulty in delegating authority to anyone"[36] and contrast his "impulsive entrepreneurship" with the temperament of Alfred Sloan—the "patient, persuasive, and systematic organization man"—who built General Motors.[37] But we should note that Ford's company grew from making 40,000 cars in 1911 to 1.4 million in 1925; it sold them through a distribution system comprising 6,400 dealers. In 1997 Ford produced 1.68 million passenger cars in North America,[38] or only about 20 percent more than in 1925. In 1925 Ford's workforce exceeded 100,000 employees, of whom 58,000 worked at the River Rouge plant. Historian David Lewis writes that in the mid-1920s the Rouge facility, which occupied more than 1,115 acres, was "easily the greatest industrial domain in the world."[39] Even today, with our considerable knowledge of large organizations, a deep pool of professional managers, and sophisticated information technology, it is difficult to imagine an entrepreneur creating an enterprise on the scale of Ford Motor Company without a considerable talent for organization. Given the conditions prevailing in the 1920s, we might fairly characterize Ford's organizational capacities as both unusual and necessary for realizing economies of mass production.

Exceptional entrepreneurs also stimulate scale-increasing innovations by their eagerness and capacity to utilize new technology. Eric von Hippel's research suggests that in many industries, the users rather than the producers often drive product innovation.[40] Ambitious entrepreneurs who want to dominate their markets may therefore push their suppliers to develop equipment that increases the minimum efficient scale. In the steel industry, for instance, Andrew Carnegie "fanatically focused on achieving cost leadership by investing heavily in process improvements," whereas his competitors "focused on making and breaking price-fixing covenants."[41] His firm was the first to adopt several innovations, such as the Thomas process. If Carnegie had had the same approach as his competitors, these innovations might well not have been developed for commercial use to the degree that they were.

There is perhaps something intrinsically different about automobiles and steel that permits greater economies of scale than in the production of lumber and furniture. To my knowledge, arguments about natural economies of scale do not make this difference clear. Rather, such arguments implicitly assume that if furniture could be mass-produced in the same way as automobiles, someone would have done so already. This Darwinian premise, I believe, flies in the face of the historical evidence about the crucial role exceptional entrepreneurs have played in bringing about product and process innovations.

Marketing and distribution economies. In many industries, ranging from soft drinks to mainframe computers, the economies of scale and scope derive more from the marketing and distribution functions than from a production process where unit costs decline steeply with output. As mentioned, some scholars argue that these economies derive from exogenous factors such as consumer "tastes" or "receptiveness to advertising"; in product categories where customers are more receptive, we find greater economies and barriers to entry.

The inherent attributes and functions of buttons and twine may doom efforts to realize marketing and distribution on a national scale. Differences in product attributes cannot easily explain why the chewing gum company Wrigley could build a global brand while lollipop companies did not. It is not obvious that the inherently greater receptiveness of consumers to advertising for cola drinks and diamonds allowed Coke and DeBeers to achieve many times the revenues of companies marketing ginger ale or rubies. Or, to use a recent example, we cannot plausibly attribute the national expansion of Starbucks coffee shops to a spontaneous change in the tastes of U.S. consumers several centuries after the availability of the beverage.

Just as Henry Ford played a critical role in the mass production of automobiles, so William Wrigley, Jr., Asa Candler (of Coca-Cola), and Howard Schultz (of Starbucks) helped create marketing and distribution economies in chewing gum, cola drinks, and coffee shops. These entrepreneurs did not merely have a "talent for marketing." Like Ford, they performed a variety of tasks involving a variety of qualities. They envisioned building large businesses in previously fragmented markets, took considerable personal risks, formulated strategies, mobilized resources, recruited and motivated talented employees and built effective organizations. As the sidebar, "Starbucks and the Coffee Connection," suggests, without Howard Schultz's ambition and capacity to build a large enterprise with a broad base of coordinated assets (such as good locations, a brand name, and buying and merchandizing capabilities), coffee retailing would have remained a "naturally" local or regional business.

Network economies. We can extend the argument about entrepreneurial ambition and ability to firms that capitalize on network economies. W. Brian Arthur and others have in recent years highlighted the phenomenon of increasing returns to scale enjoyed by certain technologies and standards. As is now well known, the value of Internet standards or computer operating systems grows with the number of users and suppliers of complementary software. These network effects can lead a technology such as the VHS format for video recorders or Qwerty keyboards to dominate the market even if the alternative beta format or Dvorak keyboard is technically superior. The benefits of network economies are not "inevitably" realized, however. For instance, in the heyday of mainframe computers and minicomputers, hardware manufacturers developed their own operating systems. Correspondingly, word processing and other applications in the 1970s generated files that could not be used across different systems. When dominant technologies or networking standards do emerge, there is no compelling reason that they be owned or controlled by a single firm; rather, we should expect that users would more likely adopt as standards,

Starbucks and the Coffee Connection

Starbucks traces its origins to a business started in 1971 by three coffee afi-cionados. By 1998 Starbucks had become the leading coffee retailer in the United States with more than sixteen hundred locations, with a new store being opened almost every day. Its evolution illustrates the nature of the entrepreneurial effort and talent involved in realizing economies in mar-keting and distribution.

Coffee retailing has traditionally been a local or a regional business. Like other firms in the field, Starbucks operated in just one city, Seattle, from 1971 to the mid-1980s. In 1982 the founders of Starbucks hired Howard Schultz to "bring marketing savvy to the loosely run company." A year later, after a buying trip to Milan, Schultz became determined to build a nation-al chain of cafés modeled after Italian coffee bars. Schultz's bosses resisted the idea because they "wanted to be in the coffee bean business, not the restaurant business." In April 1986 Schultz left to open his own coffee bars, which turned out to be instant successes. In the following year, in 1987, Schultz bought out his former bosses at Starbucks.

From 1987 to 1993 Starbucks grew from 11 stores to more than 270, expanding from Seattle to cities in the West such as Portland, to the Midwest (in Chicago), and then to the East Coast. In each market, Starbucks followed a strategy of placing multiple locations close to each other in high-traffic, high-visibility locations, acquiring competitors when it could. "Designed to be sophisticated and inviting," York writes, Starbucks stores were "fairly spacious, well-lighted places featuring lots of burnished wood, gleaming espresso machines, art work and opera music." Starbucks also published a direct-mail catalog offering its coffees and coffee-making equipment, which it believed supported its new retail stores and reinforced brand recognition in existing markets. In 1992 Starbucks went public.

Schultz hired experienced executives from companies such as PepsiCo to establish the organizational base of the company. He claimed that Starbucks had two sources of "competitive advantage"—"our coffee and our people." To ensure high-quality coffee, Starbucks ran a vertically inte-grated operation and gave its staff twenty-five hours of training before they worked behind the counter. Investments in employees took the form of an unusual level of health care and other benefits and stock options for all employees, including part-timers.

Starbucks' evolution may be contrasted with that of The Coffee Connection (TCC), launched by George Howell on the opposite coast, in Boston. In 1975 Howell, his wife, and a partner started a store in Harvard Square to teach customers how to "appreciate and care for a good cup of coffee." Started as a retailer of coffee beans, the Harvard Square store developed into a coffee bar. In 1976 Howell opened a second Boston store. Subsequent growth was slow, however. Fastlich, Knakowski, and Lesser attribute TCC's slow growth to "a lack of systems and controls and depen-dence on constant supervision from Howell ... [whose] time was split between management, recruiting, site selection, supervision, broker relationships, and purchasing." Unlike Schultz, who hired executives from PepsiCo, Howell "tried to develop some key operations people from within" because he felt that outsiders wouldn't have "the coffee background and education required to serve TCC's unique clientele."

In contrast to Starbucks' sophisticated marketing and merchandising, The Coffee Connection "persisted in maintaining a strategy that stressed quality above all else and had practically no marketing program in place." It was "managed in a 'loose, hippie-style' manner." The stores had very little in common other than the superior quality coffee and the Huichol Indian art displayed on the store walls.

In 1989 Starbucks approached Howell with an offer to acquire The Coffee Connection stores. Howell initially refused and, as a defensive measure intended to keep Starbucks out of the Boston market, formed a joint venture with Au Bon Pain, an East Coast bakery restaurant chain. Eventually, however, after the Seattle-based company decided to open its own stores in Boston, The Coffee Connection was sold to Starbucks.

---

technologies that were as close to a public good as possible. Indeed, many of the frequently cited examples of network economies—VHS, computer languages such as FORTRAN, the Qwerty keyboard, the Internet, IBM's PC architecture, and the UNIX operating system—are based on standards that are more or less in the public domain.

An entrepreneur must have exceptional abilities to create and control a significant networking standard. Microsoft's holdover personal computer operating systems (and some applications software) represent an out-of-the-ordinary outcome akin to a typewriter manufacturer's exclusive control over the layout of a keyboard. It ultimately derives, according to my analysis, from the ability of Microsoft's founder Bill Gates and (from 1980) top lieutenant Steve Ballmer to establish a nearly mythical reputation for invincibility. As discussed in the sidebar, "Self-Fulfilling Prophesies," Microsoft has been able to establish and own crucial standards because it has convinced users, hardware manufacturers, and suppliers of complementary goods that it will almost inevitably prevail in any market it chooses to dominate.

To summarize: The goals and abilities of entrepreneurs help to shape the structures of markets. As we saw in Part I, entrepreneurs tend to start businesses in niche markets. They take advantage of small opportunities, serving specialized needs or taking advantage of information gaps to buy cheap and sell dear. Their ventures usually do not have much lasting impact on industry structure. Fragmented markets remain so. But when entrepreneurs, who may have started out exploiting exogenous market conditions, have out-of-the-ordinary will and ability, their effort to build large, long-lived firms helps transform the economic landscape.

Self-Fulfilling Prophesies

The perception that Bill Gates holds little back in his drive to win has played a valuable role in Microsoft's domination of PC software. Gates's reputation in the media and computer industry is reflected, report Wallace and Erickson, in headlines such as "The Whiz They Love to Hate" in *Newsweek*, "One Day, Junior Got Too Big" in the Sunday *New York Times*, and "From Computer Whiz to Bullying Billionaire" in the *Seattle Post-Intelligencer* (p. 380). Wallace and Erickson write that as "far as Bill Gates is concerned, business is war" (p. 381). Gates looks for "any business opportunity that lets Microsoft win," they continue. Complaints about how Microsoft does business are common not just from competitors such as Philippe Kahn, chairman of Borland, and John Warnock, CEO of Adobe Systems, but also from erstwhile collaborators and partners:

Bob Metcalf, founder of 3Com Corporation, likened a disastrous joint marketing venture with Gates in the late 1980s to "black widow spiders mating—you'd be lucky to get out alive." Metcalf said Microsoft double-crossed 3Com and precipitated his company's first multimillion-dollar quarterly loss, in 1991.

Gates's reputation for ruthlessness may well derive just from the jealousy of less successful individuals. Whatever its origins, the widespread belief that he will not allow Microsoft to lose and may visit "negative inducements" on those who stand in his way have helped the company survive attacks from giants such as IBM. The perception of invincibility rather seems to have been the critical factor behind the success of Microsoft's Windows 95 over IBM's 32-bit operating system OS/2. IBM's OS/2 was fully compatible with existing Windows 3.1 programs and available in a robust state nearly two years before Windows 95. IBM management repeatedly affirmed their intent to support OS/2 for the long term and demonstrated their commitment by spending more than $1 billion in marketing and promotion. Nevertheless, the once much-feared IBM (which like Microsoft, had been the target of Justice Department investigations for anticompetitive practices) seemed unable to overcome the perception of being a spent force in personal computer software. Customers and independent software vendors were prepared to wait for Windows 95 rather than commit to an operating system they believed would ultimately lose.

6. Summary and Conclusions

Entrepreneurs have to perform different tasks and play different roles to build long-lived firms than they do when they start businesses. Their predisposition and their capacity to perform these tasks depend on a different set of qualities. The willingness of entrepreneurs to adopt audacious goals for their firms depends on the nature of their ambition and their tolerance for risk. Formulating long-term strategies to coordinate initiatives and investments requires an expansive imagination, a capacity for creative synthesis, and a capacity for abstracting general principles from specific situations. The implementation of strategies requires constancy, the capacity to inspire and intimidate others, and the willingness and ability to learn new managerial skills.

The limited correlation between the qualities involved in starting and building businesses helps explain why so few new ventures become long-lived institutions. Success at the start-up stage depends on an individual's capacity for opportunistic adaptation. As described in Part I, traits and skills such as a tolerance for ambiguity, perceptiveness, tactical ingenuity, and capacity for face-to-face selling help determine which new ventures survive. Only some of those who make the first cut have the ambition to build a large, durable business and the tolerance for the requisite sacrifices and risks. Then, from the ranks of the ambitious, the forces of competition leave standing those very select firms whose principals have (or can develop) the capacity to formulate and implement a sound, long-term strategy. The evolution of the long-lived firm turns on the effort of truly exceptional entrepreneurs.

III

Societal Implications

The next two chapters explore some broad societal implications of this study. Chapter 13 discusses the contribution of new businesses to innovation and long-term economic growth. Chapter 14 examines the conditions that foster the formation and growth of new businesses.

The current interest in the societal contribution of new and transitional businesses has its roots in Schumpeter's challenge to conventional economic theory. Schumpeter argued that new technologies and "combinations" that disrupted the prevailing equilibrium, rather than say, the steady accumulation of capital stock, led to the long-term growth and development of capitalist economies. Economist Robert Solow's 1956 and 1957 papers seemed to bear out Schumpeter's claim. They reported, according to the economist Stiglitz, the "shocking" empirical finding that "most of the growth of the economy over the past century had been due to technological progress."[1] According to Solow, an increase in the use of capital accounted for only 12.5 percent of the doubling of gross output per man-hour from 1909 to 1949; the remaining 87.5 percent was due to "technical change."[2]

Solow's results "have held up remarkably well to more than three decades of extensive and thorough investigation."[3] To some scholars, the Solow "productivity residual" points to the critical role played by entrepreneurs. According to Baumol, any technical change or innovation "will require entrepreneurial initiative in its introduction." By "ignoring the entrepreneur we are prevented from accounting fully for a very substantial portion of our historic growth."[4] Although for reasons discussed in the Introduction, most formal models of growth do not contain an explicit entrepreneurial variable, many scholars of technological change such as Stanford economist Nathan Rosenberg, popular writers such as George Gilder, and policymakers share Baumol's viewpoint.

I hesitate to add to the discourse. I have little expertise in the field of technological innovation and just a faint acquaintance with growth theory and models. I did not undertake my research with the intention of drawing inferences about the "macro" effects of what entrepreneurs do or how public policies influence their efforts. I fear the fallacy of composition. "What is good for the *Inc.* 500 is good for economic growth" is as overdrawn a proposition as the claim made in 1953 by Charles Wilson, the General Motors chairman, that what was good for General Motors was good for America. I therefore offer the ideas in the chapters that follow as provisional speculations.

The reason for saying anything at all is twofold. First, my data did suggest propositions that conflict with widespread beliefs—for instance, about the novelty of activities involved in the typical start-up, and the role that the availability of risk capital plays in the supply of entrepreneurs. Also, I want to demonstrate the contribution that a broad, case-based approach can make. A judicious aggregation of many worm's-eye views, I hope to show, can provide a valuable complementary perspective to traditional econometric and quantitative studies of innovation.

13

Reexamining Schumpeter

This chapter examines three claims made by Schumpeter about the relationship between innovation ("new combinations") and economic growth.
Section 1 discusses Schumpeter's claim about the role of large companies
in undertaking new combinations; section 2, his emphasis on radical or
discontinuous innovation; and section 3, the degree to which new combinations lead to the rapid displacement ("creative destruction") of existing
structures.

The breadth and influence of Schumpeter's ideas make them a convenient
frame for discussing the contribution of new businesses to innovation and,
by extension, to long-term growth. Schumpeter's writing spans a considerable range in content and form. The thousands of pages he wrote over
more than four decades contained sharp, unequivocal claims as well as tan-
gles of contradictions: Elster describes Schumpeter as an "elusive" writer
who could contradict himself in the course of a single paragraph.[1] The
sharp claims have proved long-lived; according to Rosenberg, "his influence has been so great" that "his model has become the accepted one for all
innovative activity."[2] This chapter reexamines some elements of what
Rosenberg calls the "Schumpeterian system." It takes for granted Schumpeter's central thesis—that innovation drives long-term growth—but
raises questions about his characterization of the process.

The discussion will make frequent references to the microcomputer
revolution of the past two decades. This reflects a long-standing personal
interest in the field, its prominence and economic significance, and the
large number of companies I encountered in my research. As mentioned,
I avoided focusing on businesses in particular sectors of the economy (such
as "high technology") because I wanted to identify patterns common to
the broad category of promising businesses. But, as discussed in Chapter
1, the turbulence generated by the microcomputer revolution has lead to
a clustering of start-ups in the field. Although microcomputer-related
products and services account for less than 5 percent of the GDP of the

United States,* they have consistently been responsible for more than a quarter of *Inc.* 500 companies.

1. The Role of Established Companies

Schumpeter placed the individual entrepreneur at the center of the innovative process in his early work but later claimed that the large corporation would inevitably usurp the entrepreneur's role. His 1911 book *The Theory of Economic Development* credited capitalist innovation to entrepreneurs with the "dream and will to found a private kingdom" and the "will to conquer." His 1942 book, *Capitalism, Socialism and Democracy* placed kingdoms ahead of conquerors. In creating the giant enterprise, Schumpeter now declared, entrepreneurs had eliminated their own function. The "perfectly bureaucratized giant industrial unit" could automatically discover and undertake the "objective possibilities" for innovation. It had "come to be the most powerful engine of progress."

The following section discusses the prior research on Schumpeter's hypothesis and my alternative view that start-ups and established companies perform complementary functions.

Prior Research

Most researchers do not directly compare the contributions of new and established firms. Rather, they study whether large firms innovate more than small firms. According to a review by Acs and Audretsch, the economic literature posits several advantages that large companies enjoy. They can support projects with high fixed costs and can diversify their risks by undertaking several initiatives. They can more easily find economic applications for the unexpected outcomes of innovative activity. Their marketing and distribution capabilities provide greater returns to the development of innovative products, and large-volume production amplifies the profit gains from cost-reducing innovations.[3]

On the other side, smaller enterprises can make "impressive contributions to innovation," according to Scherer, because "they are less bureaucratic, without layers of "abominable no-men" who block daring ventures in a more highly structured organization." They can also more easily sustain "a fever pitch of excitement" because "the links between challenges, staff and potential rewards are tight."[4] Arrow reaches a similar conclusion, relying on the information-processing capabilities of small organizations. He suggests that small firms have an advantage in pursuing novel projects

---

* As mentioned in Chapter 1, according to a U.S. Department of Commerce report, a broadly defined "Information Technology" sector, comprising all computing and communications, represented only 4.9 percent of the GDP in 1985 and 6.4 percent in 1993.

because they can efficiently share information among the individuals who are working on the innovation. Large companies cannot accurately evaluate such projects because of the distortion of information transmission within the organization; they do, however, have a superior capacity to communicate with external capital markets and can therefore fund larger-scale innovations.[5]

Empirical studies of the relationship between firm size and innovation have produced ambiguous results. The studies typically rely on two types of indirect measures: R&D expenditure, which represents a proxy for the "input" of innovative activity and patent filings, a proxy for innovative "output." Studies of R&D spending, according to Scherer, "tilt on the side of supporting the Schumpeterian hypothesis that size is conducive to vigorous conduct of R&D," whereas the evidence on patents "leans weakly against the Schumpeterian conjecture that [large companies] are especially fecund sources of patented inventions."[6] The results can have "two rather different interpretations: that the largest firms in an industry generate fewer patentable inventions per dollar of R&D than their smaller counterparts, or that they choose to patent fewer inventions."[7]

Winter has proposed that exogenous conditions (such as the importance of human capital in an industry) create "entrepreneurial regimes" conducive to innovation by small firms, or "routinized regimes" that favor the innovative efforts of large companies.[8] The empirical work of Acs and Audretsch supports the idea of the two regimes and suggests that they are the "product of the market structure environment." They find routinized regimes in industries that are "capital intensive, concentrated, highly unionized, and produce differentiated goods" and entrepreneurial regimes in "highly innovative industries, where the use of skilled labor is relatively important and where large firms comprise a large share of the market."[9]

Complementary Roles

The data and analysis in Parts I and II lead to an alternative perspective on the large vs. small company debate. As discussed below, my research suggests that corporations such as IBM and promising start-ups such as the *Inc.* 500 companies make different contributions to innovation and economic growth. They play complementary rather than overlapping roles.

Established companies. As we have seen, companies such as IBM enjoy several advantages in undertaking large initiatives. The most obvious one derives from their capacity to mobilize significant capital from investors. This intermediation function is of special importance in an era when rising incomes and retirement and pension plans have made the middle class an important source of investment funds.

Besides capital, large initiatives usually also require significant irreversible commitments by many customers, employees, and other resource providers. An established corporation's base of tangible and intangible assets provides advantages in securing such commitments. Cash flows from existing businesses and access to capital markets allow the established corporation to offer credible contractual safeguards to the resource providers. Prior reputations help engender the confidence that the corporation will not behave opportunistically in matters that cannot be contracted for and honor promises that are necessarily vague—for example, not to "punish" employees for failed initiatives, or to provide the "good" after-sales service.

Established corporations also have an advantage in solving the coordination problems involved in launching large initiatives. Major projects, which seek to exploit economies of scale and scope, involve securing the joint efforts of many personnel and solving conflicts among the providers of specialized resources. Established companies with well-developed coordination mechanisms have obvious advantages in doing so.

The microcomputer revolution illustrates the important contribution of established corporations. According to Steffens, the entry of large established companies from the computer, office products and consumer electronics industries (such as, IBM, Xerox, DEC, NEC, and Sanyo) from late 1981 to the end of 1982 "legitimized" personal computers. IBM utilized its "enormous market power and committed significant resources."[10] The company established "a highly automated, high-volume assembly plant which provided significant economies of scale." It encouraged third-party software houses to develop higher-performance applications. It "made use of bulk discounting to switch the purchasing channel from individual users to corporate buyers." IBM, which then accounted for 61 percent of the worldwide general-purpose mainframe computer market, "effectively legitimized the personal computer in the minds of data processing managers in large organizations." It broke down a "major psychological marketing barrier, namely the attitude that had existed within many DP [data processing] departments that personal computers were an unfortunate nuisance and certainly not part of the corporate management information system." IBM's penetration of the corporate market was so successful that the company could not satisfy demand for approximately eighteen months. This created an opportunity for many start-ups to develop IBM-compatible machines or "clones."[11] IBM's entry also led to "increasing professionalism in the industry" and forced competitors to invest in marketing activities, especially in advertising, distribution and service support."[12]

Substantial investments by Intel, and after the late 1980s by Microsoft, have sustained ongoing improvements in performance and reductions in costs. Intel spent more than $4 billion to develop the Pentium family of microprocessors. Development costs for the Merced (P7) chip are expected to exceed $8 billion.[13] According to cofounder Gordon Moore, the company has routinely invested 10 to 15 percent of revenues on R&D: "A plot of Intel's financial performance," writes Moore, "would show revenues dipping here and there, earnings fluctuating wildly, and R&D expenses following a smooth exponential growth curve."[14] Intel has also invested heavily in making and marketing its microprocessors. One new semiconductor fabrication facility costs well in excess of $1 billion to build, and in 1997 the company spent $3.5 billion in the Sales, General, and Administration (SG&A) category. Microsoft has spent similar amounts in recent years in developing and marketing software. In 1997 the company spent $2.5 billion on R&D (slightly under 20 percent of the $13 billion it booked in revenues) and $3.5 billion in SG&A. According to one analyst, manufacturers of PCs have essentially relied on Intel's and Microsoft's efforts, spending just 2 to 3 percent of their annual revenues on R&D.[15]

New businesses. We can think of the distinctive, complementary role of new businesses in the following way: They mitigate the constraints that result from the rules that large corporations must observe. As we saw in Part I, the institution of extensive checks and balances (or "internal control systems") allows large corporations to separate the bearing of the risks of innovative activities from the identification, evaluation, and implementation of such activities. These systems provide access to capital markets but limit the firm's capacity to pursue small, uncertain initiatives. By filling this opportunity space, bootstrapped entrepreneurs help incubate technologies whose promise is initially unknown. Many new "disruptive" technologies, according to Christensen, cannot initially compete in mainstream markets and can only be sustained in out-of-the-way niches. In 1975, for instance, the personal computer was a poor substitute for mini- and mainframe computers and was of interest mainly to hobbyists. Corporate decision-makers (or any other objective analysts, for that matter) cannot predict which offbeat products and technologies will enter the mainstream; individual entrepreneurs who have the capacity and the incentive to pursue uncertain, niche projects help select and develop the "fittest" ones. Between 1975 and 1980, for instance, tinkerers and enthusiasts conducting low-cost, and not particularly scientific, experiments with personal computers refined the technology and developed commercial applications that broadened its appeal. The cumulative efforts of a diffused band of individual entrepreneurs reduced the uncertainty about the size of the potential market and paved the way for IBM to enter the business. A similar pattern, we may note, later emerged with Internet technologies.

The willingness to pursue niche opportunities helps propagate innovations after they have become recognized. New businesses provide complementary goods and services whose revenue potential is too small to interest established companies. In the 1980s, for instance, start-ups provided services such as installation and maintenance and products such "add-on" hardware and software and educational books and videos that both took advantage of and helped advance IBM's efforts to make the PC a mainstream product. Startups also help attack the disequilibria that follow the introduction of new technologies, as manifested by the 90 percent gross margins on the retailing of printer cables. Established companies usually do not pursue these small, transient profit opportunities.

Opportunistic entrepreneurs relieve the inflexibility that arises because established companies tend to adhere to long-term strategies. In Part II we saw that companies build valuable know-how and reputations by steadfast adherence to rules about the markets they will serve and the services they will provide. These rules can preclude established companies from securing optimal contracts and lead to a misallocation of resources. For example, IBM offered standard levels of service and support for its PCs; for some sophisticated customers the standard was too much, and for some technical novices it was too little. Similarly, when PCs were in short supply, IBM's policy of treating dealers "equitably" led to a geographic distribution of machines that did not reflect differences in demand. IBM would not ship more product to regions where customers placed a high value on PCs and were prepared to pay a premium to obtain them. New businesses that took advantage of such misallocations helped mitigate their consequences. Some sold PCs at a low cost to customers who did not need much hand-holding and service; others (the "value-added-resellers") charged premium prices to customers who did. Upstart businesses also operated "gray" markets, buying surplus machines from authorized IBM dealers and selling them in territories where PCs were in short supply. Thus IBM could maintain its reputation for treating authorized dealers equitably while entrepreneurs helped place its computers in their highest-valued use.

Entrepreneurs similarly help mitigate the costs of standardized employment policies that large corporations adopt. Corporations try to recruit individuals who will fit their culture and norms in order to promote cooperation and teamwork. Such policies, however, limit their ability to employ the best individual for a given task, especially in the early stages of a technology, when many capable individuals lack the backgrounds and temperaments that suit the organizational climate of a large corporation. Corporations can reduce this problem by contracting out tasks to start-ups that can "make do" with difficult staff and where there isn't much teamwork or organizational climate for quirky individualists to disrupt. IBM can secure the use of nonconformist programmers without compromising its culture by turning to start-ups who can best utilize their talents.

Start-ups also can help established corporations, whose employment policies are optimized for long-term relationships, fill their transient needs for labor.[16] Companies such as IBM have historically adopted policies such as a commitment to promote from within and to provide job and income security in order to encourage employees to internalize organizational objectives and acquire "firm-specific" skills that have limited value to other employers. The effectiveness of such policies depends on the constancy of their application. Unlike the firm promises in written contracts, these policies often have an ambiguous "best efforts" quality—for instance, corporations "favor" internal promotions but do not rule out hiring outsiders; unless the circumstances are clear-cut, deviations impair credibility. Moreover, to promote solidarity and teamwork, the policies have to be uniformly applied: Corporations cannot easily offer job security just to employees from whom they wish to elicit high "specific" investment in human capital.

The difficulty of discriminating among employees poses an acute problem in the development of new technologies and markets. In the early stages of a product or an industry, firms have needs for labor that disappear later. For instance, marketing personal computers initially required considerable hand-holding and missionary selling; as consumers gained experience and comfort with the product, their need for such service declined. Established companies that employ staff for these transient services whom they later dismiss, risk tarnishing their reputations as good employers. They can instead rely on start-ups, whose staff do not expect much job security and who often lack many employment alternatives, to satisfy these needs.

Subcontracting to get around the rigidities of employment policies can entail some costs. "Outsiders" who invest in firm-specific assets may require higher current compensation in lieu of the employment security and promotion opportunities that employees receive. These outsiders may also not internalize their customers' goals to the same degree as loyal employees. Contrary to received theory, however, there seems little evidence that subcontractors are less responsive or more difficult to control. Several theorists, going back to Simon, assert that employees submit to hierarchical authority more readily than do subcontractors. This control hypothesis seems inconsistent with everyday experience. To take an extreme example, Detroit autoworkers have been known to attack foremen with tire irons. "Outside" management consultants and investment bankers, I can report from firsthand knowledge, will usually work longer hours to satisfy client executives than in-house staff. College professors who formulate models of employment relationships exercise greater control over graduate students than over the support staff employed by the university. My interviews with *Inc.* founders suggest that they feel the same pressure to serve their large-company customers as many graduate students do their advisers; they are more willing to submit to capricious demands than "nine-to-five" employees, not less.

The complementary nature of the roles of new and established businesses does change when ambitious entrepreneurs try to build long-lived businesses. As Microsoft stops serving IBM and begins competing with it, the roles of the two companies begin to overlap, and some of the debate inspired by Schumpeter's hypothesis about innovation in large companies becomes germane. The "transitional" Microsoft has greater access to resources than it does at the start-up stage but not to the same degree as an established IBM. Conversely, Microsoft's emerging decision-making routines and strategies give Bill Gates more room to act boldly than IBM's CEO enjoys. An analysis of these trade-offs, however, is beyond the scope of this book.

2. Discontinuous Innovation

According to Schumpeter, the economically significant innovations that disturbed the "circular flow" were "large" and "spontaneous" rather than "small" and "adaptive." They so displaced the "equilibrium point" that "the new one [could] not be reached from the old one by infinitesimal steps. Add successively as many mail coaches as you please, you will never get a railway thereby."[17]

Schumpeter also distinguished such innovations ("carrying out of new combinations of the means of production") from their antecedent inventions. "The making of the invention and the carrying out of the corresponding innovation," he wrote, "are, economically and sociologically, two entirely different things."[18] Inventions are "economically irrelevant" as long as they are not carried out into practice.[19] He also contrasted innovation from its subsequent diffusion through imitation and adaptation. Undertaking a new combination represents an unusual event and takes charismatic economic leadership. But "as soon as the various kinds of social resistance to something that is fundamentally new and untried have been overcome, it is much easier not only to do the same thing again but also to do similar things in different directions, so that a first success will always produce a cluster."[20]

Some scholars, notably Nathan Rosenberg, have questioned these claims about the importance and distinctiveness of radical innovation; the following section summarizes and then extends these critiques.

Rosenberg's Critique

In his 1976 book *Perspectives on Technology*, Rosenberg suggests that Schumpeter's sharp distinctions have created "artificial conceptual disjunctions between innovative activity and other activities with which it is not only linked, but which in fact constitute major parts of the historical process of innovation itself." This leads us to "focus disproportionately upon discontinuities and neglect continuities in the innovative process" and to overlook its crucial later stages.[21]

The inventive activity that precedes a new combination in Schumpeter's model, observes Rosenberg, is "carried on offstage and out of sight. Inventions come onto the Schumpeterian stage already fully grown"[22] and ready for commercial exploitation. In fact, we cannot easily distinguish between invention and innovation: "Whereas for some inventions no serious technical obstacles to their implementation may exist once the basic idea has been established, for other inventions such obstacles are formidable and can be overcome only after much further time-consuming search and experimentation."[23]

Rosenberg questions the association of inventions with the "initial basic conceptualization of a product or process," under the assumption that "as soon as the basic conceptual or intellectual breakthroughs have been made, all the 'real' problems are solved." Writes Rosenberg: "To date the invention of the fluorescent lamp in 1859, the gyro-compass in 1852, the cotton picker in 1889, the zipper in 1891, radar in 1922, the jet engine in 1929, or xerography in 1937 is to select years in which significant steps were indeed made. But in none of these years was the product concerned even remotely near a state of technical feasibility."[24] Solving the problems that remain after the initial conceptualization takes "protracted inventive activity." Techniques for producing a new material (such as polyethylene) under laboratory conditions may be known, but it may take years to develop ways to produce it commercially. Or an invention may be technically feasible, but its economic superiority over existing techniques may require many improvements in its "performance characteristics, often in inconspicuous and unspectacular ways." Early diesel engines for instance were too heavy for economic operation, and early jet engines had unacceptably low performance characteristics until the development of materials that could withstand high pressures and temperatures.[25] In such cases, innovators cannot, per the Schumpeter model, merely select inventions that are "already suitable for commercial introduction" and carry out the introduction of a new production function with them.[26]

Rosenberg similarly questions the distinct and secondary role Schumpeter accords to the propagation of new combinations. Schumpeter posits a "sharp disjunction" between "the high level of leadership and creativity involved in the first introduction of a new technique as compared to the mere imitative activity of subsequent adopters." In fact, Rosenberg argues, the diffusion of an innovation requires much more than simple imitation. A "stream of improvements in performance characteristics," "progressive modification and adaptation" to suit the requirements of submarkets, and the introduction of complementary inputs "decisively affect the economic usefulness of an original innovation."[27] These ongoing activities are

> ... central to the pace of the diffusion process. It is economically absurd to consider the innovation of the automobile as having been accomplished when there were a few buffs riding around the countryside terrifying horses. Innovation is, economically speaking, not a single well-defined act, but a series of acts closely linked to the innovation process. An innovation acquires economic significance only through an extensive process of redesign, modification, and a thousand small improvements which suit it

for a mass market, for production by drastically new mass production techniques, and by the eventual availability of a whole range of complementary activities, ranging, in the case of the automobile, from a network of service stations to an extensive system of paved roads. These later provisions, even if they involve little scientific novelty, or genuinely new forms of knowledge, constitute uses and applications of knowledge from which flow the productivity improvements of innovative activity.[28]

Although Rosenberg defers to Schumpeter's analysis for "major innovations" involving "significant shifts to an entirely new production function," he does not provide examples of such one-shot breakthroughs. I wonder whether many exist. As we saw in Chapter 7, even ventures such as Federal Express that start with a revolutionary concept seem to require refinement over several years before their product or service attains commercial viability. More commonly, noteworthy developments of new products or processes result from a large number of steps undertaken by many individuals and companies over several decades.

Extensions to the Critique

The evolution of microcomputers after 1975 conforms closely to the model of continuous innovation discussed in Rosenberg's 1976 book. My current laptop (a sadly out-of-date 1996 model), which provides more processing power and functionality than did the computer center of my undergraduate engineering college, seems to have little in common with its pioneering forebear, the Altair. Altair aficionados derived less practical use from their machines than did the turn-of-the-century automobile buffs. Lacking basic input or output devices (such as keyboards and printers), Altairs could not even scare horses. Numerous innovations turned this oddity into a ubiquitous artifact. Some of these innovations—the mouse, graphical user interfaces, and electronic spreadsheets—represented conceptual breakthroughs. Others (such as word-processing software) were borrowed from mainframes and minicomputers. Continuous improvements and refinements in performance and features have been a hallmark of the industry—Excel 7.0 has come a long way from the first spreadsheet, Visicalc. Complementary innovations have played a crucial role in such improvements: Excel 7.0 could not have been implemented on earlier generations of hardware. The introduction of new microprocessors, storage devices, application and operating system software, communications technologies (such as local area networks and the Internet), innovations in manufacturing and distribution (such as the "build to order" process), and the opening of new market segments (such as home computing) have reinforced each other and sustained a virtuous cycle of ever-improving price performance.

The case studies discussed in Parts I and II suggest that ongoing rather than one-shot innovation extends beyond high technology into fields such as publishing and retailing. Jann Wenner, who started *Rolling Stone*, we saw, built on the experiences of several predecessor rock and roll magazines. Sam Walton opened his first Wal-Mart (in Rogers, Arkansas) after making dozens of trips to study discount retailers that were emerging in other parts of the country, including Ann and Hope (considered the creator of the concept) in Rhode Island and Fed-Mart in California. And, as we have seen, Walton never stopped innovating, continuing to borrow and integrate new ideas into Wal-Mart practically until the day he died.

This research also suggests extensions to Rosenberg's ideas. First, the uncertainty-investment trade-off discussed in Part I provides another reason for a gradual rather than one-shot development of new combinations. Pioneering individuals who have the psychological willingness to confront the early uncertainties and do not have to answer to outside investors or bosses cannot muster the resources for a great leap forward. Corporations who have the resources to make large commitments tend to wait until the pioneers have resolved some of the uncertainties because of their due-diligence requirements.

A second extension relates to the coordination of sequential adaptations. We should expect a more opportunistic pattern in the early stages, when individual entrepreneurs add to each other's innovations in the manner of guests at a party who create a story by adding sentences to the collective narrative. This leads to a stochastic evolution of technologies, as seems to have occurred in the early years of the microcomputer industry. After some basic technological trajectories have been established, the entry or emergence of firms with the will and the resources to pursue a long-term strategy leads to a more directed or purposive sequence of innovations. The strategic players search for and select innovations that conform, not just to an innate, predetermined technological path but also to their goal of market dominance. For instance, Intel continued to develop CISC-based microprocessors to leverage its installed base when RISC-based microprocessors may have represented a superior technological choice. Strategic players also influence the initiatives of more opportunistic participants. For example, from about the early 1980s, Intel's strategies in microprocessors and Microsoft's strategies in operating systems helped determine the product choices of numerous ventures that provided complementary goods and services.

If large, well-established firms totally dominate a market (as now seems the case in the automobile, commercial aircraft, and photo-film industries) and shut out opportunistic start-ups, we would expect their strategies to more or less dictate the evolution of new products and processes and limit chance variations from a purposively determined trajectory. We may further expect that the innovative efforts of already dominant players will reflect the expected effects on their existing base of business. They will, for instance, be more concerned with the "backward compatibility" of their new products and (as I will discuss in the following section, "Creative Destruction") will attempt to avoid cannibalizing their existing revenues. Innovation will therefore follow a more predictable path.

Third, we can extend Rosenberg's propositions to the evolution of large firms. Companies such as IBM represent a "new combination" or innovative production function that transforms capital, labor, and other inputs into products and services in a unique way. And like most innovative products and processes, such companies evolve gradually. As we saw in Part II, the "radical" transformation of a fledgling C-T-R into the mature IBM takes place over many decades and involves bold moves as well as many incremental modifications and adaptive changes. Here, too, we find that complementary innovations play an important role: The effectiveness of an initiative undertaken by, say, the manufacturing function often turns on parallel changes undertaken by the others. Apparently many significant economic developments require multifaceted, multiperiod change.

3. Creative Destruction

According to Schumpeter, "a perennial gale of creative destruction" is an "essential fact about capitalism. It is what capitalism consists in and what every capitalist concern has got to live with."[29] Destruction is the price of innovation: The automobile must displace the buggy makers, and mass merchandisers must put the country store out of business. The innovator combines the roles of Shiva the Destroyer and of Brahma the Creator, of the mobs of the French Revolution who overthrew the *ancien régime* and of Napoleon, who founded an empire on its remains.

Although Schumpeter's vivid metaphor has become commonplace, the underlying proposition has not received much scrutiny. According to Jensen's 1993 article "The Modern Industrial Revolution," research on issues of exit and retrenchment have been sparse since the publication of Schumpeter's creative destruction idea in *Capitalism, Socialism and Democracy*.[30] The indirect evidence, I argue below, suggests that new combinations usually displace existing structures gradually rather than through a sudden, cataclysmic gale. And a variety of other factors overshadow the importance of new combinations in engendering business terminations and job losses.

Pace of Displacement

The gradual evolution of new technologies discussed in Section 2 limits the rate at which they displace existing products and processes. The automobile did not displace the stagecoach and the horse buggy overnight. Karl Benz and Gottlieb Daimler built a gasoline-powered vehicle in Germany in 1885. Armand Peugeot built a workable automobile in France soon thereafter. Automobile manufacture began in the United States in 1893, when the Duryea brothers of Springfield, Massachusetts, built a carriage powered by a one-cylinder motor. Six years later, in 1899, many individuals and about 30 American companies had built a grand total of some 2,500 vehicles.[31] Ten years later, reports the U.S. Bureau of the Census, total car registrations reached 32,900 vehicles, with 11,200 passenger vehicles sold in 1903.[32] The "unification" phase of the automobile industry in the United States, which, according to historians McCraw and Tedlow led to the development of a mass market, did not begin until the introduction of Ford's Model T. This was in 1908, fifteen years after the Duryea brothers and twenty-three years after the Daimler-Benz vehicles.

Moreover, unlike urban redevelopment projects that must first level decrepit structures, most innovations start out on virgin ground. Cost and unreliability often preclude new technologies from serving existing mainstream needs. The early automobiles were too unreliable a substitute for stagecoaches to deliver mail and too expensive to satisfy mainstream transportation needs; like the early PCs, they appealed instead to the enthusiasms of a few individuals for trendy products.* Customers' switching costs and prior investments make them unwilling to adopt new technologies for current needs. For instance, after the 1980s, personal computers became cheap and reliable enough to migrate from the fringe hobbyists market into commercial use. But even as PCs sprouted in offices everywhere, they did not displace many traditional mainframe applications because of the great cost that turning over the installed base entailed, not to mention the reluctance of many MIS personnel to obsolete their personal human capital. Spreadsheets, the "killer application" that created a commercial market for personal computers, allowed users, many of whom had not previously used computers extensively, to perform analyses and simulations which they would not have otherwise performed.

The "growth imperative" faced by large, well-established companies often helps channel innovations toward serving new needs and markets rather than attacking existing ones. The desire to expand revenues, profits, personnel, market power, and so on represents the main impetus in large corporations for undertaking new investments and initiatives; they generally back technologies that cannibalize existing businesses with reluctance when it becomes clear that if they don't, competitors will. Robert Cringely, who has written a popular history of the industry, suggests that IBM executives backed its PC initiative in 1980 because they thought personal computers would not reduce the demand for IBM's other products. "Every sales dollar brought in to buy a microcomputer," writes Cringely, "would be a dollar that would not otherwise have come to IBM."[33] The substantial

---

* Schumpeter himself noted that innovations create the needs they satisfy rather than fill preexisting needs. In *Business Cycles* ([1939], p. 73) he cited the example of automobiles.

assets and resources of large corporations and their dominance of some markets suggest that these corporations' bias against displacement* likely has a significant effect on the evolution of technologies.

The role of PCs in expanding the pie rather than destroying existing technologies apparently represents a common feature of the "digital revolution." New communications services—e-mail, newsgroups, and "chat"— have provided a critical mass of users for the Internet and on-line services such as AOL. These services do not seem to have significantly eroded the demand for traditional phone and mail communication. Nor is it obvious what products or services are threatened by the dissemination of information on web sites and Intranets or the upsurge in web-surfing. To be sure, some new technologies have attacked existing products from the outset. Sun and other microcomputer-based engineering workstation manufacturers targeted their products against minicomputers. New on-line services such as Travelocity, Amazon, and E-trade compete against traditional travel agencies, bookstores, and stockbrokers. It seems implausible to me, however, that the growing importance of information technology in the economy derives, to any significant degree, from displacement effects. According to a 1998 U.S Department of Commerce report, the share of the information technology (IT) sector (computing and communications) grew from 4.2 percent of the Gross Domestic Product of the United States in 1977 to 6.1 percent in 1990 to 8.2 percent in 1998.[34] This is probably not because computers have displaced traditional goods and services. Rather, IT has accounted for a disproportionate share of growth: According to the Department of Commerce, IT industries have been responsible for more than one-quarter of real economic growth[35] that is, about three times their share of the economy.

Of course, new combinations can undermine older businesses without competing for their customers, by drawing away capital, labor, and other inputs. Fast-growing companies offer investors and talented individuals opportunities for capital gains and excitement that firms in slower-growing fields cannot. The stock market provides a striking indicator of the appeal of IT companies. The Department of Commerce report on IT notes that the collective market capitalization of five large companies—Microsoft, Intel, Compaq, Dell, and Cisco—grew to more than $588 billion in 1997 from less than $12 billion in 1987.** IT industries also offered workers higher

---

* The "planned obsolescence" we have seen in durable goods is consistent with this principle. Detroit's annual model introductions and new versions of software represent attempts to stimulate new purchases of long-lived or indestructible goods.

** As of this writing the stock market has placed nearly twice as great a valuation on the stock of the virtual bookseller Amazon.com than on the stock of Barnes and Noble, the leading chain of conventional bookstores. Barnes and Noble, which has recorded "solid" profits for the last three years, has nineteen times the revenues as Amazon.com, which has never booked a profit (Mayer, 1998).

compensation. The Department of Commerce estimates that the 7.4 million people employed in the sector earned about $46,000 a year, compared to an average of $28,000 in the private sector.[36] Such differentials do sap the vitality of slow-growing companies and industries, but the process is insidious and gradual.

Similarly, in the long run, technologies that initially serve "new" needs can take over traditional markets. Automobiles and trucks did replace buggies and stagecoaches, and packet-switched Internet telephony may someday make the existing circuit-based telecommunications obsolete.* But the displacement often takes place at a much slower rate than the hype about the obsolescence suggests. In 1938 the *New York Times* observed that the typewriter was "driving out writing with one's own hand," yet Petroski reports the sale of 14 billion pencils in 1990.[37] The introduction of word processors in the 1970s in turn led to predictions of the imminent demise of typewriters. As I discovered in the course of a consulting study for a typewriter manufacturer, in spite of a fourteenfold growth in the shipment of word processing units between 1977 and 1981, the demand for typewriters in the United States had remained steady, at about 1 million units per year.

Newer computer architectures have taken away share from mainframes, but more than thirty years after the introduction of minicomputers and more than twenty years after the introduction of microcomputers, the mainframe remains an important category. Total worldwide revenues of large-scale computer processors (or mainframes) amounted to $16 billion in 1997, compared to $16.2 billion in 1982 (see Fig. 13.1). Their share of the

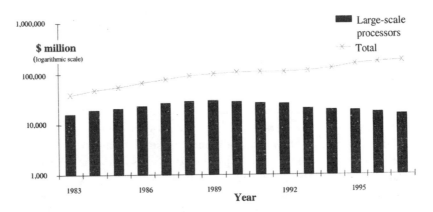

Figure 13.1. Computer Processor Revenues
Note: Includes embedded peripherals only; excludes all external peripherals and software.
Source: McKinsey database; McKinsey analysis.

---

* We should note however that the rapid growth of cellular phones has not had this effect.

total computer market dropped considerably in that period, from about 42 percent in 1982 to about 9 percent in 1997 as total demand grew from $38 billion to $183 billion. Although its share of total revenues has declined considerably, IBM's mainframe business continues to be large and profitable. In 1997, mainframes and their associated storage devices generated $5.7 billion for the company. Networks of smaller processors may eventually make mainframes extinct, but their destruction will not be the consequence of a cataclysmic "gale of creative destruction."

Salience

The magnitude of the "destruction" wrought by new combinations is sometimes as exaggerated as the rate. As we will see next, only some businesses (such as stagecoach building and typewriter manufacturing) succumb to new combinations. Other factors such as incompetence, overconfidence, and the growth imperative likely play more significant roles in the failure and contraction of businesses.

Small businesses apparently turn over at a rapid rate—a roughly similar number (about 750,000) of businesses are started and terminated in the United States every year. Most of these entries and exits have little to do with creative destruction. As we saw in Part I, most new businesses are started in fields such as lawn care, beauty salons, and construction, all of which require little technology, specialized skill, or capital. For example, Kirchoff and Phillips estimate that there are five times as many "low-innovation" start-ups as "high-innovation" start-ups.[38] The termination of such low-innovation businesses cannot be attributed to their displacement by a new combination. Indeed, except to their proprietors, exits have little significance. For instance, according to Dun & Bradstreet's estimates, nearly 90 percent of terminations do not involve losses to creditors; apparently suppliers and banks do not regard these businesses as creditworthy.

Some high-growth companies, particularly in high-technology industries, do get leapfrogged by competition from the next generation of innovation. As mentioned, Henderson has studied this phenomenon in the photolithography equipment business and Christensen in disk drives. The high-flying manufacturers of dedicated word processors of the 1970s such as Wang, CPT, and NBI, lost out in the 1980s to PC-based software that could provide the same functionality at a much lower cost. But a superseding innovation represents only one of the factors that can lead to the termination of promising businesses. Many promising start-ups, as we saw in Part I, exploit opportunities that are inherently transitory. Unless their proprietors can find a more sustainable follow-on source of profit, they have to wind up the enterprise. As discussed in Part II, the inability to manage growth also can jeopardize a business. The entrepreneur may run out of cash because of inadequate financial controls, dissipate effort by failing to formulate a coherent strategy, or engender organizational turmoil through ill-defined reporting relationships.

New combinations represent even less of a threat to the survival of mature, well-established corporations. As discussed in Part II, the diversified assets of companies such as IBM protect them from adverse innovations, such as the displacement of punch-card-based data processing by mainframe computers. Innovations usually cause mortal harm only in conjunction with protracted obstinacy and denial. I can think of few examples from the past two decades where a large corporation has failed to survive because of an innovation from which it could not defend itself. Moreover, the destructive force of new combinations represents but one, arguably minor, cause of the demise of large corporations. Many fail because of "internal" management lapses. My former employer E. F. Hutton was forced to merge into its competitor Shearson Lehman because poor internal controls led first to a check-kiting scandal and then, in the stock market crash of 1987, de facto insolvency. International Harvester is no longer with us because in 1980, management took a strike to get out of a contract with the United Automobile Workers. According to Flint, the strike "lasted six months and wrecked the company."[39] And companies can fail because of the financial policies they adopt. "The high leverage incurred in the eighties," Jensen writes, "contributed to an increase in the bankruptcy rate of large firms in the early 1990s."[40]

Creative destruction also seems to have played a modest role in the recent "downsizing" of large corporations. According to Jensen, the "Third Industrial Revolution" that started after 1973 generated significant "excess capacity and thus the requirement for exit."[41] As one manifestation of this phenomenon, Jensen notes that *Fortune* 100 firms eliminated 1.5 million jobs, or 14 percent of their workforce, in the decade from 1979 to 1989.[42] Technological changes helped generate some of the excess capacity eliminated. For example, radial tires lasting three to five times longer than the older bias ply tires created excess capacity in the tire industry. Improvements in the design of objects such as bridges and cars reduced the intensity of consumption of metals. Minimills increased the productivity of steelmaking.

Technology represents but one of the factors behind the sharp reductions in capacity in mature industries such as oil, chemicals, steel, aluminum, and automobiles. We find little evidence in these sectors of cataclysmic or unforeseeable changes. Radial tires displaced the older technology gradually. The consumption of metals and energy grew more slowly but did not actually decline because economic growth outweighed the increased efficiency in their use. And we cannot easily relate technological innovation to the widespread cutbacks in what Jensen calls "white-collar corporate bureaucracies."[43] Some large companies, report Bartlett and Ghoshal,[44] nearly halved the number of layers of their middle management.*

The pressure to grow faced by the managers of large companies in the United States and overseas was at least as important a factor as technological changes in generating excess capacity. These pressures led to investments in new capacity in the face of slow or declining demand. They also fostered the growth of managerial positions: Between 1970 and 1980, report Caves and Kreps, executive, administrative, and managerial occupations in the median industry grew 20.6 percent faster than real output.[45] The profitability of their core franchises helped mask the excess physical and managerial capacity carried by large corporations. Jensen's analysis suggests that many factors forced companies to reduce this capacity after 1973. These factors included the oil shock, which lead to a tenfold increase in prices between 1973 and 1979; changes in tax policies; deregulation of transportation, telecommunications, and financial services in the United States; the globalization of world trade; and the movement of formerly Communist and socialist economies to more market-oriented capitalist economies. Technology, of course, contributed, but per the previous discussion, many of its dramatic advances had as much to do with creating new markets as with generating excess capacity in existing ones.

4. Summary and Conclusions

The case Schumpeter made for the importance of new combinations has stood the test of time. His contributions seem exceptionally valuable when set against the great body of microeconomics that assumes known, stable production functions. Schumpeter's speculations about the process and mechanism of innovation conflicts, however, with the observed evidence in important ways: Routinized innovation by large corporations represents an important but not dominant mode for undertaking new combinations. Major innovations usually evolve through many steps rather than through a single discontinuity, and they do not rapidly blow away existing structures—new combinations typically satisfy new needs and only gradually displace existing products and processes.

Rosenberg suggests that the Schumpeterian framework does not adequately incorporate the technical difficulties and the learning by doing that major innovations entail. Schumpeter's failure to address issues of capital availability and organizational structures may also have contributed to the

---

* We do not have good aggregate estimates of the white-collar positions eliminated in the "downsizings" and "restructurings" of large corporations; announcements by companies such as AT&T, IBM, and Exxon in the 1980s suggest they were significant. Nohria (1996, p. 24) reports that about 75 percent of the layoffs by *Fortune* 100 firms between 1978 and 1992 involved white-collar employees.

limitations of his assertions. Schumpeter argued that the providers of capital, rather than entrepreneurs, bore the financial risks of undertaking new combinations. Schumpeter did not, however, adequately analyze the conditions under which the providers of capital would do so.

These conditions have important implications. Established companies such as IBM enjoy access to capital on a large scale because they have an objective process for evaluating initiatives, and this process tends to screen out great leaps into the unknown. Individual entrepreneurs can undertake uncertain initiatives because they aren't bound by rigorous vetting procedures, but they cannot raise the capital to do so on a large scale. This trade-off between the uncertainty and investment requirements of new initiatives suggests that individual entrepreneurs and large companies play complementary roles and helps explain why new combinations evolve in a gradual rather than a discontinuous way.

Financial and organizational constraints also help direct innovative effort away from displacing existing products and processes. Individual entrepreneurs lack the resources to directly attack the existing order. And large companies that do have the resources are reluctant to pursue innovations that would reduce their current revenues and profits.

14

Facilitating Conditions

This chapter analyzes the conditions that influence the formation and growth of promising businesses. The first four sections examine the following factors that influence the level new business formation: social attitudes, technology, the prevailing corporate ethos, and tax and regulatory policies. Section 5 deals with the determinants of the growth of promising businesses. Section 6 discusses the implications for public policy.

The proposition we just reviewed, that start-ups and established corporations complement each other's roles, does not imply a fixed relationship between new business and corporate activity. Indeed, we find noteworthy shifts in their relative proportions. From the turn of the century until about the early 1970s, large corporations in the United States steadily increased their share of output and employment. The trend was subsequently arrested and possibly reversed. David Birch's 1979 report, *The Job Generation Process*, which claimed that small firms created 82 percent of new jobs, sparked controversy regarding his definitions and methodology. But whatever the precise numbers, the tens of millions of new jobs created in the United States in the past two decades, in the face of shrinking of the workforces of *Fortune* 500 companies, clearly point to an increasing proportion of employment in the "entrepreneurial" sector. The data also seem persuasive in attributing much of the net growth in employment to the formation and growth of promising start-ups (or what Birch calls "gazelles") rather than to the more numerous marginal businesses.

Although new businesses and entrepreneurs are in vogue, the factors behind their renaissance do not seem to be well researched. David McClelland's 1961 book *The Achieving Society* may well represent the last major effort to systematically investigate the factors that promote self-employment; furthermore, McClelland did not distinguish between marginal and high-growth businesses. Today, policymakers and analysts often rely on the vivid but special case of VC-backed start-ups. Consider, for instance,

Acs and Audretsch's (1990) explanation for why the small-business share of manufacturing employment has grown substantially in the United States when we find decline or stagnation in the main European economies. According to Acs and Audretsch, "the main sources of these differences in the employment growth can be traced to misguided government policies in Europe supporting large firms, as well as a much larger venture capital market in the United States, and from the willingness of scientists and experienced managers to leave secure jobs and share the entrepreneurial risks in new enterprises."[1]

In fact, promising start-ups do not usually require venture capital or risk-taking by seasoned scientists and managers. As we have seen, most promising start-ups do not require much capital. Their founders have some, but usually not deep, experience in their chosen line of business, and they do not leave high-paid employment to start their ventures. This chapter explores the "exogenous" or "environmental" factors that affect the formation and subsequent expansion of such bootstrapped ventures that could help explain their recent resurgence.*

1. Social Attitudes

A few "born" entrepreneurs feel compelled to start businesses under any conditions. The following section discusses how social attitudes affect— and are affected by—the efforts of the more typical individuals—that is, those who can choose between starting promising businesses and pursuing other careers.

Status and Recognition

The degree to which society rewards and recognizes entrepreneurs can influence in several ways the willingness of individuals to start promising businesses in several ways. In societies that hold entrepreneurs in low esteem, new businesses are started mainly by deviants and "outsiders." Conversely, societies that accord entrepreneurs high status attract mainstream individuals to such careers by the provision of prestige and by influencing the nature of the psychic rewards they seek. As is well known, peer groups affect the preferences of many individuals. We often value certain activities and goals when we see others valuing them.

The attitudes of peer groups may also affect their members' willingness to confront the uncertainties of starting promising businesses. As mentioned in Chapter 4, experimental research suggests that social factors influ-

---

* The discussion of the determinants of the share of new initiatives undertaken by individual entrepreneurs does not address the more significant issue of what determines the aggregate level of entrepreneurial activity; it also has nothing to say about "marginal" businesses, which likely have very significant socioeconomic consequences.

ence ambiguity aversion. The fear of the unknown likely represents less of an impediment to starting a business if "others like us" (rather than of a few unusual deviants) seem willing to take the plunge.

Public and media interest in start-ups can indirectly increase potential entrepreneurs' estimates of the probability of significant success. Media coverage of noteworthy successes considerably exceeds their representativeness in the universe of start-ups. This celebration of big winners stands in contrast to the normal focus of the media on regrettable occurrences such as massacres, political scandals, natural disasters, and the mistakes of large company executives. This reflects the asymmetric magnitude of gains and losses involved in starting new businesses: The failure of a promising start-up (as opposed to the stumbles of an IBM, or the folding of a glamorous VC-backed company such as GO) is not sufficiently consequential to be newsworthy. Even when covered, the stories lack pizzazz. The resulting spotlight on the more interesting and memorable winners leads people (per the "availability" bias) to overestimate the likelihood of a major success.

Trust

The opportunity for entrepreneurs to realize attractive returns without much downside often turns on the willingness of customers and other resource providers to bear the risks. As we will see next, that willingness requires an optimistic trust bordering on naïveté, which is distinct from the quasi-contractual trust that facilitates ongoing exchanges in settled markets.*

Social scientists suggest that trust—which we may broadly define as the willingness to take a gamble on others—represents a prerequisite for economic development. "Virtually every commercial transaction," Arrow writes, "has within itself an element of trust, certainly any transaction conducted over a period of time. It can be plausibly argued that much of the economic backwardness in the world can be explained by the lack of mutual confidence."[2] Francis Fukuyama's 1995 book contrasts prosperous "high trust" societies of Germany and Japan with the relatively less well to "low trust" societies of Italy and China.[3] A 1988 compilation of papers by scholars from several fields, edited by Diego Gambetta (*Trust: Making and Breaking Cooperative Relationships*) offers a similar view.

This literature suggests that mutual trust facilitates economic exchange by reducing the costs of negotiating formal contracts and monitoring the performance of agreed-on duties. It permits transactions that information asymmetries might otherwise preclude: A market for secondhand cars, for example, will not clear at efficient prices if dealers are known to pass off

* The discussion relies on interviews that Howard Stevenson and I conducted with about twenty entrepreneurs on the topic of trust, and our analysis reported in Bhidé and Stevenson (1990)

lemons as good buys.[4] And it helps overcome "prisoner's dilemma"-type problems that impede cooperation. The literature also suggests that under certain conditions, rational self-interest can sustain trust. The fear of ostracism and what Axelrod calls tit-for-tat retaliation discourage breaches of trust when parties engage in repeated transactions. Axelrod cites the example of diamond markets that are "famous for the way their members exchange millions of dollars worth of goods with only a verbal pledge and a handshake. The key factor is that the participants know they will be dealing with each other again and again. Therefore, any attempt to exploit the situation will simply not pay."[5]

Rational self-interest cannot, however, easily explain the trust that facilitates the formation of new businesses. Unlike diamond merchants, the

---

The Selling of an Ad Salesman

Philippe Kahn, in an interview with *Inc.* magazine, describes with apparent relish how his company, Borland International, got its start by deceiving an ad salesman for *BYTE* magazine.

Inc.: The story goes that Borland was launched by a single ad, without which we wouldn't be sitting here talking about the company. How much of that is apocryphal?

Kahn: It's true: One full-page ad in the November 1983 issue of *BYTE* magazine got the company running. If it had failed, I would have had nowhere else to go.

Inc.: If you were so broke, how did you pay for the ad?

Kahn: Let's put it that we convinced the salesman to give us terms. We wanted to appear only in *BYTE*—not any of the other microcomputer magazines—because *BYTE* is for programmers, and that's who we wanted to reach. But we couldn't afford it. We figured the only way was somehow to convince them to extend us credit terms.

Inc.: And they did?

Kahn: Well, they didn't offer. What we did was, before the ad salesman came in—we existed in two small rooms, but I had hired extra people so we would look like a very busy, venture-backed company—we prepared a chart with what we pretended was our media plan for the computer magazines. On the chart we had *BYTE* crossed out. When the salesman arrived, we made sure the phones were ringing and the extras were scurrying around. Here was this chart he thought he wasn't supposed to see, so I pushed it out of the way. He said, "Hold on, can we get you in *BYTE*?" I said, "We don't really want to be in your book, it's not the right audience for us." "You've got to try," he pleaded. I said, "Frankly, our media plan is done, and we can't afford it." So he offered good terms, if only we'd let him run it just once. We expected we'd sell maybe $20,000 worth of software and at least pay for the ad. We sold $150,000 worth. Looking back now, it's a funny story; then it was a big risk.[6]

often young and inexperienced founders of promising businesses do not risk an established reputation; if anything, the heads-I-win, tails-I-don't-lose nature of their ventures should encourage entrepreneurs to take their chances with puffery and misrepresentation. As the sidebar, "The Selling of an Ad Salesman" suggests, an entrepreneur with his back to the wall can resort to elaborate deceptions.

Moreover, the effectiveness of reputational incentives and tit-for-tat strategies turns on the clear identification of bad faith, which is often difficult to establish in an uncertain new enterprise. The failure to pay for diamonds received, the palming off of a lemon as a good car, or defection in a "prisoner's dilemma" game can be sharply identified after they occur. An entrepreneur's dishonesty or bad faith is less clear-cut. When others take a chance on a start-up, they simultaneously rely on the founder's integrity and native ability and on favorable external circumstances. So if things go wrong, they (and third parties) often cannot tell whether the entrepreneur acted in bad faith, lacked competence, or was unlucky.

We saw in Chapter 3 that in lieu of "objectively" credible promises, entrepreneurs use a variety of strategies to exploit others' cognitive biases, reflexive behavior, and sympathy for an underdog. The success of such strategies depends on mores and attitudes that are distinct from those that sustain ongoing transactions between known parties. In a social climate conducive to start-ups, customers and resource providers do not ask many questions about entrepreneurs' backgrounds. They assume that others are usually honest. As one businessman we interviewed put it: "I tend to take people at face value until proven otherwise, and more often than not, that works. It doesn't work with a blackguard and a scoundrel, but how many total blackguards and scoundrels are there?" They disregard past incidents, such as Thomas J. Watson, Sr.'s, conviction for price fixing (later overturned on a technicality) and the repeated business failures of R. H. Macy and H. J. Heinz.[7] They attribute deceptions, such as Kahn's charade for the ad salesman to the force of circumstance, and may even enter into transactions with individuals they believe are dishonest. As one real estate developer told us: "People are really whores. They will do business with someone they can't trust if it suits their convenience. . . . I've done transactions with people knowing they were horrible. But the deal was so good, I just accepted it."

Members of a start-up-friendly society are somewhat myopic. They focus on immediate benefits and disregard the long-term risks. And if things go wrong or if their trust is violated, they shrug their shoulders and move on. "You can't get obsessed with getting even. It will take away from everything else," one businessman told us. Another called retaliation "a double loss. First you lose your money; now you're losing time. . . . [If you bite me] I won't have anything to do with you, but I'm not going to bite back. I'm not going to litigate just for the pleasure of getting even with you."

Such attitudes obviously create opportunities for fraud; a favorable climate for legitimate new businesses also facilitates the sales of titles to swampland and the operation of boiler room stock operations. Conversely, norms of the diamond market and of societies optimized for frictionless exchange may not be the most hospitable ones for start-ups. The mistrust of strangers, long memories, and belief in an-eye-for-an-eye, limit broken promises but also make it hard for young, undercapitalized entrepreneurs to start new businesses. In suspicious or retributive societies, we would expect, established entities who can bond their commitments with their name and capital would undertake a high proportion of new initiatives.

This is not to suggest that absolute tolerance for broken commitments produces an agreeable climate for start-ups. An "anything goes" system would collapse into a Hobbesian state of disorder hostile to any kind of commerce. There has to be some risk of sanction for failure to keep one's commitments, or some way to distinguish between out-and-out cheats from desperate entrepreneurs like Kahn, who use deception to build a legitimate business. My argument is simply that closed, unforgiving systems to ensure probity and frictionless exchange make it difficult to start a business. "Entrepreneurial" systems rely on weaker forces of social disapproval (rather than ostracism) and on a morality that encourages most people to behave honestly most of the time. There is a trade-off between frictionless exchange and new ventures, although a state of anarchy is good for neither.

Feedback Effects

The social factors, which influence the level of start-up activity in a certain period, are themselves affected by the start-up activity of previous periods. Up to a point, the skewed distribution of attention and returns generated by start-ups leads to positive feedback: Because the gains of successful entrepreneurs exceed the losses of the unsuccessful ones, the glamour and excitement of the activity increases, which in turn encourages more individuals to try their hand. The process snowballs as the winner's circle expands to include "mainstream" individuals (rather than "deviants"), which provides support for the belief that "anyone can do it." Casual observation suggests that we have reached this stage in the United States today, as many college students and corporate employees who would previously have sought to rise through managerial ranks dream of starting their own businesses.

The expansion has limits, however. Innate ambiguity aversion represents one limiting factor. Snowballing social acceptance will draw in increasingly ambiguity-averse individuals, but only up to a point. Starting a business requires a more conscious choice than does finding a job: There are no campus recruiters or corporate headhunters who sign people up to start a business. And some individuals will be too ambiguity-averse to make the leap to self-employment, no matter how fashionable it becomes. They may talk about it and think about it, but at the end of the day they will follow the path of least resistance into working for someone else.

The availability of profitable opportunities represents a second constraint. Most promising start-ups, we have seen, exploit situations that already exist rather than undertake their own innovations. But the supply of such opportunities is limited. The introduction of IBM PCs creates opportunities for a large but finite number of start-ups selling complementary goods and services. If the number of entrepreneurs overwhelms available opportunities, we would expect failure rates to escalate to proportions that undermine the glamour of starting a business and the "availability biases" that distort estimates of the chances of success.

Third, as the number of entrepreneurs escalates, the social attitudes and norms that help the founders of new businesses to get others to bear the risks decline. The psychic value customers derive from giving the "struggling entrepreneur" a break depends in part on the scarcity of such individuals. If they became as ubiquitous as, say, telemarketers of long-distance phone services, the founders of new businesses wouldn't enjoy the same goodwill. Increased start-up activity can increase suspiciousness and intolerance as the number of entrepreneurs who fail to live up to their commitments grows; a climate of optimism and tolerance requires that bad faith or incompetence remains within limits. Similarly, the ploys entrepreneurs use to gain credibility and orders become less effective as their use becomes more common. In other words, promising businesses provide a valuable free option to their founders only to the degree that factors such as ambiguity aversion or ignorance of sales skills limit the number of individuals who try to take advantage of them.

2. Technology

In the previous chapter we discussed how start-ups contribute to technological change. We now turn to the reciprocal role of new technology in stimulating start-ups. Although there is some literature on how technology affects economies of scale and the size distribution of firms, I will argue that these results cannot be simply extended to start-up activity, which is driven by somewhat different factors.

According to Acs and Audretsch, the "implementation of new flexible technologies" represents "the most decisive factor contributing to the [recent] emergence of small firms." For most of the twentieth century, they write, "industrial technology favored mass production, or the application of special purpose machines to produce standardized products." This technology was "inherently" inflexible and favored large firms over small firms. New technologies such as programmable robots and numerically controlled machines allow for "flexible," short-production-run manufacturing at costs comparable to those of producing standardized goods on a large scale. Changing consumer tastes have supported the shift to flexible techniques: "The proliferation of consumer tastes, away from standardized mass-produced goods and toward stylized and personalized products," write Acs and Audretsch, has mitigated "the inherent cost disadvantage of small scale production."[8]

Empirical research supports the argument that changes in manufacturing technology have affected the size distribution of firms. In their 1990 paper Acs, Audretsch, and Carlsson concluded that "there was substantial evidence that at least certain flexible technologies have promoted the viability of small firms." Subsequently they studied plant-level data from the Bureau of the Census and found that mean plant size "tended to decrease the most in those engineering industries where there has been the greatest application of programmable robots and numerically controlled machines"—that is, flexible manufacturing techniques.[9] But the historical evidence suggests that technologies that increase the viability of small firms and decrease plant size do not always lead to a proliferation of new businesses. Between 1947 and 1958, according to a study of 125 industries, the share of sales of the eight largest plants declined in 67 cases and increased in only 48. A contemporary economist, John M. Blair, attributed the declining share of large plants to "fundamental changes in the direction of technological advance away from centralizing innovations and toward decentralizing techniques" such as "the replacement of central motive power units by individual electric motors."[10] We do not find a great upsurge in the number of start-ups in the 1947–1958 period, however.

Flexible manufacturing techniques do not appear to have played much of a role in the *Inc.* start-ups I studied. I encountered just one company involved in the manufacture of robots. I did not encounter a single user of such equipment or of numerically controlled machine tools. The reported fragmentation of customer tastes also did not seem to have affected the start-ups in my sample, nearly 90 percent of whom sold to other businesses rather than to end users. Capital constraints preclude most individuals from using flexible manufacturing techniques to start their businesses. A bare-bones machine tool shop requires several hundred thousand dollars of equipment, and a state-of-the-art facility can run into the millions. VCs who can make investments on this scale did fund start-ups making robotics equipment, but I do not know of any that have backed companies using such equipment. So the techniques to customize products such as automobiles, which may produce significant changes in the operations of the incumbents, have likely not had much effect on start-up activity.

For a technological change to catalyze start-ups (rather than reduce industry concentration ratios or the average size of plants) it must mitigate the constraints faced by the typical entrepreneur. One example is the case of the "digital" or "information technology" revolution, which has

helped promising start-ups overcome capital constraints and secure customers.

Sharp declines in computing and communication costs have brought
the fixed and recurring outlays required to start a business within the reach
of a large number of capital-constrained individuals. As of this writing an
aspiring entrepreneur can purchase the equipment required for a fully
featured office—a computer, fax machine, printer, and copier—for a few
thousand dollars and rent voice mail and Internet access for fewer than fifty
dollars per month. In addition, software programs for word processing,
bookkeeping, and tax preparation that cost a few hundred dollars allow
entrepreneurs to substitute their personal labor for services that would
otherwise cost tens of thousand of dollars per year. These developments have
affected the economics of established companies as well, but their value for
the bootstrapped entrepreneurs is difficult to overestimate. Whereas leasing
a telex machine involved a serious financial and emotional commitment,
buying a fax machine and establishing an e-mail account is commonplace.

The new technologies have ameliorated the credibility problems entrepreneurs face by blurring the differences in the "appearance" of well-
established companies and shoestring start-ups. Word processing packages
(with spell checkers) and laser printers let any business generate professional-
looking business correspondence. Desktop publishing and color copiers
allow start-ups to produce slick sales brochures and newsletters at low cost.
Advances in communications have also eroded the perceptional advantages
of established companies. A cartoon in *The New Yorker* of a canine with its
paws on a computer keyboard has the caption "On the Internet, nobody
knows you are a dog." Whereas in the past, the phone manner of reception-
ists and secretaries gave callers an indication of the solidity of the enterprise,
today it is difficult for callers to tell whether they are leaving voice mail message on a multimillion-dollar PBX system or a ten-dollar-per-month service offered by the phone company.

The digital revolution has created opportunities that resource-con-
strained entrepreneurs can exploit. As mentioned in Chapter 1, many new
ventures have taken advantage of opportunities to provide ancillary goods
and services whose revenues were too small to attract large companies and
did not require much up-front investment. And, in contrast to many flexible manufacturing techniques, the advances in information technologies
have created opportunities to provide goods and services without displacing existing technologies and firms. The capital and credibility barriers
faced by start-ups have been correspondingly lower.

We may further speculate that the digital revolution has helped start-
ups by the beliefs about new technologies that it has engendered. In the
previous section I suggested that favorable social attitudes had caused start-
ups to snowball; a similar (and very likely overlapping) relationship may be
observed between expectations of advances in digital technology and the

accelerating realization of such advances. Gordon Moore's famous "law"—which he proposed in an *Electronics* magazine article in 1965—that the number of transistors that can be built on a chip doubles every eighteen months, provides a classic and important illustration of the role expectations have played in the digital revolution. Moore's claim, which we cannot properly call a natural or an economic law, has become an influential self-fulfilling prophesy. Semiconductor companies who believe in Moore's law invest the resources needed to make it come true. Downstream customers (such as PC manufacturers) and providers of complementary goods to their customers (such as applications software companies) design products in anticipation of the eighteen-month cycle. So when the new chips arrive they find a ready market, which in turn validates beliefs in Moore's law and encourages even more investment in building and using new chips.

Snowballing technological change seems to have engendered a powerful belief among large suppliers and users about the need to make rapid preemptive investments without their traditional analytical scrutiny. For instance, telephone and cable companies are rapidly providing "high-bandwidth" connections to households in the belief that the proliferation of the Internet will provide first-mover advantages. Similarly, *Fortune* 500 corporations are investing in web sites and e-commerce in anticipation of Internet ubiquity, without waiting to see what standards emerge or demanding much economic justification for their outlays. This attitude, we may note, contrasts with the corporate response to the advent of personal computers. Enthusiastic individuals first brought personal computers into the corporate world without official sanction, sometimes "diverting" departmental budgetary allocations from other uses. Corporations did not embrace personal computers until they were reassured by the entry of IBM and until applications such as spreadsheets and word processing had demonstrated their value.

The current almost unquestioning faith in new technology helps creates niche opportunities for start-ups to provide complementary products and services. For instance, the growth of the web has created a demand for HTML tools and training. And as customers are in a great rush to embrace the new technologies, they are more willing to give start-ups a chance. For instance, the urgency many corporate customers feel to establish their web sites and Intranets has led them to turn to untried entrepreneurs instead of waiting for, say, a division of IBM or Anderson Consulting to offer such services or hiring in-house staff.

3. Corporate Beliefs

Besides inducing episodic deviations from normal procedures, corporate beliefs also affect the initiatives they routinely undertake. An "optimistic" climate increases the proportion of new initiatives undertaken by corpora-

Skepticism about diversification and the belief that they had saturated their core markets encouraged executives to shrink. Surplus resources lost their perceived value as growth options. The new climate seemed to throw the Penrose and Rubin growth models into reverse gear. Recall that in those models unused managerial and other resources stimulate a search for new profit opportunities. Now companies sought ways to most profitably shed the excess resources.

Business consultants promoted the retrenchment ethos. "Reengineering" studies, which helped corporations make do with fewer employees, became a multimillion-dollar business. Stern Stewart's Economic Value Analysis and BCG's Cash Flow Return on Investment measured profits generated by businesses after taking into account the cost of the capital they employed. Such measures, which encouraged managers to shrink the capital they used in their businesses, implicitly assumed that shedding assets did not destroy valuable growth options (or employee morale). Stockholders who reacted positively to the downsizing of old-line corporations apparently endorsed this assumption.

The new beliefs, which have directly limited the initiatives undertaken by large companies, have also indirectly encouraged the formation of promising businesses. Reengineering projects have created "outsourcing" opportunities for start-ups. Many employees who have been laid off have started their own businesses. According to the outplacement firm Challenger, Gray, & Christmas, about 20 percent of laid-off managers started or bought their own businesses and consulting firms in 1990.[15] And, as faith about the security of employment has been shaken; the perceived difference in the uncertainty of starting a business and working for a large company has narrowed.

4. Tax and Regulatory Policies

The effects of tax and regulatory policies must always be examined on a case-by-case basis. The section below suggests a few heuristics about how different policies affect the mix of corporate initiatives and promising start-ups.

Tax Policies

Investment tax credits. Accelerated depreciation and similar efforts to lower the cost of capital expenditures favor initiatives undertaken by established corporations who have relatively easy access to debt and equity financing. They do little for individual entrepreneurs who rely on their sweat equity to start labor-intensive businesses. Similarly, tax credits for R&D favor large corporations that have the wherewithal to support such activity and can "segregate" it for tax purposes from their ongoing business. Promising businesses rarely use these credits because they start out by imitating or modestly refining others' ideas, and their subsequent development activities are closely intertwined with their ongoing business.

Double taxation of dividends. Dividends get taxed twice—through taxes on corporate profits and then through taxes on the incomes of individuals who receive dividends. This encourages corporations to reinvest profits in "internal" initiatives instead of paying them out to stockholders. Double taxation has a more limited impact in small, owner-managed firms, where the principals can pay themselves high salaries and bonuses instead of dividends.

Capital gains rates. Lower rates on capital gains (than on ordinary corporate incomes) also create an incentive for corporations to undertake new incentives. It encourages corporations to transform current income into increased equity value through deductible expenditures (on items such as R&D and advertising) and to develop new products and markets. Low capital gains rates have less impact on the economics of most start-ups. The founders of most bootstrapped ventures (as opposed to VC-backed companies), as we saw in previous chapters, do not expect to realize a substantial capital gain through an IPO or sale of their company.

Taxes on personal incomes. The effect of personal taxes on the formation of new businesses depends on the opportunities the system provides for avoidance or evasion. Low personal taxes should stimulate new business starts by helping individuals accumulate the savings they need to start a business. Also, as mentioned, the ongoing returns of an owner-managed business are especially sensitive to the level of personal taxes. But high rates on personal income may also encourage individuals to start their own businesses if it is easier to evade or avoid taxes as the owner of a business than as an employee.

Regulatory Policies

The effect of regulations on the mix of entrepreneurial activities will depend on a number of factors.

Fixed compliance costs. Regulations, such as those designed to promote product safety, that impose high up-front compliance costs preclude entry by capital-constrained entrepreneurs. For instance, we almost never find bootstrapped start-ups offering new pharmaceuticals or medical devices. Only the established drug companies and some VC-backed start-ups can afford the tens of millions of dollars it takes to secure Food and Drug Administration (FDA) approvals. By contrast, the unregulated health food and supplements markets have been a hotbed of start-up activity.

Small-company exemptions. Some regulations, especially regarding the terms and conditions of employment, often exempt small companies from their purview. In other cases (such as immigration or minimum-wage rules) regulators cannot effectively enforce the provisions of the law in small firms. The de jure or de facto relief from compliance costs have led large companies to rely on entrepreneurs to provide services ranging from custodial work (which is often dirty and low-paid) to contract programming (which involves securing work permits for overseas staff).

Long-tailed liabilities. Some activities, such as asbestos removal, involve risks of large, long-term liabilities. Here, too, established companies will turn to start-ups who "have nothing to lose," in the hope of protecting their assets and cash flows from future lawsuits and penalties.

Unexpected consequences. Major changes in the rules (such as airline or telecom deregulation) often lead to disruptions and unforeseen opportunities that nimble start-ups can exploit more easily than large, well-established companies.

5. Facilitators of Growth

In Part II we examined the proposition that only exceptional entrepreneurs can transform promising start-ups into long-lived corporations. The total number of start-ups should therefore help determine the number of such transformations; the greater the number of individuals who start new businesses, the greater the likelihood that some of them will have the necessary drive and capacity. Many entrants do not, however, ensure a proportionately large number of big winners. The evidence suggests that the United States and European economies have comparable numbers of small businesses and start-ups. The perception of a gap between the United States and Europe likely derives from the fewer founders of promising businesses in Europe who try to subsequently build a Microsoft or Dell Computer. As we will see next, the factors that promote the formation of new businesses do not necessarily coincide with the factors that facilitate their subsequent growth.

Social Attitudes

In his 1979 book *The Wheels of Commerce*, the economic historian Fernand Braudel distinguishes between a market economy and the system of capitalism. Simple "bourgeois principles" can sustain the former, whereas the latter requires the capacity and the drive to accumulate significant capital. We can similarly say that whereas bourgeois principles and a generally favorable view of commerce may suffice to encourage individuals to start new businesses, the social climate that encourages entrepreneurs to build a large company has distinctive features. Society must approve of, or at least grudgingly respect, the drive to accumulate substantial wealth and power and value winning over being a "good sport." It must tolerate "winner take all"-type games and the rough tactics that some entrepreneurs employ in their drive for dominance. Social attitudes that frown on individuals rising too far above the rest or think more highly of gifted amateurs than of methodical winners discourage the average entrepreneur from trying to build a substantial enterprise.*

Corporate beliefs

We see considerable overlap here—the nature of corporate beliefs has a similar effect on the growth of fledgling firms as it does on start-ups. Corporate pessimism helps ambitious entrepreneurs grow their businesses by freeing up capital and managerial personnel. If large corporations retrench, financial markets can recycle some of their surplus cash to smaller growth companies.** The downsizing of managerial staff likewise helps growing companies, by increasing the supply of employees who have the know-how of large company systems and procedures that the often inexperienced founders of promising companies lack.

Corporate attitudes toward diversification affect the competitive resistance that growing companies encounter. New businesses, we have seen, usually start in markets where they compete against other small companies. If their success attracts large companies, the stiffer competition can limit their growth. The office-products discounter Staples could more easily expand from a regional to a national scale as long as large established retailers (such as the mass merchandisers, Wal-Mart and Kmart) did not enter its category. In general, therefore, transitional companies are more likely to attain their growth goals when executives of large companies lack confidence in their capacity to enter new businesses and when the prevailing ethos is a cautious one of focus and consolidation.

Tax and Regulatory Policies

Policies that promote the formation of new businesses can sometimes discourage their subsequent growth. As mentioned, the opportunities for tax evasion afforded by the ownership of a business can encourage individuals

---

* A former student, Mauro Pretolani, speculates that the attitudes of the different socioeconomic classes also play an important role. According to Pretolani, Italy has a stronger entrepreneurial tradition than many other European countries. But its entrepreneurs have been drawn mainly from the ranks of manual or blue-collar workers who have been satisfied with building small businesses. Individuals from upper-middle-class backgrounds who might have aspired to build larger companies have been attracted to professions such as medicine and the law.

** In the past decade, for instance, stock repurchases have exceeded stock issuance, and according to a report by Needham Asset Management, large companies (i.e., those with a market capitalization of more than $1 billion) have done most of the repurchasing. The net supply of the stocks of smaller companies has increased during this period.

to start their own ventures. And the lower costs of complying with work-place safety, nondiscrimination, overtime, and other such rules enjoyed by small businesses, can lead large companies to outsource some functions to entrepreneurs. Such conditions, however, discourage firm growth. I have encountered many business owners in Europe and Asia who do not want to expand for fear of attracting the attentions of the tax authorities and government regulators. They have chosen to enjoy what Galbraith called the "quiet life" or to satisfy their ambition through owning several small firms.* Conversely, regulations that discourage small-scale entry can spur growth. For instance, the high fixed costs of complying with product safety regulations encourage businesses to expand their output to decrease the costs per unit.

Government policies such as antitrust laws can also directly limit an entrepreneur's drive to dominate a market. According to some historians, the United States has spawned more large companies than other countries partly because of a more tolerant attitude toward firm expansion. In the formative years of the country, leaders such as Jefferson directed their fear of concentrated power toward government—the issue of corporate power was moot. When the Second Industrial Revolution started in about 1880, a "tiny" government, according to McCraw, left a "vacuum of power" that allowed American companies to attain "gigantic" size.[16] Subsequently, "trust-busting" politicians did attempt to curb the power of large corporations, but as McCraw points out, their antitrust legislation was "not synonymous with antibigness law. The "most conspicuous targets" of antitrust were giant companies, but "the majority of prosecutions" had been against groups of small firms engaging in collusive behavior.[17]

In pre-Communist, imperial China, by contrast, an omnipotent state actively suppressed the emergence of large businesses, which could threaten its hegemony. The state played a ubiquitous role, writes Braudel, handling "public works, irrigation, roads [and] canals." To provide measures against famines, the state took responsibility for agricultural production, making advance payments to peasants and filling the public granaries as emergency stores. A "lynx-eyed administration" controlled and confined the activities of businessmen—for instance, the local mandarin authorized the entry and departures of all vessels in the ports. "Under such conditions, neither the merchants, the usurers, the money changers, nor the manufacturers . . . had much in the way of power. The government had the right to punish or tax anyone it saw fit to, in the name of the common good which condemned excessive wealth . . . as both immoral and unjust."

China did have "a solidly established market economy" with "chains of local markets," a "swarming population of small artisans and itinerant mer-

---

* One businessman provided a Kafkaesque story of having different firms operating the same plant in succeeding months of the year, so that each could enjoy small-firm status. (I did not, however, verify this claim.)

chants," and "busy shopping streets and urban centers." The government encouraged simple trade to facilitate agricultural production. But the accumulation of capital "could only be achieved by the state and within the state apparatus." Long before the arrival of Communist rule, a state that "uncompromisingly controlled everything and expressed unmistakable hostility to any individual making himself 'abnormally' rich" could not countenance any private large-scale enterprise.[18]

Capital and Labor Markets

The conventions and structures of financial markets have a more significant impact on the growth of fledgling businesses than they do on start-ups. The workings of financial markets make little difference to the founders of most promising businesses who face nearly insurmountable barriers to raising outside capital and can make do with meager funds. Some businesses, like Microsoft, enjoy such high profit margins that they can finance their subsequent growth entirely through retained earnings. For many other businesses the availability of additional capital represents an important determinant of growth. Wal-Mart, for instance, relied heavily on lines of credit, limited partnerships, subordinated loans from insurance companies, and the public equity markets to finance its growth. The financial markets can therefore affect the entrepreneurs' capacity and willingness to grow such businesses.

In markets that encourage the growth of companies like Wal-Mart, capital is mobile rather than locked into existing corporations. Imaginative financial intermediaries compete to offer a broad range of financial instruments. Their optimistic outlook makes them willing to weigh potential earnings more heavily than past performance and to extend credit against expected cash flows; in unfavorable markets, pessimistic capital providers invest in blue-chip companies and demand hard collateral for any loans they make to fledgling businesses.

The terms of capital availability also matter. Market conventions (and legal rules) about the separation of personal and business liability affect the willingness of entrepreneurs to seek expansion capital. If capital providers hold entrepreneurs liable for the debts of their business (e.g., through personal guarantees) or make it difficult for them to start new business after a failed venture, we would expect to see fewer entrepreneurs trying to expand. Conversely, an environment in which entrepreneurs can raise hundreds of millions of dollars in unsecured debt after declaring bankruptcy (as in the case of Donald Trump) or renege on contractual obligations (as in the case of Oscar Wyatt, the founder of Coastal Corporation) encourages them to turn small businesses into large ones.[19]

The market for experienced personnel similarly affects firm growth more than it does start-ups. Whereas improvised start-ups make do with inexperienced employees who have limited job prospects, their subsequent evolution often requires entrepreneurs to recruit seasoned employees from established companies. The willingness of such personnel to join transitional businesses depends in part on the costs they incur when they leave their jobs and the risks they face if things don't work out. For instance, the portability of pension benefits and the acceptance of "job hopping" help transitional companies attract experienced employees. Conversely, if established companies usually tie pensions to employment until retirement age and fill "good" jobs mainly from within, they will discourage experienced employees from taking a chance on a transitional enterprise.

6. Implications for Public Policy

The preceding sections raise many questions about the effectiveness and wisdom of extending public help to individual entrepreneurs. Government policies, I argue next, cannot promote the formation and evolution of new businesses to a significant degree. Nor does favoring individual entrepreneurs over the initiatives of established companies seem any more sensible than the reverse tilt in favor of large companies.

We have examined an extensive (and arguably incomplete) set of factors that affect the willingness and the capacity of individuals to start their own businesses. It is difficult to imagine how governments can affect these factors to create a more "favorable" environment for entrepreneurs. Public policies cannot easily make start-ups fashionable or turn successful entrepreneurs into popular icons. Government awards and recognition tend to follow rather than determine what's "in": The U.S. Postal Service issues Elvis stamps long after he has attained cult status. We have limited knowledge of, let alone the capacity to manage, how societies attain the optimal level of honesty (and gullibility) that facilitates start-ups, or how the corporate climate turns from optimistic expansionism to retrenchment. Similarly, whereas governments can underwrite scientific research, we cannot predict what kind of projects will generate technologies that help start-ups.

Even the factors most directly connected to the activities of government—taxes and regulations—do not provide effective instruments for helping entrepreneurs. Although individuals may start businesses to evade or avoid taxes or because small businesses can more easily circumvent workplace regulation, this does not seem like a reasonable consideration in the design of the tax and regulatory system. Similarly, although the FDA has a significant impact on entrepreneurial activity in the United States, this need not be of primary concern in the debate over its role. If public health concerns justify strict oversight of new drug development or the labeling of health foods, it is not obvious that the rules should be weakened for the benefit of undercapitalized entrepreneurs.

Policies to ameliorate the so-called capital shortage faced by entrepreneurs seem particularly questionable. Most entrepreneurs, we have seen, use their personal savings or the modest funds raised from relatives and friends to start their businesses because they don't have much verifiable human capital and intellectual property. Their success depends on their energy and adaptability. It is just as hard for a public agency as it is for professional investors to identify individuals who have the requisite innate capacity to make a go of such ventures. And providing capital to all comers will lead to large-scale misallocation of resources (even without the inducement of easy funding, nearly a million individuals try to start new businesses each year) and opportunities for fraud.

Moreover, much of the distinguishing contribution of promising start-ups derives from their capital constraints. Meager funding forces entrepreneurs to conduct low-cost experiments that help resolve market and technological uncertainties and prepare the ground for subsequent large-scale investment. It also makes entrepreneurs seek out underutilized resources such as inexperienced or fringe members of the labor force and provide them with on-the-job training.

Capital availability does represent an issue for the exceptional start-ups (such as in biotechnology) that require significant up-front investment to develop new technologies and for firms trying to expand their scale and scope. Policy choices such as the taxation of capital gains, investment tax credits, and the regulation of financial markets and intermediaries can make a difference in such situations. But at least in the United States, there seems little evidence that capital-intensive start-ups and transitional firms face a shortage of funds. Arguably, VC firms and the IPO markets have shown an excessive eagerness, bordering on what the U.S. Federal Reserve Board Chairman Alan Greenspan might term as "irrational exuberance," to provide capital to them. Expectations about the revolutionary potential of the Internet, for instance, may have engendered significant overinvestment and drawn in individuals who lack the innate capacity to start a business. The easy availability of large-scale funding can also lead inexperienced entrepreneurs to grow their businesses at a faster rate than their managerial capacities can develop. We may wonder, for instance, whether individuals such as Bill Hewlett, David Packard, or Bill Gates would have been able to build long-lived firms if they had to cope with multibillion-dollar stock market valuations within years of launching their businesses.

The personal computer industry provides a useful contrast. Bootstrapped entrepreneurs carried out the early experiments with very little capital in the 1970s. Capital became available on a large scale in the 1980s mainly to entrepreneurs and firms with demonstrable track records and technologies. Companies such as Microsoft, Lotus, and Dell issued public stock after they had established sizable ongoing revenues, profits, and an organizational infrastructure. And, by the standards of Internet IPOs, valuations were modest.

Richard Florida argues that venture capitalists fund too many start-ups by "pulling inventions out of existing companies." Florida writes that in Silicon Valley, "every new idea seems to lead to the formation of a new start-up—a wasteful and inefficient process. . . . [E]xisting firms suffer from raids and defections of key scientists, technologists, and management personnel. Promising projects are abandoned and companies find it hard to follow on breakthroughs they have made. . . . Too much venture capital, while it may lead to more start-ups, may in fact be detrimental to the national economy."[20]

We cannot easily verify Florida's impressions, but they do raise a basic question about whether public policies should even try to favor new or transitional businesses over established corporations. Many kinds of individuals and organizations carry out "entrepreneurial" activities. Their initiatives often complement each other, and in some cases overlap. This chapter has discussed some broad factors that affect the proportion of the activities of the different players but has not made any claims about the optimal mix. Individual entrepreneurs (many bootstrapped and some VC-backed) have made great economic contributions, but so have large corporations. While individuals likely have an advantage in undertaking small, uncertain initiatives, established companies are better equipped to put large amounts of capital to work. In this era of corporate retrenchment, we should not lose sight of the long-term record of publicly held corporations in the United States. Some large companies have realized poor returns: For instance, according to Jensen, General Motors spent $67.2 billion on its R&D and investment program between 1980 and 1990, only to produce a firm with a total value at the end of the period of $26.2 billion.[21] For just $21.5 billion GM could have bought all of the equity of Toyota and Honda in 1985. Fama and French's estimates of the returns earned by all nonfinancial publicly held corporations in the United States for 1950–96 tell a different story. According to Fama and French, these corporations earned a return on 12.11 percent p.a. compared, to their cost of capital of 10.72 percent over the 46-year period. These numbers are especially impressive given the trillions of dollars these companies invested.

There seems little reason, therefore, for governments to try to manage the ebbs and flows in the fortunes of the different actors. The idea of large "national champions" that so captured the fancy of European policymakers in the 1960s has, appropriately, fallen out of favor. This need not, however, lead governments to undertake the even more difficult task of directing capital and other resources to the vast and diffused population of actual and would-be entrepreneurs. An interest in the overall climate for economic enterprise seems more worthwhile than a focus on any particular manifestations of entrepreneurship.

7. Summary and Conclusions

Several factors help determine the relative proportions of promising start-ups and the initiatives of large corporations. These include social attitudes toward entrepreneurs, the nature of technological developments, the outlook and beliefs of executives in large corporations, and the tax and regulatory regimes. (See Table 14.1 for a list of some of the factors that have contributed to the increased importance of promising start-ups in recent years.) The same factors do not, however, facilitate the transformation of start-ups into large corporations—the growth of firms depends on a different set of conditions (see Table 14.2). Public policies cannot easily influence the climate for the formation and growth of promising businesses. Nor does there appear to be a compelling case for the state to even try to influence the relative proportions of the entrepreneurial initiatives undertaken by individuals, transitional firms, and large corporations.

Table 14.1. Conditions Favoring Promising Start-ups

Social attitudes	• Entrepreneurs accorded prestige and recognition • "Optimistic" trust
Technology	• Products and services that facilitate bootstrapping • Expectations of rapid and unpredictable change
Beliefs of corporate executives	• Pessimism about profitable growth and diversification opportunities
Tax and regulatory policies	• Tax advantages from business ownership • Low fixed costs of regulatory compliance • Regulatory burdens decrease with firm size • Disruptions due to radical changes in regulation

Table 14.2. Conditions Favoring Firm Growth

Social attitudes	• Emphasis on winning • Tolerance for "winner take all"
Beliefs of corporate executives	• Pessimism about profitable growth and diversification opportunities
Tax and regulatory policies	• Tax and regulatory burdens do not increase with firm size • Fixed compliance costs increase minimum efficient scale • Regulatory burdens decrease with firm size • Tolerance for market power (e.g., weak antitrust rules)
Capital and labor markets	• High mobility for capital and labor • Limited personal liability (e.g., liberal bankruptcy regime)

Conclusion

When we embarked on this journey, I stated that our purpose was to outline the principal features of an important but not-well-explored territory. This final chapter recapitulates some of the highlights of what we have observed and provides suggestions for future travels. My claims are tentative—exploratory inquiries do not lead to firm conclusions. But for the sake of clarity, I have omitted the "perhaps" and "mays" that ought to qualify the following propositions.

1. Recapitulation

Promising Start-ups

Only a small proportion of new businesses—5 to 10 percent of the total—make much of a contribution to economic growth or job creation or have the potential to provide significant returns to their owners. The great majority comprise "marginal" microenterprises providing routine services in mature fields such as lawn care and beauty salons. Their high rate of appearance and disappearance has limited economic significance.

Capital constraints. Most promising businesses start out with meager funds—only a very select subset of high potential start-ups can raise funds from professional intermediaries such as venture capitalists. Most founders of promising businesses cannot raise much outside capital because they don't have much verifiable human capital or proprietary technologies—they tend to have limited experience and often start their businesses by copying or slightly modifying someone else's idea.

Uncertain niches. Promising start-ups have low "most likely" profit potential; but because of the nature of the opportunities they pursue, they have at least a chance of earning significant returns: Promising start-ups cluster in market niches characterized by high uncertainty generated by technological, regulatory, or other such exogenous changes or by the amorphous nature of customer wants. High uncertainty and low capital and opportunity costs create a "heads I win, tails I don't lose much" proposition for entrepreneurs. In contrast, the low uncertainty of marginal businesses means that their principals don't have even an outside chance of a sizable payoff.

Opportunistic adaptation. The founders of promising ventures find their business ideas in the course of their previous employment or by chance, rather than through a systematic search. They devote little effort to prior market research or planning. They don't have the money, the opportunities are often fleeting and with high uncertainty, and extensive research and planning do not have much value. Instead, entrepreneurs rely on opportunistic adaptation to unexpected problems and opportunities.

Securing resources. To add value to their free option, entrepreneurs have to get customers and other "resource providers" to take a chance on their business. The lack of a track record and capital makes resource providers reluctant to do business with a start-up. Entrepreneurs overcome this reluctance by providing special benefits, exploiting others' cognitive biases and reflexive tendencies, and by locating resource providers with unusual needs or a willingness to bear the risks of a new enterprise.

Traits and skills. Unforeseen events play a significant role in promising start-ups because of the high uncertainty and lack of planning. Success isn't just a matter of luck, however. Starting a business with a "free option" attached requires an unusual tolerance for ambiguity. Adapting to unforeseen circumstances requires the ability to act decisively, to be both open-minded and confident, and to have a talent for reading messy or hidden data. Moreover, attracting customers and other resources requires exceptional control over one's ego, tactical ingenuity, perceptiveness, and sales skills. Some other qualities that have been traditionally associated with entrepreneurs, such as low risk or loss aversion, foresight, and charisma, do not play important roles in starting promising businesses.

Specialization of initiatives

Large, established corporations such as IBM and P&G tend to pursue different kinds of opportunities than do promising start-ups. Such large corporations have the capacity and the incentive to pursue larger projects; because large corporations have track records and checks and balances for evaluating investments, they can raise capital from diffused sources (not from just a few relatives and friends). Also, they tend to concentrate their efforts on a few initiatives that they expect will generate profits large enough to cover their high fixed evaluation and monitoring costs. Corporations avoid uncertainty: Requirements for due diligence discourage them from undertaking initiatives whose risks cannot be objectively verified or diversified away. Due process and multilevel decision-making also make it difficult to execute the quick course changes required in an uncertain environment. The corporate comparative advantage thus lies in projects that require substantial up-front capital and the execution of well-laid-out plans. The billion-dollar development of the next generation of microprocessors represents a concrete example of the natural and preferred initiatives of established semiconductor companies such as Intel.

Venture-capital-backed start-ups and "transitional" firms pursue initiatives of medium uncertainty and size. The verifiable human capital of the founders of VC-backed start-ups and the track records of transitional firms give them more credibility with investors than most new businesses have but not quite as much as "blue-chip" corporations. Similarly, the due-diligence processes of VCs (or other providers of expansion capital) and the emerging internal control systems of young firms fall between the "act first and adapt afterwards" approach of promising ventures and the extensive checks and balances of mature corporations. The "intermediate" reputations and control mechanisms lead to an incentive and a capacity to specialize in projects of in-between investment and uncertainty, such as Mitch Kapor's launch of a better spreadsheet (Lotus 1-2-3) and Wal-Mart's construction of its first in-house distribution center.

These specific archetypes suggest the general hypothesis of an inverse relationship between the investment requirements and uncertainty of new initiatives. Different types of economic agents specialize in different regions of this trade-off, depending on their track records and processes for decision-making. Inexperienced "nothing to lose" entrepreneurs represent one bookend, large and mature corporations the other, and a variety of experienced individuals and young firms occupy the space between. On rare occasions we see "revolutionary" initiatives such as Federal Express, which involve high uncertainty and large initial investment, but these are exceptions to the general rule.

Firm Evolution

Turning a promising start-up into a large, long-lived corporation entails a radical transformation, not a simple "scaling up." The fledgling firm's profits usually derive from arbitrage-type activity in an unsettled market, quasi-wage compensation for the proprietors' labor, or, in a relatively small number of cases, a differentiated product. A large and long-lived corporation's profits, in contrast, derive from many tangible and intangible assets, such as its manufacturing plants, patents, customer relationships, and know-how. Large corporations have dense, deeply embedded coordination mechanisms to coordinate their heterogeneous assets and activities, whereas in the relatively simple fledgling enterprise, the entrepreneur performs the integrative and coordination functions. And large corporations can sustain ongoing growth by virtue of the size of the markets they serve, the productive capacity of their assets, and their coordination mechanisms. The specialized nature of the fledgling firm's markets, the limited capacity of its main asset—the entrepreneur—and the lack of coordinating mechanisms all place significant constraints on its growth.

The transformation from fledgling to mature firm requires protracted, purposive investment. Firms acquire a system of coordinated assets gradually, because capital constraints limit the size of individual investments and because it takes time to build customer relationships, know-how, and other such intangible assets. The process isn't predestined, such as the normal development of an infant into an adult; entrepreneurs must consciously abandon the pursuit of short-term cash flow in favor of long-term investment. And although the sequence and pattern of investments aren't predetermined, they aren't random or opportunistic either. Building long-lived firms involves the coordination of investments and efforts across functions and time. Specifically, entrepreneurs have to adopt and articulate audacious goals, formulate a set of general rules (or strategy) for realizing these goals, and translate these rules into specific actions and decisions (i.e., implement the strategy).

The effective pursuit of a strategic rather than an opportunistic approach requires entrepreneurs to have qualities and skills that are not important in starting improvised businesses. The pursuit of audacious goals requires a high level of ambition and tolerance for risk. Formulating a strategy requires imagination, a capacity for creative synthesis, and a capacity for abstraction. And the effective implementation of a strategy requires constancy, the capacity to inspire and intimidate, and the ability to learn new skills.

Many individuals who start businesses don't have these traits; nor can they easily transfer or delegate the responsibility for critical firm-building tasks to others. Few new ventures attain significant longevity and size because only a very small number of individuals have the willingness and the capacity to both start *and* build a business.

Implications for Economic Change

Investment-uncertainty trade-offs (and the incremental nature of scientific discovery) limit the occurrence of large-scale discontinuities in technology (or the "production function"). Individual entrepreneurs who might have the disposition to confront the uncertainty don't have the capital to undertake large-scale innovations, whereas large companies that have the resources cannot tolerate the uncertainty. Major technical changes therefore occur gradually, through the complementary efforts of many entrepreneurs and firms. Improvised start-ups help resolve the early-stage uncertainties of new technologies by conducting cheap experiments as well as the subsequent diffusion of these technologies by providing complementary goods and services. Established and transitional firms and some VC-backed start-ups with access to more resources undertake R&D that requires significant up-front expenditure, invest in high-volume production, and help create a mass market.

The interests and the capabilities of the different players also direct their efforts toward technologies that create new markets rather than ones that displace existing products and firms. The founders of promising start-ups have a propensity to serve new markets and customer needs because they lack the resources to compete against incumbents in existing markets. The fear of cannibalizing their existing revenues and profits creates a similar bias in large, resource-rich firms. And when new technologies and "combinations" do provide substitutes for existing products and services, they usually threaten small firms with narrow capabilities. Schumpeter's "gale of creative destruction" sweeps away the country store and narrowly focused minicomputer manufacturer rather than the *Fortune* 100 company with a broad range of businesses and assets.

The goals and qualities of the entrepreneurs who start businesses in the formative stages of a market influence its long-run structure. Markets do not naturally converge to a certain number of competitors because of pre-ordained economies of scale and scope. Whereas exogenous innovations often provide the spark (e.g., as the microprocessor did for personal computers), the choices and investments of the participants in the market help determine the minimum efficient scale, the importance of brand names, customer switching costs, and other such long-run structural features. Entrepreneurs with the unusual drive and capacity needed to build large and dominant firms help create concentrated market structures with high barriers to entry. With less ambitious or capable entrepreneurs we are more likely to find fragmented markets and firms that are not as well entrenched.

2. Open Questions

The territory explored in this book holds great potential for advancing our understanding of important economic phenomena. The propositions summarized above merit, I believe, refinement and challenge. For instance, although my analysis of firm evolution conforms to the histories of actual firms more closely than do theories of predestined or random development, it is but a rough and incomplete sketch. I believe that more regularities in firm evolution await discovery, if only because entrepreneurs often look for successful models they can imitate. The data and analysis contained in this book also point to new questions and the need for hypotheses and theories about the topics listed below.

Opportunity evaluation. Standard discounted cash flow techniques assume a well-diversified decision-maker with free access to capital. While these assumptions may approximate the situation facing corporate decision-makers, they are not relevant for the founders of promising businesses who face severe capital constraints and can pursue only one project at a time. For these individuals, the up-front cash required, payback periods, gross margins, and other such characteristics represent critical determinants of the attractiveness of a project. But we do not have a normative or a descriptive theory for the systematic incorporation of such factors into an entrepreneur's decisions about whether to proceed with a project.

Decision-making under uncertainty. Modern theory assumes away the problem of (Knightian) uncertainty by asserting that decision-makers can (or ought to) form a subjective estimate of the probabilities of the consequences of their choices. The experimental evidence on ambiguity aversion that we reviewed in Chapter 4 suggests that in many situations this is an unrealistic assumption, but our knowledge of alternative procedures for coping with uncertainty (such as "opportunistic adaptation") is limited.

Contracting. Uncertainty and capital constraints also play an important role in a start-up's ability to contract with customers and other resource providers. Uncertainty creates considerable incompleteness by making it difficult for the parties to anticipate contingencies and leads to fuzzy promises about "best efforts," "fairness," and other such ambiguous constructs. Capital constraints make it difficult for others to recover their investment if the entrepreneur defaults on agreed-on terms (such as providing ongoing maintenance to customers). Standard contracting theory, which implicitly assumes "known" probabilities and contingencies, ignores such problems. For instance, under what Goldberg calls "the paradigmatic contract of neo-classical economics,"[1] the parties clearly determine the duties they will discharge, and there is a sharp line between breach and performance. The recent economic literature contains a growing acknowledgment of the importance of incomplete contracts. For instance, Zingales suggests that "corporate governance" exists to mitigate the contracting problems faced by the stakeholders of firms because they cannot anticipate all the events that will affect the division of the returns their specific investments will generate.[2] These ideas will perhaps also eventually help us analyze the contracting problems faced by the founders of new businesses.

Firm evolution. Instead of forcing the data into a one-size-fits-all model, we could make more progress toward developing a general theory by identifying and explaining differences in the evolution of long-lived firms. This corresponds, incidentally, to Kurt Fischer's approach to studying human development. Fischer argues that standard developmental theory overemphasizes universal consistencies and neglects the variations that represent

room for H-P's company picnics (which take up two pages in *The H-P Way*), Sam Walton's hula dances, hiring practices that trade off talent for personality "fit" with the group, or for unilateral gift-giving to firm members to create reciprocal obligations and loyalty. It does not take into account the heterogeneity and malleability of the goals and wants of individuals; it tacitly assumes that employees have fixed preferences that group norms cannot materially affect.

All theory, of course, abstracts from the reality, and for many problems, "oversimplification" may be inconsequential. The known "incompleteness" of Newtonian physics, for instance, did not stop NASA scientists from using it to land a man on the moon. The choices and reasoning of entrepreneurs suggest, however, that the variables that the theory of the firm glosses over have important economic implications for an organization's capacity to undertake new initiatives. Employees will be more willing, for instance, to specialize their human capital for a new project if they subscribe to the firm's goals and believe that managers will not exploit the limited transferability of their knowledge and skills. We may further note that the popular and scholarly management literature has long moved beyond its initial militaristic or "Theory X" focus on authority. Modern management practice accords as much importance to "Theory Y" principles for building teamwork and loyalty as it does to the design of systems and to monitoring and controlling employee behavior. It also recognizes that a focus on controls over individual behavior may impair group solidarity and effort.

The theory of the firm could relatively easily incorporate some ideas (such as investments in building employee trust) from the management literature. Incorporating other assumptions (such as the malleability of employee preferences) could impair analytical tractability. But in terms of explaining real world economic phenomena, excluding modern management practices is as problematic as neglecting the circulatory and nervous systems in a model of human anatomy and recognizing only the skeletal system. Studies of the evolution of firms and markets ought to pay as much attention to Edgar Schein's ideas of corporate culture as Alfred Chandler's histories did to the transaction costs models of Oliver Williamson.

Understanding the processes of change requires attention to exceptional phenomena. Economic analysis ought to pay as much attention to deviant phenomena as do historians, evolutionary biologists, psychologists, and sociologists. An exclusive focus on what happens "on average" leads us to attribute the creation of new profit streams and firms to chance, to the otherwise undistinguished player who got lucky. To say something systematic about such out-of-the-ordinary events, we have to use our knowledge of central tendencies to examine the distinctive features of the outliers. We may further note that the vast number of economic agents and events provides a sizable sample of special cases—the evolution of an IBM or a Microsoft is unusual, but not as extraordinary an event as a revolution or a war.

We need a special effort, I believe, to examine the psychology of "exceptional" entrepreneurs. Schumpeter put this psychology at the center of his economic theories, but most modern economists shy away from treating variations in the traits of individuals as explanatory variables. The following claim by the economist Franklin Fisher exemplifies the prevailing ethos:

> As a teacher of mine (probably Carl Kaysen) once remarked some thirty years ago, it may very well be the case that one cannot understand the history of the American rubber tire industry without knowing that Harvey Firestone was an aggressive guy who believed in cutting prices. Maybe so. But then, as someone else (probably Mordecai Kurz or Kenneth Arrow) remarked to me a few years ago, the job of theory is to discover what characteristics of the rubber tire industry made such aggressive behavior a likely successful strategy. Absolutely right. That question would be answered if we had a generalizing theory of oligopoly.[5]

For reasons discussed in Chapter 12, I consider the search for innate characteristics of the rubber industry that made it conducive to aggressive strategies as implausible* and contrived. An analogy would be a historical determinist's attempt to explain the evolution of Germany and Italy without taking into account the roles and personalities of Bismarck and Garibaldi. The neglect of individual entrepreneurs seems to derive mainly from convention. As Sutton puts it: "In seeking to explain why things went this way rather than that, we rapidly outrun those systematic and measurable influences that are the domain of the contemporary economist, and we are drawn ineluctably into the historian's realm of accident and personality."[6] The implication I draw from Sutton's statement is that to explain significant variations in important economic phenomena, we must venture out of the domain of contemporary economists and examine the issue of personality.

We can and should do so in a systematic way, however. To merely say that exceptional entrepreneurs drive economic change does not provide more insight than the claim that changes arise by chance. We have to disaggregate what entrepreneurs do under different conditions and relate

---

* As a thought experiment, I once tried to relate the vertical structure of metal extraction industries to the position of the metal in the Periodic Table thus: The oxides of metals such as sodium and potassium occupy a low position in the Periodic Table, can be found in large quantities but require considerable energy to break the metal-oxygen bond. The value added is therefore concentrated in the downstream extraction of the metal rather than upstream mining and discovery. As one progresses along the Periodic Table (through aluminum, copper, silver, and gold) the oxide become more scarce but the metal-oxygen bond easier to break. Correspondingly, the economic action progressively shifts from the extraction to mining and discovery. This is the *only* example I can think of that ties the structure of an industry to a truly innate characteristic.

specific tasks to specific traits. Fortunately, work in "behavioral economics" and related fields has given us a much deeper knowledge of the psychology of cognition and decision-making than Schumpeter had at his disposal, so it is more feasible to map tasks into traits. But here, too, we have to focus more on variations in traits and personalities rather than on the central tendencies. Much of the work in behavioral economics focuses on the cognitive biases of the typical individual, whereas my analysis suggests that *differences* in ambiguity aversion, self-control, susceptibility to framing, and so on play a crucial role in the formation and evolution of businesses.

Last, and possibly most important, we need to develop appropriate standards for scholarly inquiry. The rhetoric of economic analysis (if not always the reality) seems to crave the norms of the natural experimental sciences, which we cannot easily apply to the transient and out-of-the-ordinary processes of change. Here it would help to adapt models for research from fields such as history, literature, anthropology, or even some of the more speculative subfields of physics. Scholars who analyze the works of Shakespeare or try to explain the origins of the World War II have managed to establish high standards for research and discourse in spite of measurement problems and the lack of matched samples. Incorporating their standards for consistency of reasoning, the integrity of data, building on prior work, and so on will provide much-needed respectability and draw the best and the brightest to work on exciting, real-world issues of economic change.

Appendix 1

Background Information
1989 *Inc.* 500 Study

As described in the Introduction, I surveyed 100 founders of companies that appeared on the 1989 *Inc.* 500 list. This appendix provides further details and summary statistics on all 500 companies that comprised the list. It also contains summary statistics and individual information about the 100 companies I surveyed.

Inc. 500 Selection Process

Inc. magazine staff sent nomination forms to more than 20,000 potential candidates. Qualifying applicants had to have (1) been independent and privately held on July 3, 1989; (2) secured revenues of at least $100,000 but not more than $25 million in 1984; and (3) registered a sales increase between 1987 and 1988. Holding companies and regulated banks and utilities were not eligible. From the list of qualified nominees, *Inc.* picked the 500 companies with the greatest percentage increase in sales from 1984 to 1988. *Inc.* magazine independently corroborated the information from each application.

Summary Statistics for the 500 Companies

Revenues and Employees in 1988 and 1984

	1988	1984
Average revenues (millions)	$15.01	$0.996
Median revenues (millions)	$ 6.62	N.A.
Number of employees	138	20

Distribution by Industry

Industry	Percentage of Total
Computer-related	23
Business services	19
Consumer goods	19
Industrial equipment	9
Construction and engineering	8
Medical and pharmaceutical	7
Environmental	6
Other	5
Publishing and media	2
Telecommunications	2

Summary Statistics for 100 Founders Surveyed by the Author

As described in the text, I excluded companies that were eight years old or older from my survey, so my sample was slightly younger than the full list. The median company in my survey also had somewhat lower revenues, fewer employees, and a greater proportion of ventures in the computer industry.

Revenues and Employees in 1988 and 1984

	1988	1984
Revenues		
Average (millions)	$8.98	$0.576
Median (millions)	$5.55	$0.307
Range (millions)	$0.92 to $56.40	$0.101 to $4.10
Number of employees		
Median	100	12
Range	4 to 1147	1 to 100

Distribution by Industry

Industry	Percentage of Total
Computer-related	36
Business services	23
Consumer goods	13
Medical and pharmaceutical	13
Publishing and media	5
Construction and engineering	3
Other	3
Industrial equipment	2
Environmental	2

Profit Margins in 1988 and 1984

Average Profit Margin	No. of Companies in 1988	No. of Companies in 1984
16% or more	10	7
11–15%	9	8
6–10%	33	17
1–5%	35	20
Breakeven	0	10
Loss	12	37

List of Companies Surveyed by Author

Company Name	Company Description	1988 Revenues ($000)	Profit Margin % in 1988	No. of Employees in 1988	1984 Revenues ($000)	Profit Margin % in 1984	No. of Employees in 1984
Active Parenting, Inc.	Develops and markets parent education videos	1,300	≥16	13	107	<0	2
Advanced Computer Concepts, Inc.	Sells computer products	20,219	6–10	40	1,954	~0	5
Advanced Entry Systems	Sells and services CardKey security systems	3,777	1–5	30	198	<0	4
Advent Software, Inc.	Markets software to the investment services industry	2,267	6–10	35	167	≥16	2
Allied Computer Group Companies, Inc.	Sells and supports systems; Valcom franchisee	7,839	6–10	34	521	~0	8
Allservice Foods	Packages and distributes snack foods	1,980	6–10	17	195	1–5	3
American Medical Imaging	Provides diagnostic ultrasound imaging services	11,100	1–5	184	104	<0	3
American Rug Craftsmen, Inc.	Manufactures contemporary-style rugs	15,478	6–10	292	1,239	6–10	4
Anderson Soft-Teach	Produces and markets PC/software usage training videotapes	1,571	6–10	23	171	6–10	4
Attronica Computers	Sells computer products	8,118	<0	32	210	<0	2
Australian Wines, Inc.	Imports and distributes Australian and New Zealand wines	1,216	11–15	6	132	<0	2
Automotive Caliper Exchange	Remanufactures brake calipers and front-end systems	7,172	6–10	111	384	1–5	16
Barakat & Chamberlin	Provides consulting services on regulatory, environmental, and planning issues to electric utilities	3,469	11–15	90	222	11–15	3
Beckett Corp.	Manufactures self-adhesive labels	8,744	1–5	58	775	1–5	4
Bertucci's	Gourmet pizza restaurant chain	11,400	11–15	200	350	<0	10
Best Mailing Lists, Inc.	Sells information lists by direct mail	1,029	11–15	8	108	<0	1
Bohdan Associates	Sells hardware, software, and peripherals	48,458	1–5	102	2,900	1–5	6
Buccino & Associates	Provides "turnaround" consulting	5,724	≥16	40	307	≥16	1
Burnham Broadcasting	Operates network TV stations	48,290	<0	517	1,705	<0	100
C Text	Sells and supports PC-based newspaper publishing systems	7,318	6–10	89	652	<0	12
Cadmus Group	Provides economic and environmental policy consulting	2,009	1–5	30	117	<0	2
CCB Computer Brokers	Distributes used and refurbished computer hardware and peripherals	6,750	≥16	40	130	<0	1
CEBCOR	Provides employee leasing services	25,083	1–5	49	120	1–5	3
Chariot Eagle	Manufactures high-end RVs	10,522	1–5	89	263	<0	13
Citicam Video Services	Supplies video crews to TV productions	2,400	≥16	11	114	≥16	2
Clinical Medical Equipment, Inc.	Provides third-party equipment maintenance to hospitals	6,948	<0	84	519	<0	24
CoddBarrett Associates	Sells computer graphics systems	2,493	<0	25	249	6–10	15
Colter Bay International	Manufactures sweaters and other apparel	13,937	6–10	25	871	<0	5
Compuclassics	Sells software by mail order	11,800	1–5	40	968	1–5	2
Compu-Link	Assembles and installs cable assemblies	3,624	1–5	95	156	11–15	12
Computer Media Technology	Manufactures and brokers computer recording media	2,727	6–10	13	136	6–10	2
Computer People Unlimited, Inc.	Provides custom programming services	11,182	1–5	182	799	6–10	38
Construction Technology, Inc.	Provides general contracting services	2,700	6–10	40	305	<0	6
Continental Financial Resources	Equipment leasing to printers, business offices, and construction firms	3,777	1–5	20	433	~0	3

List of Companies Surveyed by Author *(continued)*

Company Name	Company Description	1988 Revenues ($000)	Profit Margin % in 1988	No. of Employees in 1988	1984 Revenues ($000)	Profit Margin % in 1984	No. of Employees in 1984
Corporate Research Associates	Designs and develops computer-based custom training systems	1,677	1–5	23	118	6–10	3
Creative BioMolecules	Produces proteins for medical applications	4,281	<0	61	447	<0	36
Devon Direct Marketing and Advertising	Provides direct marketing services	45,277	11–15	46	375	≥16	3
Donaldson and Co., Inc.	Sells research to money managers	2,513	11–15	4	171	6–10	2
Eaglebrook Plastics, Inc.	Recycles plastics	6,199	6–10	50	390	~0	8
Electrotek Concepts, Inc.	Provides systems to the electric utilities industry	1,996	1–5	22	159	<0	5
Exsel, Inc.	Remarkets used copiers and computer equipment	5,379	1–5	18	401	<0	6
Facter, Fox & Associates, Inc.	Provides telemarketing services for nonprofits	6,631	<0	155	555	~0	10
Gammalink	Manufactures boards and software for mainframe-fax and mainframe-PC communication	3,602	6–10	38	105	<0	3
Gateway Design Automation Corp.	CAE software tools	6,106	≥16	75	391	≥16	4
Georgia Mountain Water, Inc.	Bottles and distributes spring water	1,794	6–10	30	187	1–5	6
Gerber Alley	Sells health-care information systems	27,284	6–10	241	3,864	11–15	26
Ghafari Associates, Inc.	Provides CAD and architectural services	11,323	1–5	161	1,609	1–5	46
ICT Technologies, Inc.	PC-based CAD systems distributor	15,782	1–5	25	587	1–5	5
IG Systems, Inc.	Provides data-processing consulting	5,499	6–10	70	494	~0	10
Information America, Inc.	Provides on-line public record information and services	7,876	<0	77	307	<0	20
Interactive Learning Systems	Computerized vocational schools	5,763	≥16	133	729	<0	31
Inter-ad, Inc.	Manufactures public access computer information systems	1,667	6–10	18	133	≥16	2
Internet Systems Corporation	Sells front-end systems to international banks	10,619	<0	110	265	<0	53
Lebrecht Stephenson and Hagen	Provides advertising and PR services	1,461	1–5	8	184	<0	8
Logical Operations, Inc.	Publishes software usage training literature and provides classroom training	2,649	1–5	51	129	<0	3
MEDLINC, Inc.	Provides contract labor in health care	12,080	1–5	73	166	11–15	6
Melannco International Ltd.	Assembles and markets decorative photographic albums	5,342	1–5	43	257	<0	12
Mercury Computer Systems	Produces processors for computer applications	11,818	6–10	103	146	<0	17
Micron Separations, Inc.	Manufactures membrane filters for medical purposes	5,021	11–15	55	683	<0	20
Modular Instruments, Inc.	Manufactures PC-based neurological testing devices	1,981	6–10	15	104	<0	1
Myers-Holum	Sells and supports CA accounting sofware products	2,811	1–5	55	390	1–5	4
NAC, Inc.	Manufactures intelligent network platforms	26,745	≥16	147	345	<0	16
National Communications	Provides sales promotions services	3,890	6–10	23	547	1–5	5
National Data Products	Distributes business forms and computer hardware	7,504	1–5	45	491	6–10	15
National Engineering Service	Provides technically skilled contract laborers (i.e., engineers)	16,065	1–5	540	740	<0	40
Orbital Sciences Corporation	Aerospace manufacturer	56,400	<0	405	2,600	6–10	24
Oscor Medical Corporation	Mfrs. products for microsurgery	4,191	6–10	45	406	<0	6
Paris Gourmet	Imports and distributes gourmet food	1,891	1–5	16	119	1–5	3

List of Companies Surveyed by Author *(continued)*

Company Name	Company Description	1988 Revenues ($000)	Profit Margin % in 1988	No. of Employees in 1988	1984 Revenues ($000)	Profit Margin % in 1984	No. of Employees in 1984
PC Warehouse, Inc.	Sells hardware, software, systems, and networks	5,513	1–5	22	732	~0	3
PPOM, L.P.	PPOM (preferred provider) health care delivery management	3,147	1–5	40	101	<0	2
Practice Management Systems	Provides office automation systems for medical and dental practices in New England	6,786	6–10	79	767	11–15	5
Precision Response Corporation	Provides telemarketing and database-management services	4,573	6–10	105	245	6–10	10
Princeton Review, Inc.	Provides preparation for college and graduate school admissions exams	5,548	6–10	35	489	6–10	14
Progress Software Corporation	Develops and markets applications development software	15,371	6–10	160	296	<0	22
Progressive Peripherals and Software	Manufactures and sells personal computer peripherals	5,138	6–10	30	190	1–5	7
Quad Systems Corporation	Manufactures robots for surface-mounted components applications	12,280	<0	100	698	<0	42
Real World Systems, Inc.	Sells local area networks	3,518	1–5	14	224	1–5	3
Rizzo Associates, Inc.	Provides environmental consulting (i.e., environmental impact studies and engineering design) for public and private entities	4,160	1–5	80	272	6–10	7
Roadshow International, Inc.	Provide tour logistics planning services to recording artists	2,321	1–5	26	146	<0	5
RPM Rent-A-Car	Auto rentals	10,916	6–10	214	391	6–10	12
Russell Personnel Services	Provides permanent and temporary employment services	3,474	1–5	1147	223	11–15	22
Sampler Publications	Publishes *Country Sampler* catalog and several magazines	7,257	≥16	20	114	~0	2
SBT Corporation	Manufactures accounting and MIS computer software	8,349	6–10	85	619	1–5	10
Shawmut Design and Construction	Provides general contracting services	19,278	1–5	120	1,275	~0	20
Silton-Bookman Systems, Inc.	Develops and Markets PC applications software	1,364	6–10	14	144	1–5	3
SIR Group	Provides insurance sales and risk-management consultation	12,338	6–10	45	4,100	6–10	40
Softa Group, Inc.	Sells systems to real estate managers	2,840	6–10	41	417	<0	10
Software 2000	Develops and distributes business applications software for accounting and human resource management uses	9,780	11–15	94	678	1–5	8
Starpak, Inc.	Provides software services	918	<0	81	133	6–10	1
STAT Medical Services	Contract nursing services	14,735	6–10	1000	1,427	≥16	100
Steadi-Systems Ltd.	Sells film and videotape	4,342	6–10	13	250	6–10	1
Symplex Communications Corp.	Manufactures "datamizers" (data communications equipment)	16,532	≥16	77	2,297	<0	20
SysComm International Corp.	Sells computer hardware and software by mail order	28,292	1–5	60	2,830	1–5	13
TME, Inc.	Manages MRI diagnostic clinics	6,532	1–5	76	168	11–15	1
Transamerica Energy Associates	Provides peak-load laborers in the right-of-way industry	11,617	1–5	237	808	1–5	15
U.S. Realty Associates, Inc.	Provides real estate services to government personnel in the D.C. area	1,012	1–5	13	108	1–5	3
Unique Transportation Systems	Provides trucking services	3,905	<0	60	412	6–10	12
Venture Graphics, Inc.	Provides lithographic preprinting services	2,106	≥16	33	197	11–15	7
Wang Associates Public Relations	Provides public relations services to pharmaceutical and biotech	1,560	11–15	18	125	~0	2

Appendix 2

Partial List of Student Papers Written on Successful Entrepreneurs

Note: This list excludes papers where the subjects preferred to remain anonymous. About 60 of the papers listed below have been published (with minor editing) in: A. Bhidé, "Tales from Successful Entrepreneurs," Harvard Business School No. 396-050 (1995).

Company/Venture	Entrepreneur(s)	Author(s) of Paper
Acacia Yogurt, Inc.	Steve Harris	Don Daniels, Brent Martin
Accion	Joe Blanchford, Bill Burrus	Karin Finkelston, Silvia Barragan
ADT Engineering, Inc.	V. T. Van	Do Thu Nguyen
Advent International	Peter Brooke	Whitney Bower
Affinity VideoNet	Linda and Dave Carlson	Troy Brown, Rod Bourgeois
Aldrich, Eastman & Waltch, L.P.	Peter C. Aldrich	Victor George Dodig
Almacenes Paiz	Carlos M. Paiz	José Carlos Paiz
Alpha-Beta Technology Incorporated	Spiros Jamas, David Easson	Brian Barringe, Marcos Gonzalez, Jerome Meier
American Bailey Corporation	Douglas Bailey	David Ethridge, Skip Grow, John Hunsicker
American Business Information	Shyam P. Gupta	Vinod Gupta, Glen Humphrey
Amgen, Inc., and Icos Corp.	George Rathmann	Timothy L. Anderson
Anthra Pharmaceuticals, Inc.	Michael Walker	Stacey A. Lauren
Aquamarine	Shimon Spier	Guy Spier
Ark Capital Management	Ivan Smith	Gail L. Covington
Arnowitz Studios	Burt and David Arnowitz	Russell Ruthen, Laurie Gottlieb
Arrowstreet, Inc.	Bob Slattery	Kathryne Gambrell, Stefanie Rinza, Barbara Thornton
Art Machines, Inc.	Hugh Smyser	Marc Metis
The ASC Story	Heinz Prechter	Robert Anglin, Ricardo Elias
Autumn Ridge Farm	Dave and Sue Thompson	Alex Gilbert, David S. Milstein
Bill Warner and Avid Technology, Inc.	Bill Warner	David Feldman
Avid Technology, Inc.	Bill Warner, Curt Rawley	Michael S. Bauer, Mark Goffman
Bach Designs Limited	Stephen Bach	Dana Andrews, Ria G. Vergara
BancA Corporation	John Cook	A. Woelflein
Baskin Family Camps and Camp Balcones Springs	Bo Baskin, Steve Baskin	Michelle A. Toth
Bayside Controls	Howard Lind, Avi Telyas	Rafael Tallada
BBF Corporation	B. B. Frusztajer	Carine Barco, Carola Paschola
Sylvia Beach and the Publication of *Ulysses*		Laura R. Barnes
Belk Department Stores	William Henry Belk	Patricia Noble Birch
Benson Pump, Patterson Labs, Acupack, Rooto Corp., Stone Mountain, Bildry, 7 Seas Spa	Dr. Joon Moon	John J-H Kim
Big Dog Sportswear	Andrew Feshbach	Chris Hemmeter, Jill Langley
Big Planet Adventure Outfitters	Pretlow Majette	Mark R. Hoffman, H. Benjamin Samuels
BlackRock Financial Management	Robert Kapito	Ralph Clark, Richard Gardiner, Mark Pincus

Company/Venture	Entrepreneur(s)	Author(s) of Paper
Blockbuster Video	Wayne Huizenga	Michael Johnston, Nicolas Van Dyk, Glenn Zweig
Bloomberg L.P.	Michael Bloomberg	Jonathan Halkyard, Raji Khabbaz
Bob the Chef's Restaurant	Darryl Settles	Gisele A. Marcus
The Bombay Company	Robert E. Nourse	Adrian Jones, Michael Feerick, Alessandro Bignami
The Boston Beer Company	Jim Koch	Susan Ehrlich
Boyle Leasing Technologies	Peter von Bleyleben	Stephen J. Picazio
Bright Horizons	Linda Mason and Roger Brown	Elizabeth Gehring, Holly Haseotes, Barbara Wall
Cablecasting Limited	James Meekison	Thomas Dea, Jennifer Gilbert
Cabletron Systems	Craig Benson, Robert Levine	Stephen Gallagher, John Grund
California Pizza Kitchen	Larry Flax, Rick Rosenfield	Lisa Jacobson
Calvin Klein, Inc.	Calvin Klein and Barry Schwartz	Bethel Gorin, Gretchen Wolfe, Dana Zucker
Calyx & Corolla	Ruth Owades	Christian Johnson
Carlson Plastics LBO	Alan Price, Sam Simmons (disguised names)	Timothy Byrne, Andrew Skoler
The Carson Group	Dave Geliebter	Steve Raab, B.G. Porter
The Celex Group	Mac Anderson	Darius Adamczyk, Dominic Ianno
Chappo & Co., Inc.	Richard J. Chappo	Stan Pomichter
Chattanooga Glass Company and Flow Components, Inc.	J. Reed Boles	Spencer M. Young, Joseph I. Dowling
CHF Capital Partners	Tim Howarad, Tyler Comann, Dan Flamen	Kim Davis, Christine Reiter, Joy Winterfield
Liz Claiborne, Inc.	Elisabeth Claiborne Ortenberg; Arthur Ortenberg, Leonard Boxer; Jerome Chazen	Eduardo Fernandez
Claims Services Resource Group	Dianne Patterson	Debra S. Graham
Clayton Homes	James Clayton	Vincent Keller, Steven Anderson
Clean Air Capital Markets	John Henry	Amy R. Ericson
Clemente Capital, Inc.	Lilia Calderon Clemente	Lynn Dinwiddie, May Ann Bravo
CML	Charles M. Leighton	Shawn W. Kravetz
Coffee Connection	George Howell	Adolfo Fastlicht, Mark Knakowski, Michael Lesser
Cognitive Systems	Dr. Roger Schank	Scott Lichtman
Colonial Drug	Botindari	Howard G. Sands
Company Assistance Ltd.	Steven Buckley, Jim Van Berg	Roma B. Kusznir
Compton's New Media	Norm Bastin	Michelle Yee
Computer Aided Decisions, Inc.	Milton C. Weiler, Jr., Charles A. Hunt	Michael Roy, Mohammed Khaishgi
Consolidated Management Group, Inc.	Robert Fayne, Willie Fry	Kimberly L. Robinson, Shari Schwartzman
Course Technology, Inc.	John M. Connolly	Andrew Baldwin, Jan De Witte, Eram Hasan
Cross Country Motor Club, Inc.	Sidney Wolk	Rob Adler
Cross River, Inc.	Deaver Brown	Bob Fogarty, Randy Fuller
CUC International	Walter A. Forbes	Diana Dowling
Da Vinci Systems	Bill Nussey	Laura Fortner, David Palmieri
The Daniel Mirror Company	Daniel C. Miller	Kristin Kamon Miller
David Chu and Nautica International, Inc.	David Chu	William Chen, Kathy Lee, Steven Lee
Defense Systems Inc.	Dr. George Sebestyen	Robert L. Acker
Dell Computer Corp.	Michael Dell	Karen Angelini, Arlene Ertel
Dent and Company, Inc.	Stephen Dent	Ravin Agrawal, Temitope Lawani, David N. Capobianco
The Detwiler Corporation	John Detwiler	James Kirby
DiVA Corporation	Jonathan Harber, Hans Peter Brondmo	Kevin Foreman
Doktor Pet Center	Les Charm	Alex Martin, Richard Lerner
Domain	Judy George	Constance Capone
Donovan Enterprises, Inc.	Michael Ciferra	Thomas Morgan, Jr., Lloyd Howell
Doyle Sailmakers, Inc.	Robbie Doyle	Stefan Eishold
Easel Corporation	Doug Kahn	Wendy Mogan, Joel Schwartz
The East Coast Grill and The Blue Room	Cary Wheaton	Ann Pao
Echo	Stacy Horn	Roxane Romero, Nyna Urovitch

Company/Venture	Entrepreneur(s)	Author(s) of Paper
Education Alternatives, Inc.	John Golle	Erik Gans, Mike Quilty, Russell Jolivet
Edusoft Publishing Co., Inc.	Robert Finnegan, Peter Kaplan	Andrew Baldwin, Jan De Witte, Eram Hasan
EMC² Corporation	Richard Egan, Roger Morino	Terence C. Bruyn, Clarence V. Wesley
Expansion Publishing Company	Harvey Popell	Pablo Payro
Fabric Frontline	Andre Stutz	Brenda Young
FiberSpar	Peter Quigley	Peter Latham, Kevin Moran, Ian McKerlich
Fininvest	Silvio Berlusconi	Mircea Caraman
First Health Care Associates	Shael Bellows	Laurence Schreiber
Fitigues	Andrea Levinson, Steve Rosenstein	Ellen Schlossberg
Flow Components	Read Boles	David Kotchen
Fluent, Inc.	Neil Ferris, David Nelson	Pamela J. Kostka
France Abonnements	Phillippe Vigneron	Nina Castro
Franklin Quest	Hyrum Smith	Mei-Mei Tuan, Signe Yock
Geerlings and Wade Personal Wine Importers, Inc.	Phillip D. Wade, Huib Geerlings	Alex Woods, Joonhee Won
Geffen Records	David Geffen	David Pullan
Gensym	Bob Moore	John C. Glover, Paul E. Obsitnik, Scott P. Sullivan
Glycomed	Brian Atwood	Douglas H. Post
Bill Goff, Inc.	Bill Goff	Stuart L. Hindle
Goods!	Sigmar Willnauer	Pamela Woo
Gordon's Books	Howard Bellowe	German Herrera, Felipe Holguin, Danie Roig
Graphics Express, Inc.	Rick Dyer, Skip Dyer, Joe Glove, Rick Theder	Don Aquilano, Tim Huckaby, Sean Thompson
Great Plains Supply, Inc.	Michael Wigley	Jessy Jahn
Haemonetics	Jack Latham, Gordon Kingsley	Steve Bernt, Paal Gisholt, Eric Smith
Harmony Castings	Don Weil	Jeff Huntley, Michael Spalter, Dan Stubbs
HBO Satellite Services, Inc.	Vinton Bauer, Larry Carlson	Kendra L. Egge
Health Payment Review, Inc.	Dr. Marcia Radosevich	Brian J. Mohan
Health Stop	Kenneth Hachikian	Harold E. Brakewood
Hear Music	Kevin Sheehan	Lisa Kolker, Lisa Roseff, Bruce Shalett
James T. Heard Management Corporation	Mrs. Lonear Heard-Davis	Kenneth Fearn, Gregg Gonsalves, Willie Woods
Hero Arts Rubber Stamps, Inc.	Jackie Levonthal	Clayton B. Earle
Tommy Hilfiger, Inc.	Tommy Hilfiger	David Ronick
Hi-Port Industries, Inc.	Jay H. Golding	Todd Klein
IA	Gerry Beemiller	Mary Callahan, Katharine Kelley, Tom Roupe
IDEAssociates	Gautam Gupta, David Hunter, David Page	Paul Brient
Indivers BV	Bert W. M. Twaalfhoven	Kakha Avaliani, Anatoli Kaminov
Intuit	Scott Cook	Scott Friend, Alisa Gordon
Investban	Ramiro Crespo	Loren Blackford, Mary Donovan
Ionics	Arthur Goldstein	Gary Mueller
The Irene Marie Modeling Agency	Irene Marie	Halsted Sullivan
I.R.S. Records	Jay Boberg	Elisabeth Bentel, Tori Hackett
ISD (Information Systems by Design)	Ron Watkins	Alexis Ceballos, Franz Heinsen
Kalinat, C.A.	Teymour Farman-Farmain	Carlos E. Erban, Francesca Fiore, Enrique Tabora
Keystone Corporation	Dan Bommer	Kerry Anne McLaughlin, John E. Zdanowski
K&H Corrugated Case Corp.	Kenneth J. Hanau, Jr.	Kenneth J. Hanau III
Anne Klein & Company; The Donna Karan Company	Frank Mori	Tina M. Goldberg
Leader Enterprises, Inc	Robert Fraley	D. J. Snell, Jr.
Learning Corp.	Stephen Kapelow	C. Denver Mullican
Learningsmith	Marshall Smith	Barry Hurewitz, Richard Fadil, Jed Smith
Leeds Publishers	Cole Jones	Jon Ein, Jamie Goldstein

Company/Venture	Entrepreneur(s)	Author(s) of Paper
The Liquidity Fund	Richard G. Wollack	Sheila J. Morrissey
Logicraft	Jim Bender	Thomas B. Gillis, W. Scott Weiss
MacTemps, Inc.	John Chuang	Andrea Bloom, Jeewon Park
J. Makowski Company, Inc.	Jacek Makowski	Stanley Nowak, Charles Heskett, Jonas Lee
Manco	Jack Kahl	William Downing, Ian Morris
Manufactural Electricas De Venezuela, C.A.	Darrell V. Zander	Douglas M. Cohen, Taylor J. O'Malley, Laura R. Zander
March Irrigation	Walter Wilkie	Marc Sanderson
Marketplace Information Corp.	Doug Borchard, Richard Lim	Dave O'Reilly, Drew Sawyer, Peter Troob, John Wang
Marquip	Richard Thomas	Nina S. Ebert
The Massachusetts Bay Brewing Company	Rich Doyle	Robert E. Lewis, John A. Murphy
MBO Laboratories, Inc.	Dr. William McCormick	Valerie Hausman
McCaw Cellular Corporation	Craig McCaw	Kevin McClelland
McCue Corporation	David McCue	Brad Volin, Carlos Contreras
Media Incorporated	Michael Kubin	April C. Valenzuela
Meitec Company	Fusaro Sekiguchi	Katsue Kawabata
The Men's Wearhouse	George Zimmer	Timothy D. Belton
Merlin Metalworks	Gwyn Jones	Garrick Ahn, Molly Albrinck, Jim Yang
Miramax Films	Bob and Harvey Weinstein	Mark Lieberman
Molten Metal Technology	Bill Haney	Bogie Miltchev, Alex Terry, Jeff Zindel
Mothers Work, Inc.	Rebecca Matthias	Kara Arnold
Motif Designs	Karl Friberg, Lyn Peterson	Caitlin Gagnon, Christine Roth
Multi-instructional Design Corp.	Wynn Setia, Dick Liman	Henny Purnamawati
Munchkin Bottling Company	Steven Dunn	Warren Adams
Natural World, Inc.	Austin Furst	Floriana Spezza, Stephanie Joe
The North Face	Kenneth Klopp	Mark Beder, Brad Kwong
NutraMax Products, Inc.	Donald Lepone	Jeff David
Old Fox, Inc.	Bernard V. Buonanno, Jr.	Bernie Buonanno III
Once Upon A Time Films	Stan Brooks	Jean Cameron, Dave Edward, Tomoko Hori
Oracle Corporation	Larry Ellison	Mathews Cherian, Courtney Crowley, Fadi Majdalani
OSCAR, Work Flow Process Management System	The McAteer Group	Richard A. Goulding
Otis Spunkmeyer, Inc.	Linda E. Rawlings	Susan Beth Raskin
Oxford Health Plans	Steve Wiggins	David Koenig, Angela Piscitello, Katherine Wold
Parametric Technologies	Steven C. Walske	Mark F. Caron, Nagi Rao
The Parthenon Group	Bill Achtmeyer, John Rutherford	Catherine Bohutinsky, Jeanine DeLoche
The Payne Firm	John Payne	Gerard du Toit, Lindsey Johnson, Efrain Torres
Pei Cobb Freed & Partners James Freed	I.M. Pei; Henry Cobb,	Sheila B. Ines, Carla S. Kapikian
Phoenix Controls	Jerry Schaufeld	David Diamond
PictureTel	Jeff Bernstein, Brian Hinman	Donna Regenbaum, Troy Stovall, Thierry Tanoh
Port, Sloanman & Baggs	Steve Port, Betsy Sloanman, John Baggs	Alex Agarwal
Powersoft	Mitchell Kertzman	Mark Adams, Nelson Chu, Kelly Huang
Private Satellite Networks, Inc.	Richard Neustadt	Brett A. Perlman
Prize Possessions	Sarah Foehl	Lisa S. Tanzer
Proex	Bruce Thomson	Suzanne M. Hull
Professional Sports Publications	Jarred Metze	Tony Hill, Travis Lewis, Alan Weisenfeld
Professional Support, Inc.	Michael A. Dougherty	Cynthia A. Weber
Progress Software	Joe Alsop	Doug Mankoff, Dwayne Rush, Nick Solomou
Public Allies	Vanessa Kirsch	Linda M. Carrigan
RailTex, Inc.	Bruce Flohr	Malek Ali, Benoit Duplat
Robohand, Inc.	Nicky Borcea, Alex Ionescu	Kate Burke

Company/Venture	Entrepreneur(s)	Author(s) of Paper
Rolling Stone	Jann Wenner	Pinny Chaviv, Andrew Hauptman
Rosalie's Restaurants	Rosalie Harrington	Melissa Kent, Amy Muntner
Rykodisc	Don Rose	Mark Wachen
S & S Leather Co.	Paul Segal	Debbie Rubenstein
Seatrans Ans	B. Kyrkjebo; H. Schodt; W. Hvide	Anders Hvide
Send Me No Flowers	Robin Steif	Todd Berkley, Mina Sooch
Sentex	Bill Davis, Rick Greenthal	Robert H. Tolleson, Jr.
Shocking Gray	Cindy Cesnalis	Veronica M. Diaz
Simonds Industries, Inc.	Chuck Doulton	Ted Henderson
Sonitrol	Dennis Hickey	Robert Friedman, Michael Gorman
Spin Magazine	Stephen Swid	Michael Karsch, David Wasserman
Staples, Inc.	Tom Stemberg	Nicolas Bernardi, Andrew Sun
Starbucks Coffee Company	Howard Schultz	Paige York
Starwood Capital Group	Barry Sternlicht	Robert Greenhill, Dennis Pemberton
Storey Communications	Martha, John Storey	Jack Phillips
Strategic Data Systems	Stuart Warrington	Bernabe F. Ibanez, Peter Sallick, Ronald C. Warrington
Symantec	Gorden E. Eubanks, Jr.	Sonja L. Hoel
Talent +	Bill Brandt, William Hall, Doug Wrath, Kimberly Rath	Tracy E. Kwiker, Dawn T. Clare
Teknekron Software Systems, Inc.	Vivek Ranadive	Carlton Byrd, Georgi Petrov, Stephen Semprevivo
TheraTx	Robert Gremore, Bret Jorgensen, Kip Hallman	Michele Browne, C. Scott Fellows, Alison Fried
Thermo Cardiosystems, Inc.	Vic Poirier	Yiannis Monovoukas, Stavros Theodoropoulos, Melissa Tolblert
Thinking Machines Corporation	Danny Hillis	Victor Vescovo
Threads 4 Life d/b/a/ Cross Colours	Carl Jones	Melvin A. Glapion, Jr.
Tic Toc	Larry Rogoff	Laura Bordevieck, Rick Brockmeier, Clara Wu
TLC (The Lewis Company)	Reginald Lewis	Keith Oren Burks, Stacye Monique Brown
Tole Americana	Bob Petkun	Andy Sack
Tweeds	Jeff Aschkenes and Ted Pamperin	Christina Love, Martin Coulter, Mauro Pretolani
TVT Records	Steve Gottlieb	Julie Kahn
UNC Partners	Ed Dugger III	Erik Hovanec, Cynthia Jeffers, Jeri Slavin
The United States Surgical Corporation	Leon C. Hirsch	Cameron Fleming, Kimberly Nearing, Erik Syring
The Vacation Outlet	Joel Bernard-Cutler, David Fialkow	Erik Statten
Vera Wang Bridal House and Made-to-Order Salon	Vera Wang	Kimmeron Lisle
Vertex Pharmaceuticals	Josh Boger, Rich Aldrich, Kevin Kinsella	Alec de Changy, Tom Daniel, Marc Erzberger
Vidal, Reynaradus & Moya	Jorge Reynardus	Elena C. Crespo, Sandy A. Mendez, Francine E. Starks
Viewlogic Systems	Alain Hanover	Gurinder Singh Kalra
Virgin Atlantic Airways	Richard Branson	Davor Gjivoje, John Schiavone
Wabash National	Jerry Ehrlich	Hamsa Shadaksharappa
Wacky Wallwalkers	Ken Hakuta	Jillian A. Marcus
Wal-Mart Stores	Sam Walton	Chris Lemley
Warren Equities, Inc.	Warren Alpert	John West, Trey Flautt
Wasserstein Perella & Company	Bruce Wasserstein; Joseph Perella; Bill Lambert; Charles Ward	Justin T. Chang
Witan Associates, Ltd.	Bernice Cramer	Fiona Pak-Poy, Kjartan Vonen Skaugvoll
The Women's Referral Service	Nancy Sardella	Maureen E. Brekka
WordPerfect Corporation	Alan Ashton	Jeffrey Singer, Robert Ciappanelli
Worldwide	Sir Yue-kong Pao	Harvey C. Lee
XPRESS$$ TAX	Lewis Weinstein	Thomas W. Carhart
Zschiesche GmbH	Jens Leistner; Torsten Schmidt, Ingrid Leistner; Marie-Louise Zschiesche	Jozef Barta, Steffen Leistner, Peter Pick, Christoph Zinke

Notes

Preface

1. Chandler (1990), 1.
2. Chandler (1990), 2.
3. Galbraith (1967), 1.
4. Schumpeter (1961), 134.
5. Chandler (1990), 3–4.
6. Galbraith (1967), 2.
7. Galbraith (1967), 2.
8. Knight (1921).
9. Schumpeter (1961), 132.
10. Baumol (1993), 6.
11. Rumelt (1982).
12. Tedlow, et al. (1992).
13. Stevenson (1983).
14. Orth (1963), 50–51
15. Birch (1979).
16. *The Standard Periodical Directory*, 20th ed., 1997 (1996).
17. Bronner (1998).
18. Baumol (1993), 13.
19. Thurston (1983), 235.
20. Dooley (1983), 223.
21. Bronner (1998).
22. List posted by Jerry Katz at the web site http://www.slu.edu/eweb/phdlist.htm.
23. Bhidé (1986).

Introduction

1. Baumol (1993), 7.
2. Baumol (1993), 2.
3. Baumol (1993), 12–13.
4. Baumol (1993), 14.
5. Say (1845), 287, cited in Baretto (1989), 11.
6. Kirzner (1973), 16.
7. Schumpeter (1939), 75, cited in Barreto (1989), 30.
8. Knight (1921).
9. Barreto (1989), 43.
10. Barreto (1989), 49.
11. Barreto (1989), 53.
12. Barreto (1989), 58.
13. Barreto (1989), 59.
14. Barreto (1989), 64.
15. Barreto (1989), 65.
16. Barreto (1989), 2.
17. Barreto (1989), 132–33.

18. Barreto (1989), 2.
19. See Scherer (1980), 145; Sutton (1996), 3.
20. Gourman (1997).
21. Baumol (1993), 15.
22. Baumol (1993), 3.
23. Fisher (1989), 118
24. Fisher (1989), 117.
25. Fisher (1989), 118.
26. Baumol (1993), 117.
27. Baumol (1993), 114.
28. Baumol (1993), 282.
29. Packard (1996), 42
30. See Case (1995) for a full discussion of the studies and data summarized in this paragraph.
31. Erikson, E.H. (1969).
32. Bhidé, A. (1996), "The Road Well-Traveled."
33. Elster (1993)

Part I: The Nature of Promising Start-ups

1. Camerer (1995), 644

Chapter 1: Endowments and Opportunities

1. Friedman (1997), 108.
2. I have adapted this figure from Ghemawat (1991), 130.
3. Case (1989), 51
4. Bhidé (1995), paper by Jeffrey Singer and Robert Ciappenelli, 454.
5. Cringely (1996), 9.
6. Bhidé (1995), paper by Andrew Hauptman and Pinny Chaviv, 142.
7. Case (1989).
8. "Almanac" (1996), compiled by *Inc.* staff, 22 (*Inc.* Special Issue 1996)
9. See Hubbard (1998) for an overview.
10. Chandler (1962), 118.
11. U.S. Department of Commerce (1998), 4.
12. Bhidé (1995), "Bob Reiss and Val-dawn."
13. Bhidé (1995), paper by Andrew Hauptman and Pinny Chaviv, 141–53.
14. Sabini and Silver (1982).

Chapter 2: Planning vs. Opportunistic Adaptation

1. Wallace and Erickson (1993), 67.
2. Gates (1996), 18.
3. Case (1989), 51.
4. Lovallo and Camerer (1996), 2.
5. Lovallo and Camerer (1996), 1.
6. These inferences about the greater propensity of experts to be overconfident represent my interpretation of Lovallo and Camerer's experiments. Lovallo and Camerer's own discussion stresses other inferences.
7. Main (1990), 120.
8. Wallace and Erickson (1993), 74.
9. Elster (1993), 51.
10. Elster (1993), 71.
11. Elster (1993), 51.
12. Elster (1993), 71.
13. Elster (1993), 5.

Chapter 3: Securing Resources

1. Einhorn and Hogarth as cited in Bell, Raiffa, and Tversky (1988), 114.
2. Stovic, Fischoff, and Lichtenstein, as cited in Bell, Raiffa, and Tversky (1988), 152.
3. Thaler (1980).
4. Camerer (1995).
5. Cialdini (1993), 6.
6. Cialdini (1993), 96.
7. Cialdini (1993), 94.
8. Cialdini (1993), 12.
9. Packard (1996), 42.
10. Cialdini (1993), 61–62.

Chapter 4: Distinctive Qualities

1. Hornaday (1982), 26–27.
2. Shaver and Scott (1991), 25.
3. Brockhaus and Horwitz (1986), 30.
4. Brockhaus (1982).
5. Miner, Smith, and Bracker (1992) discuss the work of Smith and other research on entrepreneurial "types."
6. Vesper (1980), *New Venture Strategies*, cited in Hornaday (1982), 26.
7. Hornaday (1982), 26–27.
8. Wallace and Erickson (1993), 19.
9. Wallace and Erickson (1993), 21.
10. T. Jackson, *The Virgin King: Inside Richard Branson's Business Empire* (New York: Harper Collins, 1994), p. 65, cited in paper by Davor Gjivoje, Jr., and John Thomas Schiavone in Bhidé (1995), 127.
11. Bhidé (1990a).
12. Camerer (1995), 644–47.
13. Ellsberg (1961), cited in Camerer (1995).
14. Becker and Brownson (1964), cited in Camerer (1995).
15. Slovic and Tversky (1974), cited in Camerer (1995).
16. Curley and Yates (1985), cited in Camerer (1995).
17. Curley, Yates, and Abrams (1986), cited in Camerer (1995).
18. Cohen, Jaffray, and Said (1985), Hogarth and Einhorn (1990), cited in Camerer (1995).
19. Camerer (1995), 646.
20. Heath and Tversky (1991), cited in Camerer (1995).
21. The *Concise Oxford Dictionary* defines a decisive person as one who decides quickly and effectively.
22. Russo and Schoemaker (1989), 121–22.
23. Russo and Schoemaker (1989), 179.
24. Russo and Schoemaker (1989), 183.
25. Cringley (1996), 128–29.
26. Thaler (1996).
27. Wallace and Erickson (1993), 64.
28. Bhidé (1996), "The Road Well-Traveled," 13.
29. Wallace and Erickson (1993), 66.
30. Wallace and Erickson (1993), 66.

Chapter 5: Corporate Initiatives

1. Jensen (1993), 856–857.
2. Berle and Means (1932).
3. Clark (1985).
4. Fama and Jensen (1983).
5. Heath, Larrick, and Klayman (1998).
6. Fama and Jensen (1983), 107.
7. See Acs and Audretsch (1991), 42–43, for a review of the evidence.
8. Moore (1996), 169.
9. Moore (1996), 170.
10. Moore (1996), 168.
11. Moore (1996), 171.
12. Moore (1996), 170.
13. Nichols (1994), 107.
14. Pearson (1988), 106.
15. "Post-it: How a Maverick Got His Way." 1993. *Marketing* 31 (October 28).
16. Pearson (1988), 99–100.
17. Pearson (1988), 102–3.
18. Nichols (1994), 107.
19. Nichols (1994), 107–8.
20. Peters and Peters (1996).
21. Ogilvy (1980), 86, cited in Peters and Waterman (1982), 138.
22. "Post-It Notes Click Thanks to Entrepreneurial Spirit." 1984. *Marketing News* 18 (18): 21–23.
23. "Post-it: How a Maverick Got His Way." 1993. *Marketing* 31 (October 28).
24. "Post-It Notes Click Thanks to Entrepreneurial Spirit." 1984. *Marketing News* 18 (18): 21–23.
25. Rodgers (1993), 105.

26. Rodgers (1990), 88–89.
27. Argyris (1967), 34–40, cited in Peters and Waterman (1982), 49.
28. Pearson (1988), 103.
29. Nichols (1994), 105.
30. Moore (1996), 168.
31. Moore (1996), 169.
32. Peters and Waterman (1982), 136.
33. Bartlett and Mohammed (1995), 2.
34. Bartlett and Mohammed (1995), 12.
35. Bartlett and Mohammed (1995), 12.
36. Bartlett and Mohammed (1995), 12.
37. Christensen (1997), 135.
38. *Wall Street Journal* (November 5, 1997), A11.

Chapter 6: VC-Backed Start-ups

1. Bhidé (1993b), 31–51.
2. See Gompers and Lerner (1996) for a discussion of venture partnership agreements.
3. Sahlman (1990b), 508.
4. Lerner (1995).
5. Interview in *Harvard Business School Bulletin* (December 1997), 43.
6. Information in this paragraph taken from "Lotus Development Corporation," Harvard Business School Case No. 9–285–094.
7. Merrill and Nichols (1990), xiv.
8. Merrill and Nichols (1990), xxi.
9. Merrill and Nichols (1990), xix.
10. *Venture Capital Journal* (February 1995), 45. The table covers IPOs from 1984 to 1994.
11. Megginson and Weiss (1991), 886. The data in the paper covered 390 VC-backed IPOs from January 1983 through September 1987 with offering amounts of more than $3 million and offer prices of at least $5.
12. Sahlman (1990b), 482.
13. Gompers and Lerner (1999), chapt. 6.
14. Roberts and Walton (1987), 13.
15. Roberts and Walton (1987), 1.
16. Fenn, Liang, and Prowse (1995), 7.
17. Fenn, Liang, and Prowse (1995), 9.
18. Fenn, Liang, and Prowse (1995), 11–12.
19. Liles (1977), 83, cited in Fenn, Liang, and Prowse (1995), 7.
20. Gompers and Lerner (1999).
21. Sahlman and Stevenson (1985).
22. Fenn, Liang, and Prowse (1995), 2.
23. Fenn, Liang, and Prowse (1995), 19.

Chapter 7: Revolutionary Ventures

1. Shields (1986), 287.
2. Sigafoos (1983), 26.
3. Sigafoos (1983), 27.
4. Sigafoos (1983), 29.
5. Sigafoos (1983), 29.
6. Sigafoos (1983), 32.
7. Sigafoos (1983), 31.
8. Sigafoos (1983), 32.
9. Sigafoos (1983), 37.
10. Sigafoos (1983), 37.
11. Sigafoos (1983), 37.
12. Sigafoos (1983), 38.
13. Sigafoos (1983), 39.
14. Sigafoos (1983), 40.
15. Sigafoos (1983), 41.
16. Sigafoos (1983), 41.
17. Sigafoos (1983), 42.
18. Sigafoos (1983), 44.
19. Sigafoos (1983), 44.
20. Sigafoos (1983), 49.
21. Sigafoos (1983), 52.
22. Sigafoos (1983), 184.
23. Sigafoos (1983), 24.
24. Sigafoos (1983), 42.
25. Sigafoos (1983), 53.
26. Sigafoos (1983), 53.
27. Sigafoos (1983), 55.
28. Sigafoos (1983), 58.
29. Sigafoos (1983), 46.
30. Sigafoos (1983), 56.
31. Sigafoos (1983), 57.
32. Sigafoos (1983), 59.
33. Sigafoos (1983), 60.
34. Sigafoos (1983), 61.
35. Sigafoos (1983), 62.
36. Sigafoos (1983), 64.
37. Sigafoos (1983), 49–50.
38. Sigafoos (1983), 64.
39. Sigafoos (1983), 65.
40. Sigafoos (1983), 64.
41. Sigafoos (1983), 67.
42. Sigafoos (1983), 67.
43. Sigafoos (1983), 68.
44. Sigafoos (1983), 69.
45. Sigafoos (1983), 73.
46. Sigafoos (1983), 70.
47. Sigafoos (1983), 70.
48. Sigafoos (1983), 76.
49. Sigafoos (1983), 77.
50. Sigafoos (1983), 60.
51. Sigafoos (1983), 60.
52. Sigafoos (1983), 128.
53. Sigafoos (1983), 78.
54. Sigafoos (1983), 78.
55. Sigafoos (1983), 79.
56. Sigafoos (1983), 80.
57. Sigafoos (1983), 79.
58. Sigafoos (1983), 81.
59. Sigafoos (1983), 83.
60. Sigafoos (1983), 84.
61. Sigafoos (1983), 83.
62. Sigafoos (1983), 84.
63. Sigafoos (1983), 85.
64. Sigafoos (1983), 86.
65. Sigafoos (1983), 84.
66. Sigafoos (1983), 89.

67. Sigafoos (1983), 105.
68. Sigafoos (1983), 92.
69. Sigafoos (1983), 93.
70. Sigafoos (1983), 83.
71. Kinkead (1981), 102.
72. Kinkead (1981), 103.
73. Shields (1986), 2.
74. Shields (1986), 49.
75. Shields (1986), 150.
76. Shields (1986), 154–76.
77. Shields (1986), 194.
78. Shields (1986), 290.
79. Shields (1986), 290.
80. Shields (1986), 294.
81. Shields (1986), 296.
82. Kinkead (1981), 105.
83. Kinkead (1981), 103.
84. Kinkead (1981), 105.
85. Kinkead (1981), 105.
86. Kinkead (1981), 106.
87. Kinkead (1981), 106.
88. Kinkead (1981), 106.
89. Kinkead (1981), 107.
90. Shields (1986), 315.
91. Shields (1986), 312.
92. Shields (1986), 321.
93. Shields (1986), 325.
94. Shields (1986), 326.
95. Shields (1986), 326.
96. Shields (1986), 327.
97. Kinkead (1981), 110.
98. Kinkead (1981), 103.
99. Kinkead (1981), 110.
100. Shields (1986), 329.
101. Shields (1986), 331.
102. Hardy (1996).
103. Hardy (1996).
104. *Fortune* (March 11, 1991), 100.
105. Kirzner (1998), 2.
106. Loasby (1989), 17.

Part II: The Evolution of Fledgling Businesses

1. Case (1995), 24.
2. Mangelsdorf (1996), 84.

Chapter 9: Missing Attributes

1. Penrose (1959), 22.
2. Packard (1996), 46.
3. Christensen (1997), xvii.
4. Christensen (1997), xv.
5. Dixit and Pindyck (1994).
6. Watson and Petre (1990), 2.
7. Nee (1998), 54.
8. I have discussed the advantages and disadvantages of corporate diversification more fully in "Reversing Corporate Diversification," Bhidé (1990b).
9. Williamson (1975), 104.
10. Granovetter (1985), 68.
11. Granovetter (1985), 69, quoting Dalton, 32.
12. Granovetter (1985), 72.
13. Chandler (1962), 16.
14. Chandler (1962), 44.
15. Chandler (1962), 46.
16. McCraw and Tedlow (1997), 285.
17. Chandler (1962), 152.
18. Chandler (1962), 151.
19. Chandler and Salsbury (1971), 573, 580.
20. Packard (1996), 141.
21. Packard (1996), 81.
22. Rubin (1973), 939.
23. Packard (1996), 141.
24. Packard (1996), 52.
25. Kelly (1998), 26.
26. Packard (1996) 48.

Chapter 10: Existing Theories and Models

1. Henderson (1994).
2. Polyani (1964), 52, cited in Nelson and Winter (1982), 119.
3. Ip (1998), C1.
4. Case (1989), 51.
5. Walton (1993), 68.
6. Walton (1993), 67.
7. Walton (1993), 80.
8. Author's *Inc.* 500 company interviews.
9. Penrose (1959).
10. Jovanovic and MacDonald (1994), 346.
11. Jovanovic and MacDonald (1994), 322.
12. Jovanovic and MacDonald (1994), 326.
13. Churchill and Lewis (1983), 12.
14. Churchill and Lewis (1983) 9.
15. McCraw and Tedlow (1997), 285–87.
16. I am indebted to Bruce Scott for this observation.
17. Walton (1993), 140.
18. Walton (1993), 144.
19. Bhidé (1993a), 8.
20. Walton (1993), 318–19.
21. Zaleznik (1989), 61.
22. Nelson and Winter (1982), 128.
23. Nelson and Winter (1982), 134.
24. Elster (1993), 139, 147.
25. Nelson and Winter (1982), 136.
26. Nelson and Winter (1978), 524.
27. Nelson and Winter (1982), 97.
28. Penrose (1959), 8.
29. Penrose (1959), 33.
30. Packard (1996), 46.
31. Olegario (1997), 356.
32. Chandler (1990), 9.
33. Chandler (1990), 11.
34. Nelson and Winter (1982), 133.

35. Bhidé (1992b), 4.
36. Bhidé (1992b), 13.
37. Andrews (1980), 28.
38. Ghemawat (1997), 12.
39. Quinn (1980), 14.
40. Quinn (1980), 52.
41. Selznick (1957), 36.
42. See Mintzberg (1973), "Strategy Making in Three Modes."
43. Andrews (1980), 26.
44. Andrews (1980), 25.

Chapter 11: Critical Tasks

1. Kelly (1998), 60–61.
2. Bhidé (1989a), 10.
3. Bhidé (1989), 5.
4. Bhidé (1989), 16.
5. Bartlett and Ghoshal (1994), 84.
6. Packard (1996), 24.
7. Packard (1996), 40.
8. Murphy (1995), 77.
9. Case (1989), 51.
10. Bhidé (1992b), 9.
11. Bartlett and Ghoshal (1994), 85.
12. As of November 24, 1998.
13. Olegario (1997), 356.
14. Olegario (1997), 357.
15. Olegario (1997), 358.
16. Olegario (1997), 359.
17. Olegario (1997), 360.
18. Watson and Petre (1990), 218.
19. Packard (1996), 61.
20. Packard (1996), 128.
21. Packard (1996), 132.
22. Pelline (1996).
23. Packard (1996), 139.
24. Packard (1996), 76.
25. Packard (1996), 139.
26. Packard (1996), 77.
27. Packard (1996), 140.
28. Packard (1996), 80.
29. Packard (1996), 141–42.
30. Packard (1996), 142–43.
31. Walton (1993), 265.
32. Walton (1993), 111.
33. Interview in *Forbes* (August 10, 1987).
34. Walton (1993), 65–66.
35. Walton (1993), 107.
36. Walton (1993), 117.
37. Walton (1993), 163.
38. Walton (1993), 165.
39. Bhidé (1992b), 12.
40. Walton (1993), 38–39.
41. Caves (1980), 88.
42. Kreps (1990), 91.
43. Henderson (1994), 607
44. *Consultants News*, June 1998, 9.
45. Porter (1980), 368.
46. Porter (1980), 369.
47. Hamel and Prahalad (1994), 55.

48. Walton (1993), 81.
49. Walton (1993), 62.
50. Adler (1993), discusses the issue of transplanting manufacturing pratices. Adler (1999), discusses human relations practices.
51. Wallace and Erickson (1993), 163.
52. Pitta (1992).
53. Khanna (1997).
54. Nakache (1997), 275.
55. Bhidé (1989), "Vinod Khosla and Sun Microsystems (A)," 12–13.
56. Bhidé (1989), "Vinod Khosla and Sun Microsystems (C)," 1.
57. Pitta (1992).
58. Schein (1985), 225.
59. Walton (1993), 201.

Chapter 12: Exceptional Qualities

1. Cited in Elster (1993), 116.
2. Penrose (1959), 35.
3. Walton (1993), 101–2.
4. Walton (1993), 104.
5. Walton (1993), 319.
6. Walton (1993), 101–2.
7. Walton (1993), 241–42.
8. Kelly (1998), 58.
9. Walton (1993), 56.
10. Walton (1993), 248.
11. Walton (1993), 243.
12. Kelly (1998), 26.
13. Kelly (1998), 31.
14. Walton (1993), 141.
15. Walton (1993), 140.
16. Walton (1993), 142.
17. Packard (1996), 61.
18. Kelly (1998), 115.
19. Simon (1976).
20. Brokaw (1993), 56.
21. Walton (1993), 117.
22. Mangelsdorf (1996), 84.
23. Pelline (1996), B1.
24. Scherer (1980), 145.
25. Scherer (1980), 72.
26. Sutton (1996), 3.
27. Chandler (1990), 18.
28. Chandler (1990), 20.
29. Chandler (1990), 22–23.
30. Chandler (1990), 22.
31. McCraw (1997), 324.
32. Sutton (1996), 25.
33. Cited in Elster (1993), 121.
34. McCraw and Tedlow (1997), 275.
35. McCraw and Tedlow (1997), 273.
36. McCraw and Tedlow (1997), 272.
37. McCraw and Tedlow (1997), 288.
38. *Automotive News 1998 Market Data Book.*
39. Lewis (1976), 160–61.
40. von Hippel (1988).
41. Unpublished paper by Mark Casey.

Part III: Societal Implications

1. Stiglitz (1990), 53.
2. Solow (1957), 320.
3. Stiglitz (1990), 53.
4. Baumol (1993), 4.

Chapter 13: Reexamining Schumpeter

1. Elster (1993), 118–19, 247.
2. Rosenberg (1976), 66.
3. Acs and Audretsch (1991), 39–40.
4. Scherer (1988), 4–5, cited in Acs and Audretsch (1991), 40.
5. Arrow (1982).
6. Scherer (1982), 234–235, cited in Acs and Audretsch (1991), 42.
7. Scherer (1983), 115–116, cited in Acs and Audretsch (1991), 43.
8. Winter (1984), 267.
9. Acs and Audretsch (1991), 59.
10. Steffens (1994), 197.
11. Steffens (1994), 179–81.
12. Steffens (1994), 197.
13. Estimates supplied by Joanne Guiniven, electronics consultant, McKinsey & Co.
14. Moore (1996), 166.
15. Correspondence with Joanne Guiniven, electronics consultant, McKinsey & Co.
16. The discussion on sub-contracting draws on and extends an unpublished working paper by Bhidé and Stevenson (1988).
17. Schumpeter (1934), 64, note 1 cited in Elster (1993), 114.
18. Schumpeter (1939), 85, cited in Rosenberg (1976), 67.
19. Schumpeter (1934), 88, cited in Baumol (1993), 6.
20. Schumpeter (1944), 10, cited in Rosenberg (1976), 67.
21. Rosenberg (1976), 77.
22. Rosenberg (1976), 67.
23. Rosenberg (1976), 71.
24. Rosenberg (1976), 71.
25. Rosenberg (1976), 72–73.
26. Rosenberg (1976), 67.
27. Rosenberg (1976), 75.
28. Rosenberg (1976), 75–76.
29. Schumpeter (1961), 81, 83–84.
30. Jensen (1993), 833.
31. McCraw and Tedlow (1997), 267–68.
32. U.S. Department of Commerce, Bureau of the Census (1975), 716.

33. Cringely (1996), 125–26.
34. U.S. Department of Commerce (1998), 4.
35. U.S. Department of Commerce (1998), 6.
36. U.S. Department of Commerce (1998), 6.
37. Petroski (1990).
38. Kirchoff and Phillips (1989).
39. Flint (1998).
40. Jensen (1993), 838.
41. Jensen (1993), 835.
42. Jensen (1993), 841.
43. Jensen (1993), 841.
44. Bartlett and Ghoshal (1993), cited in Nohria (1996), 22.
45. Caves and Kreps (1993), cited in Nohria (1996), 22.

Chapter 14: Facilitating Conditions

1. Acs and Audretsch (1990), 15.
2. Arrow (1972).
3. Fukuyama (1995).
4. Akerlof (1970).
5. Axelrod (1984), 178.
6. "Management by Necessity," *Inc.* (March 1989): 33.
7. McCraw (1997), 316.
8. Acs and Audretsch (1990), 4–5.
9. Acs, Audretsch, and Carlsson (1990), 141–42.
10. Scherer (1980), 98.
11. Sahlman (1990a).
12. Copeland and Weston (1979), cited in Nohria (1996), 10.
13. Chandler (1990).
14. Nohria (1996), 16.
15. Brokaw (1993).
16. McCraw (1997), 327.
17. McCraw (1997), 330.
18. Braudel (1986), 586–89.
19. Bhidé and Stevenson (1990).
20. Florida (1994), 58.
21. Jensen (1993), 858.

Conclusion

1. Goldberg (1976).
2. Zingales (1997).
3. Donna Coch (1997) provides a good lay overview of Fischer's work.
4. Schumpeter (1939), 44.
5. Fisher (1989), 119.
6. Sutton (1996), 324.

References

Books and Articles

Acs, Z. J., and D. B. Audretsch. 1990. *The Economics of Small Firms: A European Challenge.* Dodrecht, Netherlands: Kluwer Academic Publishers.

———. 1991. *Innovation and Small Firms.* Cambridge, Mass.: The MIT Press.

Acs, Z. J., D. B. Audretsch, and B. Carlsson. 1990. "Flexibility, Plant Size and Industrial Restructuring." In Z. J. Acs and D. B. Audretsch, eds., *The Economics of Small Firms: A European Challenge.* Dodrecht, Netherlands: Kluwer Academic Publishers.

Adler, P. S. 1993. "The Learning Bureaucracy: New United Motors Manufacturing, Inc." In Barry M. Staw and Larry L. Cummings, eds., *Research in Organizational Behavior* 15: 111–94, Greenwich, Conn.: JAI Press.

———. 1999. "Hybridization of Human Resource Management at Two Toyota Transplants," In J. Liker, M. Fruin, and P. S. Adler, eds., *Remade in America: Transplanting and Transforming Japanese Management Systems.* New York: Oxford University Press.

Akerlof, G. 1970. "The Market for 'Lemons': Qualititive Uncertainty and the Market Mechanism." *Quarterly Journal of Economics* 84: 488–500.

Alchian, A. A., and H. Demsetz. 1972. "Production, Information Costs, and Economic Organization." *American Economic Review* 62 (December): 777–95.

Alter, M., and A. Bhidé. 1994. *Selling as a Systematic Process.* Harvard Business School Note No. 395–091. Boston: Harvard Business School Press.

Andrews, K. R. 1980. *The Concept of Corporate Strategy*, Homewood, Ill.: Richard D. Irwin.

Argyris, C. 1967. 'Today's Problems with Tomorrow's Organizations." *Journal of Management Studies* February: 34–40.

———. 1990. *Overcoming Organizational Defenses.* Needham Heights, Mass.: Allyn & Bacon, 12–44, 67–117.

Arrow, K. J. 1972. "Gift and Exchanges." *Philosophy and Public Affairs*: 1, 3, 242–362.

———. 1974. *The Limits of Organization.* New York: W. W. Norton.

———. 1982. "Innovation in Large and Small Firms." In. J. Ronen, ed., *Entrepreneurship.* Lexington, Mass.: Lexington Books.

Axelrod, R. 1984. *The Evolution of Cooperation.* New York: Basic Books.

Barnard, C. I. 1968. *The Functions of the Executive.* Cambridge, Mass.: Harvard University Press.

Barreto, H. 1989. *The Entrepreneur in Microeconomic Theory.* London and New York: Routledge.

Bartlett, C. A., and S. Ghoshal. 1993. "Beyond the M-form: Toward a Managerial Theory of the Firm." *Strategic Management Journal* 14 (Winter: 23–46).

———. 1994. "Changing the Role of Top Management: Beyond Strategy to Purpose." *Harvard Business Review* (November-December 1994): 79–88, repr. 94601.

Bartlett, C. A., and A. Mohammed. 1995. *3M: Profile of an Innovating Company.* Harvard Business School Case No. 395–016. Boston: Harvard Business School Press.

Baumol, W. J. 1993. *Entrepreneurship, Management and the Structure of Payoffs*, Cambridge, Mass.: MIT Press.

Becker, S. W., and F. O. Brownson. 1964. "What Price Ambiguity? Or the Role of Ambiguity in Decision-making." *Journal of Political Economy* 72: 62–73.

Begley, T. M., and D. Boyd. 1987. "Psychological Characteristics Associated with Performance in Entrepreneurial Firms and Smaller Businesses." *Journal of Business Venturing* 2: 79–93.

Bell, D. E., H. Raiffa, and A. Tversky, eds. 1988. *Decision-making: Descriptive, Normative, and Prescriptive Interactions.* Cambridge, Eng.: Cambridge University Press.

Berle, A., and G. Means. 1932. *The Modern Corporation and Private Property.* New York: Macmillan.

Bhidé, A. 1986. "Hustle as Strategy." *Harvard Business Review* 64 (5): 59–65.

———. 1989. "Vinod Khosla and Sun Microsystems (A)." Harvard Business School Case No. 390–049. Boston: Harvard Business School Press.

———. 1990a. "The DAG Group," with V. Rayzman and C. J. Hackett. Harvard Business School Case No. 392–077. Boston: Harvard Business School Press.

———. 1990b. "Reversing Corporate Diversification." *Journal of Applied Corporate Finance* 3 (2): 70–81.

———. 1992a. "Bootstrap Finance: The Art of Start-ups." *Harvard Business Review* 70 (66): 109–17, repr. 92601.

———. 1992b. "McKinsey & Co. (A): 1956." Harvard Business School Case No. 393–066. Boston: Harvard Business School Press.

———. 1993a. "McKinsey & Co. (B): 1966." Harvard Business School Case No. 393–067. Boston: Harvard Business School Press.

———. 1993b. "The Hidden Costs of Stock Market Liquidity." *Journal of Financial Economics* 34: 31–51.

———. 1994a. "How Entrepreneurs Craft Strategies That Work." *Harvard Business Review* 72 (2): 150–61.

———. 1995. "Tales from Successful Entrepreneurs." Harvard Business School Case No. 396–050. Boston: Harvard Business School Press.

———. 1996a. "The Road Well Traveled." Harvard Business School Case No. 396–277. Boston: Harvard Business School Press.

———. 1996b. "The Questions Every Entrepreneur Must Answer." *Harvard Business Review* 74 (6): 120–30.

———. 1996c. "Building the Professional Firm: McKinsey & Co.: 1939–1968." Working Paper 95–010, Harvard Business School.

Bhidé, A., and H. Stevenson. 1988. "Employment vs. Subcontracting: The Real Trade-offs." Working Paper 88–046, Harvard Business School.

———. 1990. "Why Be Honest if Honesty Doesn't Pay." *Harvard Business Review* (September–October): 121–29.

———. 1992. "Trust, Uncertainty, and Profit." *Journal of Socioeconomics* 21 (3): 191–208.

Birch, D. L. 1979. *The Job Generation Process.* Cambridge, Mass.: MIT Program on Neighborhood and Regional Change 8.

Blundy, D. 1976. "After Getty, Who Is the World's Richest Man?" *Sunday Times* (London), June 13.

Braudel, F. 1986. *The Wheels of Commerce.* New York: Harper and Row.

Brockhaus, R. H. 1982. "The Psychology of the Entrepreneur." In C. A. Kent, D. L. Sexton, and K. H. Vesper, eds., *Encyclopedia of Entrepreneurship.* Englewood Cliffs, N.J.: Prentice-Hall, 39–57.

Brockhaus, R. H., and P. Horwitz. 1986. "The Psychology of the Entrepreneur." In D. L. Sexton and R. Smilor, eds., *The Art and Science of Entrepreneurship.* Cambridge, Mass.: Ballinger, 25–48.

Brokaw, L. 1993. "The Truth About Start-ups." *Inc.* magazine (March): 56.

Bronner, E. 1998. "Students at B-Schools Flock to the E-Courses." *New York Times*, special supplement on entrepreneurship (September 23).

Camerer, C. 1995. "Individual Decision-making." In J. H. Kagel and A. E. Roth, eds., *The Handbook of Experimental Economics*. Princeton, N.J.: Princeton University Press: 588–703.

Carr, E. H. 1961. *What Is History*. New York: Random House, 3–69.

Case, J. 1989. "The Origins of Entrepreneurship." *Inc.* magazine (June): 51.

———. 1995. "The Wonderland Economy." *State of Small Business 1995*, *Inc.* magazine (special issue): 14–29.

Caves, R. E. 1980. "Industrial Organization, Corporate Strategy and Structure." *Journal of Economic Literature* 5 (18): 64–92.

Caves, R. E., and M. B. Kreps. 1993. "Fat: The Displacement of Nonproduction Workers from U.S. Manufacturing Industries." *Brookings Papers: Microeconomics* 2: 227–88.

Chandler, A. D., Jr. 1962. *Strategy and Structure*. Cambridge: The MIT Press.

———. 1977. *The Visible Hand: The Managerial Revolution in American Business*. Cambridge, Mass.: Harvard University Press.

———. 1990. *Scale and Scope: The Dynamics of Industrial Capitalism*. Cambridge, Mass.: Belknap Press.

Chandler, A. D., Jr., and S. Salsbury. 1971. *Pierre S. DuPont and the Making of the Modern Corporation*. New York: Harper and Row.

Christensen, C. M. 1997. *The Innovator's Dilemma: When New Technologies Cause Great Firms to Fail*. Boston: The Harvard Business School Press.

Churchill, N. C., and V. L. Lewis. 1983. "The Five Stages of Small Business Growth." *Harvard Business Review*, repr. 83301.

Cialdini, R. B. 1993. *Influence: Science and Practice*, 3rd ed. New York: HarperCollins.

Clark, R. 1985. *Principals and Agents: The Structure of Business*. Boston: Harvard Business School Press.

Coase, R. H. 1937. "The Nature of the Firm." In O. E. Williamson and S. G. Winter, eds., *The Nature of the Firm*. New York: Oxford University Press.

Coch, D. 1997. "Order in the Chaos." *Harvard University Gazette* (July 3): 3.

Cohen, M., J-Y. Jaffray, and T. Said. 1985. "Individual Behavior under Risk and under Uncertainty: An Experimental Study." *Theory and Decision* 5 (18): 203–28.

Cringely, R. X. 1996. *Accidental Empires*. New York: HarperCollins.

Curley, S. P., and J. F. Yates. 1985. "The Center and Range of the Probability Interval as Factors Affecting Ambiguity Preferences." *Organizational Behavior and Human Decision Processes* 5 (36): 272–87.

Curley, S. P., J. F. Yates, and R. A. Abrams. 1986. "Psychological Sources of Ambiguity Avoidance." *Organizational Behavior and Human Decision Processes* 5 (38): 397–427.

Dasgupta, P. 1988. "Trust as a Commodity," In D. Gambetta, ed., *Trust: Making and Breaking Cooperative Relationships*. New York: Basil Blackwell.

Delbridge, R. 1998. *Life on the Line in Contemporary Manufacturing*. Oxford: Oxford University Press.

Dixit, A., and R. Pindyck. 1994. "Investment under Uncertainty." Princeton, N.J.: Princeton University Press.

Dooley, A. 1983. "The Explosion of Interest in Entrepreneurship: Concern in the Midst of Celebration," in J. J. Kao and Howard H. Stevenson, eds. *Entrepreneurship: What It Is and How to Teach It*. Boston: Harvard Business School.

Economist. 1997. "Conglomerates on Trial" (April 5): 59.

Einhorn, H. J., and R. M. Hogarth. 1988. "Behavioral Decision Theory: Processes of Judgment and Choice." In D. E. Bell, H. Raiffa, and A. Tversky, eds., *Decision-making: Descriptive, Normative, and Prescriptive Interactions*. Cambridge, Eng.: Cambridge University Press.

Ellsberg, D. 1961. "Risk, Ambiguity, and the Savage Axioms." *Quarterly Journal of Economics* 5 (75): 643–9.

Elster, J. 1993. *Explaining Technical Change*. Cambridge, Eng.: Cambridge University Press.

Erikson, E. H. 1969. *Gandhi's Truth*. New York: Norton.

Fama, E. F., and M. C. Jensen. 1983. "Separation of Ownership and Control." *Journal of Law and Economics* 26 (June): 301–25.

———. 1985. "Organizational Forms and Investment Decisions." *Journal of Financial Economics*, 14: 101–119.

Fastlich, A., M. Knakowski, and M. Lesser. 1993. "The Coffee Connection." Unpublished paper.

Fenn, G. W., N. Liang, and S. Prowse. 1995. "The Economics of the Private Equity Market," Board of Governors of the Federal Reserve System. Washington, D.C.

Fisher, F. M. 1989. "Games Economists Play: A Noncooperative View." *RAND Journal of Economics* 20 (1): 113–23.

Flint, J. 1998. "Was This Strike Really Necessary?" *Forbes* (July 27): 64.

Florida, R. 1994. "Keep Government out of Venture Capital." In C. Beltz, ed., *Financing Entrepreneurs*. Washington, D.C.: AEI Press.

Friedman, A. 1997. "The New Economy Almanac." *State of Small Business 1997, Inc.* magazine (special issue): 108.

Fukuyama, F. 1995. *Trust: The Social Virtues and the Creation of Prosperity*. New York: Free Press.

Galbraith, J. K. 1967. *The New Industrial State*. Boston: Houghton Mifflin.

Gambetta, D. 1988. "Foreword." In D. Gambetta, ed., *Trust: Making and Breaking Cooperative Relationships*. New York: Basil Blackwell.

Gasse, Yvon. 1982. "Elaborations on the Psychology of the Entrepreneur." In C. A. Kent, D. L. Sexton, and K. H. Vesper, eds., *Encyclopedia of Entrepreneurship*. Englewood Cliffs, N.J.: Prentice-Hall, 57–71.

Gates, B., with N. Myhrvold and P. Rinearson. 1996. *The Road Ahead*. New York: Penguin Books.

Ghemawat, P. 1991. *Commitment: The Dynamic of Strategy*. New York: The Free Press.

———. 1997. *Competition and Business Strategy in Historical Perspective*. Harvard Business School Note No. N9-797–136. Boston: Harvard Business School Press.

Goldberg, V. 1976. "Toward an Expanded Theory of Contract." *Journal of Economic Issues* 45, 49, 51.

Gompers, P., and J. Lerner. 1996. "The Use of Covenants: An Empirical Analysis of Venture Partnership Agreements." *Journal of Law and Economics* 39 (October): 463–98.

———. 1999. *The Venture Capital Cycle,* Cambridge, Mass.: MIT Press.

Good, D. 1988. "Individuals, Interpersonal Relationships, and Trust." In D. Gambetta, ed., *Trust: Making and Breaking Cooperative Relationships*. New York: Basil Blackwell.

Gourman, J. 1997. *The Gourman Report*. Los Angeles: National Educational Standards.

Granovetter, M. 1985. "Economic Action and Social Structure." *American Journal of Sociology* 5 (91): 53–81.

Hamel, G. S., and C. K. Prahalad. 1994. *Competing for the Future*. Boston: Harvard Business School Press.

Hannan, M. T., and J. Freeman. 1977. "The Population Ecology of Organizations." *American Journal of Sociology* 82 (5): 929–64.

Hardy, Q. 1996. "Higher Calling: How a Wife's Question Led Motorola to Chase Global Cell-Phone Plan." *Wall Street Journal* (December 16), Section A, l.

Heath, C., R. P. Larrick, and J. Klayman. 1998. "Cognitive Repairs: How Organizational Practices Can Compensate for Individual Shortcomings." *Research in Organizational Behavior* 20: 1–37.

Heath, C., and A. Tversky. 1991. "Preference and Belief: Ambiguity and Competence in Choice under Uncertainty." *Journal of Risk and Uncertainty* 4: 5–28.

Henderson, R. 1993. "Underinvestment and Incompetence as Responses to Radical Innovation." *Rand Journal of Economics* 24 (2): 248–70.

———. 1994. "The Evolution of Integrative Competence: Innovation in Cardiovascular Drug Discovery." *Industrial and Corporate Change* 3 (3): 607–30.

Henderson, R., and K. B. Clark. 1990. "Architectural Innovation: The Reconfiguration of Existing Product Technologies and the Failure of Established Firms." *Administrative Science Quarterly* 5 (35): 9–30.

Hoch, S., and Y-W. Ha. 1986. "Consumer Learning: Advertising and the Ambiguity of Product Experience." *Journal of Consumer Research* 13: 21–233.

Hogarth, R. M., and H. J. Einhorn. 1990. "Venture Theory: A Model of Decision Weights." *Management Science* 5 (36): 780–803.

Holmstrom, B. 1982. "Moral Hazard in Teams." *Bell Journal of Economics* 13(2): 324–40.

Hornaday, John A. 1982. "Research About Living Entrepreneurs." In C. A. Kent, D. L. Sexton, and K. H. Vesper, eds., *Encyclopedia of Entrepreneurship*. Englewood Cliffs, N.J.: Prentice-Hall, 26–27.

Hubbard, R. G. 1998. "Capital Market Imperfections and Investment." *Journal of Economic Literature* 36 (March): 193–225.

Ip, G. 1998. "Dominant Firms' Wealth Attracts Investors—and Antitrust Probes." *The Wall Street Journal* (May 12): C1

Jacobsen, T. C. 1993. *Waste Management: An American Corporate Success Story*. Washington, D.C.: Gateway Business Books, 49–51.

Jensen, M. C. 1993. "The Modern Industrial Revolution, Exit, and the Failure of the Internal Control Systems." *The Journal of Finance* 47 (3): 831–81.

Jovanovic, B., and G. M. MacDonald. 1994. "The Life Cycle of a Competitive Industry." *Journal of Political Economy* 102(2): 322–47.

Kagel, J. H., and A. E. Roth. 1995. *The Handbook of Experimental Economics*. Princeton, N.J.: Princeton University Press.

Kelly, P., with J. Case. 1998. *Faster Company*. New York: John Wiley.

Kent, C. A., D. L. Sexton, and K. H. Vesper, eds. 1982. *Encyclopedia of Entrepreneurship*. Englewood Cliffs, N.J.: Prentice-Hall.

Khanna, V., 1997. "The King of Network Computing: Leveraging Off the Internet/Cisco Systems," *Business Times* (Singapore) (July 26).

Kinkead, G. 1981. "Trouble in D. K. Ludwig's Jungle." *Fortune* (April 20): 102–17.

Kirchoff, B., and B. Phillips. 1989. "Innovation and Growth Among New Firms in the U. S. Economy." *Frontiers of Entrepreneurship Research*: 173–88.

Kirzner, I. M. 1973. *Competition and Entrepreneurship*. Chicago: University of Chicago Press.

———. 1998. "Creativity and/or Alertness: A Reconsideration of the Schumpeterian Entrepreneur." Presentation to the Entrepreneurship Research Seminar, Sloan School of Management, MIT (February 2).

Knight, F. H. 1921. *Risk, Uncertainty, and Profit*. Boston: Houghton Mifflin.

Kreps, D. 1990. "Corporate Culture and Economic Theory." In J. Alt and K. Shepsle, ed., *Perspectives on Positive Political Economy*. Cambridge, Eng.: Cambridge University Press, 90–143.

Kuhn, T. 1970. *The Structure of Scientific Revolutions*. Chicago: The University of Chicago Press.

Lerner, J. 1995. "Venture Capitalists and the Oversight of Private Firms." *Journal of Finance* 50: 301–18.

Lewis, D. L. 1976. *The Public Image of Henry Ford: An American Folk Hero and His Company*. Detroit: Wayne State University Press.

Loasby, B. J. 1989. *The Mind and Method of the Economist: A Critical Appraisal of Major Economists in the Twentieth Century*. Aldershot, Eng.: Edward Elgar.

"Lotus Development Corporation." 1985. Harvard Business School Case No. 9–285–094. Boston: Harvard Business School.

Lovallo, D., and C. F. Camerer. 1996. "Overconfidence and Excess Entry: An Experimental Approach." California Institute of Technology Working Paper No. 975.

Luhmann, N. 1988. "Familiarity, Confidence, Trust: Problems and Alternatives." In D. Gambetta, ed., *Trust: Making and Breaking Cooperative Relationships*. New York: Basil Blackwell.

Main, J. 1990. "A Golden Age for Entrepreneurs." *Fortune* (February 12): 120.

Mangelsdorf, M. E. 1996. "The Startling Truth about Growth Companies." *State of Small Business 1996, Inc.* magazine (special issue).

Mayer, C. 1998. "Does Amazon.com = 2 Barnes & Nobles?" *New York Times* Sunday Business Section (July 19).

McClelland, D. C. 1961. *The Achieving Society*. Princeton, N.J.: Princeton University Press.

McCraw, T. K. 1997. "American Capitalism." In T. K. McCraw, ed., *Creating Modern Capitalism*. Cambridge, Mass.: Harvard University Press.

McCraw, T. K., and R. S. Tedlow. 1997. "Henry Ford, Alfred Sloan, and the Three Phases of Marketing." In T. K. McCraw, ed., *Creating Modern Capitalism*. Cambridge, Mass. Harvard University Press.

Megginson, William L., and K. A. Weiss. 1991. "Venture Capital Certification in Initial Public Offerings." *Journal of Finance* 46 (3).

Merrill, R. E., and G. E. Nichols. 1990. *Raising Money: Venture Funding and How to Get It*. New York: AMACOM.

Miner, J. B., N. R. Smith, and J. Bracker. 1992. "Defining the Inventor-Entrepreneur in the Context of Established Typologies." *Journal of Business Venturing* 7: 103–13.

Mintzberg, H. 1973. "Strategy Making in Three Modes." *California Management Review* 16 (2).

Moore, G. E. 1996. "Some Personal Perspectives on Research in the Semiconductor Industry." In R. S. Rosenbloom and W. J. Spencer, eds., *Engines of Innovation*. Boston: Harvard Business School Press.

Moskowitz, M., R. Levering, and M. Katz. 1990. *Everybody's Business*. New York: Doubleday Currency.

Mossberg, W. S. (1998). "Microsoft's Outlook 98 Is a Flawed Improvement." *Wall Street Journal* (April 16), B1.

Murphy, A. 1995. "Enemies, a Love Story." *Inc.* magazine (April): 77.

Nakache, P. 1997. "Cisco's Recruiting Edge." *Fortune* (September 29): 275.

Nee, E. 1998. "Defending the Desktop." *Forbes* (December 28): 53–54.

Nelson, R., and S. Winter. 1978. "Forces Generating and Limiting Competition Under Schumpeterian Conditions." *Bell Journal of Economics* 9: 524–48.

———. 1982. *An Evolutionary Theory of Economic Change*. Cambridge, Mass.: The Belknap Press of Harvard University Press.

Nichols, N. 1994. "Medicine, Management and Mergers: An Interview with Merck's P. Roy Vagelos." *Harvard Business Review* (November-December): 104–14.

Nohria, N. 1996. "From the M-form to the N-form: Taking Stock of Changes in the Large Industrial Corporation." Harvard Business School Working Paper No. 96–054.

Ogilvy, D. 1980. *Confessions of an Advertising Man*. New York: Atheneum, 86.

Olegario, R. 1997. "IBM and the Two Thomas J. Watsons." In T. K McCraw, ed., *Creating Modern Capitalism*. Cambridge, Mass.: Harvard University Press.

Orth, C. D. 1963. *Social Structure and Learning Climate: The First Year at the Harvard Business School*. Boston: Harvard Business School.

Packard, D. 1996. *The HP Way: How Bill Hewlett and I Built Our Company*. Ed. D. Kirby with Karen Lewis. New York: HarperBusiness.

Pearson, A. 1988. "Tough-Minded Ways to Get Innovative." *Harvard Business Review* (May–June): 99–106., repr. 88311.

Pelline, J. 1996. "Cisco on a Winning Streak." *San Francisco Chronicle* (July 10), B1.

Penrose, E. T. 1959. *The Theory of the Growth of the Firm*. White Plains, N.Y.: M. E. Sharpe.

Peters, B., and J. Peters. 1996. "Research Budgets up Overall; Staffing Levels Flat." *Marketing News* 30 (11): 22, 24.

Peters, T. J., and R. H. Waterman. 1982. *In Search of Excellence*. New York: Harper and Row.

Petroski, H. 1990. *The Pencil: A History of Design and Circumstance*. New York: Alfred A. Knopf.

Pitta, J. 1992. "Long Distance Relationship." *Forbes* (March 16): 136.

Popper, K. 1968. *The Logic of Scientific Discovery*. New York: Harper and Row, 27–112.

Porter, M. E. 1980. *Competitive Strategy: Techniques for Analyzing Industries and Competitors*. New York: Free Press.

———. 1996. "What Is Strategy?" *Harvard Business Review* (November-December): 61–78.

Quinn, J. B. 1980. *Strategies for Change*. Homewood, Ill.: Irwin.

Roberts, M. J., and E. J. Walton. 1987. "National Demographics and Lifestyles (A)." Harvard Business School Case No. 388–043. Boston: Harvard Business School Press.

Rodgers, T. J. 1990. "No-Excuses Management." *Harvard Business Review* (July-August): 84–98, repr. 90409.

———. 1993. *No-Excuses Management: Proven Systems for Starting Fast, Growing Quickly, and Surviving Hard Times*. New York: Currency/Doubleday.

Rosenberg, N. 1976. *Perspectives on Technology*. Cambridge, Eng.: Cambridge University Press.

Rubin, P. H. 1973. "The Expansion of Firms." *Journal of Political Economy* 81 (July-August): 936–49.

Rumelt, R. P. 1982. "Diversification Strategy and Profitability." *Strategic Management Journal* 3: 359–69.

Russo, J. E., and P. J. H. Schoemaker. 1989. *Decision Traps: The Ten Barriers to Brilliant Decision-making and How to Overcome Them*. New York: Fireside.

Sabini, J., and M. Silver. 1982. "Some Senses of Subjective." In P. F. Secord, ed., *Explaining Human Behavior*. Beverly Hills, Calif.: Sage, 71–91.

Sahlman, W. A., 1990a. "A Cautionary Tale about Discounted Cash Flow Analysis." Harvard Business School Working Paper No. 90–069.

———. 1990b. "The Structure and Governance of Venture-Capital Organizations." *Journal of Financial Economics* 27: 473–521.

Sahlman, W. A., and H. H. Stevenson. 1985. "Capital Market Myopia." Harvard Business School Working Paper No. 9–785–066.

Schein, E. 1985. *Organizational Culture and Leadership*. San Francisco: Jossey Bass.

Scherer, F. M. 1980. *Industrial Market Structure and Economic Performance*. 2nd ed. Boston: Houghton Mifflin Company.

———. 1982. "Inter-Industry Technology Flows in the United States." *Research Policy* 11: 227–45.

———. 1983. "The Propensity to Patent." *International Journal of Industrial Organization* 1 (March): 107–28.

———. 1988. Testimony Before the Subcommittee on Monopolies and Commercial Law, Committee of the Judiciary, U. S. House of Representatives, February 24.

Schumpeter, J. A. 1911; rprt. 1934. *The Theory of Economic Development*. Cambridge, Mass.: Harvard University Press.

———. 1939. *Business Cycles*. New York: McGraw-Hill.

———. 1942; rprt. 1961. *Capitalism, Socialism and Democracy*. London: George Allen & Unwin.

———. 1944. "The Analysis of Economic Change." Repr. in *Readings in Business Cycle Theory*. Philadelphia: The Blakiston Company.

Selznick, P. 1957. *Leadership in Administration: A Sociological Interpretation*. Berkeley: University of California Press.

Shaver, K. G., and L. R. Scott. 1991. "Person, Process, Choice: The Psychology of New Venture Creation." *Entrepreneurship Theory and Practice* 15 (Winter): 23–45.

Shields, J. 1986. *The Invisible Billionaire*. Boston: Houghton Mifflin.

Sigafoos, R. A. 1983. *Absolutely, Positively Overnight*. Memphis, Tenn.: St. Luke's Press.

Simon, H. A. 1976. *Administrative Behavior*. New York: The Free Press.

Slovic, P., and A. Tversky. 1974. "Who Accepts Savage's Axiom?" *Behavioral Science* 5 (19): 368–373.

Slovic, P., B. Fischhoff, and S. Lichtenstein. 1988. "Response Mode, Framing, and Information-Processing Effects in Risk Assessment." In D. E. Bell, H. Raiffa, and A. Tversky, eds., *Decision-making: Descriptive, Normative, and Prescriptive Interactions*. Cambridge, Eng.: Cambridge University Press, 152–166.

Smith, N. R. 1967. *The Entrepreneur and His Firm: The Relationship Between Type of Man and Type of Company*. East Lansing: Bureau of Business and Economic Research, Graduate School of Business Administration, Michigan State University.

Solow, R. M. 1957. "Technical Change and the Aggregate Production Function." *Review of Economics and Statistics* 39 (3): 312–20.

The Standard Periodical Directory. Twentieth Edition 1997. 1996. New York: Oxbridge Communications.

Steffens, J. 1994. *Newgames: Strategic Competition in the PC Revolution*. Oxford: Pergamon Press.

Stevenson, H. H. 1983. "Who Are the Harvard Self-Employed?" Harvard Business School Case No. 783–042. Boston: Harvard Business School Press.

Stiglitz, J. 1990. "Comments: Some Retrospective Views on Growth Theory." In P. Diamond, ed., *Growth/Productivity/Unemployment: Essays to Celebrate Bob Solow's Birthday*. Cambridge, Mass.: The MIT Press.

Sutton, J. 1996. *Sunk Costs and Market Structure*. Cambridge, Mass.: The MIT Press.

Tedlow, R. S., et al. 1992. "Making Choices: Aspects of the History of the Harvard Business School MBA Program." Project team: Nancy F. Koehn, Thomas R. Piper, V. Kasturi Rangan, Richard S. Tedlow, chair, and Amy Schalet, research assistant. Boston, Mass.: Harvard Business School, Leadership and Learning.

Thaler, R. H. 1980. "Towards a Positive Theory of Consumer Choice." *Journal of Economic Behavior and Organization* 1: 39–60.

Thaler, R. H. 1996. "Doing Economics Without Homo Economicus." In S. G. Medema and W. J. Samuels, eds., *Exploring the Foundations of Research in Economics: How Should Economists Do Economics?* Cheltenham, Eng.: Edward Elgar.

Thurston, P. H. 1983. "The Initial Steps of Enterprise." In J. J. Kao and H. H. Stevenson, eds., *Entrepreneurship: What It Is and How to Teach It.* Boston: Harvard Business School.

U. S. Department of Commerce. 1975. *Historical Statistics of the United States, Colonial Times to 1970, Bicentennial Edition, Part 2*, Washington, D.C.: U.S. Government Printing Office.

———. 1998. *The Emerging Digital Economy.* Washington, D.C.: U.S. Government Printing Office.

Vesper, K. H. 1980. *New Venture Strategies.* Englewood Cliffs, N.J.: Prentice-Hall.

von Hippel, E. A. 1988. *The Sources of Innovation*, New York: Oxford University Press.

Wallace, J., and J. Erickson. 1993. *Hard Drive: Bill Gates and the Making of the Microsoft Empire.* New York: HarperBusiness.

Walton, S., with J. Huey. 1993. *Sam Walton: Made in America, My Story.* New York: Bantam Books.

Watson, T. J., Jr., and P. Petre. 1990. *Father, Son & Co.: My Life at IBM and Beyond.* New York: Bantam Books.

Williamson, O. E. 1975. *Markets and Hierarchies.* New York: Free Press.

———. 1985. *The Economic Institutions of Capitalism.* New York: Free Press.

Winter, S. 1964. "Economic 'Natural Selection' and the Theory of the Firm." *Yale Economic Essays* 4: 225–72.

———. 1984. "Schumpeterian Competition in Alternative Technological Regimes." *Journal of Economic Behavior and Organization* 5: 287–320.

Zaleznik, A. 1989. "Real Work." *Harvard Business Review* (January-February), repr. 97611.

Zingales, L. 1997. "Corporate Governance." *The New Palgrave Dictionary of Economics and the Law.* London: Macmillan.

Case Studies Written by the Author

"The Road Well Traveled." 1996. Boston: Harvard Business School No. 396–277.

"Johnson-Grace: March 1994." 1995. Harvard Business School No. 396–096.

"Bob Reiss and Valdawn (A)." 1995. Harvard Business School No. 396–063.

"Metropolis Software: May 1995." 1995. Harvard Business School No. 396–005.

"Stonyfield Farm: September 1994," with M. Thurber. 1995. Harvard Business School No. 395–157.

"Physician Sales & Service, Inc.: June 1992 (A)," with J. Dial. 1994. Harvard Business School No. 395–066.

"Marcia Radosevich and Health Payment Review: 1989 (A)." 1994. Harvard Business School No. 394–204.

"McKinsey & Co. (A): 1956." 1992. Harvard Business School No. 393–066.

"McKinsey & Co. (B): 1966." 1993. Harvard Business School No. 393–067.

"Deaver Brown and Cross River, Inc." 1993. Harvard Business School No. 394–042.

"Cherrill Farnsworth and TME, Inc.: 1990 (A)." 1993. Harvard Business School No. 394–021.

"National Communications Inc. (A): 1988," with L. Pochup. 1993. Harvard Business School No. 393–103.

"The DAG Group," with V. Rayzman and C. J. Hackett. 1990. Harvard Business School No. 392–077.

"Momenta Corporation (A)." 1991. Harvard Business School No. 392–013.

"Momenta Corporation (B)." 1991. Harvard Business School No. 392–014.

"Momenta Corporation (C)." 1991 Harvard Business School No. 392–048.

"Granite Broadcasting Corporation (A)," with S. J. Bryant, Y. R. Daniels, N. T. Henderson, and M. B. Robinson. 1991. Harvard Business School No. 392–008.

"Granite Broadcasting Corporation (B)," with S. J. Bryant, Y. R. Daniels, N. T. Henderson, and M. B. Robinson. 1991. Harvard Business School No. 392–009.

"Paul Olsen (A)," with L. Pochop. 1991. Harvard Business School No. 392–011.

"Peanut Butter Fantasies: June 1989," with M. Hart. 1990. Harvard Business School No. 391–072.

"Image Presentations, Inc.," with K. Hinton. 1990. Harvard Business School No. 390–140.

"Vinod Khosla and Sun Microsystems (A)." 1989. Harvard Business School No. 390–049.

"Vinod Khosla and Sun Microsystems (B)." 1989. Harvard Business School No. 390–050.

"Vinod Khosla and Sun Microsystems (C). 1989. Harvard Business School No. 390–051.

Index

Imitation, 15, 17, 32–36, 52, 196, 197, 326–30, 360
Immortality of firms, 210, 210n
Imperial Chemical Industries (ICI), 248, 304
Inc. companies: background information about, 371–75; and capital constraints, 37–38; customers of, 325; descriptive statistics about, 13–14, 372; employees of, 174; and endowments and opportunities, 29–30, 32–34, 37–38, 39, 40, 43, 45, 46, 47, 48, 49, 51; and entrepreneurs' value added, 47, 48, 49, 51; goals of, 261, 264; growth/maturation of, 29–30, 29n, 234, 240, 318, 320; initial investments in, 141; and innovation, 320, 321, 325; list of, 373–75; and most popular fields, 30–31; and niche markets, 40; and planning vs. adaptation, 54–55, 57, 61, 63; and prior experience, 37; profits/revenues of, 29–30, 211; and qualities of entrepreneurs, 94, 97, 108–9, 174, 294, 303, 305; and revolutionary ventures, 194; sales of, 49, 51; and Schumpeter's concepts, 320; and securing resources, 29n, 77, 78, 82, 176; selection of, 371; societal implications of, 318; as source for information, 15, 210-11; as start-ups, 25; survival rate among, 207; and technology, 345; and turbulent markets, 43, 45, 46, 47; and VC-backed ventures, 141, 148–49, 152, 153, 161, 165
Inc. magazine: Kahn interview in, 341
Industry/industries: and clustering of companies, 307–8; entrepreneur's role in, 308–14; how to conduct analysis of, 279; maturation of, 243; and qualities of entrepreneurs, 306–14, 315; structure of, 243, 249, 279, 306–14, 315, 366; and VC-backed ventures, 145–46
Information technology (IT), 45, 76, 332–33
Ingenuity, 104–5, 200, 315, 361

Initial concepts/conditions: and corporate-backed ventures, 20, 114–16, 196–97, 199, 201; and endowments and opportunities, 31–36, 39, 52; as imitation of others, 15, 17, 32–36, 52, 196, 197, 360; implications of, 152; overview/summary about, 17, 196–97; and planning vs. adaptation, 61–63, 199; and revolutionary ventures, 167, 197, 198, 199; and success requirements, 201; uniqueness of, 16, 32, 34, 39; and VC-backed ventures, 16, 17, 141-52, 155–56, 157, 158–59, 197, 200, 201. *See also* Specialization; *specific firm*
Initial public offering. *See* IPO
Innovation: business school teaching about, 9–11; and capital, 321; complementary, 328, 330; and corporations, 263–64, 320–26; discontinuous/radical, 326–30; and displacement of existing structures, 330–34; and economic theory, 5–9; and evolution of firms, 207–8; and functions/roles of entrepreneurs, 5–9; and growth, 319–37; as imitation and adaptation, 326–30; and invention, 326–28; and qualities of entrepreneurs, 26, 364; routinized, 10–11, 133, 134, 336; Schumpeter's views about, 319–37; and start-ups, 200, 263–64, 317–18; and success requirements, 200
Inspiration, 201, 298, 299, 301, 302, 315, 363
Institutional Venture Partners, 151, 151n
Insurance, 217–22, 228
Intel: capitalization of, 332; corporate-backed projects of, 114, 117, 121–22, 131, 133, 151, 198, 362; and endowments and opportunities, 44; and evolution of firms, 237, 329; and innovation, 322–23, 329; Pentium development by, 114, 131, 155n; and qualities of entrepreneurs, 298; R&D at, 121, 122, 123, 133, 322–23; and Schumpeter's concepts, 329; and securing

resources, 198, 202; strategies of, 278; and turbulent markets, 44; as VC-backed venture, 25, 153
Inter-Ad, 40, 81
International Business Machines Company. *See* IBM
International Harvester, 335
International Olympic Committee, 117
International Record Syndicate (IRS), 105
Intimidation, 298, 299, 301, 302, 315, 363
Intuit, 12, 15, 253
Invention: and innovation, 326–28
Investment tax credits, 350–51, 357
Investment-uncertainty-profit diagram: and corporate-backed ventures, 20, 114; and corporations, 3–4; and evolution of firms, 3–4, 239, 259; function of, 3–4; and new businesses, 3–4, 17; terms in, 26; and transitional firms, 3–4, 21, 211; and venture capital/capitalists, 16, 164, 165. *See also* Revolutionary ventures
Investments/investors: and endowments and opportunities, 38–39, 52; and entrepreneurs' value added, 52; institutional, 151, 151n; irrational, 8; and nature of opportunities, 59; and transitional firms, 211. *See also* Investment-uncertainty-profit diagram; *type of investor*
IO (industrial organization) research, 5, 8, 243, 244n, 256–57, 256n, 259, 276, 306, 307–8
Iomega, 136
Ip, G., 240
IPO (initial public offering), 163, 164n, 351, 357, 358
Iridium project (Motorola), 25, 167, 193–94, 195, 197, 199, 262, 263
IT&T, 257

Jacob, François, 67
Jacobs, Irwin, 297
Jacobson, Allen, 134
James O. McKinsey & Co., 272, 297. *See also* McKinsey & Co.
Japanese Export-Import Bank, 192
Jari Development (Ludwig),